PELICAN BOOKS

A236

FACTS FROM FIGURES

M. J. MORONEY

D0925352

FACTS
FROM FIGURES

—

M. J. MORONEY

PENGUIN BOOKS
BALTIMORE · MARYLAND

Penguin Books Ltd, Harmondsworth, Middlesex
U.S.A.: Penguin Books Inc., 3300 Clipper Mill Road, Baltimore 11, Md
AUSTRALIA: Penguin Books Pty Ltd, 762 Whitehorse Road,
Mitcham, Victoria

—

First published 1951
Second and revised edition 1953; reprinted 1954
Third and revised edition 1956; reprinted 1957, 1958, 1960

TO

MY WIFE

Made and printed in Great Britain
by William Clowes and Sons, Limited
London and Beccles

Contents

Acknowledgements

I am indebted to many people directly and indirectly. Many of them will be found mentioned in the bibliography. My recommendation is my thanks. If I have inadvertently adopted or adapted where I should have sought permission, I hope it will be excused as oversight or ignorance. In particular, I have to acknowledge my indebtedness to the following:

Professor Sir Ronald Fisher, Cambridge, Dr. Frank Yates, Rothamsted, and Messrs. Oliver & Boyd, Ltd, Edinburgh, for permission to reprint abridged tables of the Ordinate and Area of the Normal Curve (page 116), the graph of Student's t (Fig. 81), abridged tables of the Variance Ratio (pages 234 and 235), and the graph of χ^2 (Fig. 82), all based on their book *Statistical Tables for Biological, Agricultural and Medical Research*.

Professor E. S. Pearson and Mr. L. H. C. Tippett, for material utilized in the chapter on Control Charts.

Professor M. G. Kendall, some of whose tables for significance in ranking tests I have compressed into approximate formulae which are adequate for the purposes of a book such as this yet not suitable for those who might later wish to use the techniques described in serious work.

Messrs H. F. Dodge and H. G. Romig, from whose extensive and valuable Sampling Tables I have given a simplified extract to supplement my description of the tables.

Dr J. Wishart for persuading me to stress Hotelling's T^2 test rather than the discriminant function and for suggesting better figures for the numerical example.

Her Majesty's Stationery Office, by whose permission Figures 2, 3, 4 and 6 (a) are reproduced from *Survey '49* and Figure 10 from *The Budget and Your Pocket*.

Mrs C. N. McCaig, for her skill and diligence in translating my rough sketches into drawings for the blockmaker.

My publishers, especially for their great care during production and for the many things they have helped me with when, alone, I would have floundered.

Those who have been kind enough to point out errors in the earlier printings.

Preface

This book attempts to take the reader on a conducted tour of the statistician's workshop. The reader is shown many tools and machines, given a quick explanation of their purpose and method of operation, and then encouraged, after watching the craftsman for a while, to try for himself. It does not claim to do everything. It does not claim to be exhaustive on what it does attempt. But it does aim at giving enough information to satisfy a man on a conducted tour and to let him see enough of the game as he goes around to really learn something. If the reader finishes up with a smattering of the workshop jargon, a rough idea of the jobs tackled and of the tools required to do them, I shall be more than satisfied. Moreover, I believe he will, too.

There are many to whom a conducted tour of this sort should appeal: not only students, but those whose work calls for a general knowledge of the capabilities of this subject in the industrial and research world. They must be the judges of whether the book serves a useful purpose. And those critics whose excellent books I have not been able to write and whose pet theories I have not hesitated to ignore or make fun of will perhaps treat me lightly when they realize that I am not trying to do more than I have here said.

M. J. M.

Preface to the Second Edition

It is fair to judge from the rapid sale and many kind letters from readers that this little book does serve a useful purpose. I am particularly indebted to those who sent in details of errata, the elimination of which should increase the usefulness of the book.

The contents remain almost unchanged, except for the latter part of Chapter II which I have revised to include a new approach to modified limit control charts.

I am sorry still to remain *persona non grata* to the index number men and the fortune tellers, but there it is. I give way to none in my admiration for the theory (may its shadow never be less!), but when it comes to a great deal of the practice I simply cannot help chuckling.

M. J. M.

1

Statistics Undesirable

'Lasciate ogni speranza, voi ch'entrate.' DANTE

There is more than a germ of truth in the suggestion that, in a society where statisticians thrive, liberty and individuality are likely to be emasculated. Historically, Statistics is no more than State Arithmetic, a system of computation by which differences between individuals are eliminated by the taking of an average. It has been used – indeed, still is used – to enable rulers to know just how far they may safely go in picking the pockets of their subjects. A king going to war wishes to know what reserves of manpower and money he can call on. How many men need be put in the field to defeat the enemy? How many guns and shirts, how much food, will they need? How much will all this cost? Have the citizens the necessary money to pay for the king's war? Taxation and military service were the earliest fields for the use of Statistics. For this reason was Domesday Book compiled.

We are reminded of the ancient statisticians every Christmas when we read that Caesar Augustus decreed that the whole world should be enrolled, each man returning to his own city for registration. Had it not been for the statisticians Christ would have been born in the modest comfort of a cottage in Nazareth instead of in a stable at Bethlehem. The story is a symbol of the blindness of the planners of all ages to the comforts of the individual. They just didn't think of the overcrowding there would be in a little place like Bethlehem.

But Statistics suffers from other drawbacks in the public eye. No one who has lived through recent years can have failed to notice the uses to which statistics are put in times of economic desperation. John Citizen is assumed to develop a sudden and remarkable aptitude for contemplating thousands of millions of pounds. He is supposed to brush up his knowledge of index numbers and respond with enthusiasm to the tables and charts flung at his head by benevolent authority. He is even expected to pay his sixpences to see exactly what his elected representatives are doing with £3,778 million in the brief space of 52 weeks. The people who issue these things would get a shock if they knew the proportion of the adult population that does not even know its multiplication table. Having looked at the charts, John Citizen feels less able than ever to put his resentment into words. He feels a fool, blinded by science, and he resents the clever statisticians who have made him feel so inferior.

Statistics has other claims to unpopularity. It lends itself only too easily to the pinchbeck taradiddle to which advertising is by nature prone. The public is told that 'nine people out of ten' in a certain class for whom the reader will have the greatest admiration use a certain excellent product. No doubt this is plain truth. But we must be forgiven for suspecting that it is obviously artful. Were the ten people specially chosen so as to include one who was less wise than the nine knowing virgins who had the gumption to agree with the advertiser? There is undoubted cozenage in saying 'nine out of ten' in the confident hope that the reader will unsuspectingly lend at least partial credence to the idea that 'nine out of *every* ten' of the excellent people in question do what the reader is urged to do.

What we have already said is amply sufficient to make clear the origin of the popular mistrust in statistics and to show that it has very real justification. But the worst has not yet been said. There still remains the sorry spectacle of opposing factions in politics and medicine (to mention only two of the most obvious cases) who bolster up their respective cases by statistics in the confident hope that 'figures cannot lie' or, as they often hope, that 'you can't dispute the figures'. All this is very sad indeed, for these ardent computers are usually truly sincere in their convictions, even where they are rash with their statistical deductions. The cynic sums it up in the old tag: 'There are lies, damned lies, and statistics.'

If no more were to be said about Statistics, this book would end here. But it is just about to begin. It is true that it is extremely difficult to interpret figures when they relate to some concrete problem. It is equally true that it is extremely easy to do arithmetic. Herein lies the real difficulty. Averages can be calculated to nineteen places of decimals with astonishing ease. When the job is done it looks very accurate. It is an easy and fatal step to think that the accuracy of our arithmetic is equivalent to the accuracy of our knowledge about the problem in hand. We suffer from 'delusions of accuracy'. Once an enthusiast gets this disease, he and all who depend on his conclusions for their welfare are damned.

For the most part, Statistics is a method of investigation that is used when other methods are of no avail; it is often a last resort and a forlorn hope. A statistical analysis, properly conducted, is a delicate dissection of uncertainties, a surgery of suppositions. The surgeon must guard carefully against false incisions with his scalpel. Very often he has to sew up the patient as inoperable. The public knows too little about the statistician as a conscientious and skilled servant of true science. In this small book it is hoped to give the reader some insight into the statistician's tools and some idea of the very wide range of problems to which these tools are applied. We shall try to see the scientist with no axe to grind other than the axe of truth and no product to advertise save the product of honest and careful enquiry.

2

The Laws of Chance

'Quoth she: "I've heard old cunning stagers
Say fools for arguments use wagers." ' S. BUTLER (*Hudibras*)

There are certain notions which it is impossible to define adequately. Such notions are found to be those based on universal experience of nature. Probability is such a notion. The dictionary tells me that 'probable' means 'likely'. Further reference gives the not very helpful information that 'likely' means 'probable'. It is not always that we are so quickly made aware of circularity in our definitions. We might have had an extra step in our circle by bringing in the word 'chance', but, to judge from the heated arguments of philosophers, no extension of vocabulary or ingenuity in definition ever seems to clear away all the difficulties attached to this perfectly common notion of probability.

In this chapter we shall try to get some idea of what the statistician has in mind when he speaks of probability. His ideas are at bottom those of common sense, but he has them a little more carefully sorted out so that he can make numerical statements about his problems instead of vague general comments. It is always useful when we can *measure* things on a ruler instead of simply calling them 'big' or 'small'.

THE PROBABILITY SCALE

We measure probability by providing ourselves with a scale marked zero at one end and unity at the other. (In reading what follows, the reader will do well to keep Fig. 1 constantly before his attention.) The top end of the scale, marked unity or 1, represents *absolute certainty*. Any proposition about which there is absolutely no doubt at all would find its place at this point on the scale. For example: The probability that I shall one day die is equal to unity, because it is absolutely certain that I shall die some day.* The mathematician would here write $p = 1$, the letter p standing for probability. The bottom end of the scale, marked zero or

* Quia pulvis es, et in pulverem reverteris (Gen. iii, 19).

0, represents *absolute impossibility*. For example: The probability that I should succeed in an attempt to swim the Atlantic is zero, because failure would be absolutely certain. The statistician would here write $p = 0$.

If all the affairs of life were as clear-cut as this, statisticians would be out of a job, and scientific research would shoot ahead at an intolerable rate, losing most of its interest. Life and nature

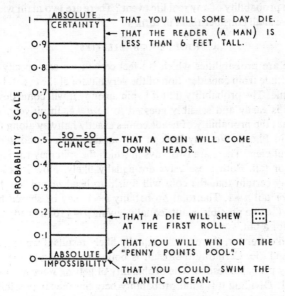

Fig. 1. The Probability Scale

may be simple enough to the Almighty who designed them and keeps them going, but to the human mind there is presented an unending stream of problems that cannot be given a clear-cut answer of the type $p = 1$ or $p = 0$. The doctor knows that penicillin is excellent for your particular disease, but he cannot absolutely guarantee that you will be cured by using it. At most he can be very sure. He may say that for all practical purposes he is prepared to put $p = 1$ for your recovery. But this is an approximation; we have already slipped from the realm of absolute certainty. In fact, we may suppose, $p = 0.999$. What the doctor then says is: 'We may without noticeable error put $p = 1$.' Fig. 1 shows the sort of position occupied on the scale of probability by various common affairs. The thing to notice is that there is no greater certainty than $p = 1$, and nothing less likely than $p = 0$.

So far, then, we have set up our scale on which the probability of events may be specified. How do we arrive at an actual measure of the probability of any real life event? There are two main ways, and we shall consider them in turn.

A PRIORI PROBABILITIES

These are probabilities which we feel certain we can specify in magnitude from consideration of the very nature of the event. For example: The probability that if I spin a penny it will come down heads is easily and sensibly guessed to be $p = \frac{1}{2}$. Intuitively, we feel that the probability of heads comes exactly halfway along the scale in Fig. 1. We may look at it from another commonsense point of view. There are two ways in which the spin may turn up: head or tail. Both these ways are equally likely. Now it is absolutely certain that the coin will finish up head *or* tail, i.e. for head *or* tail $p = 1$. The total probability $p = 1$ may be shared between the two possible results equally, giving $p = \frac{1}{2}$ for a head, and $p = \frac{1}{2}$ for a tail.

In like manner, there are six equally likely results if we roll an unbiased die. Certainly the result is bound to be one of the six equally probable results. The probability of getting *some* number is $p = 1$. Dividing this total probability between the six possibilities, we say that there is a probability of $p = \frac{1}{6}$ for each of the possible results. (We ignore in all cases the preposterous suggestion that the coin will land on its edge or the die stand up on one corner.)

EMPIRICAL PROBABILITY

The problem of probabilities in card and dice games may be tackled from another point of view. Say, having made a die, we roll it 600 times. We should *expect* that each face would have shown uppermost 100 times. What do we mean by 'expect'? We don't really expect anything of the sort. In fact, we should be rather surprised at the 'coincidence' if any practical trial gave a result in perfect agreement with our 'expectation'. What we really expect is that each face would turn up *roughly* 100 times – not *too* roughly, of course, or we should suspect bias; nor too *exactly*, either, or we might suspect jiggery-pokery. This suggests to us another way of measuring the probability of an event: by counting the number of times the event occurs in a certain number of trials. We take it that a very long series will give a closer indication of the probability than a short series. We believe from our experience of things that while short trials are easily upset by 'chance' a long trial is protected by the mysterious laws of this very same 'chance'. We may express the empirical probability of an event as:

$$\text{Probability} = \frac{\text{Total number of occurrences of the event}}{\text{Total number of trials}}$$

Thus, for example, if a surgeon performs a certain operation on 200 people and 16 of them die, he may assume the probability of death to be $p = \frac{16}{200} = 0\cdot08$. This empirical method of finding probabilities as the ratio of the number of occurrences to the total number of trials is the method that has to be used in many fields of research.

Having seen how probabilities may be measured, we must now consider some of the laws of probability, so that we can analyse more complex situations.

ADDITION LAW

Consider the phrase 'Heads I win; tails you lose'. This is the simplest possible illustration of the Law of Addition. To calculate my total chance of winning, I have, according to this law, to add up the probabilities of each of the several ways in which I may win. In the first place, I shall win if the coin turns up heads, and this has $p = \frac{1}{2}$. In the second place I shall also win if the coin turns up tails, and this also has $p = \frac{1}{2}$. Adding the two probabilities together, we see that the total probability of my winning is $p = \frac{1}{2} + \frac{1}{2} = 1$. That is, it is absolutely certain that I shall win.

The probability that an event will occur in one of several possible ways is calculated as the sum of the probabilities of the occurrence of the several different possible ways.

It is assumed that the occurrence of the event in one way

excludes the possibility of its occurrence in any of the other possible ways, on the occasion in question.

As a simple example, let us suppose that 10 Englishmen, 8 Irishmen, 2 Scotsmen, and 5 Welshmen apply for a job to which only one man will be appointed. Altogether there are 25 applicants. Let us suppose that the interviewing board are completely unable to agree with each other on the respective merits of the applicants, and so decide to draw a name out of the hat. The probability of the job going to an Englishman will evidently be $\frac{10}{25}$; to a Scotsman, $\frac{2}{25}$; to a Welshman, $\frac{5}{25}$; and to an Irishman, $\frac{8}{25}$. Then the Law of Addition gives us the following results:

Probability of a Celt $=\frac{2}{25}+\frac{5}{25}+\frac{8}{25}=\frac{15}{25}=0\cdot6$.

Probability of native of Gt. Britain $=\frac{10}{25}+\frac{2}{25}+\frac{5}{25}=\frac{17}{25}=0\cdot68$

Probability of NOT a native of Gt. Britain $=\frac{8}{25}=0\cdot32$

Other simple examples will be found at the end of this chapter for the reader to work for himself.

MULTIPLICATION LAW

We shall now prove, to the no little satisfaction of the fair sex, that every woman is a woman in a billion. It is hoped that menfolk will find salve for their consciences in this scientific proof of the age-old compliment. ('Statistics show, my dear, that you are one in a billion.') It will be obvious to the reader that the more exacting we are in our demands, the less likely we are to get them satisfied. Consider the case of a man who demands the simultaneous occurrence of many virtues of an unrelated nature in his young lady. Let us suppose that he insists on a Grecian nose, platinum-blonde hair, eyes of odd colours, one blue and one brown, and, finally, a first-class knowledge of statistics. What is the probability that the first lady he meets in the street will put ideas of marriage into his head? To answer the question we must know the probabilities for the several different demands. We shall suppose them to be known as follows:

Probability of lady with Grecian nose: $0\cdot01$

Probability of lady with platinum-blonde hair: $0\cdot01$

Probability of lady with odd eyes: $0\cdot001$

Probability of lady with first-class knowledge of statistics: $0\cdot00001$

In order to calculate the probability that all these desirable attributes will be found in one person, we use the Multiplication Law. Multiplying together the several probabilities, we find for our result that the probability of the first young lady he meets, or indeed any lady chosen at random, coming up to his requirements is $p = 0.000\,000\,000\,001$, or precisely one in an English billion. The point is that every individual is *unique* when he is carefully compared, point by point, with his fellows.*

We have considered here the case of the *simultaneous occurrence* of events. The Multiplication Law is also used when we consider the probability of the occurrence of two or more events in succession, even where the successive events are dependent. Consider the following example: A bag contains eight billiard balls, five being red and three white. If a man selects two balls at random from the bag, what is the probability that he will get one ball of each colour? The problem is solved as follows:

The first ball chosen will be either red or white, and we have:

Probability that first ball is red $= \frac{5}{8}$. If this happens, then there will be four red balls and three white balls in the bag for the second choice.

Hence the probability of choosing a white after choosing a red will be $\frac{3}{7}$.

The Multiplication Law tells us that the probability of choosing white after red is $\frac{5}{8} \times \frac{3}{7} = \frac{15}{56}$.

In like manner, the probability of the first ball out being white is $\frac{3}{8}$.

This will leave two white balls in the bag for the second choice. Hence the probability of choosing a red ball after choosing a white one will be, by the Multiplication Law: $\frac{3}{8} \times \frac{5}{7} = \frac{15}{56}$.

Now the man will have succeeded in getting one ball of each colour in either case. Applying the Addition Law, we find the probability of his success to be $\frac{15}{56} + \frac{15}{56} = \frac{30}{56} = \frac{15}{28} = 0.535$.

* The different applications of the Laws of Addition and Multiplication of probabilities may be remembered in terms of betting on horse racing. If I bet on two horses in the same race the probability of my winning is the *sum* of the probabilities for winning on each of the two horses separately. If I have an 'accumulator bet', i.e. bet on one horse in the first race and direct that my winnings, if any, be placed on one horse in the second race, then my chance of winning the accumulator bet is the *product* of the probabilities that each of my chosen horses will win its own race.

The Addition Law and the Multiplication Law are fundamental in Statistics. They are simple; but sufficient to carry us a long way, if we make good use of them. We shall meet them in full sail in Chapter 7.

What we have discussed so far is known as the *Direct* Theory of probability. Basically, all the problems commonly met with in this branch of the subject turn on counting the number of ways in which events can occur. For example: if we ask ourselves what is the probability that three pennies on being tossed will all show heads, we can arrange all the possible results in a table as follows:

Result	1st coin	2nd coin	3rd coin
3 Heads	H	H	H
2 Heads {	H H T	H T H	T H H
2 Tails {	T T H	T H T	H T T
3 Tails	T	T	T

In the table, *H* represents head and *T* represents tail. If we assume all the possible results to be equally likely, then of the eight possible results, only one will be a success. Hence the probability of all three coins showing heads is $p = \frac{1}{8}$. In like manner, the probability is again $p = \frac{1}{8}$ that all the coins will show a tail. Hence, by the Addition Law, the probability of three heads *or* three tails will be $p = \frac{1}{8} + \frac{1}{8} = \frac{1}{4}$.

This is a suitable point to introduce some fallacious arguments for the reader to consider.

Fallacious argument Number 1. There are two possible results: either all the coins show alike or they don't. Hence the probability of all the coins showing the same face is $p = \frac{1}{2}$.

Fallacious argument Number 2. There are four possible results: all heads, all tails, two heads and a tail, or two tails and a head. Two of these results would be satisfactory. Hence the probability of all the coins showing the same face will be $p = \frac{1}{2}$.

These arguments are invalid because they assume events to be equiprobable which in fact are not so. Inspection of the table will show that there is only one way of getting the result three heads. There is similarly only one way of getting the result three tails. But the result two heads and a tail can occur in three different coin arrangements, as also can the result two tails and a head.

It is a simple enough matter to write out all the possible arrangements where these are relatively few in number. The introduction of permutations in football pools recognized the difficulty of writing out complex cases by the punter and the enormous labour of checking them. It will be useful to spend a few moments on the idea of Permutations and Combinations.

COMBINATIONS AND PERMUTATIONS

Suppose a race were run by seven children and that we attempted to predict the first three children home. It is one thing to name the three children irrespective of their placing, and quite another to get not only the first three correct but also their placing. When a problem concerns groups without any reference to order within the group it is a problem in *combinations*. When the problem asks us to take arrangements into account it is a problem in *permutations*. Thus what is commonly called a combination lock is really a permutation lock, since order is vitally important. On the other hand, the football pools fan who enters six teams for the 'four aways' and writes on his coupon 'Perm. 4 from 6, making 15 lines at 6d. Stake 7s. 6d.', is really talking about a combination, since there is no question of arranging the correct four teams in any way. It is sufficient to name them in any order whatsoever. The 'penny points pool', on the other hand, is indeed a permutation; it is not sufficient to get the correct number of wins away and at home and the correct number of draws; correct arrangement within the column is essential.

Permutations are more numerous than combinations, for each

combination can be permuted. As an example the group of letters *ABC* which make a single combination, whatever their order, gives rise to six permutations, viz. *ABC, ACB, BCA, BAC, CAB, CBA.*

We shall now give some of the main results in the theory of permutations and combinations with simple illustrations of each type. Further examples will be found at the end of the chapter for the reader to work for himself.

SIMPLE CASES OF CHOICES

If there are *m* ways of performing one operation, *n* ways of performing a second operation, and *p* ways of performing a third operation, then there are $N = m \times n \times p$ ways of performing the whole group of operations.

Example. A man travelling from Dover to Calais and back has the choice of ten boats. In how many ways can he make the double journey, using a different boat in each direction?

Going, he has the choice of all ten boats, i.e. the first operation (going) can be performed in $m = 10$ ways. Coming back, he will only have nine boats to choose from, i.e. the second operation (returning) can be performed in $n = 9$ ways. Hence, there are $N = m \times n = 10 \times 9 = 90$ ways of making the double journey.

Example. How many lines would be required for a full permutation on a fourteen-match 'penny points pool'?

Regarding the forecasting of each match as an operation, we have fourteen operations to perform. Each operation can be dealt with in three ways, viz. 1, 2, or X. Hence the total number of ways of forecasting the result will be

$$N = 3 \times 3 \times 3 \times 3 \times 3 \times 3 \times 3 \times 3 \times 3 \times 3 \times 3 \times 3 \times 3 \times 3 = 4,782,969,$$

This number of entries at 1d. per line would cost roughly £20,000. It is the author's considered opinion that the amount of skill one can bring to bear in forecasting is a relatively negligible quantity. In so far as this is true, no amount of permuting is likely to be of great assistance while the old lady with a pin is in the running. It would be salutary for readers of expert permutationists in the newspapers to remember that armies of gullible fans, sending in massive permutations week after week, are bound to produce some successes for the expert to advertise. The real test is: how many weeks in the season does the columnist himself bring home a really substantial prize?

Example. A factory call light system has four colours. The lights may be on one, two, three, or four at a time. If each signal combination can be made to serve for two people, being steady for one and flickering for the other, how many people can be accommodated on the system?

This problem is very easily dealt with. Ignore for the moment the question of flickering. There are two ways of dealing with the first lamp – switch it on or leave it off. There is the same choice for each lamp. Evidently, then, the total number of ways in which the system may be set will be $N = 2 \times 2 \times 2 \times 2 = 16$. But this would include the case where all the lights were left off. We must leave this case out as being of no use as a signal. We are left with fifteen signals. Each of these fifteen signals may be either steady or flickering, so the system can accommodate thirty people.

PERMUTATIONS

If all the things to be arranged are different, it is very simple to calculate the total number of permutations.

Example. In how many ways can the letters of the word BREAD be arranged?

In the first position we can have a choice of five letters. Having filled the first place, we shall be left with a choice of four letters for the second place. In turn, there will be a choice of three letters for the third place, two letters for the fourth place, and, finally, only one letter to go into the last place. Applying our previous rule we find the total number of ways of arranging the letters is $N = 5 \times 4 \times 3 \times 2 \times 1 = 120$.

Example. How many three-letter words can be made using the letters of the word BREAD?

Similar reasoning to that used above yields the answer

$$N = 5 \times 4 \times 3 = 60$$

The mathematician has a simple piece of shorthand for permutations. In our first example we were arranging five things in every possible way, each thing appearing in each arrangement, i.e. we were arranging, or permuting, five things in groups of five at a time. The shorthand for this is 5*P*5. In the second problem we were arranging the five things in groups of three. The shorthand for this is 5*P*3. The letter *P* stands for 'the number of permutations'. The number *before* the *P* tells us how many things we have to choose from; and the number *after* the *P* tells us how many things are to be in each arrangement. Thus if we saw 43*P*7, we should know that there were forty-three things to be made up into every possible arrangement (order counting), there being seven things in each arrangement.

It is convenient here to introduce one other piece of shorthand, which is easy to understand and which saves a great deal of time in writing things down. It will be remembered that the result for our first problem in permutations (arranging the letters of the word BREAD in every possible five-letter arrangement) was $N = 5 \times 4 \times 3 \times 2 \times 1$. Here we have multiplied together a string of numbers, starting with 5, each number being one less than the one before it, the last number in the sequence being 1. Such an arrangement is called a 'factorial'. One or two examples will make the meaning clear.

Factorial $5 = 5 \times 4 \times 3 \times 2 \times 1 = 120$

Factorial $7 = 7 \times 6 \times 5 \times 4 \times 3 \times 2 \times 1 = 5,040$, and so on.

The shorthand sign for the factorial of a number is made by writing an exclamation mark after the number. Thus factorial 7 is written 7! and factorial 93 is written 93! The use of this factorial sign will enable us to write down further results in the theory of permutations and combinations compactly.

What happens if we have to make permutations of things that are not all different? Obviously we shall have to allow for the fact that the identical things can be interchanged without disturbing the permutation.

If we have *n* things, *p* being alike of one kind, *q* alike of another kind, and *r* alike of another kind still, then the total number of ways in which all the *n* things can be arranged so that no arrangement is repeated is:

$$N = \frac{n!}{p! \times q! \times r!}$$

Example. How many different permutations may be made each containing the ten letters of the word STATISTICS? Here we have the letter S three times, the letter T three times, the letter I twice, and the letters A and C once each. Applying our rule, we get:

$$N = \frac{10!}{3! \times 3! \times 2!} = \frac{10.9.8.7.6.5.4.3.2.1}{3.2.1 \times 3.2.1 \times 2.1} = 50,400$$

COMBINATIONS

It remains for us now to consider the problem of calculating the number of combinations (i.e. irrespective of order) which can be made from a group of things. We have already seen that any combination can give rise to a set of permutations, the combination *ABC* yielding, for example, the six permutations *ABC, ACB, BCA, BAC, CAB, CBA.* Very little thought is required to see that a combination of n things can generate $n!$ permutations. Thus in any problem, if we knew the number of combinations that could be made, and knew the number of permutations to which each combination could give rise, we should know that the total number of permutations was equal to the number of combinations multiplied by the number of permutations within a combination. *Number of Combinations × Number of permutations within a Combination = Total Number of Permutations.*

Just as, previously, we denoted the number of permutations of five things taken three at a time by the symbol $5P3$, so now we shall denote the number of combinations of five things taken three at a time by the shorthand symbol $5C3$. The letter C stands for 'the number of combinations that can be made'. The number *before* the C tells us how many things we have to choose from, and the number *after* the C tells us how many things are to appear in each combination. The number of combinations of n things taken r at a time will thus be denoted by nCr and the number of permutations of n things taken r at a time will be denoted by nPr. Now we know that r things forming a combination can give us $r!$ permutations, so we have our previous result in mathematical form as:

$$nCr \times r! = nPr$$

from which, dividing both sides by $r!$, we find that the number of combinations of r things at a time chosen from a group of n things is to be calculated as:

$$nCr = \frac{nPr}{r!}$$

It is clear, too, that whenever we make a choice of items to *include* in a combination, we thereby automatically also make a choice of the remaining items to *exclude* from our combination. For example, if we are forming combinations of three things from five things, every time we choose a group of three (to include) we also choose a group of two, the remainder (to exclude). It follows that

$$nCr = nC(n - r)$$

This result is often useful in calculating, as a time saver.

Example. From a group of seven men and four ladies a committee is to be formed. If there are to be six people on the committee, in how many ways can the committee be composed (a) if there are to be exactly two ladies serving, (b) if there are to be *at least* two ladies serving?

Consider first the case where there are to be *exactly* two ladies. There are two distinct operations to be performed: (i) choosing the ladies, (ii) choosing the men. The number of ways of choosing two ladies from four ladies is $4C2 = \dfrac{4P2}{2!} = \dfrac{4 \times 3}{2 \times 1} = 6$. The number of ways of choosing four men to make the committee up to six is $7C4 = \dfrac{7P4}{4!} = \dfrac{7 \times 6 \times 5 \times 4}{4 \times 3 \times 2 \times 1} = 35$. Hence there are six ways of performing the first operation (choosing ladies) and thirty-five ways of performing the second operation (choosing men). The total number of ways of selecting the committee is therefore $N = 6 \times 35 = 210$.

Consider, now, the second problem, where there are to be *at least* two ladies. In addition to the 210 ways of having exactly two ladies, we shall have the number of ways in which we can have three ladies and three men, or four ladies and two men (there are only four ladies available). Arguing exactly as before, we find the number of ways of having three ladies and three men is

$4C3 \times 7C3 = 140$, and the number of ways of having four ladies and two men is $4C4 \times 7C2 = 21$. Adding up all these results, we find that the total number of ways of having at least two ladies on the committee is $210 + 140 + 21 = 371$.

Permutations and combinations make nice brain-teasers. The arithmetic is dead easy, but it is essential to think very clearly.

NOW SEE HOW MUCH YOU HAVE LEARNT

1. Two dice are thrown simultaneously. What is the probability that the total score will be five? It will be a good help if you lay out the calculation in the form of a table, as follows:

First die	1	2	3	4
Second die	4	3	2	1
Probability				

2. A group of four cards is drawn from a pack. What is the probability that it will contain the four aces?

3. An entry in the 'Four Aways' section of a football pool has seven teams marked with the instruction 'Perm, 4 from 7' (it is a combination, actually). Find the cost of the entry at sixpence per line.

4. In an Analysis of Variance investigation (Analysis of Variance is dealt with in Chapter 19, but you don't need to know anything about it to answer this question) five different factors, A, B, C, D and E, are considered. To investigate what are known as 'Interaction Effects' the factors are considered in combinations. How many interactions of the type AB, CE, etc. are there? How many of the type ABC, BCE, etc.?

5. Six men each spin a penny, the results being recorded against the men's names. How many possible different results are there?

6. A school governor sends the headmistress six books from which the senior prefect is to choose four as a prize. One of the six books is entitled *No Orchids for Miss Blandish*, the headmistress quickly notices. In how many ways can the senior prefect choose her four books if the headmistress forbids her to have *No Orchids*? In how many ways may the senior prefect choose her four books if the headmistress, being more advanced, insists that the famous book be included in the selection? How many ways are there if the headmistress lets the girl pick freely from the six books? Write your answers down symbolically and the relation between them. Do you think this is a general rule, or does it only apply to this particular example?

7. Find the value of the following: (a) $8C3$, (b) $7C6$, (c) $5P2$, (d) $10P3$.

8. Find the value of $\dfrac{7!3!}{2!4!}$

9. How many different permutations, each containing all the letters of the following words, may be used?

   (a) *STATESMEN*   (b) *PROCRASTINATOR*

How many can be made from all the letters of the two words combined?

10. In how many different ways can ten draughtsmen appear simultaneously on the board during a game of draughts?

3

The Magic Lantern Technique

'Ultra proprium videre nemo libenter ducitur.' THOMAS À
KEMPIS

Very few people can look at a balance sheet and get a quick idea
of what it is all about – yet a good* balance sheet is laid out in
nice orderly fashion to make it as comprehensible as possible. A
balance sheet is a *summary* drawn up to show the overall state of
affairs brought about by a large number of transactions. Most
people look at a balance sheet, note in amazement that it does

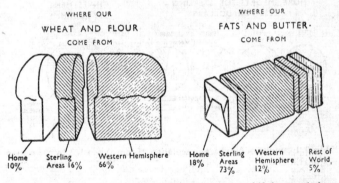

WHERE OUR
WHEAT AND FLOUR
COME FROM

Home 10%
Sterling Areas 16%
Western Hemisphere 66%

WHERE OUR
FATS AND BUTTER·
COME FROM

Home 18%
Sterling Areas 73%
Western Hemisphere 12%
Rest of World, 5%

Fig. 2. Information that is easy to grasp. (From *Survey '49*, by permission
of H.M.S.O.)

balance, and look for the balance in hand. Beyond that they do
not venture. Yet the balance sheet tells a story, if only we have the
skill to bring it to life. An income tax officer, looking at a balance
sheet, sees it, not as a list of figures which must be accepted as
they stand, but as a story whose verisimilitude it is his duty to
assess. He sees just how the various items of expense are related to
each other. He asks himself whether this is a reasonable story, and

* Most readers will be aware that skill is not infrequently used to hide the
moral truth in balance sheets while obeying to the letter the laws of accoun-
tancy.

whether the various items have a likely-looking magnitude, both absolutely and in relation to the other items in the statement. He seizes on doubtful-looking points and asks for explanations. He looks at the balance sheet from many points of view – always asking the question: 'Does this make sense?'. While it is true that there is a certain amount of gift about it, it is also true that skill can be acquired by practice.

Cold figures are uninspiring to most people. Diagrams help us to see the *pattern and shape* of any complex situation. Just as a map gives us a bird's-eye view of a wide stretch of country, so diagrams help us to visualize the *whole meaning* of a numerical complex *at a single glance*. Give me an undigested heap of figures

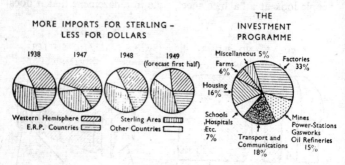

Fig. 3. Examples of pie chart presentation. (From *Survey '49*, by permission of H.M.S.O.)

and I cannot see the wood for the trees. Give me a diagram and I am positively encouraged to forget detail until I have a real grasp of the overall picture. Diagrams register a meaningful impression almost before we think.

A very common device is the presenting of an actual picture to the reader. Effective examples of this type frequently occur in government pamphlets and advertisements addressed to the general public. Some examples are shown in Fig. 2, based on *Survey '49*, published by the Stationery Office. A similar device (capable of more accurate representation) is the Pie Chart. Here a 'pie' is cut into slices corresponding in size with various quantities to be compared. Fig. 3 gives an example of this type of chart.

Another effective method of pictorial representation is the ideograph, examples of which are shown in Fig. 4. The ideograph depends on the idea of giving each item to be compared a *group* of

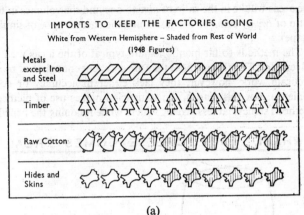

(a)

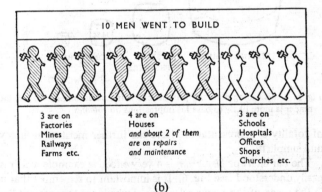

(b)

Fig. 4. Examples of Ideograph method of presenting information. (From *Survey '49*, by permission of H.M.S.O.)

the pictorial units, *all the units being of the same size*. This should be compared with the idea shown in Fig. 5, where each item has only *one* of the pictorial units and the comparison is made via the *size* of the unit. In this latter case, trouble in interpretation arises.

Is it the *heights* of the cheeses, or their *areas* on the printed page, or their *volumes* that are intended to illustrate the comparison? This is a serious matter, for if the heights are in the ratio of *three* to one, the areas will be in the ratio of *nine* to one and the volumes in the ratio of *twenty-seven* to one (assuming the cheeses to be of similar shape).

The methods so far mentioned are typical of the ideas used in advertising. For this purpose they are excellent enough. For more accurate work, however, they lack either in accuracy or convenience. For this reason, the statistician makes use of pictorial methods somewhat less artistic which, while retaining the benefits

WHERE YOUR CHEESE COMES FROM

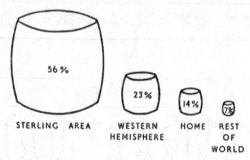

56% STERLING AREA

23% WESTERN HEMISPHERE

14% HOME

7% REST OF WORLD

Fig. 5. A misleading diagram, proportions being based on *heights*, but the reader is more likely to base his impressions on *volumes*

of totality of representation, have the further merit of accuracy and simplicity.

The bar chart or *histogram* is a very effective example which is easily understood (see Fig. 6). It is important to remember that it is the *areas*, of the rectangular blocks which are to represent the relative frequencies in the various classes. In the case where the width of the rectangles is constant, of course, the heights are proportional to the areas and so to the frequencies. Diagrams of this type should be arranged, wherever possible, so that the rectangles do have equal widths. In this way confusion is avoided. A similar idea is the horizontal or vertical line chart of the type shown in

Fig. 7. The length of the line is made proportional to the frequency in each class. Yet another device is the *frequency polygon* shown in Fig. 8. This is akin to the ordinary graph, though, of course, it is not sensible to read off at intermediate points as is made clear in the figure.

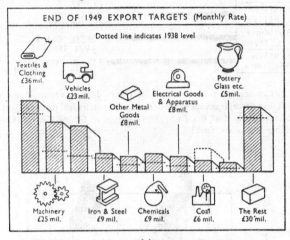

(a)

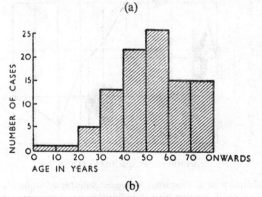

(b)

Fig. 6. Bar Charts

(a) From *Survey '49*, by permission of H.M.S.O.
(b) Age incidence of gastric ulcer at autopsy (after John O. Gibbs) [U.S.A.], 1946

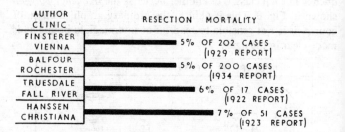

AUTHOR CLINIC	RESECTION MORTALITY
FINSTERER VIENNA	5% OF 202 CASES (1929 REPORT)
BALFOUR ROCHESTER	5% OF 200 CASES (1934 REPORT)
TRUESDALE FALL RIVER	6% OF 17 CASES (1922 REPORT)
HANSSEN CHRISTIANA	7% OF 51 CASES (1923 REPORT)

Fig. 7. Example of a Horizontal Line Chart. Lowest reported resection mortality percentages taken from a first-class statistical report by Livingston and Pack: *End Results in the Treatment of Gastric Cancer* (Paul B. Hoeber Inc., New York)

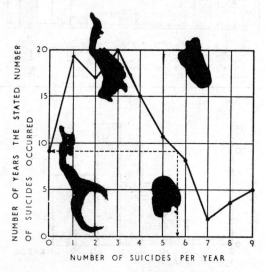

Fig. 8. Example of a Frequency Polygon. Suicides of women in eight German states in fourteen years. Von Bortkiewicz (1898) quoted by M. G. Kendall, *Advanced Statistics*, Vol. 1. (*Note:* It would be silly to read off' from the graph that in nine years there were $5\frac{1}{2}$ suicides per year)

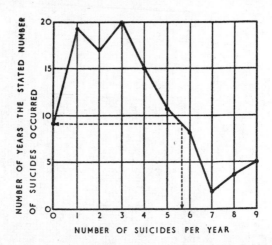

Fig. 8. Example of a Frequency Polygon. Suicides of women in eight German states in fourteen years. Von Bortkiewicz (1898) quoted by M. G. Kendall, *Advanced Statistics*, Vol. 1. (*Note:* It would be silly to 'read off' from the graph that in nine years there were $5\frac{1}{2}$ suicides per year)

It is regretted that in the book itself Fig. 8 has been printed faultily. The correct form is shown above.

Very frequently it is desired to show in diagrammatic form, not the relative frequency of occurrence in the various intervals, but the cumulative frequency above or below a given value. For example, we may wish to be able to read off from our chart the number or proportion of people whose height does not exceed any stated value, or the proportion of people whose income is not less than any given amount. Charts of this type are known variously as *cumulative frequency diagrams*, *ogives*, '*more than curves*', or

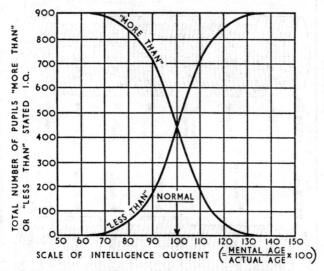

Fig. 9. Ogives or Cumulative Frequency Curves. Distribution of intelligence quotient in children, based on material in Terman, *The Measurement of Intelligence* (see also Fig. 16)

'*less than curves*'. Typically they look like a somewhat straggling letter *S*. Study of Fig. 9 will make their nature clear to the reader.

There is scope for the extension of the basic ideas in each case. For example, one frequently sees compound bar charts of the type illustrated in Fig. 10. Some people have a strange predilection for making charts of this type which are so compound that they become utterly incomprehensible. One might say that confusion is worse compounded. It is useless to expend great ingenuity in

2

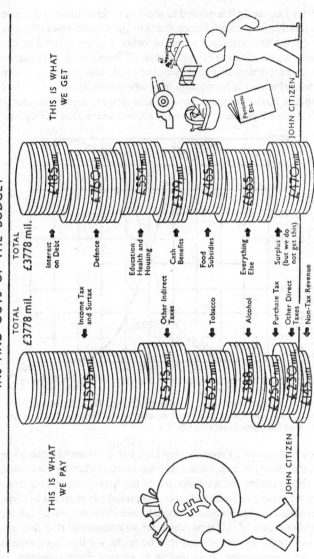

INS AND OUTS OF THE BUDGET

THIS IS WHAT WE GET

TOTAL £3778 mil.

£485 mil.	Interest on Debt
£760 mil.	Defence
£551 mil.	Education Health and Housing
£379 mil.	Cash Benefits
£465 mil.	Food Subsidies
£665 mil.	Everything Else
£470 mil.	Surplus (but we do not get this)

JOHN CITIZEN

TOTAL £3778 mil.

THIS IS WHAT WE PAY

£1595 mil.	Income Tax and Surtax
£545 mil.	Other Indirect Taxes
£625 mil.	Tobacco
£388 mil.	Alcohol
£250 mil.	Purchase Tax
£230 mil.	Other Direct Taxes
£145 mil.	Non-Tax Revenue

JOHN CITIZEN

Figures shown are estimates for the year starting 1st April 1949 making a diagram perplexing, when the whole purpose of a diagram is to render the meaning as plain as a pikestaff.

Quite frequently, use is made of graphs. It is as well to point out that there are rules to be obeyed if the graph is not to lose in value. Not infrequently one sees graphs in advertisements where the basic rules have deliberately been broken so as to create a more attractive impression. This may be good advertising but it certainly is not honest.

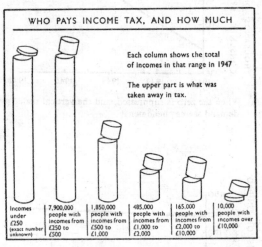

Fig. 10 (b). Another good example of a Compound Bar Chart (source as Fig. 10 (a)). The reader will notice that these charts have been drawn with heights in strict proportion to the total *incomes* within the stated ranges. This diagram may be compared with Fig. 18 which shows the *numbers of people* in the same ranges

It pays to keep wide awake in studying any graph. The thing looks so simple, so frank, and so appealing that the careless are easily fooled. Some examples are shown in the figures of bad manners in graph drawing. Fig. 11 shows how misleading the suppression of the zero line can be, especially with a change of scale. In cases where the zero and full scale cannot sensibly be shown, good manners will call attention to the fact. A nice way of doing this is to show the zero and then break the axis. It is a good

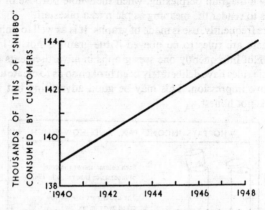

Fig. 11 (a). When the zero is suppressed, and the vertical scale 'stretched' the rise in demand seems phenomenal

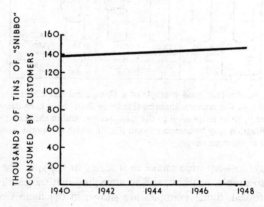

Fig. 11 (b). But this is the modest progress actually made. (With apologies and grateful thanks to 'Beachcomber' for the excellently facetious trade name 'Snibbo')

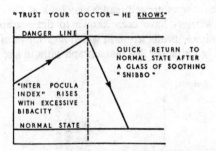

Fig. 12. The Advertiser's Graph – devoid of scales. After consumption of alcohol, your 'Inter Pocula Index' rises to what may prove a dangerous level, with serious risk of muscular atony. In such cases the taking of a therapeutic nostrum has untold effect as a sedative and restorative. There is no finer nostrum than 'Snibbo'

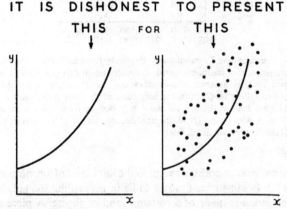

Fig. 13. When a trend line is drawn on a graph the original points should not be erased

thing to emphasize the zero and, in the case of percentage charts, the 100% line. Data and formulae should be given along with the graph, so that the interested reader may look at the details if he wishes. Advertisers have been known to draw graphs for the general public to 'profit' from in which *no scale at all* is shown, deliberately ignoring the fact that a graph without a scale on each

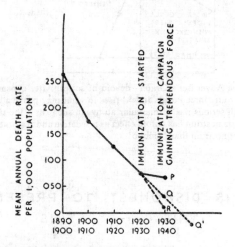

Fig. 14. Overconfident Extrapolation – Example (from an author who shall be anonymous) of reasoning based on overconfident extrapolation. It was claimed that, in absence of immunization, the death-rate would have continued falling to Q, in fact it only reached P. Some point such as R would have been necessary to show any benefit from immunization. But if to Q, why not to Q^1 in the next decade, with the 'Resurrection of the Dead'? (negative death rate)

axis means next to nothing except in the fairy land of a profession whose job is sometimes thought to lie in persuading the gullible that the moon is made of a certain brand of cheese. A piece of self-deception – often dear to the heart of apprentice scientists – is the drawing of a 'smooth curve' (how attractive it sounds!) through a set of points which have about as much trend as the currants in plum duff. Once this is done, the mind, looking for order amidst chaos, follows the Jack-o'-lantern line with scant attention to the protesting shouts of the actual points. Nor, let it be whispered, is it unknown for people who should know better to rub off the offending points and publish the trend line which their foolish imagination has introduced on the flimsiest of evidence. Allied to this sin is that of overconfident *extrapolation*, i.e. extend-

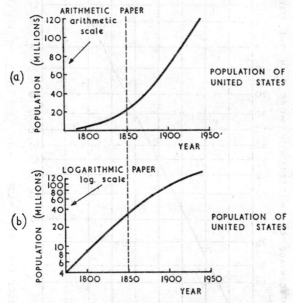

Fig. 15. Logarithmic Paper – used in rate of growth problems. Each paper creates a different impression. The graph on arithmetic paper shows that after about 1850 the population grew steadily by about the same number of citizens each decade. From this it follows that the population increased by a decreasing percentage or ratio in each succeeding decade. This is brought out by the flattening out of the graph on logarithmic paper

ing the graph by guesswork beyond the range of factual information. Whenever extrapolation is attempted it should be carefully distinguished from the rest of the graph, e.g. by showing the extrapolation as a dotted line in contrast to the full line of the rest

of the graph. The writer recently heard of a mathematician of undoubted skill who drew a graph through a *single point*, explaining
that 'that is the way it must go'! No doubt he was quite correct,

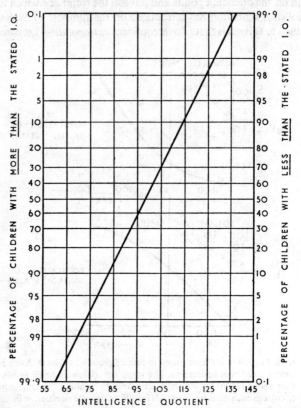

Fig. 16. The ogives of Fig. 9 presented as a straight line by using probability
paper. Note how scale is crowded at the centre – just as I.Q. itself tends
to bunch around the average value

but he must have had a lot of information to help him in addition
to the small amount contained in the single point in his graph.
Extrapolation always calls for justification, sooner or later. Until

this justification is forthcoming, it remains a provisional estimate, based on guesswork. Economists and politicians have been great offenders against us all in this matter of extrapolation. The economic crisis after the last war brought forth a spate of prognostication as to when slumps would come, when loans would run out and the rest, for which, as it proved in the event, there was usually little or no justification.

Special types of paper are often used by experts, e.g. logarithmic and probability papers. These are extremely useful to the expert (if he goes carefully) but are next to useless for the layman, as they are invariably misleading to the uninitiated. Figs. 15 and 16 show examples of special papers commonly in use.

YOU SHOULD NOW BE ABLE TO DO THE FOLLOWING:

Annual wage £	Number of employees
0– 99	10
100–199	54
200–299	184
300–399	264
400–499	146
500–599	40
600–799	1
700–899	1

1. Draw a horizontal line chart, histogram, frequency polygon, ascending and descending ogives for the data in the table showing the number of employees earning different salaries in a certain company.

Display the data in ideograph form using the symbol ⚛ to represent 10 employees.

2. Convert Fig. 4 (b) to Pie Chart form.
3. Convert Fig. 6 (a) to Pie Chart form.
4. Put Fig 4 (b) in the form of Fig. 10 (a).
5. Convert Fig. 6 (b) to an ogive in 'less than' form.

4

On the Average

'The figure of 2·2 children per adult female was felt to be in some respects absurd, and a Royal Commission suggested that the middle classes be paid money to increase the average to a rounder and more convenient number.' (*Punch*)

In former times, when the hazards of sea voyages were much more serious than they are today, when ships buffeted by storms threw a portion of their cargo overboard, it was recognized that those whose goods were sacrificed had a claim in equity to indemnification at the expense of those whose goods were safely delivered. The value of the lost goods was paid for by agreement between all those whose merchandise had been in the same ship. This sea damage to cargo in transit was known as 'havaria' and the word came naturally to be applied to the compensation money which each individual was called upon to pay. From this Latin word derives our modern word *average*. Thus the idea of an average has its roots in primitive insurance. Quite naturally, with the growth of shipping, insurance was put on a firmer footing whereby the risk was shared, not simply by those whose goods were at risk on a particular voyage, but by large groups of traders. Eventually the carrying of such risks developed into a separate skilled and profit-making profession. This entailed the payment to the underwriter of a sum of money which bore a recognizable relation to the risk involved.

The idea of an average is common property. However scanty our knowledge of arithmetic, we are all at home with the idea of goal averages, batting and bowling averages, and the like. We realize that the purpose of an average is *to represent a group of individual values* in a simple and concise manner so that the mind can get a quick understanding of the general size of the individuals in the group, undistracted by fortuitous and irrelevant variations. It is of the utmost importance to appreciate this fact that the average is to act as a *representative*. It follows that it is the acme of nonsense to go through all the rigmarole of the arithmetic to calculate the average of a set of figures which do not in some real sense constitute a single family. Suppose a prosperous medical man earning £3,000 a year had a wife and two children none of whom were gainfully employed and that the doctor had in his household a maid to whom he paid £150 a year and that there was a jobbing gardener who received £40 a year. We can go through all the processes of calculating the average income for this little group. Six people between them earn £3,190 in the year. Dividing the total earnings by the number of people we may determine the average earnings of the group to be £531 13s. 4d. But this figure is no more than an impostor in the robes of an average. It represents not a single person in the group. It gives the reader a totally meaningless figure, because he cannot make one single reliable deduction from it. This is an extreme example, but mock averages are calculated with great abandon. Few people ask themselves: What conclusions will be drawn from this average that I am about to calculate? Will it create a false impression?

The idea of an average is so handy that it is not surprising that several kinds of average have been invented so that as wide a field as possible may be covered with the minimum of misrepresentation. We have a choice of averages; and we pick out the one which is appropriate both to our data and our purpose. We should not let ourselves fall into the error that because the idea of an average is easy to grasp there is no more to be said on the subject. Averages can be very misleading.

The simplest average is that which will be well known to every reader. This common or garden average is also called the *mean*, a word meaning 'centre'. (All averages are known to statisticians as 'measures of central tendency', for they tell us the point about which the several different values cluster.) The *arithmetic mean* or average of a set of numbers is calculated by totalling the items in the set and dividing the total by the number of individuals in the set. No more need be said on this point, save that the items to be averaged must be of the same genus. We cannot, for example, average the wages of a polygamist with the number of his wives.

A second kind of average is the *harmonic mean*, which is the reciprocal* of the arithmetic mean of the reciprocals of the values

* The reciprocal of a number is found by dividing that number into unity, e.g. the reciprocal of $4 = \frac{1}{4} = 0.25$.

we wish to average. The harmonic mean is the appropriate average to use when we are dealing with rates and prices. Consider the well-known academic example of the aeroplane which flies round a square whose side is 100 miles long, taking the first side at 100 m.p.h., the second side at 200 m.p.h., the third side at 300 m.p.h., and the fourth side at 400 m.p.h. What is the average speed of the plane in its flight around the square? If we average the speeds using the arithmetic average in the ordinary way, we get:

$$\text{Average speed} = \frac{100 + 200 + 300 + 400}{4} = 250 \text{ m.p.h.}$$

But this is not the correct result, as may easily be seen as follows:

> Time to travel along the first side   = 1 hour
> Time to travel along the second side = 30 minutes
> Time to travel along the third side   = 20 minutes
> Time to travel along the fourth side = 15 minutes
> Hence total time to travel 400 miles = 2 hours 5 minutes
> $= \frac{25}{12}$ hours

From this it appears that the average velocity is $\frac{400}{1} \div \frac{25}{12} = 192$ m.p.h.

The ordinary arithmetic average, then, gives us the wrong result. A clue as to the reason for this will be found in the fact that the different speeds are not all maintained for the same time – only for the same distance. The correct average to employ in such a case is the harmonic mean.

In order to give the formula for this we shall here introduce a little more mathematical notation which will be of great benefit to us later in this book. In calculating averages we have to *add up* a string of items which make up the set whose average is required. The mathematician uses a shorthand sign to tell us when to add up. He calls adding up 'summing' and uses the Greek letter S which is written Σ and called 'sigma' to indicate when terms are to be added. (This is actually the capital sigma. Later we shall have a lot to say about the small letter sigma which is written σ.) Each of the numbers which have to be taken into account in our calculation is denoted by the letter x. If we wish to differentiate between the various quantities we can number them thus: x_1, x_2, x_3, x_4, etc., the labelling numbers being written as subscripts so that they will not be confused with actual numbers entering into the calculation. (This may sound as confusing to the novice as it will be boring to the learned. Let the learned turn over the pages till they find something more interesting, while we explain this simple and useful shorthand to the novice.) Let us take as an example the calculation of the arithmetic average of the five numbers 5, 6, 8, 7, 6. We could, if there were any reason for keeping track of these, label them as follows:

$$x_1 = 5 \qquad x_2 = 6 \qquad x_3 = 8 \qquad x_4 = 7 \qquad x_5 = 6$$

Now the advantage of using algebraic notation (i.e. letters to stand for any numbers we care to substitute for them according to the problem in hand) is that we can write down in a very compact way the rules for performing the calculation which will give us the correct answer to the type of problem we are dealing with. In fact, a formula is nothing else than the *answer to every problem* of the type to which it applies. We solve the problem once and for all when we work out a formula. The formula *is* the answer. All we have to do is to substitute for the letters the actual quantities they stand for in the given problem. Suppose, now, we denote the number of quantities which are to be averaged in our problem by the letter n (in our case here, $n = 5$). To calculate the arithmetic average we have to add up all the five quantities thus: $5 + 6 + 8 + 7 + 6 = 32$. This adding part of the calculation would appear in algebraic form as $x_1 + x_2 + x_3 + x_4 + x_5$. The next step would be to divide the total by the number of items to be averaged, viz. 5, giving the result $6 \cdot 4$ for the average. In algebraic notation this would appear as

$$\text{Average} = \frac{x_1 + x_2 + x_3 + x_4 + x_5}{n}$$

This method of writing the formula would be very inconvenient if there were a large number of items to be averaged; moreover, there is no need to keep the individual items labelled, for in an average the identity of the individuals is deliberately thrown away as irrelevant. So we introduce the summation sign, Σ, and write our formula in the very compact form:

$$\text{Average} = \frac{\Sigma x}{n}$$

The formula thus tells us that to get the average we 'add up all the x values and divide their total by the number of items, n'.

In similar fashion, now, the *harmonic mean*, which we have said is the average to be used in averaging speeds and so on and which is defined as the reciprocal (the reciprocal of a number x is equal to $\frac{1}{x}$) of the arithmetic mean of the reciprocals of the values, x, which we wish to average, has the formula:

$$\text{Harmonic mean} = \frac{n}{\sum\left(\frac{1}{x}\right)}$$

To illustrate the use of this formula let us use it on our aeroplane problem. The four speeds, which were each maintained over the same distance, were 100, 200, 300, and 400 m.p.h. These are our x values. Since there are four of them the value of n in our formula is 4, and we get:

$$\text{Harmonic mean} = \frac{n}{\sum\left(\frac{1}{x}\right)} = \frac{4}{\left(\frac{1}{100} + \frac{1}{200} + \frac{1}{300} + \frac{1}{400}\right)} = \frac{4}{\left(\frac{25}{1200}\right)}$$

$$= \frac{4 \times 1200}{25} = 192 \text{ m.p.h.}$$

which we know to be the correct answer.

The reader should note carefully that the harmonic mean is here appropriate because the times were variable, with the distances constant. Had it been that times were constant and distances variable the ordinary arithmetic average would have been the correct one to use. The type of average which is appropriate always depends on the terms of the problem in hand. Formulae should never be applied indiscriminately.

Yet a third type of average is the *geometric mean*. This is the appropriate average to use when we wish to average quantities which are drawn from a situation in which they follow what W. W. Sawyer in *Mathematician's Delight* calls the 'gangster law of growth', i.e. a geometric progression or the exponential law. Many quantities follow this type of law. For example, the population of a city, given a stable birth-rate and death-rate with no migration, will increase at a rate proportional to the number of people in the city. Suppose that in the year 1940 a certain city had a population of 250,000 and that in the year 1950 its population were 490,000. If we wished to estimate the population in the year 1945 (estimating populations at various times between successive censuses is an important matter in public health statistics) then we might, as a rough approximation, take the average of the populations at the two known dates, thus:

$$\text{Population at 1945} = \frac{250,000 + 490,000}{2} = 370,000$$

This would only be a sensible method if we were able to assume that the population increased by the same number every year. This is not likely, however, for, as the city grows in size, so the number of citizens is likely to grow at an ever increasing rate (see Fig. 17). A better estimate is likely to be obtained, in normal circumstances, by calculating the *geometric mean* of the population at the two known dates. To calculate the geometric mean, we multiply together all the quantities which it is desired to average. Then, if there are n such quantities, we find the nth root of the product. Denoting our n quantities by $x_1, x_2, x_3, \ldots x_n$, we may write the formula for the geometric mean as follows:

$$\text{Geometric mean} = \sqrt[n]{x_1 \times x_2 \times x_3 \times \ldots x_n}$$

Applying this to the problem given above where we wish to estimate the population of a city in 1945, given that in 1940 the population was 250,000 and in 1950 was 490,000, we have $n = 2$ items to average, and we find:

$$\text{Geometric mean} = \sqrt[2]{250,000 \times 490,000} = 350,000$$

as our estimate for the population of 1945. This result, it will be noted, is appreciably lower than we obtained using the arithmetic average (370,000). If the reader considers Fig. 17 he will see that it is the more likely estimate.

Collecting together, at this point, our three different averages, we have:

Arithmetic Mean (usually denoted as $\bar{x}$ and called x-bar)

$$\bar{x} = \frac{\Sigma x}{n}$$

Harmonic Mean (usually denoted by H)

$$H = \frac{n}{\sum\left(\frac{1}{x}\right)}$$

Geometric Mean (usually denoted by G)

$$G = \sqrt[n]{x_1 \times x_2 \times x_3 \times \ldots x_n}$$

Each of these measures of central tendency has its own special applications. All of them are obtained by simple arithmetical pro-

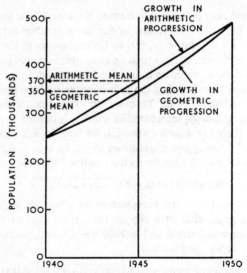

Fig. 17. Comparison of Interpolation by Arithmetic Mean and Geometric Mean. The population of a city often grows according to the exponential law. This would certainly be true with stable birth-rate and death-rate and in absence of migration. Under these conditions, the geometric average would be more appropriate than the arithmetic average to interpolate the population at a given date between two dates at which the population was known

cesses which take into account the magnitude of every individual item.

We emphasized the important idea of any average or measure of central tendency as the *representative* of a homogeneous group in which the members are recognizably similar. Now many distributions, while being undoubtedly homogeneous in the sense that there is continuity between the various members of the group, nevertheless are such that very great differences exist between the largest and smallest members, and, moreover, exhibit a marked lack of symmetry, the family tending to cluster much nearer to one extreme than the other. Fig. 18 is a typical example. It shows the

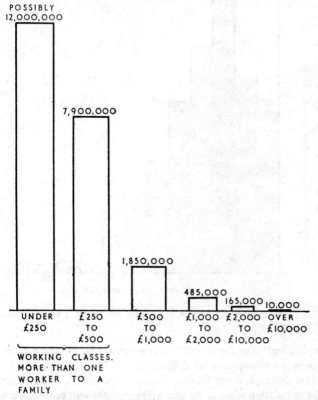

Fig. 18. Numbers of people in different income ranges forming a positively skew distribution. Compare with Fig. 10 (b) with regard to shape of distribution, noticing (a) the large combined income of the vanishingly small numbers in the top ranges and (b) the effect of taxation

way in which annual income is distributed. There is certainly continuity, but small incomes are the norm. The reader will appreciate at once that to calculate averages for distributions of this type using the arithmetic mean would be very misleading. The relatively few people with extremely high incomes would pull up the average appreciably, so that it could not be taken as truly

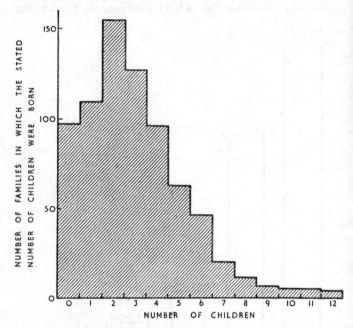

Fig. 19. Distribution of number of children per family is also positively skewed

representative of the population in general. Fig. 19, which shows the relative frequency of different sizes of family, presents the same difficulty. Some families are *very* well off for children and the calculation of an arithmetic average might well be misleading – particularly if our purpose is purely descriptive.

It is evident that what we need in such cases is a measure of central tendency which is unaffected by the relatively few extreme values in the 'tail' of the distribution. Two ideas suggest themselves. The first is that if we were to take all our families and set them down in a long column starting with the smallest and working up to the largest, we could then use the size of that family which came halfway down the column as our measure of central tendency. This measure is called the *median* (meaning 'middle item'). Half of all families would have a size not less than that of the median family and half not more than that of the median family. Notice that in this way we do not take account at all of the actual numbers of children except for ranking purposes. It is evident that the number of children in the largest family could be increased to 50,000 without in any way disturbing our measure of central tendency, which would still be the middle item.

A second method of getting a measure of central tendency which is not upset by extreme values in the distribution is to use the *most commonly occurring value*. This is the fashionable value, the value *à la mode*, so to say. It is called the *mode* or *modal value*. For example, in Fig. 19 the modal value for the size of family is seen to be two children. This is really a typical value and seems real to us compared with the arithmetic average which in this case works out to 2·96. It is difficult to imagine 2·96 children. Notice that the arithmetic mean is markedly affected by the relatively few very large families. Which is correct? Neither and both. Both averages serve a purpose. The mode would form a very poor basis for any further calculations of an arithmetical nature, for it has deliberately excluded arithmetical precision in the interests of presenting a typical result. The arithmetic average, on the other hand, excellent as it is for numerical purposes, has sacrificed its desire to be typical in favour of numerical accuracy. In such a case it is often desirable to quote *both* measures of central tendency. Better still, go further and present a histogram of the distribution as in Fig. 19.

A problem which not infrequently arises is to make an estimate of the median value of a distribution when we do not have the actual values of each individual item given, but only the numbers of items in specified ranges. We shall deal with this matter in Chapter 6 where the question of class limits and boundaries will be considered.

We shall now say a few words about frequency distributions. If we have a large group of items each of which has connected with it some numerical value indicative of its magnitude, which varies as between one member of the group and another (as, for example, when we consider the heights of men or the amount of income tax paid by them), and if we draw up a table or graph showing the relative frequency with which members of the group have the various possible values of the variable quantity (e.g. proportion of men at each different height, or proportions of the

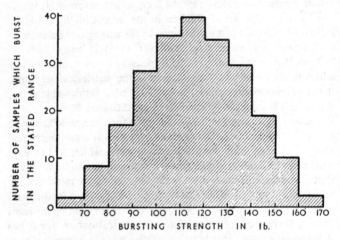

Fig. 20. Distribution for the bursting strength of samples of vinyl coated nylon exhibiting symmetry

population falling into various income tax groups), then we have what is called a *frequency distribution* for the variable quantity in question. This is usually called simply the *distribution*. Thus we have distributions for height, weight, chest size, income, living rooms per person, and so on. Similarly we have distributions for the number of deaths according to age for different diseases, number of local government areas with specified birthrates and death-rates, and so on. The quantity which varies (height, birthrate, income, and so on) is called the *variate*. Some variates are *continuous*, i.e. they can assume *any* value at all within a certain

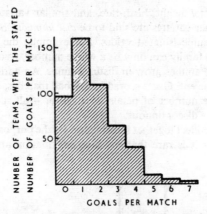

Fig. 21. The number of goals scored per team per match gives a positively skewed distribution of a discontinuous variable

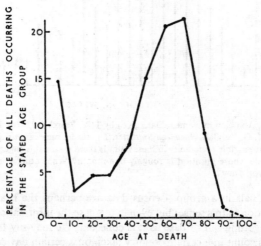

Fig. 22. Example of a Bimodal (double peaked) Distribution. The peak in the first years of life reflects the serious loss of potential life due to the infantile mortality rate. (From the *Registrar General's Report, Years 1930–32*, quoted by M. G. Kendall in *Advanced Statistics*)

range. Income, height, birth-rate, and similar variates are continuous. Other variates are said to be *discontinuous* because they can only assume isolated values. For example, the number of children in a family can only be a whole number, fractions being impossible. Families grow in distinct jumps. An addition to the family is an event. Goals scored in football matches, articles lost in buses, the number of petals on a flower – all such variable quantities are discontinuous.

When we collect together information for the purposes of statistical analysis it is rare that we have information about all the

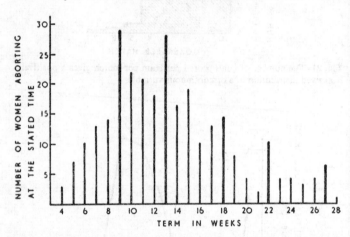

Fig. 23. Abortion in women. Data given by T. V. Pearce (1930) and quoted by M. G. Kendall, *Advanced Statistics*. The reader may care to speculate about possible periodicity in these data. Is there reasonable suggestion of a cycle whose duration is roughly one month? What other conclusion can you draw?

individuals in a group. Census data are perhaps the nearest to perfection in this sense; but even in this case the information is already getting out of date as it is collected. We may say that the census count in a certain country taken on a certain day came to 43,574,205, but it would be nothing short of silly to keep quoting the last little figure 5 for the next ten years – or even the next ten minutes. Such accuracy would be spurious. In general it is not possible to investigate the whole of a population. We have to be content with a *sample*. We take a sample with the idea of making inferences from it about the population from which it was drawn, believing, for example, that the average of a good sample is closely related to the average of the whole population. We shall say more about samples in Chapter 10. The word *population* is used in statistics to refer not simply to groups of people, but, by a natural extension, to groups of measurements associated with any collection of inanimate objects. By drawing a sufficiently large sample of measurements, we may arrive at a frequency distribution for any population. Figs. 20–24 give examples of various types of distribution.

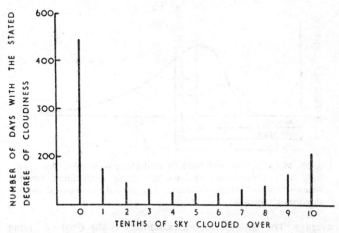

Fig. 24. Peculiar distribution of cloudiness at Greenwich. Based on data given by Gertrude Pearse (1928) for month of July 1890–1904 (excluding 1901) and quoted by M. G. Kendall, *Advanced Statistics*, Vol. 1. Note tendency for sky to be either very clear or very cloudy

Some distributions, as will be seen from the diagrams, are *symmetrical* about their central value. Other distributions have marked asymmetry and are said to be *skew*. Skew distributions are divided into two types. If the 'tail' of the distribution reaches out into the larger values of the variate, the distribution is said to show *positive skewness*; if the tail extends towards the smaller values of the variate, the distribution is called *negatively skew*. In the next chapter we shall take up the question of the concentration of the members of the distribution about their central value, for it is clearly a matter of the greatest importance to be able to measure the degree to which the various members of a population may differ from each other.

Fig. 25 illustrates an interesting relationship which is found to hold approximately between the median, mode, and mean of moderately skew distributions. Figs. 26 and 27 illustrate geometrical interpretations of the three measures of central tendency.

We shall close this chapter with an elementary account of Index Numbers, which are really nothing more than a special kind of

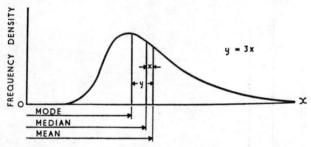

Fig. 25. Mean, Median and Mode in moderately skew cases. For moderately skew distributions we have the simple approximate relation: Mean − Mode = 3 (Mean − Median). For a perfectly symmetrical distribution they all coincide

average. The best known index number is the Cost of Living Index, which, as readers will know, is a rough measure of the average price of the basic necessities of life. In many industries, the Cost of Living Index is a strong chain which keeps a man's reward tied strictly to his necessity rather than to his ambition. But index numbers are a widespread disease of modern life, or, we might better say, a symptom of the modern disease of constantly trying to keep a close check on everything. We have index numbers for exports, for imports, for wage changes, and for consumption. We have others for wholesale and retail prices. The Board of Trade has an index. The Ministry of Labour has an index. *The*

Economist has another. It is scarcely possible to be respectable nowadays unless one owns at least one index number. It is a corporate way of 'keeping up with the Joneses' – the private individual having been forced by taxation to give up this inspiring aim long ago.

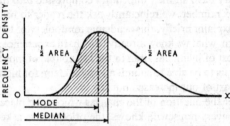

Fig. 26. Geometrical interpretation of Mode and Median. The vertical line at the median value divides the area under the frequency curve into halves (area is proportional to frequency). The vertical line at the modal value passes through the peak of the curve, i.e. it is the value at which the frequency density is a maximum

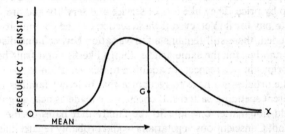

Fig. 27. Geometrical interpretation of the Mean. The vertical line at the mean will pass through the centre of gravity of a sheet of uniform thickness and density cut to the shape of the distribution. The mean is the abscissa of the centre of gravity *G*

It is really questionable – though bordering on heresy to put the question – whether we would be any the worse off if the whole bag of tricks were scrapped. So many of these index numbers are so ancient and so out of date, so out of touch with reality, so completely devoid of practical value when they have been computed, that their regular calculation must be regarded as a widespread compulsion neurosis. Only lunatics and public servants with no other choice go on doing silly things and liking it. Yet, since we become more and more the servants of our servants, and since they persist in tying us down to this lugubrious system whereby the housewife, the business man, and the most excellent groups of the citizenry have all their difficulties compressed into the brevity of an index number, we reluctantly ask the reader to bear with us while we explain, briefly, this academic tomfoolery of telling us in cryptic form what we knew already from hard experience: namely, that the cost of living has risen in the last couple of months, sufficiently for us to be able to submit a humble claim for higher wages to offset part of our increased burden.

Consider the question of the changes which take place in retail prices. As every housewife knows, the price we are asked to pay bears only the faintest resemblance in many cases to the worth of the article. She knows, too, that for many commodities it is more accurate to speak of prices rather than price. Tomatoes in one shop may be 6d. per pound; the same tomatoes in another shop may be 10d. or 1s. Some people are well enough off to be able to shop by price. They like lots of service and servility and are willing to pay for it. Yet, even if these sections of the community are excluded, there still remains a fair variation between one district and another for the same article, things like fish and fruit being notorious in this respect. In addition to this variation in the price of the articles, we have to recognize that different families have different spending patterns. If cheese were made as dear as gold it would not matter one iota to the family that hates cheese like poison. Conscientious vegetarians would probably regard it as an excellent thing if the price of meat rose to prohibitive levels. Total abstainers positively loathe the idea of beer and spirits being cheap. Non-smokers love to see the Chancellor raise the money by piling the tax on 'non-essentials' like tobacco. It is evident that we shall get nowhere if all this individuality is to run riot. It is far too inconvenient for the statistician.

We get over the difficulty by shutting our eyes to it. All we have to do is to invent a 'standard family'.* We might, for example,

* Composed of one underpaid male, one overworked female, and 2·2 underfed children.

choose the standard urban working-class family. We then do a sample survey, to find out what quantities of the various articles we are considering they consume in a week under normal conditions, and draw up a table as follows:

EXPENDITURE OF THE STANDARD WORKING-CLASS FAMILY
(1949)

	Quantity	Price	Expenditure	Weight
Bread and Flour	39 lb.	4d./lb.	156d.	31·2
Meat	7 lb.	24d./lb.	168d.	33·6
Potatoes	35 lb.	2d./lb.	70d.	14·0
Tea	1 lb.	36d./lb.	36d.	7·2
Sugar	2 lb.	5d./lb.	10d.	2·0
Butter	1 lb.	18d./lb.	18d.	3·6
Margarine	1 lb.	12d./lb.	12d.	2·4
Eggs	1 doz.	30d./doz.	30d.	6·0
		Total	500d.	100·0

Now, it is a relatively simple matter to keep track of the changes in prices as time goes on. It would be very much more troublesome to keep a check on whether the spending pattern, as indicated by the amounts of the various items bought by the standard family, was tending to change. One line of approach would be to assume that our standard family will not change its demands from year to year. Suppose for the year 1950 the prices were as in the following table.

EXPENDITURE OF THE STANDARD WORKING-CLASS FAMILY
(1950)

	Quantity	Price	Expenditure	Weight
Bread and Flour	39 lb.	5d./lb.	195d.	30·1
Meat	7 lb.	30d./lb.	210d.	32·6
Potatoes	35 lb.	3d./lb.	105d.	16·3
Tea	1 lb.	36d./lb.	36d.	5·6
Sugar	2 lb.	6d./lb.	12d.	1·9
Butter	1 lb.	27d./lb.	27d.	4·2
Margarine	1 lb.	15d./lb.	15d.	2·3
Eggs	1 doz.	45d./doz.	45d.	7·0
		Total	645d.	100·0

The reader should ignore, for the moment, the last column, headed 'Weight', in each table. The obvious thing, at once, is that to buy the same quantities of the same articles, and therefore to get the same 'satisfaction', as the economists have it, cost the standard family 645d. in 1950 as against 500d. in 1949, i.e. the cost in 1950 as compared with 1949 was $\frac{645}{500} \times 100 = 128 \cdot 8\%$. We could then say that the index of retail prices, as represented by this group of items, stood at 129 in 1950 (1949 = 100).

We could get a similar indication of the rise in retail prices as follows. Consider, first, the amount of money our standard family spent on the various items in our 'base year, 1949'. These can be reduced to percentages of the total expenditure (on the group of items considered in the index). For instance, out of a total expenditure of 500d., bread and flour claimed 156d. or $31 \cdot 2\%$. Similarly, meat took $33 \cdot 6\%$ of the total expenditure, potatoes $14 \cdot 0\%$, and so on. These figures are entered in the column headed 'Weight' since they tell us the relative importance of the different items in the household budget. Meat is a very heavy item, sugar a relatively small one. These weights give us a pattern of expenditure as it actually appeared to the standard housewife in the base year. They take account of both quantity and price. The first thing that is obvious from this pattern of weights is that, while a 50% increase in the cost of sugar is not a matter of great importance to the housewife, even a 10% increase in the price of meat would be a serious extra burden to carry in the standard family where income is usually closely matched to expenditure. We must remember that our standard family is a standardized family. Its wants are not supposed to change. It is supposed to be devoid of ambition. It only gets a rise in salary when such a rise is absolutely necessary.

Now while it is true (in the absence of subsidies and purchase tax or price fixing by combines) that all commodities tend to rise in price together, nevertheless, superimposed on this general tendency, there will be a certain irregularity. Comparing the price of bread and flour in our two years we find that the 'price relative', as it is called, of this item is $\frac{5}{4} \times 100 = 125\%$ in 1950 as compared with the base year, 1949.

The following table shows the 'prices relative' for the several items, together with the weights corresponding to the base year.

The weights have been quoted to the first decimal place, further places being condemned as coming under the heading 'delusions of accuracy'.

	Price relative	Base year weight	Price-rel. × weight
Bread and Flour	125	31·2	3,900
Meat	125	33·6	4,200
Potatoes	150	14·0	2,100
Tea	100	7·2	720
Sugar	120	2·0	240
Butter	150	3·6	540
Margarine	125	2·4	300
Eggs	150	6·0	900
	Total	100·0	12,900

If, now, we divide the total of the 'prices relative × weight' by the total of the weights, we get the average price of the commodities in 1950, as compared with the base year, 1949, equals 129·00, which we certainly quote no more accurately than 129. This would now be our index of retail prices. For every hundred pennies spent in 1949 we need to spend 129 in 1950 to get the same amount of 'satisfaction'. Evidently, every succeeding year – or month, for that matter – can be compared with our base year.

The economists, of course, have great fun – and show remarkable skill – in inventing more refined index numbers. Sometimes they use geometric averages instead of arithmetic averages (the advantage here being that the geometric average is less upset by extreme oscillations in individual items), sometimes they use the harmonic average. But these are all refinements of the basic idea of the index number which we have indicated in this chapter. Most business men seem to thrive without understanding this simple matter. Perhaps they half realize that it doesn't mean a lot, except in regard to wage negotiations between themselves and Trade Unions – and in such cases experts on both sides of the fence do all the statistics required. The employer and employee don't much mind how much of this arithmetic goes on, so long as the final agreement is reasonably fair to both sides.

The snags in this index number game will be apparent to the reader. First of all, if he will inspect the pattern of weights in the tables for 1949 and 1950, he will see that they are not identical. Over a reasonable period of years the pattern can change appreciably. Then, again, if we try to measure the cost of living of our standard family by including heating, lighting, rent, beer, cigarettes, football pools, and the rest, we soon get into deep water. For example, if we find that in the base year the standard family spends one-tenth of its income on football pools, are we to argue that since this is a heavy item of expenditure it shall be supported somehow in the cost of living calculations? Until very recently the cost of living index in this country took account of the cost of paraffin and candles for lighting purposes, and assumed that no working-class family had heard of electricity. Then there is the difficulty that the standard family tends to become a standardized family in so far as its wages are tied to an index which is slow to recognize the right of its standard family to be anything but standard in its requirements from year to year. The reader should consider carefully the full implication of 'subsidies on essentials' (included in cost of living index) and 'purchase tax on non-essentials' (not included in the index or only modestly represented). The pernicious nature of tying wages to cost of living indexes while this jiggery-pokery is official policy will be apparent. The whole scheme is positively Machiavellian in its acceptance of deception as a necessity in politics. And does it really work so well, after all? The truth is that it is too inefficient even to keep the worker standardized. As new items are available from manufacturers, the public has to be given the power to purchase them, whether they are included in the cost of living index or not. Shall we ask the economists: What good do your indexes do – really?

NOW HAVE A GO AT THE FOLLOWING:

1. Find the arithmetic average of the numbers from 1 to 10. Now see if you can find a simple rule by getting the average of the numbers 1 to 3; 1 to 5; 1 to 7 and so on. Does the rule also work for finding the average of an even number of terms, e.g. 1 to 6; 1 to 14, etc.?

2. A physics student, in finding the formula for the vibration time of a pendulum, made the following repeat readings at one particular

length of the pendulum. How do you account for the variations? Use an assumed mean to find the arithmetic average of the readings.

50·4, 50·2, 50·7, 49.8, 50·1, 50·3, 49·8, 50·0, 49·9, 50·3, 49·6

3. A man goes by car from town X to town Y and back. The outward journey is uphill and he gets only 20 miles to the gallon of petrol. On the return journey he gets 30 miles to the gallon. Find the harmonic mean of his petrol consumption in miles per gallon. Then, by assuming that the distance from X to Y is 60 miles, verify that the harmonic mean is the correct average to calculate. Find the arithmetic average for comparison.

4. Groups of boys and girls are tested for reading ability. The forty boys make an average score of 76%. The sixty girls have an average score of 37%. Calculate the arithmetic average for boys and girls combined. Have you any comments to make?

5. On March 1st a baby weighed 14 lb. On May 1st it weighed 20 lb. Use the geometric mean to estimate its weight at April 1st. Talk to a mother or a doctor and see if your answer is a sensible one. If not, have you any suggestion?

Scatter

'The words figure and fictitious both derive from the same
Latin root, fingere. Beware!' M. J. M.

We have discussed various ways of measuring the central tendency of distributions and have seen that such measures are
characteristic of the distribution of any quantity, so that different
populations are distinguished from each other by different values
of these measures. For example, the average value for the height

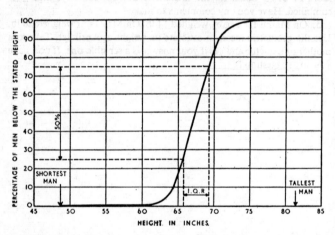

Fig. 28(a). Ogive for heights for young men (I.Q.R.=interquartile range).
(Based on W. T. Martin, *Physique of the Young Male*, by permission of
H.M.S.O.)

of women differs from the average height for men. Numerical
characteristics of populations are called *parameters*. Having dealt
with parameters of central tendency, we now turn to the no less
important matter of parameters of dispersion. According to
Memorandum No. 20 issued by the Medical Research Council
(W. J. Martin: *The Physique of the Young Male*) the height of young
males, aged between 20 and 21 years, has an average value of 5

feet 7½ inches. This is information. But we should like to know more,* for it is evident that not all the young men were exactly of this height. The adjoining ogive (Fig. 28a) shows the percentages of men less than stated heights in a total of 91,163 who were measured. Fig. 28b shows the data displayed in histogram form. It is evident that very considerable variability exists, so that, whilst the great majority of men differ relatively little from the average height, very noticeable departures from it are not at all infrequent. How are we to get a measure of the variability about the mean value?

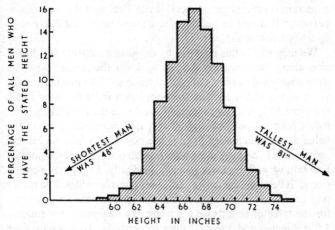

Fig. 28b. Histogram corresponding to the ogive of Fig. 28a

The easiest way is to state the height of the tallest man seen and the shortest, thus. Tallest: 6 feet 9 inches. Average: 5 feet 7½ inches, Shortest: 4 feet 0 inches. Alternatively, we might state the *range*, i.e. the difference between the tallest and the shortest, viz. 6 feet 9 inches *minus* 4 feet 0 inches = 2 feet 9 inches. This is not a very good way. A moment's thought will make it clear that we might very easily not have met these two extreme heights. It might well have been that we should have found the shortest man to be

* The author does not disappoint us in this desire.

3

4 feet 4 inches and the tallest 6 feet 6 inches. This would give us a range of 6 feet 6 inches *minus* 4 feet 4 inches = 2 feet 2 inches – a result which is appreciably different from the previous one. Again, it might have happened that among those examined in this group for military service were the giant and the dwarf from some circus. Supposing the giant to be 9 feet 7 inches and the dwarf 3 feet 2 inches, we should have obtained for our range the value 6 feet 5 inches. It is obviously undesirable to have a measure which will depend entirely on the value of any freaks that may occur. It is impossible for a measure based on freaks to speak as the *representative* of the ordinary population. The range, then, although it is used in certain circumstances, is not ideal as a measure of dispersion.* It would be better to have a parameter less likely to be upset by extreme values.

We may tackle this problem by devising a measure for dispersion along the same line that we took for the median when we were discussing measures of central tendency. The median was the value above which 50% of the population fell and below which the other 50% fell. Suppose, now, we divide the population, after it has been set out in order of size, into *four equal groups*. The value above which only 25% of the population falls we call the *upper quartile*, and the value below which only 25% of the population falls we call the *lower quartile*. Evidently, 50% of the population falls between the upper and lower quartile values. The reader may care to check for himself that the upper and lower quartiles, for the table of heights we are using as an example, are roughly 5 feet 9 inches and 5 feet 6 inches respectively. Thus, we may see at once that roughly 50% of the population differ in height by amounts not exceeding three inches, despite the fact that the tallest man observed was no less than 2 feet 9 inches taller than the shortest man. This, of course, is a consequence of the way in which the large majority of heights cluster closely to the average. This is a very common effect. Intelligence Quotients behave in the same sort of way. Most people are little removed from average intelligence, but geniuses and morons tend to occur in splendid isolation. (We may recall here that the modal ('fashionable') value

---

* The range is very efficient when the samples contain very few items (see Chapter 11 for its use).

tends to coincide with the arithmetic mean when the distribution is fairly symmetrical.) Thus the *interquartile range*, i.e. the difference between the upper and lower quartile values, makes a good measure of dispersion. It is immune from the disturbances occasioned by the incidence of extreme values. It is easy to calculate. It has a simple and meaningful significance in that it tells us the range of variability which is sufficient to contain 50 % of the population. The interquartile range is frequently used in economic and commercial statistics for another reason. Often, data are collected in such a way that there are indeterminate ranges at one or

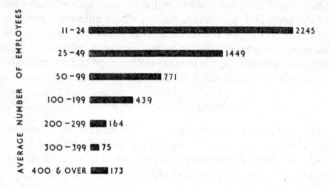

Fig. 29. Showing numbers of firms with the stated number of employees in the food, drink, and tobacco trades of Great Britain. (Based on Census of Production 1930, quoted by M. G. Kendall, *Advanced Statistics*, Vol. I)

both ends of the table. An example is shown in Fig. 29. The largest group is labelled '400 and over'. This is vague, and it would obviously be impossible to do a precise calculation for any measure depending on arithmetical processes involving the actual values in the unbounded upper class. (We shall show in the next chapter how the limited vagueness in the other *bounded* classes is dealt with.) The median and the interquartile range provide us with measures of central tendency and scatter respectively in such cases.

Median and quartiles are simply special cases of a quite general scheme for dividing up a distribution by *quantiles*. Thus, we may arrange our distribution in order of size and split it up into *ten* groups containing equal numbers of the items. The values of the variable at which the divisions occur are known then as the first, second, third, and so on, *deciles*. This idea is used by educational psychologists to divide pupils into 'top 10%, second 10%, third 10%', and so on, with regard to inherent intelligence in so far as that characteristic may be measured by tests.

Yet another measure of dispersion, which depends on all the measurements, is the *mean deviation*. In order to calculate this parameter, we first of all find the arithmetic mean of the quantities in the distribution. We then find the difference between each of the items and this average, calling all the differences positive. We then add up all the differences thus obtained and find the average difference by dividing by the number of differences. Thus the mean deviation is the average difference of the several items from their arithmetic mean. In mathematical form we have

$$\text{Mean Deviation} = \frac{\Sigma |x - \bar{x}|}{n}$$

where as before the symbol $\bar{x}$ stands for the arithmetic mean of the various values of x. The sign $|x - \bar{x}|$ indicates that we are to find the difference between x and the average of the x values, ignoring sign. The sign Σ means 'add up all the terms like'.

Example. Find the arithmetic mean and mean deviation for the set of numbers: 11, 8, 6, 7, 8.

Here we have $n = 5$ items to be averaged. As previously shown, the average of the items is

$$\bar{x} = \frac{\Sigma x}{n} = \frac{11 + 8 + 6 + 7 + 8}{5} = \frac{40}{5} = 8$$

In order to get the mean difference, we calculate the several differences of the items from their average value of 8 and sum them, thus:

$$|11 - 8| + |8 - 8| + |6 - 8| + |7 - 8| + |8 - 8|$$
$$= \quad 3 \quad + \quad 0 \quad + \quad 2 \quad + \quad 1 \quad + \quad 0 \quad = 6$$

We then calculate the mean deviation by dividing this total of the deviations by $n = 5$, and so find the mean deviation as $\frac{6}{5} = 1 \cdot 2$.

The mean deviation is frequently met with in economic statistics.

The measures so far suggested are often used in elementary work on account of their being easy to calculate and easy to understand. They are, however, of no use in more advanced work because they are extremely difficult to deal with in sampling theory, on which so much of advanced work depends. The most important measure of dispersion is the *standard deviation*, which is a little more difficult to calculate and whose significance is less obvious at first sight. Calculation and interpretation, however, soon become easy with a little practice, and then the standard deviation is the most illuminating of all the parameters of dispersion. The standard deviation will be familiar to electrical engineers and mathematicians as the *root-mean-square deviation*.* The general reader will do well to remember this phrase as it will help him to remember exactly how the standard deviation is calculated. We shall detail the steps for the calculation of the standard deviation of a set of values thus:

Step 1. Calculate the arithmetic average of the set of values.

Step 2. Calculate the differences of the several values from their arithmetic average.

Step 3. Calculate the squares of these differences (the square of a number is found by multiplying it by itself. Thus the square of 4 is written 4^2 and has the value $4 \times 4 = 16$).

Step 4. Calculate the sum of the squares of the differences to get a quantity known as the *sample sum of squares*.

Step 5. Divide this 'sample sum of squares' by the number of items, n, in the set of values. This gives a quantity known as the *sample variance*.

Step 6. Take the square root of the variance and so obtain the standard deviation. (The square root of any number, x, is a number such that when it is multiplied by itself it gives the number x. Thus, if the square root of x is equal to a number y then we shall have $y^2 = y \times y = x$.)

This sounds much more complicated than it really is. Let us work out an example, step by step.

* It is strictly analogous to radius of gyration in the theory of moments of inertia.

Example. Find the standard deviation of the set of values 11, 8, 6, 7, 8.

Step 1. We calculated the arithmetic average previously as $\bar{x} = 8$.

Step 2. The differences of the items from this average (sign may be ignored) are: 3, 0, 2, 1; 0.

Step 3. The squares of these differences are:

$3 \times 3 = 9 \qquad 0 \times 0 = 0 \qquad 2 \times 2 = 4 \qquad 1 \times 1 = 1 \qquad 0 \times 0 = 0$

Step 4. The sample sum of squares is: $9 + 0 + 4 + 1 + 0 = 14$.

Step 5. Dividing the sample sum of squares by the number of items, $n = 5$, we get the sample variance as $s^2 = \frac{14}{5} = 2 \cdot 8$ (s^2 is the accepted symbol for sample variance).

Step 6. The standard deviation is found as the square root of the sample variance thus: $s = \sqrt{2 \cdot 8} = 1 \cdot 7$.

The formula for the standard deviation is:

$$s = \sqrt{\frac{\Sigma(x - \bar{x})^2}{n}}$$

We shall meet later with the quantity called the *variance*. It is a very important quantity used in the analysis of variation.* For the present it will suffice if the reader will just make a mental note that *the variance is simply the square of the standard deviation*. It is calculated exactly like the standard deviation, except that the final step of taking the square root is omitted.

We have seen how to calculate the standard deviation. What use is it to us in interpretation? Actually it is very easy to visualize. If we are given *any* distribution which is reasonably symmetrical about its average and which is *unimodal* (i.e. has one single hump in the centre, as in the histogram shown in Fig. 28b) then we find that we make very little error in assuming that two-thirds of the distribution lies less than one standard deviation away from the mean, that 95% of the distribution lies less than two standard deviations away from the mean, and that less than 1% of the distribution lies more than three standard deviations away from the mean. This is a rough rule, of course, but it is one which is found to work very well in practice. Let us suppose, for example, that we were told no more than that the distribution of intelligence, as

* See Chapter 19.

measured by Intelligence Quotients (a person's I.Q. is defined as $\frac{\text{Mental Age}}{\text{Chronological Age}} \times 100$) has an average value $\bar{x} = 100$, with standard deviation $s = 13$. Then we might easily picture the distribution as something like the rough sketch shown in Fig. 30.

The reader may care to compare the rough picture thus formed from a simple knowledge of the two measures $\bar{x}$ and s with the histogram shown in Fig. 31 which is based on results obtained by

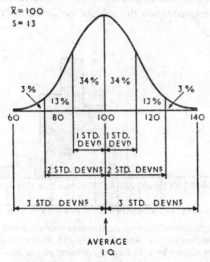

Fig. 30. Knowing only that we have a fairly symmetrical, unimodal distribution whose mean value is I.Q. 100 units and whose standard deviation is I.Q. 13 units, we can at once picture in our minds that the distribution looks something as shown. Compare this with Fig. 31

L. M. Terman and quoted by J. F. Kenney from his book *The Measurement of Intelligence*. This is typical of the use of measures of central tendency and dispersion in helping us to carry the broad picture of a whole distribution (provided it be reasonably symmetrical and unimodal) in the two values x and s. Such measures properly may be said to *represent* the distribution for which they were calculated.

The measures of dispersion which we have so far dealt with are all expressed in terms of the units in which the variable quantity is measured. It sometimes happens that we wish to ask ourselves whether one distribution is relatively more variable than another. Let us suppose, for example, that for the heights of men in the British Isles we find a mean value 67 inches with standard deviation 2·5 inches, and that for Spaniards the mean height is 64 inches with standard deviation 2·4 inches. It is evident that British men are taller than Spaniards and also slightly more variable in height. How are we to compare the *relative* variability bearing in mind

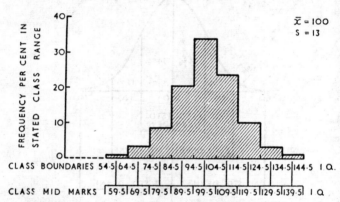

Fig. 31. Distribution of Intelligence Quotient (compare with Figs. 30 and 32). Distribution of I.Q. with $\bar{x}=100$. $s=13$. Based on data by L. M. Terman and quoted by J. F. Kenney, *Mathematics of Statistics*, Vol. I

that the Spaniards are shorter in height than the British? Karl Pearson's *coefficient of variation* is the most commonly used measure in practice for such a case.

It is defined as: $v = \dfrac{100s}{\bar{x}}$

If we calculate the coefficient of variation for our two cases, we get:

British $v = \dfrac{100 \times 2·5}{67} = 3·73\%$

Spaniards $v = \dfrac{100 \times 2·4}{64} = 3·75\%$

We conclude that, though the British are more variable in an absolute sense, the variability of the Spaniards, expressed as a percentage of the mean height, is just slightly greater.* In Chapter 9, when we consider the 'standard form' of the so-called Normal curve, we shall find that we have a further excellent way of comparing two distributions with respect, *not* to their relative variability, but to their skewness and other characteristics.

We have now provided ourselves with all the necessary basic ideas with regard to measures of central tendency and dispersion. We have a good selection of measures at our disposal, each of them appropriate to some common type of problem in numerical representation. This knowledge, together with what we know about pictorial methods of representation, is sufficient to carry us through the greater part of what is known as descriptive statistics, i.e. the sort of statistics the layman is most likely to meet with. With the previous chapters reasonably well understood, he will be able to follow intelligently and critically the major part of descriptive material. There is a vast mass of this type of statistics, and many an interesting story in it for those who are interested and able to read it.

But the ideas so far presented for consideration would leave the reader in very poor shape for working up a mass of data from the raw on his own account. There is an awful lot of arithmetic to be done in most cases, and, if we were to try to do the necessary calculations in accordance with the simple definitions and procedures so far outlined, anything but the simplest collection of data would prove an insupportable burden. But the statistician makes his task very much lighter by the use of special short cuts in calculation such as we shall meet with in the next chapter.

HERE IS THE NEXT LOT TO TEST YOUR SKILL

1. Find the arithmetic mean and standard deviation for the data of exercise 2 of Chapter 4.
2. Find the mean deviation for the same data.
3. Find the interquartile range for the same data.
4. Find the coefficient of variation for the same data.

* The question of the significance of difference between sample results is considered in Chapter 13.

6

Speeding up Calculations

'Rome wasn't built in a day? I wasn't in charge of that job.'
                                                    ANON.

There are certain short cuts in computation which suggest themselves quite naturally. Suppose, for example, we had to calculate
the arithmetic mean of the five values: 130, 120, 110, 130, 110. It
is obvious that the answer is approximately 100. We may therefore assume this value, provisionally, as the mean value, and then
proceed to calculate a correction to it. The correction will obviously be one-fifth of the total 30 + 20 + 10 + 30 + 10, i.e. 20. This
gives us for the correct value of the mean of the original data
100 + 20 = 120. Such a trick will often be of considerable value in
computing the average of a large set of values, as we shall see later.
We commonly refer to this device as *taking an assumed mean*.

Another useful dodge is the one commonly made use of in the
following type of case. Find the average of the values 4,000, 2,000,
3,000, and 1,000. What we do in such a case is to work in
thousands, and find the average as

$$\frac{4+2+3+1}{4} = 2 \cdot 5 \text{ (thousand)}$$
$$\therefore \quad \text{Average} = 2,500$$

We shall refer to this trick (for reasons which will appear later) as
working in units of the cell interval, the cell or class interval in our
example here being 1,000. There is no question of approximation
in these tricks. The answer is absolutely accurate.

Yet another handy idea is that of working with what are known
as *grouped frequencies*. Suppose, for example, we wished to find
the average of the following set of values: 4, 3, 2, 3, 5, 6, 3, 4, 6, 7,
9, 2, 2, 9, 1, 2, 5, 4, 4, 1, we could sort them out in the following
way:

Value	1	2	3	4	5	6	7	8	9
Frequency of occurrence	2	4	3	4	2	2	1	0	2

Now, instead of finding the total of the items in the original list (=82) and dividing this total by the number of items (n=20) to get the average value =4·1, we might proceed as follows:

$$\text{average} = \frac{(2\times1)+(4\times2)+(3\times3)+(4\times4)+(2\times5)+(2\times6)+(1\times7)+(0\times8)+(2\times9)}{2+4+3+4+2+2+1+0+2}$$

$$= \frac{2+8+9+16+10+12+7+0+18}{20} = \frac{82}{20} = 4·1$$

Thus, if we multiply each value by the number of times it occurs, find the total of these products, and then divide that total by the number of items we get the average. This is simple common sense, of course. Expressing this idea in mathematical form, we let x denote any value and f the frequency with which that value occurs. Then, evidently, the sum of the products fx will be the total of the values in the original list, and the total of the f values will be equal to the total number of items in the list. The formula for the average will thus be:

$$\bar{x} = \frac{\Sigma fx}{\Sigma f}$$

Again there is no question of approximation.

Suppose, now, that we were asked to find the average of the following set of values obtained for the Intelligence Quotients of 100 children.

I.Q. OF 100 CHILDREN

75	112	100	116	99	111	85	82	108	85
94	91	118	103	102	133	98	106	92	102
115	109	100	57	108	77	94	121	100	107
104	67	111	88	87	97	102	98	101	88
90	93	85	107	80	106	120	91	101	103
109	100	127	107	112	98	83	98	89	106
79	117	85	94	119	93	100	90	102	87
95	109	142	94	93	72	98	105	122	104
104	79	102	104	107	97	100	109	103	107
106	96	83	107	102	110	102	76	98	88

This is by no means a long or difficult table to find the average of by the straightforward method of addition of the items and division by the number of entries in the table. Nevertheless the work involved would be heavy enough. How can the labour in this case be made more reasonable? Inspection of the table shows that the largest I.Q. recorded was 142 and the smallest 57. The following is what is known as a *grouped frequency table* for the data:

I.Q. FOR 100 CHILDREN

Class marks	Class boundaries	Class mid-mark	Tally marks	Frequency
55– 64	54·5– 64·5	59·5	|	1
65– 74	64·5– 74·5	69·5	||	2
75– 84	74·5– 84·5	79·5	⊦⊦⊦⊦ ||||	9
85– 94	84·5– 94·5	89·5	⊦⊦⊦⊦ ⊦⊦⊦⊦ ⊦⊦⊦⊦ ⊦⊦⊦⊦ ||	22
95–104	94·5–104·5	99·5	⊦⊦⊦⊦ ⊦⊦⊦⊦ ⊦⊦⊦⊦ ⊦⊦⊦⊦ ⊦⊦⊦⊦ ⊦⊦⊦⊦ |||	33
105–114	104·5–114·5	109·5	⊦⊦⊦⊦ ⊦⊦⊦⊦ ⊦⊦⊦⊦ ⊦⊦⊦⊦ ||	22
115–124	114·5–124·5	119·5	⊦⊦⊦⊦ |||	8
125–134	124·5–134·5	129·5	||	2
135–144	134·5–144·5	139·5	|	1
	Total number of values = Total frequency =			100

Before proceeding further, there are certain things which the reader should observe. In the first place, he should distinguish carefully between the meanings of the terms 'class marks' and 'class boundaries'. The values in this case were *recorded to the nearest whole number* in our table of I.Q.'s so that a value recorded as 55 may, in fact, have been anywhere between 54·5 and 55·5. Therefore the class that contains all the values *recorded* as between 55 and 64 inclusive will contain all the values which *in fact* lay between 54·5 and 64·5. That is to say, the class *marks* 55–64 *imply* class *boundaries* 54·5–64·5. Grouped frequency tables should always be drawn up with this distinction clearly in mind, so that the class boundaries cover the whole range of observed values without gap or overlap. It is erroneous (though not uncommon) for tables to be drawn up in such a way that we should be in doubt which class to assign borderline values to. If the distinction between class marks and boundaries is kept clearly in mind, and considered in conjunction with the accuracy to which the values are originally recorded, there is no need for such ambiguity. The reader will observe that the *class mid-mark* may be obtained either by taking the average of the class marks or by taking the average of the class boundaries. In general, the number of classes into which the whole range of the values is divided should be not less than ten (or serious error becomes possible in the succeeding calculations) nor more than about twenty-five (or the saving due to grouping is much less than it might be). In our case we break this rule by having only nine classes. Class marks are often referred to, for obvious reasons, as class *end-marks*. The classes themselves are frequently called *cells*. The width of a cell, i.e. the difference between its class *boundaries*, is known as the *class interval* or the *cell interval* and denoted usually by the letter c. Inspection of our grouped frequency table will show that the width of all cells is $c = 10$.

Having decided on our classes, the original values are transferred to the group frequency table as *tally marks* in the appropriate cell. It is convenient in practice to use every fifth tally mark in a given cell to cross out the previous four, thus making it easy to count up the tally marks in each cell in groups of five at a time. Finally, the total of the tally marks in each cell is entered in the frequency column, and the total of this column tells us the total number of values recorded in the original table. It is not essential, though often convenient, to have all the cells of the same width. It will be noticed that the tally marks draw for us a rough histogram of the distribution. In drawing a histogram proper for the data, the vertical blocks representing the frequencies in each subrange have to be properly located on the scale of values of the variable with reference to the class *boundaries* (see Fig. 31).

If, now, we are prepared to make some small approximation in our calculation of the average of all the readings, we may without serious error regard each value in a given cell as having, not its true value, but the value of the class *mid-mark*. Sometimes the error will be positive and sometimes negative, so that in a large number of values we can be reasonably confident that the errors will substantially cancel one another out. The calculation of the arithmetic average would then be as follows:

Class mid-mark x	Frequency f	Frequency × mid-mark fx
59·5	1	59·5
69·5	2	139·0
79·5	9	715·5
89·5	22	1,969·0
99·5	33	3,283·5
109·5	22	2,409·0
119·5	8	956·0
129·5	2	259·0
139·5	1	139·5
	$\Sigma f = 100$	$\Sigma fx = 9,930·0$

Whence, the average value for I.Q. is found as:

$$\bar{x} = \frac{\Sigma fx}{\Sigma f} = \frac{9930 \cdot 0}{100} = 99 \cdot 3$$

The true value is actually 99·28, so that our result is reasonably close to the true value, the error being of the order of 0·02% in this case (with rather a scanty number of cells).

The arithmetic may be considerably simplified, however, if we introduce the ideas of working with an *assumed mean* and in *units of the cell interval*. The cell interval in our grouped frequency table is $c = 10$. Inspection of the table suggests at once that we should not be far out in assuming the mean to be the *class mid-mark* 99·5. It is essential in this method to take as our assumed mean a class mid-mark and essential, also, to have all cells of the same width. It does not matter at all *which* class mean we assume, though the better our assumption the simpler the subsequent arithmetic. The assumed mean is denoted by the symbol x_0. The deviation of each class from the assumed mean, measured in units of the cell interval, is denoted by t. The class which contains our assumed mean is given the value $t = 0$. Classes whose mid-marks are *smaller* than the assumed mean are given *negative* values of t, and classes whose mid-marks are *larger* than the assumed mean are given *positive* values of t. Thus the t value measures how many classes a given class is away from the assumed mean, and the sign of t tells us whether the members of the class in question have values smaller or larger than the assumed mean. If the reader will follow this explanation with the following table in front of him, the meaning should be quite clear. The reader will appreciate that what we have done is this: (a) chosen an assumed mean, (b) measured our values in units of t instead of in the original units – much as we might measure a length in feet instead of inches. The mathematician would say that we had 'made the substitution $t = \dfrac{x - x_0}{c}$'. We now calculate in our t units the correction to be applied to the assumed mean in order to get the correct mean, this correction being derived from the average value of t calculated from our table. Thus we get:

Class mid-mark		Frequency	Frequency × mid-mark
x	t	f	ft
59·5	−4	1	− 4
69·5	−3	2	− 6
79·5	−2	9	−18
89·5	−1	22	−22
99·5	0	33	0
109·5	+1	22	+22
119·5	+2	8	+16
129·5	+3	2	+ 6
139·5	+4	1	+ 4
$x_0 = 99\cdot5$ $c = 10$		$\Sigma f = 100$	$\Sigma ft = -2$

Assumed Mean → (99·5 row)

The correct value of the average would then be calculated as

$$\bar{x} = x_0 + c\frac{\Sigma ft}{\Sigma f}$$

$$= 99 \cdot 5 + 10\left[\frac{-2}{100}\right] = 99 \cdot 5 - 0 \cdot 2 = 99 \cdot 3$$

a result which agrees with our previous one. Notice that this method is subject to exactly the same grouping error as our previous method – no more, no less. The arithmetical labour is, however, now reduced to the barest minimum, involving us in no more than multiplication by very small whole numbers. Both labour and the risk of computational error are as small as it is possible to make them. But the full benefit of this method is not even faintly approached until we come to more elaborate calculations, such as the computation of standard deviations.

It will be recalled that the standard deviation is to be calculated as

$$s = \sqrt{\frac{\Sigma(x - \bar{x})^2}{n}}$$

It is a simple matter to show (the proof is given at the end of this chapter) that the standard deviation may also be expressed as:

$$s = \sqrt{\frac{\Sigma x^2}{n} - (\bar{x})^2}$$

As a numerical check on this alternative formula, we shall calculate the standard deviation of the numbers 14, 10, 8, 11, 12.

We know
$$\bar{x} = \frac{\Sigma x}{n} = \frac{55}{5} = 11$$

We may then say

$$s = \sqrt{\frac{\Sigma(x - \bar{x})^2}{n}} = \sqrt{\frac{3^2 + 1^2 + 3^2 + 0^2 + 1^2}{5}} = \sqrt{\frac{20}{5}} = \sqrt{4} = 2$$

Or, alternatively, we may use our new formula and say

$$s = \sqrt{\frac{\Sigma x^2}{n} - (\bar{x})^2} = \sqrt{\frac{14^2 + 10^2 + 8^2 + 11^2 + 12^2}{5} - 11^2}$$

$$= \sqrt{\frac{196 + 100 + 64 + 121 + 144}{5} - 121} = \sqrt{\frac{625}{5} - 121}$$

$$= \sqrt{125 - 121} = \sqrt{4} = 2$$

which is the same result as before. The numbers entering into the computation often get very large by this method, but this is no disadvantage given a machine to do the work.

Neither of these methods is much use for the man who has to do his calculations for himself. In such cases, use is usually made of the grouped frequency table method, and it may be shown that when we use this method the formula for the standard deviation may be expressed in the form

$$s = c \cdot \sqrt{\frac{\Sigma f t^2}{\Sigma f} - \left(\frac{\Sigma f t}{\Sigma f}\right)^2}$$

The proof of this formula is given at the end of this chapter.

We shall now proceed to illustrate the use of this formula by applying it to the computation of the standard deviation for our distribution of I.Q.'s.

Class mid-mark		Frequency		
x	t	f	ft	ft^2
59·5	−4	1	− 4	16
69·5	−3	2	− 6	18
79·5	−2	9	− 18	36
89·5	−1	22	− 22	22
99·5	0	33	0	0
109·5	+1	22	+ 22	22
119·5	+2	8	+ 16	32
129·5	+3	2	+ 6	18
139·5	+4	1	+ 4	16
$x_0 = 99 \cdot 5$ $c = 10$		$\Sigma f = 100$	$\Sigma f t = - 2$	$\Sigma f t^2 = 180$

Assumed ⟶ Mean (at row 99·5)

The values in the ft^2 column are obtained by multiplying together the terms in the ft column and the t column, thus $-4 \times -4 = 16$. $-6 \times -3 = 18$, etc. The ft^2 terms are necessarily all positive.

The calculation of average and standard deviation would then appear as follows:

$$\bar{x} = x_0 + c\frac{\Sigma ft}{\Sigma f} = 99 \cdot 5 + 10\left[\frac{-2}{100}\right] = \underline{99 \cdot 3}$$

$$s = c\sqrt{\frac{\Sigma ft^2}{\Sigma f} - \left(\frac{\Sigma ft}{\Sigma f}\right)^2} = 10\sqrt{\frac{180}{100} - \left(\frac{-2}{100}\right)^2}$$

$$= 10\sqrt{1.80 - 0 \cdot 0004} = 10\sqrt{1 \cdot 80} = \underline{13.41}$$

As a rough check on the accuracy of these calculations, we may remember that in a unimodal (single humped) distribution substantially all the values should be within three standard deviations of the average value, provided the distribution is reasonably symmetrical. Applying this to our distribution we have average value 99 with three standard deviations equal to 40 (in round figures). We expect the smallest value in the distribution, therefore, to be in the neighbourhood of $99 - 40 = 59$, and the largest value in our distribution to be in the neighbourhood of $99 + 40 = 139$. It will be seen that this check works very well. The reader may care to remember this as the *three standard deviations check*.

There is a very simple and useful check on the accuracy of the arithmetic in the body of the table, known as *Charlier's Check*. It depends on the fact that

$$\Sigma f(t+1)^2 = \Sigma ft^2 + 2\Sigma ft + \Sigma f$$

We already have all the terms on the right-hand side of this equation calculated in our grouped frequency table. All that remains in order to be able to use the check is to add a further column on the right of the table, whose terms are calculated as follows for each cell.

To the value of t for the cell add 1. Square the result and then multiply it by f. Thus, in the first cell, at the top of our table, we have $t = -4$. Adding 1 gives us -3. Squaring this gives us 9, and finally, multiplying the 9 by the value of f for this cell gives us $1 \times 9 = 9$. This value is entered in the $f(t+1)^2$ column on the right of the table, as shown below. Similarly, for the class whose midmark is $79 \cdot 5$ we get $t = -2$. Adding 1 gives -1. Squaring gives 1. Multiplying by the cell frequency gives 9 for the value of $f(t+1)^2$.

We now give the full table for the calculation of mean and standard deviation, including Charlier's check, calculation of mean and standard deviation and the three standard deviation check on the final result, in the form in which it should be laid out. It will be observed that we have interchanged the position of the f and t columns, as in practice this is a more convenient layout for computing the ft^2 column from the ft column and the t column.

Mid-mark x	Frequency f	t	ft	ft^2	$f(t+1)^2$
59·5	1	−4	− 4	16	9
69·5	2	−3	− 6	18	8
79·5	9	−2	−18	36	9
89·5	22	−1	−22	22	0
99·5	33	0	0	0	33
109·5	22	+1	+22	22	88
119·5	8	+2	+16	32	72
129·5	2	+3	+ 6	18	32
139·5	1	+4	+ 4	16	25
$x_0 = 99·5$	100		− 2	180	276
$c = 10$	Σf		Σft	Σft^2	$\Sigma f(t+1)^2$

Charlier's Check

$$\Sigma f(t+1)^2 = \Sigma ft^2 + 2\Sigma ft + \Sigma f$$
$$276 = 180 + 2(-2) + 100$$

Charlier's check on tabular calculations O.K.

Computation of Arithmetic Average

$$\bar{x} = x_0 + \frac{c\Sigma ft}{\Sigma f}$$

$$= 99·5 + 10\left[\frac{-2}{100}\right] = \underline{99·3}$$

Computation of Standard Deviation

$$s = c\sqrt{\frac{\Sigma ft^2}{\Sigma f} - \left(\frac{\Sigma ft}{\Sigma f}\right)^2}$$

$$= 10\sqrt{\frac{180}{100} - \left(\frac{-2}{100}\right)^2} = \underline{13·41}$$

Three Standard Deviations Check on Final Calculations

Expected minimum value $= \bar{x} - 3s = 99 - 40 = 59$ } roughly
Expected maximum value $= \bar{x} + 3s = 99 + 40 = 139$ }

Three standard deviations check agrees well with the end values in the table.

Result   Mean $\bar{x} = 99{\cdot}3$
             Standard deviation $s = 13{\cdot}41$

We should mention that Charlier's check is not an *absolute* guarantee. It is possible – though very unlikely – for compensating errors to occur in the computation of the tabular values which would not be detected by Charlier's check.

Some idea of the time saved can be got if we remember that to calculate the standard deviation by the formula first given we should have to find the difference between the mean value $99{\cdot}3$ and every one of the hundred items in the original table. These differences would then have to be squared, and totalled to give the sum of squares. The standard deviation would then be found by dividing this total by $n = 100$ and finally taking the square root. Moreover, arithmetical mistakes in this lengthy bit of work would not be unlikely. The grouped frequency table method is quite accurate enough for most purposes, having a small amount of error given sufficient cells (the number in our worked example was purposely chosen on the small side). Moreover, we have two checks to our working. The arithmetic is reduced to the manipulations of small whole numbers, so that errors are at once unlikely and easy to trace if they should occur.

LINEAR INTERPOLATION OF THE MEDIAN

We shall now explain how the median value may be estimated by linear interpolation from a grouped frequency table, using our grouped frequency table for I.Q.'s as an example. (The reader will recall that the median is a measure of central tendency, being the value which is less than the value observed in 50% of cases and greater than the value observed in 50% of cases.) The number of the item which falls in the centre of our list we shall refer to as the *median cumulative frequency*, or simply the *median frequency*.

Having this clear in our minds, we can now proceed to calculate the value of I.Q. which corresponds to the median frequency, and this will, of course, be the median we are looking for.

If the reader will imagine the class boundaries of Fig. 31 to be milestones along a road, and that he is driving along that road, making a note at each milestone of the TOTAL number of people he has seen in the distribution of I.Q. as he travels from the milestone labelled I.Q. = 54·5 to the milestone labelled 144·5, the result will be as shown in Fig. 32. In statistical terminology, the reader will be constructing a *cumulative frequency table*, which is usually laid out as shown below.

Class boundary	Cum. f
54·5	0
64·5	1
74·5	3
84·5	12
94·5	34
104·5	67
114·5	89
124·5	97
134·5	99
144·5	100

The column headed Cum. f shows the cumulative frequency at any class boundary. We have, in fact, found the necessary figures for drawing the *ogive* or cumulative frequency chart mentioned in Chapter 3. Now, since there are in this case 100 values recorded in the data, it is evident that the *median frequency* will be Cum.$f = \frac{100}{2} = 50$ and this value of the Cum. f occurs somewhere in the class whose boundaries are 94·5 and 104·5. Evidently, then, the median value for I.Q. lies between these limits.

How is the linear interpolation carried out? We apply the formula:

$$\frac{\text{Upper boundary} - \text{Lower boundary}}{\text{Upper boundary} - \text{Median value}}$$

$$= \frac{\text{Cum. } f \text{ at upper boundary} - \text{Cum. } f \text{ at lower boundary}}{\text{Cum. } f \text{ at upper boundary} - \text{Median frequency}}$$

If we put this in symbolic form, writing:

Upper boundary value	X
Lower boundary value	x
Median value	M
Frequency at upper boundary	F
Frequency at lower boundary	f
Median frequency	p

then our formula becomes:

$$\frac{X-x}{X-M} = \frac{F-f}{F-p}$$

In our example we have to determine M, given that $X = 104 \cdot 5$, $x = 94 \cdot 5$, $F = 67$, $f = 34$, and $p = 50$.

Substituting these values in our formula, we get:

$$\frac{104 \cdot 5 - 94 \cdot 5}{104 \cdot 5 - M} = \frac{67 - 34}{67 - 50}$$

which leads to

$$\frac{10}{104 \cdot 5 - M} = \frac{33}{17}$$

$$\therefore \quad 170 = 3448 \cdot 5 - 33M$$

$$\therefore \quad 33M = 3278 \cdot 5$$

$$\therefore \quad \underline{M = 99 \cdot 3}$$

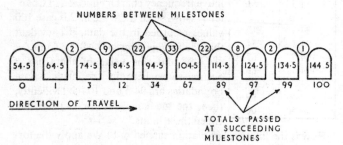

Fig. 32. Cumulative Frequency (compare with Fig. 31)

We have thus estimated the median value. Since, in this case, the distribution is so very symmetrical, we are not surprised that the median agrees with the arithmetic average, which we calculated as $\bar{x} = 99 \cdot 3$. Fig. 33 shows the actual ratio assumed in order to interpolate the median.

In the example used in this chapter, the total number of values in our data was $n = 100$. This, of course, would not normally be the case. The calculations are exactly the same whatever the number of values, n. Often, however, the actual numbers in each class are reduced to percentages before the calculations are commenced. In such cases the actual number of values on which the

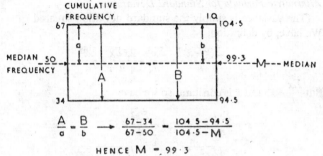

Fig. 33. Linear Interpolation of Median Value

results are based should always be quoted, since results based on large numbers are more trustworthy, in general, than results based on small samples and the person studying statistical data is always entitled to know how much reliance he may properly place on the results quoted.

MATHEMATICAL PROOFS

The general reader may skip this short section in which formulae given in the body of the chapter are considered mathematically.

Grouped Frequency Formula for the Mean

If we write

$$\frac{x - x_0}{c} = t$$

we have

$$x = x_0 + ct$$

i.e.

$$fx = fx_0 + cft$$

whence, summing and dividing through by Σf, we get:

$$\frac{\Sigma fx}{\Sigma f} = \frac{\Sigma fx_0}{\Sigma f} + \frac{\Sigma cft}{\Sigma f}$$

But x_0 and c are constants and may therefore be taken outside the summations. Moreover, $\frac{\Sigma ft}{\Sigma f}$ is, by definition, the mean, $\bar{t}$.

So we have

$$\bar{x} = x_0 + c.\frac{\Sigma ft}{\Sigma f} = x_0 + c\bar{t}$$

which is the relation used in computing.

Alternative Formula for Standard Deviation

(The variance is simply the standard deviation squared.)
We have, by definition,

$$s^2 = \frac{\Sigma(x - \bar{x})^2}{n} = \frac{\Sigma x^2}{n} - \frac{2\bar{x}\Sigma x}{n} + \frac{\Sigma \bar{x}^2}{n}$$

But $\dfrac{\Sigma x}{n} = \bar{x}$, and $\bar{x}$ is constant, so we have

$$s^2 = \frac{\Sigma x^2}{n} - 2\bar{x}^2 + \bar{x}^2 = \frac{\Sigma x^2}{n} - \bar{x}^2$$

i.e.
$$s = \sqrt{\frac{\Sigma x^2}{n} - \bar{x}^2} \quad \text{or} \quad \sqrt{\frac{\Sigma x^2}{n} - \left(\frac{\Sigma x}{n}\right)^2}$$

The same alternative formula, using the grouped frequency notation, may be proved by starting with the definition of the variance in the form

$$s^2 = \frac{\Sigma f(x - \bar{x})^2}{\Sigma f}$$

which leads to the form

$$s = \sqrt{\frac{\Sigma f x^2}{\Sigma f} - \left(\frac{\Sigma f x}{\Sigma f}\right)^2} \quad \text{or} \quad \sqrt{\frac{\Sigma f x^2}{\Sigma f} - \bar{x}^2}$$

Grouped Frequency Formulae for Variance and Standard Deviation

We have already shown that the variance may be written as

$$s^2 = \frac{\Sigma f x^2}{\Sigma f} - \bar{x}^2$$

This is identical with

$$s^2 = \left(\frac{\Sigma f x^2}{\Sigma f} - \bar{x}^2\right) + (2x_0\bar{x} - 2x_0\bar{x}) + (x_0{}^2 - x_0{}^2)$$

Rearranging, we get

$$s^2 = \left(\frac{\Sigma f x^2}{\Sigma f} - 2x_0\bar{x} + x_0{}^2\right) - (\bar{x}^2 - 2x_0\bar{x} + x_0{}^2)$$

$$= \left(\frac{\Sigma f x^2}{\Sigma f} - \frac{2x_0\Sigma f x}{\Sigma f} + \frac{x_0{}^2\Sigma f}{\Sigma f}\right) - (\bar{x} - x_0)^2$$

$$= \frac{\Sigma f(x - x_0)^2}{\Sigma f} - (\bar{x} - x_0)^2$$

This may be written as

$$s^2 = c^2\left[\frac{\Sigma f\left(\dfrac{x-x_0}{c}\right)^2}{\Sigma f} - \left(\frac{\bar{x}-x_0}{c}\right)^2\right]$$

But $\dfrac{x-x_0}{c}$ is what we call t and $\dfrac{\bar{x}-x_0}{c}$ we have shown to be $\bar{t}$ so we have as our formula for the variance

$$s^2 = c^2\left[\frac{\Sigma ft^2}{\Sigma f} - \bar{t}^2\right] = c^2\left[\frac{\Sigma ft^2}{\Sigma f} - \left(\frac{\Sigma ft}{\Sigma f}\right)^2\right]$$

Taking the square root, we find the standard deviation as

$$s = c\sqrt{\frac{\Sigma ft^2}{\Sigma f} - \bar{t}^2} = c\sqrt{\frac{\Sigma ft^2}{\Sigma f} - \left(\frac{\Sigma ft}{\Sigma f}\right)^2}$$

NOW SEE IF YOU CAN DO THESE QUESTIONS USING THE RAPID METHODS

Percentage Loss in weight of 40 samples of cloth in passing from the greasy to the clean state during manufacture

9·3	7·4	10·4	9·3	8·8	10·2	9·5	11·3
9·7	10·3	9·4	6·8	10·4	9·6	11·2	8·6
8·2	9·2	10·6	7·6	9·4	9·8	8·5	9·7
10·4	8·8	9·3	10·7	8·2	9·1	5·9	10·5
10·6	9·2	10·4	8·3	9·4	12·1	11·3	9·6

1. Lay out the above data in a grouped frequency table, showing class limits, class boundaries, class midmarks and tally marks. Then find the mean, and standard deviation, including Charlier's Check and the three standard deviations check in your working.

2. Draw a histogram for the data. What is the modal value?

3. Set up a cumulative frequency table for the data and find the median by linear interpolation.

4. Draw a frequency polygon for the data.

7

Fault-Finding – The Binominal Distribution

'When I was younger, Statistics was the science of large numbers. Now, it seems to me rapidly to be becoming the science of no numbers at all.' DR OSWALD GEORGE

Undoubtedly one of the finest gambling games ever invented is Crown and Anchor. The excellence of this game is shown by the strict way in which it is driven underground by authority in this most puritan of lands where all pleasure is either taxed, or restricted to certain hours, or forbidden altogether. It is strange that a people which took so poor a view of the medieval malpractice of the sale of indulgences should now raise over £1,000 million out of a budgetary income of £3,778 million by the sale of indulgences to drinkers, smokers, and gamblers. Maybe one day the swings will be opened to children on Sunday on condition that an indulgence is bought from the Chancellor of the Exchequer. There are few left in England to-day who could raise even a smile – let alone a howl of protest – if such a policy were introduced in the solemnity of the Budget.

But let us return to our Crown and Anchor. In this game there is a wise man who owns the board and makes a steady and tidy profit. There are others, less wise, who cock a snook at the laws of chance by playing on the first man's board. The board is divided into six sections, labelled with a heart, a club, a spade, a diamond, a crown, and an anchor respectively. Each player having staked so much on the section which takes his fancy, the owner of the board throws three dice simultaneously. Each die has its six faces marked heart, diamond, spade, club, crown, and anchor respectively to correspond with the sections of the board. In the event of the three dice all showing the same face, those who were lucky enough to back this section of the board receive back their stake money plus three times that amount. In the event of two of the dice being the same the banker pays back stake money plus twice that amount to those who staked on the double section of the board, and stake money plus the same amount to those who bet on the section of the board corresponding to the odd die. When all three dice show different faces the banker returns stake plus the same amount to anyone who has bet on the appropriate sections of the board. Moneys on other sections of the board are collected by the banker in all cases. It is commonly held by those who play this game that it is to the banker's advantage to get money placed evenly over the board. This is quite untrue in the long run. The belief arises from the fact that when the money is evenly staked on all sections it is impossible for the banker to lose even on a single throw. With money unevenly staked, his fortune can fluctuate a little from throw to throw, both up and down, but the ultimate outcome of any game lasting for an appreciable time is profit for the banker, as we shall now see.

The laws of probability apply to each individual stake, whatever section it be laid on and however big or small. If we consider the long run – which is what matters – we can most clearly see the situation by imagining bets of one unit placed on each of the six sections for each throw of the dice. If we call the case when all three dice show the same face a *treble*, the case where two of the three dice show the same face a *double*, and the case where all three different faces a *singles* throw, then the position will be as follows, so far as the banker is concerned:

Singles: Pays on three sections, collects on three sections. Profit = nothing.

Doubles: Pays on one unit to one section, pays two units to one section, collects from four sections. Profit = 1 unit.

Trebles: Pays three units to one section, collects on five sections. Profit = 2 units.

The question now arises: What is the relative frequency with which singles, doubles, and trebles come up?

This is the type of problem where, if we assume that there is no bias in the dice, we can write down all possible results. In this way the relative frequencies of singles, doubles, and trebles can be ascertained. Suppose you were the Goddess of Chance. Then there would be six possible ways of making the first die show. With any one of these six ways of settling the first die there would be six ways of settling the fate of the second die, making a total of thirty-six ways of settling the first two dice. Finally, with any one of these thirty-six ways there would be six ways of settling the fate of the third die, making a total of 216 ways in which the three dice could show up after any throw. Even as Goddess of Chance you would be limited to these 216 ways. The whole system of possibilities can be represented as in the following table, which shows the possibilities when the first die is to show club and diamond respectively. The reader will be able to write down at once, for himself, the possibilities when the first die is to show heart, spade, crown, and anchor respectively.

FIRST DIE CLUB

ccc	cdc	chc	csc	c♛c	c⚓c
ccd	cdd	chd	csd	c♛d	c⚓d
cch	cdh	chh	csh	c♛h	c⚓h
ccs	cds	chs	css	c♛s	c⚓s
cc♛	cd♛	ch♛	cs♛	c♛♛	c⚓♛
cc⚓	cd⚓	ch⚓	cs⚓	c♛⚓	c⚓⚓

FIRST DIE DIAMOND

dcc	ddc	dhc	dsc	d♛c	d⚓c
dcd	ddd	dhd	dsd	d♛d	d⚓d
dch	ddh	dhh	dsh	d♛h	d⚓h
dcs	dds	dhs	dss	d♛s	d⚓s
dc♛	dd♛	dh♛	ds♛	d♛♛	d⚓♛
dc⚓	dd⚓	dh⚓	ds⚓	d♛⚓	d⚓⚓

In each of the two sections shown there are seen to be thirty-six possibilities. In the whole table, if the reader will take the trouble to write it out, there will be our 216 possibilities which exhaust the system. Inspection will show the reader that in each section of the table there occurs one treble. There will therefore be six possible trebles altogether, viz. *ccc, ddd, hhh, sss,* ♛ ♛ ♛ , and ⚓ ⚓ ⚓. So much will have been evident to the reader from the start. With regard to doubles, the table is a real help. In each section the reader will observe that there are fifteen doubles, five in a row, five in a column, and five along the diagonal of the section. These groups of five will be seen to correspond to the cases
   (a) where the double is made by first and second dice (column)
   (b) where the double occurs between first and third dice (row)
   (c) where the double occurs between second and third dice (diagonal)
(The reader will notice that the treble in each section occurs where

row, column, and diagonal intersect. This business of getting hold of patterns is one of the mathematician's most useful tricks.)

We see, then, that there must be a total of $6 \times 15 = 90$ ways in which doubles can arise – against 6 ways of getting a treble. Now it is clear that we must get a singles in those cases which do not result in a treble or double. The remainder of 216 possibilities will therefore be the singles. Hence number of ways of getting singles $= 216 - 90 - 6 = 120$.

Let us now think of 216 throws in which this expectation is satisfied. If one unit be staked on each section of the board for each throw of the dice, there will have been $6 \times 216 = 1,296$ units staked in the series of throws. There will have been 6 throws which resulted in a treble, making a profit to the banker of 12 units. There will have been 90 throws in which the result will have been a double, thus giving the banker a further 90 units profit. Since, on singles, the banker breaks even, his total profit on this series in which expectation is realized will be 102 units out of 1,296 units staked. The banker, therefore, can expect to make about $7 \cdot 8 \%$ of the total staked in any run of play for himself. This is a fairly good rake-off. The game is beautifully designed, however. In over half the throws the banker sees nothing for himself. Whenever he makes a profit, he pays out more bountifully to other people, so that the losers' eyes turn to the lucky winner in envy, rather than to the banker in suspicion. Spectacular wins are kept to the minimum, but when they do fall the blow is always softened by apparent generosity. With a throw every two minutes (not a fast rate) and unit stakes of 1s. the banker would make himself 14s. an hour.

The general reader may feel that to analyse a fairly complex case of this sort, by writing out all the possibilities, is a little laborious. He may ask whether the mathematicians have not found a formula for such a problem as we have just discussed. The answer is: Yes, the Multinomial Theorem.

MULTINOMIAL THEOREM

Suppose we have an event which is characterized by a variable x, which can take on one of k values, $x_1, x_2, x_3, \ldots x_k$. To make this concrete for the reader, let him think of a die being rolled. The value of k is then 6, and the six possible values of our variable x are the six values stated on the faces of the die, viz. 1, 2, 3, 4, 5, and 6. Then the probability that the value x_1 occurs t_1 times, the value x_2 occurs t_2 times, the value x_3 occurs t_3 times, and so on *in a specified order* in N trials will be the product

$$p_1^{t_1} p_2^{t_2} p_3^{t_3} \dots p_k^{tk}$$

where the p's are the probabilities of the corresponding x's. Now, as we learnt previously, the number of ways in which the order can be specified is the number of permutations possible among N objects of which t_1 are of one sort, t_2 of another sort, and so on. If we denote this number by the symbol P, we have

$$P = \frac{N!}{t_1! t_2! t_3! \dots t_k!}$$

Hence, the probability that t_1 times we shall get the value x_1, t_2 times the value x_2, and so on, will be

$$P p_1^{t_1} p_2^{t_2} p_3^{t_3} \dots p_k^{tk}$$

Now it may be shown, mathematically, that this is the general term of the expansion of the multinomial

$$(p_1 + p_2 + p_3 + \dots + p_k)^N$$

We thus have a simple way of computing the various probabilities.

This will seem a little complex to the non-mathematical reader. Perhaps an example will clear up the idea. Consider, again, the dice. Each face has a probability $= \frac{1}{6}$ of turning up, i.e. in this case $p_1 = p_2 = p_3 = p_4 = p_5 = p_6$, so that each of them is equal to $\frac{1}{6}$.

Suppose, now, we wish to apply the Multinomial Theorem to calculate the probability that when a die is rolled three times in succession (or what amounts to the same thing, three dice rolled simultaneously), the result will be treble 1. Here we have all the p's equal to $\frac{1}{6}$, N equal to 3. Moreover, we want t_1 (the number of times 1 is to appear) to be equal to 3. Since

$$t_1 + t_2 + t_3 + t_4 + t_5 + t_6 = N = 3,$$

it is evident that all values of t except t_1 will be zero. Also,

$$P = \frac{N!}{t_1! t_2! t_3! t_4! t_5! t_6!}$$

$$= \frac{3!}{3!0!0!0!0!0!}$$

Now it can be shown that the value of 0! is 1. It follows that in this case $P=1$, so the probability of treble 1 is simply

$$(\tfrac{1}{6})^3(\tfrac{1}{6})^0(\tfrac{1}{6})^0(\tfrac{1}{6})^0(\tfrac{1}{6})^0(\tfrac{1}{6})^0$$

all the terms of which, except the first, are equal to 1. The probability of treble 1 is therefore $(\tfrac{1}{6})^3 = \tfrac{1}{216}$.

The probability of a treble, irrespective of whether it be treble 1, 2, 3, 4, 5, or 6, may then be obtained by asking ourselves in how many ways a treble may arise. This simply boils down to asking in how many ways we can choose one face out of six possible faces. The answer is $6C1$. We see, then, that in a game such as crown and anchor, the probability of a treble is

$$6 \times \tfrac{1}{216} = \tfrac{1}{36}$$

So far, the Multinomial Theorem will strike the reader as more of a hindrance than a help. However, if we go on to ask in how many ways a double can arise, we see its value. Previously, to solve this problem we had to write down all the possible results. This is no longer necessary. In terms of our theorem we have for any proposed double (e.g. 212, order not counting) an expression of the type

$$(\tfrac{1}{6})^2(\tfrac{1}{6})^1(\tfrac{1}{6})^0(\tfrac{1}{6})^0(\tfrac{1}{6})^0(\tfrac{1}{6})^0$$

to be multiplied by

$$P = \frac{3!}{2!1!0!0!0!0!}$$

whence we find the probability of any specified double to be

$$\frac{3!}{2!}\left(\frac{1}{6}\right)^3 = \frac{1}{72}$$

But there are $2 \times 6C2 = 30$ doubles, all equally likely. (The factor 2 before $6C2$ arises because once the pair of denominations has been chosen *either* may be doubled.) It follows that the probability of obtaining a double irrespective of what double it may be is

$$30 \times \tfrac{1}{72} = \tfrac{5}{12}$$

Again, for any proposed singles result (e.g. 265, order not counting), we get an expression of the type

$$(\tfrac{1}{6})^1(\tfrac{1}{6})^1(\tfrac{1}{6})^1(\tfrac{1}{6})^0(\tfrac{1}{6})^0(\tfrac{1}{6})^0$$

to be multiplied by

$$P = \frac{3!}{1!1!1!0!0!0!}$$

whence we find the probability of any specified single result to be

$$3! \times (\tfrac{1}{6})^3 = \tfrac{1}{36}$$

But the number of such singles it is possible to form is found, simply, as the number of ways of choosing three denominations from the six possible, viz. $6C3 = 20$. All these are equally likely, hence the probability of a singles result, irrespective of which of the possible ones it may be, is

$$20 \times \tfrac{1}{36} = \tfrac{5}{9}$$

It is certain that we shall get treble, double, or singles as our result, so the probabilities for these three events should total unity.

$$\frac{1}{36} + \frac{5}{12} + \frac{5}{9} = \frac{1 + 15 + 20}{36} = 1$$

BINOMIAL DISTRIBUTION

A particular case of the Multinomial Distribution which is of very great practical use in research and industrial inspection problems is the Binomial distribution. The reader will find this very much easier to understand than the general Multinomial Distribution. Suppose we have a bag containing a very large number of balls, all identical except with regard to colour. Let 10% of these balls be painted black, and the rest white. Then clearly the chance of a ball picked out of the bag at random being black will have a probability $p = \tfrac{1}{10}$. By the multiplication law for probabilities (Chapter 2), the probability that two balls picked at random will both be black has $p = \tfrac{1}{10} \times \tfrac{1}{10} = \tfrac{1}{100}$. And the probablitiy that three balls chosen at random will all be black will be $p = \tfrac{1}{10} \times \tfrac{1}{10} \times \tfrac{1}{10} = \tfrac{1}{1000}$. In general, the probability that n balls chosen at random will all be black will have $p = (\tfrac{1}{10})^n$. In similar fashion, the probability that n balls chosen at random will all be white will have $p = (\tfrac{9}{10})^n$, since the probability of choosing a single white ball in one trial is $p = \tfrac{9}{10}$.

So much is very easy, but, as a rule, the chosen balls will not all be of the same colour, and the question arises: What are the probabilities of getting 0, 1, 2, 3, 4, 5, etc., black balls in a group (or *sample* as we shall in future call it) of n balls? This problem is of fundamental importance in sampling inspection in industry in cases where the sampling is on a qualitative basis, the items being classified as 'O.K.' or 'defective'.

Let us start with a simple case, where we choose a sample of two items from a large batch containing 10% defectives. (It is necessary for the valid application of this theory that the batch be so large that we may consider the proportion of defectives in the batch to be virtually unaffected by the drawing of our sample. This is no serious limitation in practice, as very small batches will normally be 100% inspected.) The probability of a single item chosen at random being defective has a probability $p = 0.1$. The probability of such an item being O.K. we shall denote by $q = 0.9$. Since the item will certainly have to be classified as either O.K. or defective, we have

$$p + q = 1$$

The probability of *both our items* being defective in a random sample of two items will be $p^2 = 0.01$. The probability that *both our items* will be O.K. will be $q^2 = 0.81$. Hence, by the addition law for probabilities (Chapter 2), the probability that *both our items* will be either O.K. or defective will be $p^2 + q^2 = 0.01 + 0.81 = 0.82$. There still remains the probability that we shall get one O.K. and one defective. Since this is the only remaining possibility its probability will be $1 - 0.82 = 0.18$.

We obtained the probability of one O.K. and one defective simply by subtracting from 1, the total probability, the probability of an 'all or none' result. This would prove an unsatisfactory method in more complex cases, so we must look for a more direct method, based on the nature of the problem. The result 'one O.K. and one defective' can arise in two ways: either the first item chosen will be O.K. with the second defective, or the first item will be defective with the second O.K. By the multiplication law, the probability of the first way will be $q \times p = pq$ and the probability of the second way will be $p \times q = pq$. If, then, we are concerned only with the final result – irrespective of the order in

4

which it comes about – the probability of one O.K. and one defective will be written simply as $pq + pq = 2pq = 2 \times 0 \cdot 1 \times 0 \cdot 9 = 0 \cdot 18$ (the result obtained by subtraction). These results may be gathered together as follows:

RESULT	Both defective	One O.K. and one defective	Both O.K.
PROBABILITY	p^2	$2pq$	q^2

The reader who has done even first-year algebra will at once recognize here the terms of the expansion of $(p+q)^2$. This gives us a clue to follow up. Let us now analyse the case of a sample of three items:

Type of Result	Ways of arising			Prob. of way	Prob. of type of result
3 defectives	def.	def.	def.	p^3	p^3
2 defectives with 1 O.K.	O.K.	def.	def.	qp^2	
	def.	O.K.	def.	pqp	$3p^2q$
	def.	def.	O.K.	p^2q	
1 defective with 2 O.K.	O.K.	O.K.	def.	q^2p	
	O.K.	def.	O.K.	qpq	$3pq^2$
	def.	O.K.	O.K.	pq^2	
3 O.K.	O.K.	O.K.	O.K.	q^3	q^3

This will be seen to give us in the right-hand column the terms of the expansion of $(p+q)^3$. We shall expect, rightly, that the probabilities of 4, 3, 2, 1, and 0 defectives in a sample of $n=4$ items will be the successive terms of the expansion of $(p+q)^4$, viz.

$p^4 + 4p^3q + 6p^2q^2 + 4pq^3 + q^4$. Thus, with $p = 0 \cdot 1$ and q therefore $= 0 \cdot 9$, we have:

4 defectives have a probability $p^4 = (0 \cdot 1)^4$		0·0001
3 defectives have a probability $4p^3q = 4(0 \cdot 1)^3(0 \cdot 9)$		0·0036
2 defectives have a probability $6p^2q^2 = 6(0 \cdot 1)^2(0 \cdot 9)^2$		0·0486
1 defective has a probability $4pq^3 = 4(0 \cdot 1)(0 \cdot 9)^3$		0·2916
0 defectives have a probability $q^4 = (0 \cdot 9)^4$		0·6561

Total probability, covering all possible results   1·0000

Thus we have arrived at the very simple rule for finding the probabilities of various numbers of defectives in a sample of n items drawn from a large batch whose proportion defective is p.

The probabilities of 0, 1, 2, 3, 4, etc., defectives in a sample of n *items drawn at random from a population whose proportion defective is* p, *and whose proportion O.K. is* q *are given by the successive terms of the expansion of* $(q + p)^n$, *reading from left to right.*

The numerical coefficients in this expansion can be obtained, without actual multiplication, as $nC0$, $nC1$, $nC2$, $nC3$, $nC4$, etc., proceeding term by term from left to right. Alternatively, they may be obtained from Pascal's Triangle, as shown in the following table.

PASCAL'S TRIANGLE

Number in the sample n	Coefficients in expansion of $(q+p)^n$
1	1 1
2	1 2 1
3	1 3 3 1
4	1 4 6 4 1
5	1 5 10 10 5 1
6	1 6 15 20 15 6 1
7	1 7 21 35 35 21 7 1
8	1 8 28 56 70 56 28 8 1

Inspection will show that each term in the table is derived by adding together the two terms in the line above which lie on either side of it. Thus, in the line for $n=5$, the term 10 is found by adding together the terms 4 and 6 in the line for $n=4$.

Let us think, now, for a moment, about the problem of sampling inspection in industry. Why do we sample? There are several possible reasons. Firstly, it may be uneconomic to inspect every individual item. Secondly, it may be impossible. Some tests (e.g. testing the life of electric light lamps) are by their nature destructive. We sample, in short, whenever we believe that 100% inspection is not a sensible procedure. Why do we inspect? To determine quality; to remove defective items; to protect the customer; to protect the reputation of the manufacturer. Inspection is a means of ensuring quality in the product which has been inspected. There is no such thing as perfection in the world of industry. With quantity production, in particular, even 100% inspection cannot give an absolute guarantee that *every single item* passed will be O.K. All the customer can reasonably ask is that his chance of getting a defective item will be suitably small, considering the nature of the product. There is probably no higher standard of inspection anywhere than in industries such as the aircraft, telephone, and optical industries. Yet prototypes fail on maiden flights, faulty condensers find their way into telephone exchanges, and errors in lens grinding or assembly will occasionally get past the inspector. When such things happen the customer is very surprised – and rightly so, considering the enormous pains taken by the manufacturer. But it is part of human frailty. So important is this human frailty that firms build reputations, not only on the quality of their goods, but also on the efficiency of their after-service.

Bearing this in mind, we might say that the function of inspection is to keep defective items to a small proportion in goods passed on to the customer. The same is true of sampling inspection. It follows that in one way or another sampling inspection results are to be used as a pointer to the proportion of defectives in batches of items. In statistical terms, we do not know the value of p, but are trying to infer something about that value. This means we need a knowledge of how samples drawn from a bulk behave. We shall return to this problem in more detail in Chapter 10. Meantime, the reader will notice one or two things which are apparent when we consider the case just worked out where we had samples of $n = 4$ items being drawn from a population containing 10% defectives.

Figure 34 shows the results in histogram form. The probabilities have been expressed in terms of the percentage of all samples in a long run which we should expect to give the stated number of defectives. The first thing the reader will observe is that a small sample, in isolation, can give only a very crude estimate of

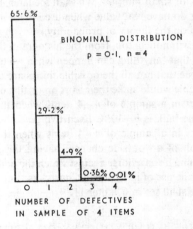

Fig. 34. Expected percentage of samples with the stated number of defectives. Samples of four items drawn from a population 10% defective

the value of the proportion defective. As the histogram shows, if the population is 10% defective then

65·6% of samples will contain no defectives, i.e. will suggest that the bulk from which they were drawn is perfect,

29·2% will contain one defective, i.e. will suggest that the bulk from which they were drawn contains 25% defectives,

4·9% of samples will contain two defectives, suggesting that the bulk from which they were drawn contains 50% defectives, roughly one-third of 1% of samples will suggest that the bulk is 75% or 100% defective.

A very crude scale indeed. Notice also the paradox. Two-thirds of the samples give an optimistic estimate of the proportion of defectives in the bulk. This, of course, is quite natural. When the proportion of defectives in the bulk is relatively small, samples *cannot be very much better* in proportion defective than the bulk from which they were drawn, but they *can be very much worse*. A very bad sample can be offset only by two or three better than average samples. On this showing there would seem to be very little use for small samples. We shall see later, however, that small samples do have real value when used in an understanding manner based on the theory of probability.

The reader will notice, too, from the histogram, that while it is certainly true that 'anything can happen when we take samples', it is equally true that not all the possible things are equally likely. Not many people would stake their shirt on getting either three or four defectives in a sample of $n = 4$ items when the proportion defective in the bulk is $p = 10\%$. Even two defectives in a single four defectives in a sample of $n = 4$ items when the proportion sample is a bit of an outside chance, having the same sort of chance of coming up as a horse against which the odds are 20 to 1. This fact is made use of in 'Control Charts' used in industrial inspection as we shall see in Chapter 11.

NOW SEE WHAT YOU CAN DO WITH THE BINOMIAL DISTRIBUTION

1. If the probability that any person thirty years old will be dead within a year is $p = 0.01$, find the probability that out of a group of 10 such people (a) none, (b) exactly one, (c) not more than one, (d) more than one, (e) at least one, will be dead within a year.

2. Samples of $n = 5$ items are drawn at random from a production process which is making 10% defectives. Draw a histogram showing the probabilities of 0, 1, 2, 3, 4, and 5 defectives in a sample.

3. I enter three telephone booths in succession and notice that the number of the phone in each case ends in the digit 1. A friend who is with me says it is just chance. I bet him 5s. that all the phones in call boxes have a number ending in 1. Was I rash? What is the probability of finding three phones in succession whose number ends with the digit 1? (Check on the phone boxes in your area and see if there is any

peculiarity about the numbers. Is there anything apart from the last digit which is peculiar?)

4. Male and female children are born in approximately equal numbers. If twins are born, in what relative proportions would you expect (a) two boys, (b) two girls, (c) one of each?

5. Sometimes, but not always, twins of the same sex are 'identical'. Twins of different sexes are never identical. Identical twins are born from a single ovum and called monozygotic. Ordinary twins are born from different ova and called dizygotic. If in a certain group of twins we find 40 pairs are of mixed sex, how many like sex pairs would you expect, in terms of your answer to number 4, where the theory you used applies only to dizygotic twins? If the whole group consists of 100 pairs of twins, the balance not so far accounted for will give an estimate of monozygotic twins. What percentage of all twins are monozygotic on these data? (This is an example of Weinberg's Rule for estimating the relative frequency of identical twins.)

8

Goals, Floods, and Horse-kicks – The Poisson Distribution

'If a man will begin with certainties he shall end in doubts; but if he will be content to begin with doubts he shall end in certainties.' FRANCIS BACON

In the previous chapter we considered the Binomial Distribution in application to cases where we take a sample of a definite size and count the number of times a certain event (e.g. occurrence of a defective) is observed. In such cases we know (a) the number of times the event *did* occur and (b) the number of times it *did not* occur. There are problems, however, in which the number of times an event occurs can be counted without there being any sense in asking how many times the event did not occur. If I watch a thunderstorm for half an hour, for example, I can report having seen the lightning flash 142 times. I cannot state *how many times* the lightning did *not* flash. We are dealing in such cases with the occurrence of isolated events in a continuum of time. The number of goals scored in a football match is another case of isolated events in a continuum of time. The number of flaws in a given length of electric cable provides us with the occurrence of isolated events in a continuum of length. The number of organisms seen in one square of a haemocytometer is an example of the occurrence of isolated events in a continuum of area (or volume). To all such cases the Binomial Distribution is inapplicable precisely because we do not know the value of n in the fundamental expression $(p+q)^n$.

To deal with events of this type we make use of the Poisson Distribution. Before giving the form of this distribution we must introduce the reader to the famous mathematical constant denoted by the letter e. This constant arises in the study of the natural law of growth (the exponential law), and has the value

$$e = \frac{1}{0!} + \frac{1}{1!} + \frac{1}{2!} + \frac{1}{3!} + \frac{1}{4!} + \frac{1}{5!} + \cdots$$

the terms on the right-hand side going on indefinitely, getting smaller and smaller all the time. The value of e, in a less interesting but more meaningful form, is obtained by working out the individual terms:

$$e = 1 + 1 + 0.5 + 0.16667 + 0.04167 + 0.00833 + 0.00139 + 0.00020 + 0.00002 + \ldots$$

which gives us $e = 2.7183$, correct to four decimal places. This number e is the basis of the natural or Napierian logarithms, where it takes the place of the base 10 used in common logarithms. Now, if this number e be raised to any power z, thus $e^z = (2.7183)^z$, then the result can be expressed in the form of an infinite series similar to the series for e itself. We get

$$e^z = \frac{z^0}{0!} + \frac{z^1}{1!} + \frac{z^2}{2!} + \frac{z^3}{2!} + \frac{z^4}{4!} + \frac{z^5}{5!} + \ldots$$

Since z^0, $0!$, and $1!$ are each equal to unity, the result is usually written at once as

$$e^z = 1 + z + \frac{z^2}{2!} + \frac{z^3}{3!} + \frac{z^4}{4!} + \frac{z^5}{5!} + \ldots$$

In order for any distribution to be useful as a probability distribution, the sum of all its terms must equal unity (the value of the total probability), and, moreover, we must be able to assign a useful meaning to the value of each term. Thus in the case of the Binomial Distribution, we had $(p+q)^n$, where $p+q = 1$ and so the nth power of $(p+q)$ must also be equal to unity, no matter what value is given to n. We were also able to give a useful meaning to each of the terms p^2, q^2, $2pq$, etc., of the expansion. With a very slight 'ruse de guerre' we can utilize the expansion of e^z as a probability distribution. The algebra of the first form tells $e^{-z} \cdot e^z = e^0 = 1$. This suggests that the product $e^{-z} \cdot e^z$ might form a handy probability distribution when written in the form

$$1 = e^{-z} \cdot e^z = e^{-z}\left(1 + z + \frac{z^2}{2!} + \frac{z^3}{3!} + \frac{z^4}{4!} + \frac{z^5}{5!} + \ldots\right)$$

It only remains to find useful work for this distribution by finding a meaning which may be attached to the several terms of the expansion. It is found that this distribution describes very beautifully the occurrence of isolated events in a continuum, if we take

z to represent the expected or average number of occurrences of the event, for then the successive terms of the expansion, viz.

$$e^{-z}, \quad ze^{-z}, \quad \frac{z^2}{2!}.e^{-z}, \quad \frac{z^3}{3!}.e^{-z}, \quad \frac{z^4}{4!}.e^{-z}, \text{ etc.,}$$

give us the probability of observing the occurrence of 0, 1, 2, 3, 4. etc., events. This is a very remarkable fact. All we need to know is the average number of occurrences of the event, z, and we can at once work out the probabilities of observing all the various possible numbers of occurrences. The only condition is that the expected number shall be constant from trial to trial. If z varies, as for example if we inspect different lengths of cable at each trial, then it is not valid to apply the distribution.

As an example, let us consider the following data, collected by Bortkewitch and quoted by R. A. Fisher, showing the chance of a cavalryman being killed by a horse-kick in the course of a year. The data are based on the records of ten army corps for twenty years, thus supplying us with 200 readings.

Deaths	Number of years this number of deaths occurred
0	109
1	65
2	22
3	3
4	1
5	0
6	0

We have total number of deaths = 122, so that the average number of deaths per year per corps is 0·61.

We may therefore take our expectation as

$$z = 0 \cdot 61$$

The value of e^{-z} is 0·543 (very nearly), so we have that the probabilities of 0, 1, 2, 3, 4, etc., deaths per year per corps will be the successive terms of

$$e^{-z}\left(1 + z + \frac{z^2}{2!} + \frac{z^3}{3!} + \frac{z^4}{4!} + \ldots\right)$$

i.e. $0 \cdot 543\left(1 + 0 \cdot 61 + \dfrac{0 \cdot 61^2}{2!} + \dfrac{0 \cdot 61^3}{3!} + \dfrac{0 \cdot 61^4}{4!} + \dfrac{0 \cdot 61^5}{5!} + \dfrac{0 \cdot 61^6}{6!} + \ldots\right)$

Working these out term by term, we enter them into the following table:

Number of deaths per year per corps	0	1	2	3	4
Probability	0·543	0·331	0·101	0·021	0·003
Frequency expected in 200 readings (approx.)	109	66·3	20·2	4·1	0·6
Actual	109	65	22	3	1

Comparison with the original data will convince the reader that the fit is remarkably good – especially when we bear in mind that a repeat of the investigation would give a result which, while similar, would not be identical, unless by some freak of chance.

In medical and biological research, the Poisson distribution is useful in describing the distribution of organisms in the squares of a haemocytometer. For example, the haemocytometer is used for making counts of red corpuscles in the blood. A small sample of the patient's blood is taken and diluted down in known amount with pure water. Then a drop of this dilution is placed on a special recessed slide (Fig. 35) and covered with a second glass slide whose surface is ruled into small squares. Since the depth of the recess in the bottom slide is known, each square of the haemocytometer corresponds with a known volume of blood. The number of cells in each of twenty or thirty squares is then counted under the microscope, and from the average value the number of corpuscles in a unit volume of blood can be estimated. The same principle is followed in making counts of bacteria by the dilution method. Since a very considerable variation in the number of organisms per square occurs, it is essential to count an adequate number of squares, where the average number of organisms per square is small. Agreement of the observed frequencies with the Poisson distribution can be made the basis of testing whether the experimental technique is satisfactory.

The mean value of a Poisson type distribution, z, is equal to its variance, so that the standard deviation will be equal to the square root of z.

As we have already stated, the Poisson distribution may only be

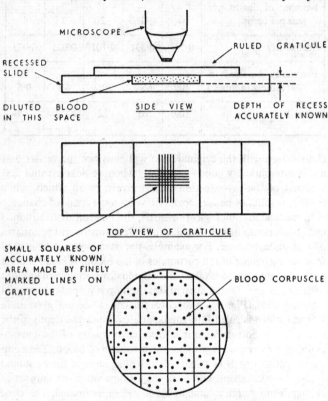

Fig. 35. Haemocytometer. Each square corresponds to a known volume of blood of a known dilution. From the average number of corpuscles per square the 'Blood Count' is determined

applied in cases where the expectation, z, is constant from trial to trial. Thus, it does not apply to the number of suicides per year in a given community, because the temptation to commit suicide

GOALS, FLOODS, AND HORSE-KICKS 101

varies with the stress of the times, as was dramatically shown during the slump in the 1930's in America. Again, we should not expect the Poisson distribution to give a perfect description of the number of goals scored per team per match at football, since the expected number of goals depends, among other things, on which teams are opposed, on the weather conditions, and so on. Fig. 21 showed the sort of distribution obtained for goals in a football match. The actual figures on which Fig. 21 is based are as follows:

Number of goals	0	1	2	3	4	5	6	7
Number of times teams scored that number of goals in a match	95	158	108	63	40	9	5	2

Thus 480 recorded scores give a total of 812 goals, which works out, very nearly, to an average of 1·7 goals per team per match. Our value for z in this problem is therefore $z = 1·7$, and the value of e^{-z} may be taken as 0·18 (or 0·1827 more exactly). For our Poisson we then have:

$$e^{-z}\left(1 + z + \frac{z^2}{2!} + \frac{z^3}{3!} + \frac{z^4}{4!} + ...\right)$$
$$= 0·18\left(1 + 1·7 + \frac{1·7^2}{2!} + \frac{1·7^3}{3!} + \frac{1·7^4}{4!} + ...\right)$$

Working out the successive terms of this distribution we get, as before, the following table (results expressed to the nearest whole number):

Goals per match	0	1	2	3	4	5	6	7
Poisson Frequency	88	150	126	72	30	10	3	1
Observed Frequency	95	158	108	63	50	9	5	2

This is not too bad a result as a prediction. It suggests that the disturbing factors of weather and team-matching do not exert so great an effect as is often supposed. However, the χ^2 test (see

Chapter 15) indicates that the fit is not altogether as good as we might expect if the Poisson were a suitable distribution for this kind of case.

In cases such as the one just discussed, where the expectation, z, varies from trial to trial, we may use a modification of the Poisson distribution, which allows for this variability in the expectation. What we have to do in this modification is to calculate the mean of the observed distribution and its variance. We leave this as an exercise for the reader, and simply state the result:

$$\text{Mean} = 1 \cdot 7 \qquad \text{Variance} = 1 \cdot 9$$

(The reader will not be surprised that the value of the variance is so close to the mean value, since the actual distribution is, as we have already seen, fairly close to a Poisson, and mean and variance for a Poisson are identical.)

We then set $\qquad \bar{x} = \dfrac{p}{c} \qquad$ i.e. $\qquad \dfrac{p}{c} = 1 \cdot 7 \qquad$ (1)

and $\qquad \bar{x} + \dfrac{\bar{x}}{c} = \sigma^2 \qquad$ i.e. $\quad 1 \cdot 7 + \dfrac{1 \cdot 7}{c} = 1 \cdot 9 \qquad$ (2)

The second equation gives us, on solving for c, $c = 8 \cdot 5$. Substituting this value of c in equation (1) and solving for p gives $p = 14 \cdot 5$. The probabilities of 0, 1, 2, 3, 4, etc., goals per team per match will then be given according to this modification as the successive terms, passing from left to right, of the expansion

$$\left(\frac{c}{c+1}\right)^p \left\{ 1, \frac{p}{c+1}, \frac{p(p+1)}{2!(c+1)^2}, \frac{p(p+1)(p+2)}{3!(c+1)^3}, \text{etc.} \dots \right\}$$

Substituting for p and c the values calculated above, we get:

$$\left(\frac{8 \cdot 5}{9 \cdot 5}\right)^{14 \cdot 5} \left\{ 1, \frac{14 \cdot 5}{9 \cdot 5}, \frac{(14 \cdot 5)(15 \cdot 5)}{2!(9 \cdot 5)^2}, \frac{(14 \cdot 5)(15 \cdot 5)(16 \cdot 5)}{3(9 \cdot 5)^3}, \text{etc.} \dots \right\}$$

Calculating these probabilities and multiplying each term by 480 in order to get the expected frequency of each score, we arrive at the following table:

Number of goals	0	1	2	3	4	5	6	7
Predicted frequency	96	147	119	69	32	12	4	1
Actual frequency	95	158	108	63	40	9	5	2

The χ^2 test (Chapter 15) confirms what the reader may judge for himself by comparison of the two predictions: that the modified distribution gives a better overall fit than the ordinary Poisson distribution. Fig. 36 gives a visual comparison between the Poisson prediction and the actual observations, on the one hand,

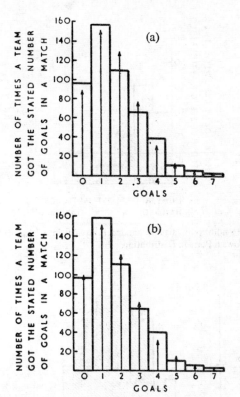

Fig. 36. Correspondence between observed and predicted frequencies of isolated events such as goals scored in football matches

(a) The blocks of the Histogram show the observed frequencies. The arrows show the frequencies predicted by the Poisson

(b) The blocks of the Histogram show the observed frequencies. The arrows show the frequencies predicted by a modified distribution which allows for a slight variation in the expectation

and between the modified distribution and the actual observations on the other hand. Figs. 37 and 38 give other examples of distributions of the Poisson type, being occurrences of isolated events.

Poisson probability paper is a graph paper with specially ruled

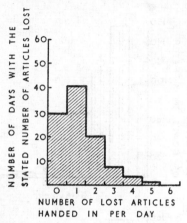

Fig. 37. The number of articles handed in as lost in a large department store follows a Poisson Distribution

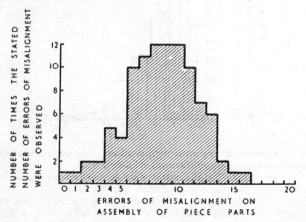

Fig. 38. Example of a Poisson Distribution of a fairly symmetrical type

grids which has several uses in this type of problem. As will be seen by study of Fig. 39, the left-hand vertical scale is a probability scale. The bottom horizontal scale is logarithmic, representing values of z, the expectation. The face of the graph is crossed by curved lines, labelled $c = 1$, $c = 2$, $c = 3$, etc.

Suppose, now, that we were dealing with a Poisson type distribution for which we knew the value of the expectation, z. From the graph we could read off at once the probability that the event in question would occur *at least* c times. For example, suppose

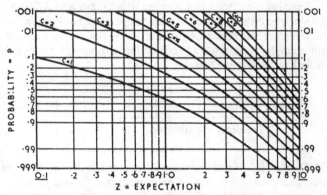

Fig. 39. Poisson probability paper, showing the probability, P, that an event will occur C times *at least* (i.e. C times or more) when the expected number of occurrences has the value of z

$z = 0.5$, then running our finger up the vertical line at $z = 0.5$ we find, by reading off the value on the probability scale opposite the various values of c, that:

The event will occur *at least* once   with a probability 0·4
  ,,   ,,   ,,   ,,   ,,   twice   ,, ,,   ,,   0·09
  ,,   ,,   ,,   ,,   ,,   ,,   three times ,, ,,   ,,   0·02

and so on. (The reader is advised to notice carefully that the probability scale has its small values at the top and larger values at the bottom, contrary to the usual convention in graphs.) It is obvious that, knowing these values, we can obtain the probabilities that the event will occur *exactly* 0, 1, 2, 3, 4, etc., times by differencing.

Thus, knowing that the event occurs in this case at least once with a probability 0·40, we know at once that the event must occur 0 times with a probability $(1 - 0·40) = 0·60$. Again, we know that the event occurs at least twice with a probability 0·09. Evidently, then, it occurs less than twice with a probability $(1 - 0·09) = 0·91$, and since we have just found that the event occurs 0 times with a probability 0·60, it is easy to see that it must occur exactly once with a probability $(0·91 - 0·60) = 0·31$. In like manner, we may calculate the probabilities of the event occurring other exact numbers of times.

A second use of the paper is to test whether any actual distribution in observed data may well be described by the Poisson law, and, if so, what the expectation for the distribution is. Consider, for example, the data already quoted for the deaths of cavalrymen from horse-kicks. We had:

Deaths	0	1	2	3	4
Frequency	109	65	22	3	1

The probability of each number of deaths can be derived from the frequencies corresponding to each group by dividing these frequencies by the total number of readings, viz. 200. Doing this, we get:

Deaths	0	1	2	3	4
Probability	0·545	0·325	0·11	0·015	0·005

From this table we can arrive, easily, at the following:

At least one death occurs with probability $= 0·455$
At least two deaths occur with probability $= 0·13$
At least three deaths occur with probability $= 0·02$
At least four deaths occur with probability $= 0·005$

If the reader will plot these on the Poisson paper, placing each point on its proper line, $c = 1$, $c = 2$, etc., opposite the computed value of the probability, he will find that they lie on a vertical straight line, at the value $z = 0.6$. Thus we may test whether a given distribution follows a Poisson type law by plotting it as just described above. If the points plot on a vertical straight line the distribution follows a Poisson law, with expectation, z, equal to the abscissa for the vertical line.

We shall meet with yet another use for this type of paper when we come to discuss 'operating characteristics' of sampling schemes in Chapter 10.

NOW SEE IF YOU KNOW ANYTHING ABOUT THE POISSON DISTRIBUTION

1. Experience of a certain disease indicates that it has a fatality rate of 10%. A new treatment tried out on 30 patients results in 7 deaths. Is the evidence sufficiently strong to show that this treatment is inimical to the best interests of the patients?

2. A class of 20 students is prepared for an examination at which experience shows that 20% of candidates fail. Only 10 of this class pass the examination. Have the class reasonable grounds for complaint? (Or – if the reader is a teacher – has the teacher reasonable grounds for complaint?)

3. A carnival organizer wishes to buy 500 balloons and does not want more than 1% to be defective. He goes into a chain store and buys a packet of 10 balloons, of which one is found to have a leak. What is the probability of getting a packet as bad as or worse than this if the balloons in that store are, in fact, only 1% defective?

4. The amount of dust in the atmosphere may be estimated by using an ultramicroscope. A very small volume of air is illuminated by a spark and the observer counts the number of particles of dust he sees. By repeating this operation a large number of times, the amount of dust in each cubic centimetre of air can be estimated. Suppose that the following test results were obtained in a series of 300 spot checks by the flash method. Calculate the expected frequencies for each number of particles for comparison with the observed frequencies shown in the table.

Number of particles	0	1	2	3	4	5	more than 5
Frequency of occurrence	38	75	89	54	20	19	5

5. Compute the variance for the data in question 4 and see how closely it agrees with the mean value (remember that the mean and variance of a Poisson distribution are supposed to be equal theoretically).

9

The Normal Distribution

'If you will have your laws obeyed without mutiny, see well
that they be pieces of God Almighty's Law; otherwise, all the
artillery in the world will not keep down mutiny.' CARLYLE

In previous chapters we have seen that the idea of a 'frequency
distribution' is of the utmost value in statistical work, and we
have noted how frequency distributions which arise in practice
can be assigned to different mathematical families such as the
Binomial and Poisson families with the great advantage that we
can picture the form of the distribution from a knowledge of one
or two compact measures. While the Binomial and Poisson distributions enable us to deal with the occurrence of distinct events,
such as the number of defective items in a sample of a given size,
or the number of accidents occurring in a factory during the working day, we have not, so far, got a mathematical distribution for
dealing with quantities whose magnitude is continuously variable.
This problem we now take up with the introduction of what is
variously known as the *Normal Law*, the *Error Law*, or the *Gaussian Law*. The reader should be on his guard, however, against
thinking that there is necessarily anything abnormal about any
observed distribution that does not follow this law. It is unlikely
that any distribution observed in practice follows exactly any of
the common distributions used as types by mathematicians. Careful enough study would in every case bring to light discrepancies.

It will be a good thing at this point for the reader to give a
moment's thought to the matter of the use of typical distributions
by the mathematician. In the first place, it will be evident that to
treat every distribution in isolation on its own merits would be
very uneconomic. Someone (probably G. K. Chesterton) once
said that the world of reality is a world of limitations. This is never
truer than in regard to applied mathematics. The mathematician
can work to an unlimited number of mathematically significant
figures. Probably not more than two or three of these are significant in practice in most cases. An accuracy of 1 % is ample for

most of the real things in life. This being the case, the approximation in assigning any observed distribution to the mathematical family to which it bears the greatest resemblance is not a matter for misgivings, but rather for confidence since it renders the mechanism of battle simpler.

If the reader will consider some of the Figures, such as Figs. 28b and 31, which show histograms for continuously variable quantities, such as height and intelligence which have a symmetrical distribution, he will see that they approximate in shape to a bell. If, now, he will imagine the class intervals to be made smaller and smaller in width, it will be apparent to him that the jumps in frequency in passing from one class to the next would

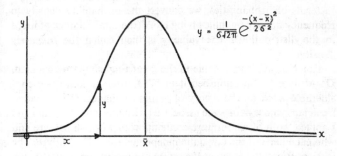

Fig. 40. The normal curve

become less and less perceptible to the eye, until eventually the diagrams would have the appearance of a smooth bell shape such as the Normal Curve shown in Fig. 40.

The mathematical equation to this curve is rather fearsome at first sight:

$$y = \frac{1}{\sigma\sqrt{2\pi}} e^{\frac{-(x-\bar{x})^2}{2\sigma^2}}$$

The quantity y, which is the height of the curve at any point along the scale of x, is known as the *probability density* of that particular value of the variable quantity, x. Thus, for example, if x represents Intelligence Quotient, we see that the probability density has a maximum value at the average intelligence value, falling

away on either side. In other words, people with about average
intelligence are much more frequently found than people who are
either geniuses or morons. The symbol σ is the small Greek letter
s and stands for standard deviation. The difference between s and
σ is that, while s is the standard deviation as measured by a sample
of finite magnitude, σ is the true value of the standard deviation in
the population. We may regard s as an estimate of the value of σ,
based on a sample. We shall have more to say on this point later.
The symbol $\bar{x}$ is, as before, the average value for the distribution.
The symbol e is the base of the Napierian logarithms ($=2\cdot7183$),
and π is well known as the ratio of the circumference of a circle to
its diameter ($=3\frac{1}{7}$).

When we wish to think in terms of numbers of cases rather than
in terms of probabilities, we convert the probability density to
frequency density by multiplying by N (the total number of items
in the distribution). The value y is then called the *frequency
density*.

This Normal Curve is due to the great English mathematician,
De Moivre,* who published it in 1733, after he had done considerable work on the theory of games of chance. Other mathematicians whose names are associated with this law are Gauss and
Laplace, both of whom were contemporary with De Moivre and
who each derived the law quite independently of De Moivre. The
law was found to represent the errors of observation in astronomy
and the other physical sciences remarkably well – hence the reason
for the name 'Law of Errors', the errors being the deviations of
actual observations from the true value. This law occupies a central position in statistical theory.

The reader will remember that in statistics one of our aims is to
represent the whole of a body of data by a few simple parameters.
The parameters of the Normal Curve are the mean, $\bar{x}$, and the
standard deviation, σ. We referred to this idea of parameters in
Chapter 5, where we showed that, given a knowledge of the mean
and standard deviation, we could form a very good mental picture of the whole of a distribution. The reader is asked to look
again at Figs. 30 and 32 in order to refresh his memory on this
point. The rule given in Chapter 5 as an arbitrary rule was, in

* An Englishman of French origin.

fact, based on the Normal Law. What we were really saying then was that our distribution was symmetrical and unimodal, so that it was a reasonable assumption for most practical purposes to assign it to the Normal Curve family. The percentages between various limits quoted in Fig. 30 belong to the Normal Curve, which is a mathematical model with fixed and definite characteristics which are known and tabulated for us by the mathematicians.

In order to go further, we must meet the Normal Curve in what is known as *standard form*. It will be apparent to the reader that all distributions in the Normal Law family are fundamentally the same. They can in fact differ from each other only in respect to their average value, $\bar{x}$, and their standard deviation, σ. Their

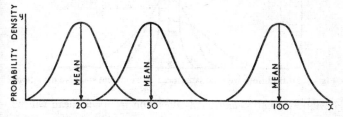

Fig. 41. Distribution with same standard deviation or spread, but different mean values

shapes will all be similar. Fig. 41 shows distributions with different values for their mean, $\bar{x}$, all having the same standard deviation or spread, σ. They are identical curves, located at different points on the scale of the variable quantity, x. For this reason, measures of central tendency are often called measures of location. Fig. 42 shows the case where we have distributions whose mean value is the same but whose standard deviation or spread is different from distribution to distribution. The reason why the curves differ in height is that the area under the curve is taken as unity, so as to represent the total probability. It follows that as the base of the curve shrinks the height must be increased so as to keep the area constant. In order to make all such distributions immediately comparable with each other we have to reduce them all to their essential nature. That is to say, their individuality, as expressed by their particular mean and standard deviation, has to be suppressed. This is done, very simply, by regarding the mean of each distribution as having the value *zero*, and measuring all deviations from this mean, not in terms of the original units, but in terms of the standard deviation of the distribution. When this is done, *every* distribution in the family will have a mean value *zero*, and *every* distribution in the family will have a standard

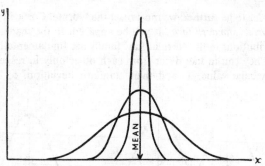

Fig. 42. Distributions with the same mean, but different standard deviations

deviation equal to *unity*. Any deviation from the mean will be represented in the new scale of units by a 'code' value $t = \frac{x - \bar{x}}{\sigma}$. To illustrate this, let us take a value 126 for I.Q. We know that the mean and standard deviation for our I.Q. distribution were $\bar{x} = 100$ and $s = 13$ respectively. Taking s as σ, we see that the value $x = 126$ on our original scale of values would become

$$t = \frac{126 - 100}{13} = 2$$

on our new scale of values. All we are saying, in fact, is that the value 126 is two standard deviations away from the mean value of the distribution. If, then, in our equation for the Normal Probability Curve

$$y = \frac{1}{\sigma\sqrt{2\pi}} e^{\frac{-(x - \bar{x})^2}{2\sigma^2}}$$

we write $t = \frac{x - \bar{x}}{\sigma}$ then $\frac{(x - \bar{x})^2}{\sigma^2}$ will become t^2, and, since we are now in the new scale, σ has the value unity. The Normal Probability Curve then becomes, simply,

$$y = \frac{1}{\sqrt{2\pi}} e^{\frac{-t^2}{2}}$$

It may be shown mathematically that the area under this curve is equal to unity – in fact, the constant $\frac{1}{\sqrt{2\pi}}$ has been specially chosen by the mathematicians to ensure this. It is important to remember that it is *the area under the curve which represents probability*. The area under the curve between any two values of t represents the probability that any item chosen at random from

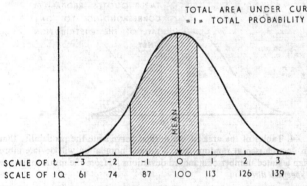

SCALE OF t -3 -2 -1 0 1 2 3
SCALE OF IQ   61   74   87   100   113   126   139

Fig. 43. Area under the probability curve is equal to the probability that an individual chosen at random will have an I.Q. within the range indicated

the distribution in question will fall between the values of the variable which correspond to those two values of t. Thus, in Fig. 43, the area under the curve between $t = -1\frac{1}{2}$ and $t = +\frac{1}{2}$ represents the probability that any individual in the population has an I.Q. between $80\frac{1}{2}$ and $106\frac{1}{2}$.

The Normal Curve extends infinitely in either direction, getting closer and closer to the axis of x; for most practical purposes, however, we may regard it as terminating at three, or at most four, standard deviations on either side of the average. Actually, $99\cdot73\%$ of the area falls between the values $t = -3$ and $t = +3$ standard deviations, and $99\cdot994\%$ within the limits $t = -4$ and

$t = +4$ standard deviations. 50% of the area is contained between the limits $t = -0.6745$ and $t = +0.6745$ standard deviations. The term *probable error* was used in former times to denote 0.6745σ, this being the deviation just as likely to be exceeded as not. The term, a poor one, is now very much obsolescent. It has been said that 'it is neither an error nor probable'.

The table on page 116 gives the probability that any item chosen at random from a Normal distribution will fall outside the value of t quoted. The reader should notice carefully that the probability as stated applies only to deviations in *one direction* (see Fig. 44). To get the probability of a deviation in *either* direction

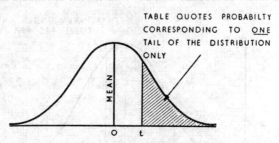

Fig. 44. Tables of the area of the normal curve state the probability that an item chosen at random from a normal population will deviate more than a stated number of standard deviations (t) from the mean value – *in a specified direction*

greater than the stated value of t the value of the probability in the table should be doubled. We illustrate the uses of the table by a couple of examples.

Example. The local authorities in a certain city instal 2,000 electric lamps in the streets of the city. If these lamps have an average life of 1,000 burning hours, with a standard deviation of 200 hours, what number of the lamps might be expected to fail in the first 700 burning hours?

In this case we want to find the probability corresponding to the area of the probability curve *below* $t = \dfrac{700 - 1000}{200} = -1\frac{1}{2}$. We ignore the sign and enter our table at $t = 1\frac{1}{2}$ to find that the probability for lives less than 700 hours is $p = 0.067$. Hence the expected number of failures will be $2,000 \times 0.067$, i.e. 134.

Example. What number of lamps may be expected to fail between 900 and 1,300 burning hours?

This problem is tackled in two stages.

The number of lamps which will fail under 900 hours: The corresponding value of t is $\frac{900 - 1000}{200} = -0.5$. Entering the table with this value of t, we find for the probability of failure below 900 hours $p = 0.309$.

The number of lamps which will fail over 1,300: The corresponding value of t is $\frac{1300 - 1000}{200} = 1.5$. Entering the table with this value of t, we find for the probability of failure over 1,300 hours $p = 0.067$.

Hence the probability of failure outside the limits 900 to 1,300 hours will be $0.309 + 0.067 = 0.376$. It follows that the number of lamps we may expect to fail outside these limits is $2,000 \times 0.376 = 752$. But we were asked to find the number which are likely to fail *inside* the limits stated. This is evidently $2,000 - 752 = 1,248$.

These answers are predictions. In the normal course of events we should expect our predictions to be reasonably close to the truth. Predictions of this sort always presuppose a continuance of the *status quo*. They make no allowance for the manufacturer who accidentally uses inferior materials in a batch of lamps or for the small boy who comes along with his catapult.

Example. After what period of burning hours would we expect that 10% of the lamps would have failed?

What we want here is the value of t corresponding to a probability $p = 0.10$. Looking along our table we find that when $t = 1.25$ the probability is $p = 0.106$. This is near enough for our purpose of prediction. Hence we may take it that 10% of the lamps will fail at 1.25 standard deviations. Since one standard deviation is equal to 200 hours, it follows that 10% of the lamps will fail before $1,000 - 1.25(200) = 1,000 - 250 = 750$ hours.

The problem of street lighting is an excellent example of a case where variability about the average is of the greatest importance.

Concerns with mass lighting problems often prefer to replace their lamps at regular intervals instead of piecemeal as the lamps fail. When the standard deviation is small, this becomes a reasonable proposition, for as soon as any number of lamps worth speaking of have failed the remaining lamps have little life left to run. Psychologically, also, it is a good thing for the lamp manufacturer's reputation for his lamps to have a uniform life. The odd bulb that fails soon after it is bought attracts much more attention than the many which burn on year after year until the customer has no idea of the length of time it has given him faithful service.

TABLE OF AREAS OF THE NORMAL CURVE*
(ONE TAIL ONLY)

t	0	0·25	0·50	0·75	
Probability	0·500	0·401	0·309	0·227	
t	1·0	1·25	1·50	1·75	
Probability	0·159	0·106	0·067	0·040	
t	2·0	2·25	2·50	2·75	3·0
Probability	0·023	0·012	0·006	0·003	0·001

TABLE OF ORDINATES OF THE NORMAL CURVE*

t	0	0·25	0·50	0·75	
Ordinate	0·399	0·387	0·352	0·301	
t	1·0	1·25	1·50	1·75	
Ordinate	0·242	0·187	0·130	0·086	
t	2·0	2·25	2·50	2·75	3·0
Ordinate	0·054	0·032	0·018	0·009	0·004

* See acknowledgements, p. vi

The probability density (height of the curve) at any value of t is given in the tables of the Ordinate of the Normal Curve, an abbreviated version of which we have given under the Table of Areas of the Normal Curve (page 116). This table enables us to draw correctly the shape of the Normal Curve, if, for example, we wish to superimpose over a histogram the Normal Curve with the same mean and standard deviation. To illustrate the technique of fitting a Normal Curve to a given distribution, we shall fit a curve to the I.Q. data for which we worked out the mean and standard deviation as $\bar{x} = 99 \cdot 3$ and $s = 13 \cdot 3$ in Chapter 6. In order to keep the arithmetic simple we shall take $\bar{x} = 100$ with $\sigma \ (=s) = 13$. In this distribution we had $N = 100$ values recorded in our histogram. The equation to the Normal Curve, when the area under the curve is made equal to unity so as to represent the total probability, is

$$y = \frac{1}{\sigma\sqrt{2\pi}} e^{\frac{-(x-\bar{x})^2}{2\sigma^2}}$$

If we wish to make the area under the curve equal the total *frequency*, N, for a given distribution, we have to multiply the right-hand side by N, which gives

$$y = \frac{N}{\sigma\sqrt{2\pi}} e^{\frac{-(x-\bar{x})^2}{2\sigma^2}}$$

In our particular case, we have $N = 100$, $\bar{x} = 100$, $\sigma = 13$, and the equation takes the form

$$y = \left(\frac{100}{13}\right)\left(\frac{1}{\sqrt{2\pi}} e^{\frac{-(x-100)^2}{2\times(13)^2}}\right)$$

Now the quantity $\left(\dfrac{x-100}{13}\right)$ is what, in our tables, we have called t. Hence, we have

$$y = \left(\frac{100}{13}\right)\left(\frac{1}{\sqrt{2\pi}} e^{\frac{-t^2}{2}}\right)$$

The expression in the right-hand bracket is simply the standard form of the equation to the Normal Curve, and, therefore, our Table for the height of the ordinate applies to this bracket. In order to get the actual height of the curve to be applied to our histogram, our equation tells us to multiply the ordinate height given in the table by the factor $\frac{100}{13} = 7.7$. It will be ample, as a demonstration, to calculate the ordinates for our curve at intervals of half a standard deviation. We show the results in the following table:

t	0	0·5	1·0	1·5	2·0	2·5	3·0
y (from table)	0·399	0·352	0·242	0·130	0·054	0·018	0·004
7·7y	3·07	2·70	1·86	1·00	0·42	0·14	0·03
x	100	106·5 and 93·5	113 and 87	119·5 and 80·5	126 and 74	132·5 and 67·5	139 and 61

The values of x are derived from the values of t, and of course there is a value of x on either side of the mean for both of which the t value is the same. We may now draw the Normal Curve for the distribution as in Fig. 45, by setting up a horizontal scale to represent I.Q. and a vertical scale to represent the values 7·7y calculated in the table.

When the Normal Curve has thus been plotted, we may add the histogram. The heights of the several blocks in the histogram are obtained by dividing the frequency the block has to represent by the value of the class interval. Thus, in our example, the class

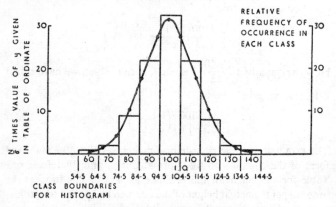

Fig. 45. Normal curve fitted to I.Q. data

whose boundaries are 94·5 and 104·5 has a frequency 33. Since the class interval, c, is 10, this block should be given a height of 3·3 units on the left-hand scale. The scale on the right of Fig. 45 is obtained by multiplying the left-hand scale by the class interval, 10, and so shows the frequency of occurrence of items in each class. Such a scale is possible only when the class interval is the same for all classes.

YOU MAY NOW DEAL WITH THE FOLLOWING

1. You work out the mean and standard deviation for a set of data and find $\bar{x} = 24$ with $s = 3$. Now try to find the answers to the following questions:

    (a) within what limits would you expect almost the whole of the distribution to lie?

    (b) within what limits would you expect about 95% of the distribution to lie?

    (c) within what limits would you expect about two-thirds of the distribution to lie?

2. Draw a histogram for the data of Chapter 6 examples. You will have found the mean and standard deviation already (if you have thrown the result away get it from the answers at the back of the book). Now fit a Normal Curve on top of your histogram.

3. Draw a histogram for the coefficients of the terms of $(p+q)^5$. Superimpose on it the Normal Curve whose mean is 2.5 and whose variance is 1·25. The area under the Normal Curve is to be taken as 32.

10

What Happens when we take Samples

'And tell by Venus and the Moon
Who stole a thimble or a spoon.'
s. BUTLER (*Hudibras*)

The statistician's job is to draw general conclusions from fragmentary data. Too often the data supplied to him for analysis are
not only fragmentary but positively incoherent, so that he can do
next to nothing with them. Even the most kindly statistician swears
heartily under his breath whenever this happens. Before he looks
at it he knows just what the position is going to be. It is a common
pastime in many organizations, and even laboratories, to collect
vast quantities of data on a routine basis, using apprentice labour,
with the vague intention of submitting them to analysis 'one day
when things are not so busy'. Of course, things are never slack, so
the 'piles of useful stuff in the files' get more comprehensive –
and out of date – as the years go by. Pious intentions to analyse
some day are of little value. If data are not worth analysis at a
suitably near date they are rarely worth the labour of collection.
Less time collecting and more time analysing would be a valuable
aim in many laboratories.

But it is not simply because the road to hell is paved with good
intentions that the miserly acquisition of data is to be deplored.
There is a more serious reason. Data should be collected with a
clear purpose in mind. Not only a clear purpose, but a clear idea as
to the precise way in which they will be analysed so as to yield the
desired information. Many ambitious schemes are finally acknow-
ledged as nugatory with the phrase: 'If only we had kept a record
of the pressure, or the cost of the leather, or the number of men
we had on the job from time to time.' It is astonishing that men,
who in other respects are clear-sighted, will collect absolute
hotch-potches of data in the blithe and uncritical belief that
analysis can get something useful out of it all – especially if a
statistician once starts to juggle with it. It cannot be too often repeated that there are only a limited number of analytical techniques in statistics. Each technique asks certain questions of the

inquirer, as a preliminary to answering his question. Unless he can *give* a satisfactory reply he will never be able to *receive* one. The man who needs the services of a statistician usually knows little about statistical method himself beyond what is elementary common sense. For this reason it is important that he should get advice from his statistical expert before he commences the work of collecting data, whenever possible. In this way he will save himself a lot of disappointments. It is surprising, when we consider the enormous volume of research that is done by physicists and engineers, biologists and economists, by essentially statistical methods, that their professional training so often is virtually devoid of any guidance in how to handle this type of material. The physicist, as a student, meets nothing but nice smooth curves in his experiments – by kindly arrangement of his tutors. When he gets out doing research in an industrial lab., all too often his graphs are plum puddings, through which he helplessly and hopefully tries to draw a trend line. The chemist is in even worse case – especially if he is doing research on some natural material such as rubber or leather. If only such people had a short course as postgraduates, sufficient to make them 'general practitioners' in statistics, with sufficient knowledge to deal with the everyday matters and sufficient insight to call in the professional statistician to complex cases at a suitably early time, we should see a marked improvement in the productivity of industrial and other research.

But even if the data presented to statisticians were not incoherent owing to the causes just dealt with, they would still be fragmentary. There would still be difficulties. Bias will creep into data despite the most careful and refined attempts (some of which we shall discuss later) to eliminate it. Often we have perforce to make do and mend with imperfect raw data. Often, the statistician knows what he wants but simply cannot have it. Medical statisticians are regularly in this plight. Then again, the collection of data can be a slow and laborious process which cannot be speeded up, however anxious we may be. An instance of this will be found in the *British Medical Journal* (9 April, 1949), where H. J. B. Atkins, Director of Surgery at Guy's Hospital, explaining a project he wished to start with regard to carcinoma of the breast, ends by saying: 'so that we may be sure of answering at least one fundamental question about breast cancer by the year 2030'. It is relevant, too, to observe that the answer might be a negative one, telling us only that something was *not* concerned with the development of this disease. The whole medical profession of England would be willing to work without food or rest for a year to get the answer to this question. But there must be patience. There is no quick or royal road.

All sampling enquiries are aimed at discovering something about a particular population. We must be clear as to what population we are interested in. As M. G. Kendall in his *Advanced Statistics* puts it: 'Is the enquiry to be made among children? among inhabitants of the British Isles? among those who habitually drink milk? among townspeople or among country folk? and so on.' The condenser engineer might equally ask himself: among all condensers? or among mica condensers only? condensers of all capacities? dry-stack or silvered? potted or unpotted? We must sample the right population and confine our conclusions to that population.

Again, we must know very clearly what it is we are trying to find out about our population. To quote Kendall again, 'it is no use returning the facile reply "all about it" to this question'. As he pertinently points out, our sample will be of limited size and so will contain only limited information. A man may set out with a pint pot to fetch himself a pint of ale. If on his way he half fills his pot with paraffin he will bring back that much less ale – and neither ale nor paraffin is likely to be of overmuch use when he comes to sort them out. Every sampling investigation is a pint pot. It can never bring back more than its own capacity of information. Often, indeed, it will bring back less. If we can only carry out a limited investigation, we had best have a strictly limited target. Many investigations are extremely loose in design. They are like nets which are indeed spread wide but have a mesh so large that all but the most giant fish escape. In statistical work, the giant fish is the one that everyone can catch for himself, without the statistician's tackle.

It is perhaps unnecessary to stress that we should take into account knowledge about our population derived from other sources. It sometimes happens that a statistician working as a consultant in a strange field will announce what he takes to be an interesting discovery, only to get the reply: 'So what? We've always known that'. A pity, perhaps, that he wasn't informed beforehand. It would have saved him the trouble of finding out. All the wasted effort could have gone to finding something that the specialists in that particular field did *not* know, or were only wondering about. It is a valuable and instructive discipline, after every investigation, to divide the conclusions into three groups: (a) the ones that were well known to start with, (b) the ones that confirm or refute previous 'hunches', (c) the ones that no one ever thought of (and possibly cannot be believed, in some cases). Consideration of other knowledge about the population prior to the investigation has a further value in suggesting what parameters are likely to be suitable, what the form of the final distribution is likely to be, what significance tests will be suitable, and so on. Very often, prior knowledge of this kind gives us very valuable clues as to the size of the sample likely to be needed in order to make firm conclusions possible in the final analysis. In absence of such prior knowledge, a preliminary pilot survey is often to be recommended.

We must remember, also, that all sampling investigations are subject to experimental error. Careful consideration to design enables this error to be kept to a minimum. No sampling investigations can give a result, except in terms of probability. What order of probability will satisfy us? The confidence we are able to extend to our final results depends both on the magnitude of interfering effects and on the size of our sample. Only very careful forethought and hindsight can make any sampling investigation other than an incoherent pile of data.

All these points we have made are the sort of thing the intelligent reader will at once recognize as true. They are fundamentally common sense. There are other factors in sampling which, while they are common sense, are not obvious and not common knowledge. We arrive at knowledge of them only by consideration of what is called 'sampling theory'. It is to such matters that we devote the rest of this chapter.

Let us first consider the behaviour of samples drawn from the Binomial distribution. We have already seen (Chapter 7) how to calculate the probability that samples of n items drawn from a population whose proportion defective (or, more generally, the proportion having a certain characteristic not belonging to the remainder of the population) is p shall contain 0, 1, 2, 3, etc., items defective (or having the characteristic in question). We did this by expanding the binomial $(q + p)^n$, and found that the probabilities were the terms of this expansion, proceeding from left to right. The mean of a distribution of this type will be the expected number of defectives in our sample of n items, viz. np. For example if the population is 10% defective, and we take samples of 50 items, then the average number of defectives in such samples will be 5, which is $np = 50 \times 0.1$. It can also be shown that the variance of the distribution for the number of defectives will have the value npq, so that the standard deviation will be $\sqrt{npq}$. In the example just given we have $n = 50$, $p = 0.1$, and therefore $q = 0.9$. We shall thus have variance equal to $50 \times 0.1 \times 0.9 = 4.5$, and standard deviation equal to $\sqrt{4.5} = 2.12$.

As we have to give these results in arbitrary fashion, it may help to convince the reader if we work out one case as a check. He may work others for himself if he is so inclined. Take the case of samples of four items drawn from a population for which $p = 0.1$. The probabilities of 0, 1, 2, 3, 4 defectives will be given by the successive terms of the expansion of $(0.9 + 0.1)^4$, i.e. of

$$(0.9)^4 + 4(0.9)^3(0.1) + 6(0.9)^2(0.1)^2 + 4(0.9)(0.1)^3 + (0.1)^4$$

Evaluating these terms, and multiplying by 10,000 to get whole numbers, we have that in 10,000 samples of four items the defectives should occur with the frequencies shown in the following table:

No. of defectives (x)	0	1	2	3	4
Frequency predicted (f)	6,561	2,916	486	36	1

We then have, using our standard formula for calculating the average:

$$\bar{x} = \frac{\Sigma f x}{\Sigma f} = \frac{6,561(0) + 2,916(1) + 486(2) + 36(3) + 1(4)}{10,000}$$

$$= \frac{4,000}{10,000} = 0.4$$

Check: $\bar{x} = np = 4(0{\cdot}1) = 0{\cdot}4$

Likewise for the variance, using the formula:

$$*\text{Var}(x) = \frac{\Sigma f x^2}{\Sigma f} - (\bar{x})^2$$

we get

$$\text{Var}(x) = \frac{6{,}561(0)^2 + 2{,}916(1)^2 + 486(2)^2 + 36(3)^2 + 1(4)^2}{10{,}000} - (0{\cdot}4)^2$$

$$= \frac{2{,}916 + 1{,}944 + 324 + 16}{10{,}000} - (0{\cdot}16)$$

$$= 0{\cdot}52 - 0{\cdot}16 = 0{\cdot}36$$

Check: $\text{Var}(x) = npq = 4(0{\cdot}1)(0{\cdot}9) = 0{\cdot}36$

This is a very useful quick way of calculating the mean and standard deviation of a Binomial distribution.

Let us now convert the frequencies of this example to probabilities, by dividing by 10,000. We get:

Number of defectives	0	1	2	3	4
Probability	0·6561	0·2916	0·0486	0·0036	0·0001

These results are shown in histogram form in Fig. 46. If the reader will compare them with the Poisson distribution shown in Chapter 8 he will at once be struck by the similarity with regard to skewness. The comparison suggests that we might use the Poisson distribution as an approximation to the Binomial distribution under certain conditions. As a trial, let us see what sort of a result we should get using this approximation. The expected number of defectives per sample is 0·4. We make this the z of our Poisson expansion, thus:

$$e^{-z}\left(1 + z + \frac{z^2}{2!} + \frac{z^3}{3!} + \frac{z^4}{4!} \text{ with other terms ignored}\right)$$

We have to ignore terms above z^4 in our Poisson distribution, since it is obvious we cannot have more than four defectives in a sample of four items. Writing $z = 0{\cdot}4$, we have:

$$e^{-0.4}\left(1 + 0{\cdot}4 + \frac{(0{\cdot}4)^2}{2!} + \frac{(0{\cdot}4)^3}{3!} + \frac{(0{\cdot}4)^4}{4!}\right)$$

* The symbol 'Var(x)' is often used for the variance.

From tables of the exponential function (or, if we have no tables at hand, by substitution in the formula

$$e^{-z} = 1 - z + \frac{z^2}{2!} - \frac{z^3}{3!} + \frac{z^4}{4!} - \dots +)$$

we find $e^{-0.4} = 0.6703$, so the probabilities of 0, 1, 2, 3, 4 defectives in a sample of four items when the expected number in the sample is 0·4 are given by the successive terms of

$$0.6703\left(1 + 0.4 + \frac{(0.4)^2}{2!} + \frac{(0.4)^3}{3!} + \frac{(0.4)^4}{4!}\right)$$

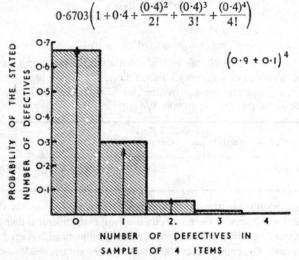

Fig. 46. Number of defectives in random samples of four items drawn from a population containing 10% defectives ($P = 0.1$). The vertical arrows in each block show the approximation using the Poisson distribution

Working these out, we enter them in the following table, with the true probabilities as given by the Binomial distribution for comparison.

Number of defectives	0	1	2	3	4
Poisson prediction	0·6703	0·2681	0·0536	0·0071	0·0007
Binomial prediction	0·6561	0·2916	0·0486	0·0036	0·0001

It will be agreed that the approximation is extremely good as a practical guide (see Fig. 46). The Poisson distribution can always be used as an approximation to the Binomial distribution whenever either p or q in the Binomial is fairly small. The nearer p or q is to zero the better the approximation. This is very handy, because in a very considerable number of problems we are concerned with either p small or q small. For example, the proportion of defective items produced in a factory under usual conditions is likely to be less than 10% for any specified fault – even if the overall rejection rate is higher than 10%. We are able to read off the answers to quite a lot of sampling questions of the Binomial type from the Poisson probability paper which we studied in Chapter 8. But more of this in a moment. The reader will observe, in passing, that when p is small, then q must be nearly equal to unity, so the variance for a skew Binomial distribution of the type we are discussing will be approximately $\text{Var}(x) = np$. Now np is the expected number of defectives in the sample, and it will be remembered that the variance of a Poisson distribution was said in Chapter 8 to be equal to the expectation.

Having considered a skew Binomial distribution and found it to be closely akin to a Poisson distribution, the reader will perhaps not be surprised that a symmetrical Binomial distribution is closely related to the Normal Curve. The symmetrical Binomial will have $p = q = 0.5$, so that the average number of defectives in a sample will be $np = 0.5n$ and the standard deviation will be $\sqrt{npq} = \sqrt{0.25n} = 0.5\sqrt{n}$. If we consider the expansion of $(0.5 + 0.5)^n$ we see at once that the part of each term involving the product of powers of p and q is always the same, namely $(0.5)^n$, and the several terms of the expansion differ only by the numerical multiplying factors given in Pascal's triangle (see Chapter 7). We find for $n = 8$ that these coefficients are:

$$1 \quad 8 \quad 28 \quad 56 \quad 70 \quad 56 \quad 28 \quad 8 \quad 1$$

so the frequency of occurrence of 0, 1, 2, 3, ... 8 defectives in samples of eight items drawn from a population whose percentage of defectives was 50% would be proportional to these numbers. In like manner, if the reader cares to work out the coefficients he will find that when the value of n gets larger and larger, the distribution approaches more and more closely to the Normal Curve. He may also check roughly that the sum of the coefficients (i.e. frequencies) lies more and more closely to the values between certain limits as predicted by the Normal Distribution. (It is handy, in doing this, to notice that the sum of *all* the coefficients given in Pascal's triangle for any values of n is simply 2^n, e.g. for $n = 4$ the coefficients are 1, 4, 6, 4, 1. Their sum is

$$1 + 4 + 6 + 4 + 1 = 16 = 2 \times 2 \times 2 \times 2 = 2^4.)$$

Thus, in the case where $n = 9$, we have for the symmetrical Binomial a standard deviation $= 0 \cdot 5 \sqrt{n} = 0 \cdot 5 \sqrt{9} = 0 \cdot 5(3) = 1 \cdot 5$. The coefficients are:

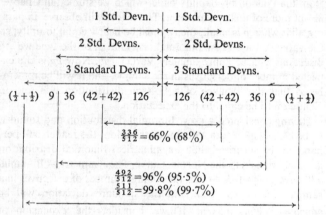

	1 Std. Devn.	1 Std. Devn.	
	2 Std. Devns.	2 Std. Devns.	
	3 Standard Devns.	3 Standard Devns.	

$(\frac{1}{2} + \frac{1}{2})$ 9 | 36 (42 + 42) 126 | 126 (42 + 42) 36 | 9 $(\frac{1}{2} + \frac{1}{2})$

$\frac{336}{512} = 66\%$ (68%)

$\frac{492}{512} = 96\%$ (95·5%)
$\frac{511}{512} = 99 \cdot 8\%$ (99·7%)

Some of the terms are shown divided into halves. This is because the standard deviation is $1\frac{1}{2}$ units, and as a rough approximation we have assigned half the frequency in the borderline cases to each group. The figures quoted in brackets are the percentages of the total frequency ($= 2^9 = 512$) which are predicted by the Normal Curve between the various limits.

The approximation is seen to be remarkably good. Actually the rough method we have followed in assigning half the frequency of borderline cases to each group gives a smaller proportion to the inner groups than is strictly correct.

More surprising still is that if n is made *very large* then, even when either p or q is quite small, the binomial distribution loses a great deal of its skewness and is well approximated by the Normal Curve. Clearly, the more nearly equal p and q are, the smaller n may be in order to make the distribution approach the Normal form; when either p or q is very small, n must be so much the larger in order to achieve approximate normality in the distribution. As a guide to the orders of magnitude we give Figs. 47 and

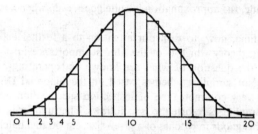

Fig. 47. Binomial $(0\cdot8+0\cdot2)^{50}$ approximates the normal distribution closely

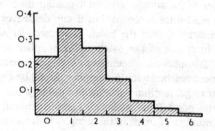

Fig. 48. Binomial $(0\cdot95+0\cdot05)^{30}$ is still markedly skew

48, showing $(0\cdot8+0\cdot2)^{50}$ which is a good approximation to the Normal form, and $(0\cdot95+0\cdot05)^{30}$ which is still markedly skew.

A very useful approximation, due to De Moivre and Laplace, for the number of defectives in the range d_1 to d_2 inclusive is as follows. If we have a Binomial distribution $(q+p)^n$, then, as before, its standard deviation will be $\sigma=\sqrt{npq}$. If, now, we write

$$t_1=\frac{d_1-np-\frac{1}{2}}{\sigma} \text{ and } t_2=\frac{d_2-np+\frac{1}{2}}{\sigma}$$

then the probability of a number of defectives in a sample of n lying in the range d_1 to d_2 inclusive is equal to the area under the Normal Curve between the limits t_1 and t_2. We saw how this is to be evaluated from the Table of Areas of the Normal Curve in Chapter 9. The theorem, as we should expect from what we have already seen, assumes that n is large. Provided that d_1 and d_2 lie at roughly equal distances away from the expected value, np, on either side, the approximation is quite good, even when n is fairly small.

It is time, now, to turn our attention to a further aspect of sampling theory which is of the utmost importance in practice, namely the question of what are known as 'operating characteristics' of sampling schemes based on the Binomial Distribution. A very common type of inspection specification adopted when sampling is resorted to is as follows. The supplier is told to deliver his goods in batches of a given size, e.g. 50 to a batch. The arrangement then is that from each batch a certain number of items will be drawn at random and inspected. This is the so-called *sample number*. If the sample is found to contain no defectives the whole batch is at once accepted, but if any defectives at all are found in the sample, then the batch is rejected. Rejection may result either in return of the batch to the supplier or in a subsequent 100% inspection, depending on the circumstances and the arrangement reached with the supplier. It will be a good thing for the reader to get familiar with the terminology and shorthand notation at this point. The batch or lot size is denoted by N, the sample size (number of items in the sample) is denoted by n, and the allowable number of defectives in a sample by d. This is a very compact notation. For example, '$N=50$, $n=10$, $d=0$' tells us that the goods are to be delivered in batches of fifty, that a sample of ten will be drawn at random for inspection, that provided no defectives at all are found in this sample the whole batch will be accepted, but that if any defectives at all are found in the sample it will be rejected. Now whenever a customer performs a 'goods-inward inspection' his idea is to protect himself against accepting defective goods from the supplier. What does this mean? His *aim* is that *all* goods accepted and paid for shall be of acceptable quality, but this is an ideal which he knows he cannot achieve absolutely. He knows that human fallibility will frustrate the most diligent efforts – even by 100% inspection – to guarantee this year in and year out. More usually, the customer will take his stand on the basis of economic considerations, arguing that inspection is a non-productive function in a manufacturing organization – an overhead cost to be kept to an economic minimum. He will strike a balance between inspection overhead charges and loss due to less than perfect inspection. There is, moreover, sound practical common sense in this approach. There is something absurd in treating a supplier who has built up a first-class reputation on the basis of high and consistent quality as if he were an itinerant huckster with catchpenny business methods.

What factors have we to allow for in a good sampling scheme? First of all the inevitable risk. The scheme should be designed in such a way that this risk is equitably shared by the supplier and the consumer. Secondly the fact that a sampling scheme is a line of defence against a threat whose seriousness varies from time to time. When we lay down '$N = 50$, $n = 10$, $d = 5$' we have laid down a fixed scheme irrespective of the threat. It is as if a general put a hundred men to defend a line irrespective of the forces attacking it. What we have to consider, then, is how any given sampling scheme will operate under different conditions. What will be the effect when the supplier is sending in batches of normal standard? What will happen as the supplier's goods fall off in quality? What we are asking, in fact, is: How will the rate of rejection enforced by the sampling scheme (N, n, d) change as the value of p, the percentage of defectives in the producer's goods, increases? This is a question we can answer quite easily by making use of the Poisson probability paper.

The first thing to be clear about is that the judgement 'accept or reject' is made on the basis of the *sample* – irrespective of what the conditions may be in the remainder of the batch. In general, the industrial supplier supplies goods for which the percentage of defectives is relatively small, so that, even when the number of items in the sample, n, is fairly large, the distribution $(q + p)^n$ will be quite skew and well approximated by the Poisson. Mathematical refinement is out of place in a problem such as we are discussing. What we need is a rapid method of assessing any suggested sampling scheme. Let us consider, first, the sampling scheme $N = 100$, $n = 10$, $d = 0$. This means that every time we find *one or more* defectives in a sample of ten items the whole batch of 100 will be rejected.

To calculate the operating characteristic, we assume a series of hypothetical values for p, the proportion defective in the goods supplied by the manufacturer. The corresponding expected number of defectives in our sample will then be np. We then look up on the Poisson probability graph (Fig. 39) the probabilities of one or more (shown by the line $c = 1$) defectives when the expectation takes each of the hypothetical values. The result is shown in the following table.

Supplier's proportion defective $= p$	0·01	0·02	0·03	0·04	0·05	0·1	0·2	0·3	0·4
Expected number of defectives in sample of n items $= np$	0·1	0·2	0·3	0·4	0·5	1	2	3	4
Probability of finding one or more defectives $=$ probability of rejection	0·1	0·18	0·27	0·33	0·4	0·63	0·87	0·95	0·97
Per cent of batches rejected by the scheme under the assumed conditions	10	18	27	33	40	63	87	95	97

The results are shown in graphical form in Fig. 49, which is the operating characteristic of the scheme. What comments are we to make on such a scheme? It is certainly *stringent*, but it is not very discriminating. By its very nature it is asking for perfection and makes no allowance at all for the poor manufacturer when he falls slightly from grace. Even when his goods are only 1 % defective he is to have 10% of batches rejected. What if the customer agrees that 1 % is a very reasonable proportion of defectives for the type of product in question? It is no use shouting at a man to keep on his toes when he is already doing his best. Batch rejection on such a heavy scale is uneconomic under such conditions (and the cost will surely be passed back to the customer in the long run). Our first lesson, then, is that stringency, like all other virtues, can be undesirable in excess. We have to make allowances for the other fellow's fallibility.

The reader may be tempted at this stage to suggest that the ideal operating characteristic would be of the form shown in Fig. 50a. If we agree that the manufacturer will be doing a good job in sending us batches containing 1% defective, then we should reject every batch with more than this proportion of defectives and accept batches as good or better than 1% defective. Such a scheme would certainly be discriminating to perfection. But do

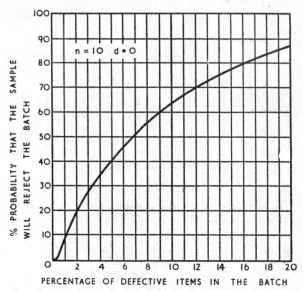

Fig. 49. Operating characteristic of sampling scheme which is certainly stringent but shows poor discrimination between good and bad quality in the batch

we want perfection of this hard and fast type? If we are prepared to accept a batch with 1% defectives with unfailing regularity, do we really wish to reject with the same regularity whenever the percentage of defectives reaches 1·1%? The very idea is ludicrous. What we want, clearly, is to have it, say, 98% sure that batches will be accepted at 1% defective or better, and rejected at a rate which mounts very steeply as the region of 1% defectives is left behind. The ideal scheme should in fact look something as shown in Fig. 50b. The reader will observe that there are two values specially marked off on the percentage defective scale: one corresponding to the quality the manufacturer can normally maintain, the so-called *process average* per cent defective, and the

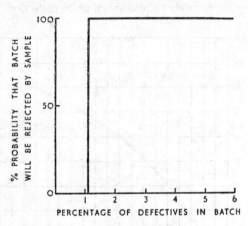

Fig. 50(a). First suggestion for ideal operating characteristic when up to 1% defectives are acceptable

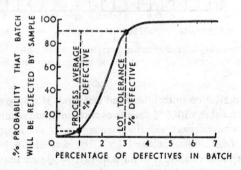

Fig. 50(b). A more realistic suggestion for ideal operating characteristic which adequately safeguards the interests of both producer and consumer

other which we have called the *tolerance* per cent defective, a quality at which the customer would want to be sure of rejecting batches with a very high degree of certainty. Such a scheme, in practice, would be fair to both parties. Operating schemes for various values of sample size and allowable defect number can rapidly be drawn in this way, and give producer and consumer a clear picture of what is involved in any sampling scheme before it is agreed upon. We shall deal with more complex cases of operating characteristics in Chapter 12 where we consider the question of economy in sampling.

A point over which confusion sometimes arises is the value of increasing the *inspection density*. (Density of inspection is simply the average amount of inspection carried out using any sampling scheme.) *Our information as to the quality of a homogeneous batch of goods is in no way related to the size of the batch which is sampled. We get information in return for the work we do in actual inspection.* Thus, if we have two batches of goods, one containing 10,000 items and the other containing 1,000, and we draw a sample of 100 items from each batch, the information about the quality of the two batches will be the same, although the inspection density in one case is 10% and in the other case 1%. Providing, then, that the batches are homogeneous in quality, it will be more economic to inspect large batches than small ones. The general rule should be that batch sizes are to be made as large as possible, though, of course, good batches should not be 'poisoned' by admixture of bad batches, simply to get economy in sampling.

We leave for the time being the problem of sampling by attributes, and turn now to a consideration of some of the basic facts in sampling theory dependent on the Normal Law. We have seen that the Normal Curve has two parameters, $\bar{x}$ and σ, which take care respectively of the central tendency and dispersion of the distribution, that is of the average and the variability about the average. If now we consider not the distribution of the values of individual items themselves but the distribution of the average value in a sample of n items, what shall we expect? To make the matter concrete, let us suppose that we were to consider the distribution for the average weight in samples of five men. One thing will be plain at once: these averages will cluster more closely round the grand average than will the weights of individual men, for the simple reason that when five men are chosen to make up a random sample the chances are that some will be lighter than average and some will be heavier. It will be a very rare thing to get five men all over twenty stone in a single sample chosen at random. The larger the sample the more closely will we expect the average weight in the sample to agree with the grand average. This means that the distribution for sample averages will have a smaller

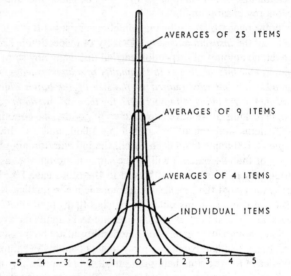

AVERAGES OF 25 ITEMS

AVERAGES OF 9 ITEMS

AVERAGES OF 4 ITEMS

INDIVIDUAL ITEMS

-5 -4 -3 -2 -1 0 1 2 3 4 5

Fig. 51. The distribution for the averages of samples becomes more and more compact as the sample size increases, the standard deviation being inversely proportional to the square root of the number of items in the sample
  Note: O on horizontal scale is equal to the grand average value for the whole population

spread or standard deviation than the distribution for the weights of individual men. Fig. 51 shows how the distribution of sample averages will become more and more compact as the sample size increases. The distribution retains its Normal character, but its standard deviation decreases as the square root of n, the number of items in the sample. Thus, if we denote the standard deviation for the averages of samples of n items by σ_n, we have $\sigma_n = \dfrac{\sigma}{\sqrt{n}}$, where σ is the standard deviation for the distribution of the individual items. If the average weight of men were 140 lb with a standard deviation of 20 lb then the standard deviation for the average weight of four men at a time would be $\sigma_4 = \dfrac{\sigma}{\sqrt{4}} = \dfrac{20}{2} = 10$ lb. The standard deviation for the weight of 100 men at a time would be $\sigma_{100} = \dfrac{20}{\sqrt{100}} = 2$ lb, and so on. This has a very useful application in the theory of *large* samples. Suppose, having measured the heights of 90,000 men for the army medical examination, we found that the distribution for the heights of individual men had a mean value 67·5 with a standard deviation 2·62 inches, we should know that the true result must be very close to 67·5 inches. In order to get an idea of how close we were to the true value, we should calculate $\sigma_n = \dfrac{2·62}{\sqrt{90,000}} = \dfrac{2·62}{300} = 0·0087$. This would be a measure of the degree of uncertainty in a sample of this size. We should be pretty confident that the true result for the whole population of the country, in this age group, did not lie more than two standard deviations $= 2 \times 0·0087 = 0·0174$ inch away from the average value found, viz. 67·5 inches, and almost certain that it was not more than three standard deviations, 0·0261 inch, away from 67·5 inches. The quantity $\dfrac{\sigma}{\sqrt{n}}$ is referred to as the *standard error of the mean*. It may be shown that the degree of uncertainty inherent in an estimate of the standard deviation from a sample is given by the quantity $\dfrac{\sigma}{\sqrt{2n}}$ which is known as the *standard error of the standard deviation*. Other results of a similar nature are as follows:

Standard error of the variance $= \sigma^2 \sqrt{\dfrac{2}{n}}$.

Standard error of the coefficient of variation, $V = \dfrac{V}{\sqrt{2n}}$.

Standard error of the median $= \dfrac{1·25\sigma}{\sqrt{n}}$.

A further matter which we shall have to make use of later when we come to look at control chart techniques is the question of how the range, i.e. the difference between the greatest and least values

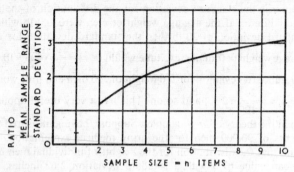

Fig. 52. How the average range in samples increases with the size of the sample

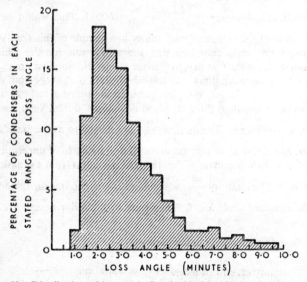

Fig. 53a. Distribution of loss angle for electrical condenser showing very marked positive skewness. Compare this with Fig. 53b for the distribution of the logarithms of the loss angles of the condensers

in a sample, changes as the sample size is increased. It will suffice for the present to say that the average range likely to be met with in a sample increases as the size of the sample increases. Fig. 52 shows how the mean sample range (expressed in units of the standard deviation) grows as the sample size, *n*, increases. The graph starts at *n* = 2 (since we cannot get a range at all until we have two items in the sample), climbs rapidly at first, and then flattens out.

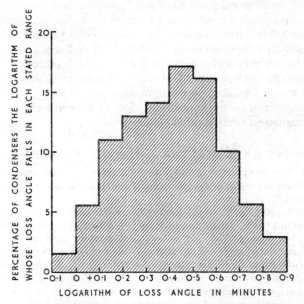

Fig. 53b. The same data as those in Fig. 53a but plotted after taking the logarithm of the variable quantity. If anything the positive skewness has been over-corrected by the logarithmic transformation into a much less serious negative skewness

So much of the useful theory of sampling turns around the Normal Law that when distributions are met with which depart seriously from the normal type – usually by being excessively skew – the statistician will force such data into a better approximation by using 'transformations'. He may, for example, work, not with the original values, *x*, but with their logarithms, log *x*, or with their square roots, $\sqrt{x}$. This sometimes strikes the onlooker as a 'bit of a fiddle'. In fact, it is nothing of the sort. The author was once accused of 'a fiddle' by some chemists with whom he was working when he recommended a logarithmic transformation. One sharp fellow, who had been as worried as the rest, suddenly saw light. 'You know,' he said, 'if these data had been pH readings, we should never have thought there was anything funny at all. In other words, if *we* had put the logs in, there would have been no query; our only grouse seems to be that *you* are putting them in.' It is true, of course, that when transformations are inserted for analytical purposes pure and simple the results have to be interpreted afterwards, and will then lack obvious symmetry. But the lack of symmetry was there to start with – that was the reason for doing the transformation in the first place. Figs. 53a and b show the normalizing effect of a logarithmic transformation on a very skew distribution.

WHAT HAVE YOU LEARNT ABOUT SAMPLING?

1. Plot the operating characteristic for a scheme in which samples of 50 items are to be drawn at random, the allowable defect number being 1.

2. Suppose that goods delivered in batches of 500 items are inspected according to the inspection scheme laid down in the first example, and that whenever a batch fails to be accepted on the basis of sample evidence the remainder of the batch will be submitted to 100% inspection. Investigate how the inspection density (percentage of the total batch submitted which is inspected on the average) varies with the percentage of defectives in the bulk consignment.

3. A certain variety of peas is found to have an average pod length of 4 inches with a standard deviation of $\frac{1}{2}$ inch. What will be the standard deviation for the average length of samples of sixteen peas?

4. Samples of four items drawn from a mass production line are measured for a particular dimension. It is found that the average range in these samples is four thousandths of an inch. What do you estimate the standard deviation of the dimension to be?

11

Control Charts

'Quality control is achieved most efficiently, of course, not by
the inspection operation itself, but by getting at causes.'
DODGE AND ROMIG

We saw previously that small samples, in isolation, are a very
unsatisfactory basis for estimating the quality of a batch. We
recognized that the degree of confidence it was reasonable to
attach to an estimate of any parameter based on a sample was
closely related to the size of the sample, i.e. to the amount of
effort expended in collecting information. Small samples are slip-
pery customers whose word is not to be taken as gospel; to cope
with their nimble behaviour statisticians have had to develop a
special branch of theory called 'Small sample theory' – a sort of
psychological study of delinquency in juvenile samples. Being
immature, small samples are unsuitable for some of the work
which large samples take in their stride; yet, sympathetically
handled, they can be very useful fellows indeed; capable, by their
nimbleness, of doing many jobs for which large samples would be
too clumsy and too expensive.

The small sample can never be more than a spot check. There
are, of course, some cases where a spot check tells us everything
we need to know, but, in the nature of things, spot checks will
suffice to detect only really impressive features. We shall see small
samples doing this kind of work in Chapter 14. There are other
cases where, having carefully investigated the circumstances, spot
checks are useful to keep us reasonably satisfied that no serious
change has come about. Any such change of a dramatic nature
will be spotted at once, even by the spot check; more insidious
changes will force themselves on the attention as successive small
changes in several spot checks create a cumulative impression.
That is the fundamental idea underlying statistical Quality Control Charts. But the idea is carried forward in a systematic way.

It is at this point that we should devote a little thought to the
inspector in industry. We may epitomize industrial history since

the Industrial Revolution as follows. Prior to the Industrial Revolution, goods were made by craftsmen (many of them fresh-water sailors and jacks-of-all-trades with never an artistic idea in their lives). For the most part these men designed, executed, and inspected their own jobs. They were in a happy position compared with the modern man working to designer's limits on a drawing – if they cut too deeply with their saw they could usually modify the design a little to make the error correct. Smaller crudities they just left – little dreaming how a later age would admire these as evidence of artistic talent in handmade articles. It was the everyday work of very modest competence done by these men which set the standards by which average men and women were judging when the Industrial Revolution came along. The merit of the first machinery was soon recognized to be its speed. One man could turn out five shabby jobs where his father had made only one very modest one. With productivity came the advantage of cheapness – and the disadvantage of unemployment. Shoddy goods find their market amongst the needy. It was only natural that factory owners (curiously, still called manufacturers) should press home this advantage of volume of production – and no less natural that, under conditions where workers were paid by systems that demanded quantity, the virtues of quality should rapidly vanish. But there is a limit to all things. Goods can become so shabby that no market can be found for them at any price – the more so when free competition floods the market. When cheapness begins to fail as a distinguishing feature, the manufacturer has to revert to quality, so that he can offer goods that are not only as cheap as those of his competitors but of better quality.

This, logically, is how the modern inspector was born. The employer paid one set of men to produce goods as fast as possible – attention to quality resulting in a smaller pay packet. At the same time there was set up (often in a different room) a sort of Gestapo whose job it was to see that quality was maintained at as high a level as possible. The antipathy between men in the shops and inspectors which is ever present in many organizations is only a natural outcome of both sides doing their best to obey orders. The inspector is despised by the workman because he is a critic who never makes anything himself, and despised by his employer because he is an overhead cost – 'non-productive labour' is his official classification. For the general reader let it be said as a corrective to this highly coloured account that more sensible ideas on interdepartmental relations are beginning to prevail, some organizations, indeed, being quite near to perfection.

In admitting that the picture is highly coloured we wish to convey to the reader that the South Sea Islands are not quite as brilliant in hues as they are presented in Technicolor. Do not let him imagine that the truth lies in simple black and white. The truth is that the inspector in industry does usually occupy an anomalous position where his daily task is to make invidious decisions. Very often he can fault the man on the machine by using measuring gear superior to that given to the man on the job – the very gear from which the worker's measuring instruments derive their authority. The inspector has the last say. The fact that the best instruments are – rightly – in the inspection department tends to create the impression that micrometers, Kelvin Bridges, and the like are the inspector's tools in trade. Some unimaginative heads of inspection departments have the same idea themselves, and devote their energies to worshipping the accuracy to which they can measure. It is a tenable point of view – and certainly a more promising one – that the inspector's real tools in trade are graph paper and pencil. The unerring sign of the good inspector is that he keeps lots of graphs and charts. He is a statistician by inclination and instinct, as his hawklike manner of spotting half-baked conclusions as to the significance about trends in rejection rates shows. The good inspector distinguishes clearly between his preliminary function as the man who sorts goods out into 'O.K.' and 'Reject' and his ultimate function as the guardian and defender of quality whose aim it is to see that as little product as possible is classified as defective. In cricket, a run saved is a run made. So, in the factory, a defective prevented is a positive contribution to production. It is an insult to classify this type of inspector as 'non-productive labour'.

Bad work is done in the shops. The correct place for inspection, whenever this can conveniently be arranged, is where the goods are being made; the correct time, as the goods are coming off the production line. This is recognized in the concept of the 'patrol inspector', who wanders round in a more or less systematic way taking spot checks during production runs and stopping the machine whenever adjustment seems necessary. Better prevent the making of a defective item than find it the next day at a grand inspection in the next room. The tendency of a machine to drift 'out of limits' can often be spotted *before* defective material is actually produced. This is a return to the continuous inspection of the craftsman, and the man on the machine has something of the craftsman's satisfaction in the assurance that the job he is doing is correct.

Wherein lies the snag to this patrol inspection? Clearly in the fact that the inspector can only carry out spot checks, inspecting a

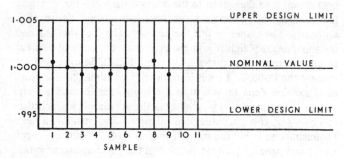

Fig. 54. Control Chart for average of sample of four items

small sample every now and again. We already know how misleading small samples can be in isolation. It may be suggested that machinery such as is used in an engineering factory produces articles which differ from each other very little indeed. This is true; but no truer than that engineers work to close limits on their jobs. The best course is for the inspector to *record* his sample findings at each visit to the machine so that his spot checks form a cumulative impression, from which tendencies to drift can be detected. Suppose, for example, that a machine were cutting off lengths of steel which were supposed to be 1·000 inch long with a tolerance of 0·005 inch either way, and that the inspector's graphical record for the average length of four items measured at each visit developed as shown in Fig. 54. The inspector would be justified in regarding the variability between successive average values as of no significance. He would argue that his averages were comfortably within the design limits; that, since the pieces produced by the machine were not *absolutely* identical, and since he had taken small samples only, such an amount of variability did no more than reflect the inherent lack of absolute precision of the machine, inflated a little by the inherent lack of absolute precision in his micrometer, inflated in turn by his inability to read the micrometer with more than a certain degree of accuracy. He would feel that so long as the sample results continued to fluctuate to the same extent about the same average value there was no need to worry. With a record such as this he would be much more confident than would be justified as the result of a single sample.

Suppose, now, that on his next visit he got the result 0·996 for the average of four items (the reader should plot this result in Fig. 54). What is he to say? The result lies within the designer's tolerance, yet it is lower than previous samples would have led him to suspect. Even if all the individual items in his sample were within the designer's limits, his suspicions would be aroused. He most certainly would 'take action', by measuring more items immediately. He would not feel justified in waiting another twenty minutes possibly before resampling. Had he not had his chart, had he been doing spot checks in isolation, his suspicions might well not have been aroused. Some patrol inspectors, of course, insist on adjustment whenever a sample seems on the high side, but the reader will see at once that this is likely to make for a lot of unnecessary adjustments, since the averages of small samples are, by nature, bound to fluctuate. The line must be drawn somewhere.

Where whall we draw this line? Obviously, at the point which marks the probable limit of non-significant fluctuations. We may do this, crudely, by guesswork after a series of samples has been taken. The statistician has made it easy to do it accurately.

There is a drawback to drawing this line roughly, which the reader will not have failed to see. The line has to be drawn after contemplation of the results obtained on a series of samples. Suppose these samples themselves were *already* giving unstable results, owing to the existence of some trouble, how are we, by guesswork, to differentiate between inevitable variability and that extra variability caused by the existence of trouble? The problem is easy if the trouble is causing major fluctuations in the sample results, less easy if the trouble, while important for the job in hand, is not of colossal proportions. The statistical method of drawing our 'Action Limit' has to face the same difficulty, but it faces it with greater chance of success, as we shall see shortly.

We have based our argument, so far, on inspection where some actual measurement is made on the individual items. Not all inspection, however, is so careful. Often, on grounds of simplicity and economy, items are tested on the 'Go – No go' principle, using a gauge. This 'all or nothing' technique is obviously less sensitive than actual measurement. We know whether the items are right or wrong but we have no indication as to how right or how wrong. On other occasions we do not measure because we cannot, the inspection being essentially qualitative, as, for example, when we inspect for that nebulous characteristic 'finish'. The dangers of the small sample will in this case be even greater; the need for a soundly based technique of assessment all the more necessary. We shall have to have techniques both for inspection by measurement and for inspection by attributes ('go – no go' type). Let us consider them in turn.

QUALITY CONTROL CHART FOR SAMPLING BY ATTRIBUTES

If we have a product being made in large numbers, we take a sample of n items at suitable regular intervals and determine the number of defectives in the sample. This number is recorded until twenty or thirty samples have been taken (all the samples, as a routine, being of the same size). From the total number inspected and the total number of defectives found we can determine the expected number per sample. This expected number will apply only provided the manufacturing process is stable in the sense that it produces a steady proportion of defectives. As an example, suppose that successive samples of fifty items yielded the following numbers of defectives:

1, 0, 1, 2, 2, 0, 0, 1, 3, 0, 2, 0, 1, 4, 0, 1, 0, 0, 2, 0

so that there were a total of 20 defectives in twenty samples of 50 items each. The percentage defective is thus estimated at 2%, i.e. proportion defective $p = 0.02$. The expected number of defectives, so long as these conditions remain stable, will be np in a sample of n items. Suppose, now, we decide to continue taking samples of $n = 50$ items. The expectation will be 1 defective per sample. Such sampling will strictly be described by the Binomial $(q + p)^n$, i.e. $(0.98 + 0.02)^{50}$, and we could calculate the probabilities of 0, 1, 2, etc., defectives in our samples by calculating the successive terms of the expansion. This would be rather hard work, but we have an easy way out. The Binomial distribution will be markedly skew, as we know, and therefore we can use the Poisson distribution as a good approximation, and save awkward computation by reading off our results on Poisson probability paper.

What is our aim? To find the probable limits of random fluctuation in the number of defectives found per sample. Violation of these limits we shall take to be *prima facie* evidence that the production set-up has changed significantly. We want, in short, to draw the line at the point where the number of defectives becomes unlikely on the basis of pure chance fluctuations. The question arises: What do we mean by 'unlikely'? A convenient practical convention, which is found to work well, is to draw the line so as to indicate that number of defectives per sample which will only be exceeded by chance, in the long run, in one sample in a thousand. We draw a line on our control chart at this number of defectives and call it the *Upper Action Limit*. It is common practice, also, to add to the chart another line called the *Upper Warning Limit* which indicates that number of defectives per sample which will only be exceeded by chance, in the long run, in only twenty-five samples in a thousand. Fig. 55 is a chart derived from Poisson probability paper, showing only the probability levels corresponding to Action and Warning Limits. Let us use it to find the Upper Action and Warning Limits for the problem we are considering, where the expectation is 1 defective per sample. Consulting the graph the reader will find that the Upper Warning line cuts the vertical at the expectation 1 on the curve $c = 4$. Thus, the number 4 or more defectives is our Warning Limit. We expect 4 or more defectives once in every forty samples, in the long run. In the same way the Upper Action line will be found to cut the vertical line at the expectation 1 at the value $c = 5 \cdot 9$. Now of course we can never have actually $5 \cdot 9$ defectives in a sample, but it is useful to use this fractional value as the point at which we draw the Action Limit on our chart, since it tells us that 6 defectives is already over the border line. We thus have:

Upper Action Limit $= 5 \cdot 9$ Upper Warning Limit $= 4$

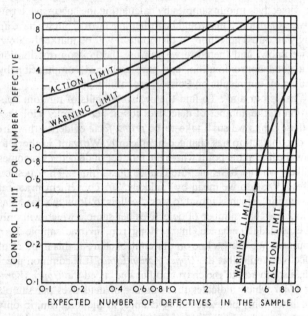

Fig. 55. Chart for upper and lower warning and action limits for control charts for number of defective items in a sample

Fig. 56 shows the Quality Control Chart drawn up with the limits marked in. In accordance with actual practice we have shown the first twenty sample results plotted on the chart. We find that the results lie nicely within the limits of variability we have calculated. This gives us confidence to believe that the process is in a state of *statistical control*, since the observed differences between sample results are explainable by the laws of chance. We have what we expect. One of our points lies on the Warning Limit. The reader will realize, however, that we expect one sample in forty to give a number of defectives as great as 4 or more. We are not surprised, then, that this result should have occurred in our first twenty samples. The position is almost the same as the chance of the ace of spades being in half a pack of cards.

So long as succeeding samples lie within our calculated limits

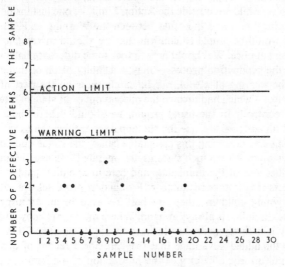

Fig. 56. Control Chart for number defective

we shall have reasonable grounds for supposing that the production process is stable. Suppose, however, that we draw a sample later on and find 7 defectives, what are we to think? The first thing to think of is the meaning of our limit. In the long run, we expect the Action Limit to be violated by one sample in a thousand. That odd chance will come up every now and then, but we have agreed that whenever it does occur we shall be exceedingly suspicious and *take action*. The first action to take will be to draw further samples, so as to confirm whether we have met the odd chance, or whether something has happened to the production set-up which has caused a significant change in the proportion of defectives being produced. Suppose we draw two further samples immediately and they both lie well within the warning limit, then we should feel that probably it was the odd chance. False alarms of this sort will be rare, precisely because of the probability level associated with our Action Limit, which is deliberately chosen so that we do not spend half our time chasing red herrings. Suppose, on the other hand, that our two next samples, while not outside the Action Limit, lie one just inside the Warning Limit and the other between the Warning and Action. This would be ample to confirm that we should investigate the process at once. We should believe that some difference had crept into the production process – maybe a faulty batch of material, maybe wearing of a tool, maybe carelessness on the part of an operator – which had thrown the process out of its state of 'statistical control'. In the usual jargon, we should believe there existed an *assignable cause* for the apparent trouble, and that, by finding and removing this assignable cause, the status quo could be restored. Where such systems are operated it is usually found that because of the immediate and careful attention paid to the process it is improved notably. Production processes are rather like young children; they are best behaved in an atmosphere where discipline is always at hand. Where the stick is known to be ready it is rarely necessary to have to use it. Charts of this sort have the added advantage that they provide a record of quality and uniformity, a history of the production of the item in question. For this reason, samples should be plotted in historical order, and notes made on the chart of any factors such as change of method or material which might be reflected in the quality of the product, as well as brief notes of assignable causes of trouble found whenever limits are violated. Such information can be of the utmost value both to designers and to methods and planning engineers.

Quality Control can also be used for samples of unequal sizes, being based on the *percentage* of defectives found in samples. This is a useful technique applied to good inward inspection of large batches, especially when used in conjunction with the Dodge and

Romig Sampling Schemes. We leave consideration of the matter until Chapter 12, where those schemes are dealt with.

Before we pass on from this type of chart the reader might like to have a handy way of getting the 'feel' of the meaning of the Warning and Action Limits. In Chapter 8 we discussed the distribution of the number of goals scored by a football team per match. We found the expected number of goals to be 1·7 per team per match. Now we may regard each goal scored as the occurrence of a defect in the defence of the opposing side. From Fig. 55 the reader may read off the Action and Warning Limits when the expectation is 1·7 as

Action Limit = 7·5   Warning Limit = 5·0

If he will now place himself in the position of the manager of the team against which the goals are scored, he will have a pretty good idea of the significance of the limits. Either the attack was very strong or the defence was pretty weak is the most likely conclusion when 8 goals are scored against a team, and 6 goals is nothing to boast about – it *might* be just bad luck, but a wise manager would look for an 'assignable cause'.

There are cases sometimes when the expectation per sample is so large – either because the sample itself is large or because the proportion defective in the bulk from which the sample is taken is large – that we can draw not only *Upper* Action and Warning Limits, but also *Lower* ones. At first sight, some people say they do not see the point of lower limits, arguing that, after all, it is only when things look suspiciously *bad* that we are interested. This is true only up to a point. When samples show significantly *good* results there will be an assignable cause no less than when they show results that are significantly bad. Sometimes, the tracking down of the assignable cause gives a clue as to how the process might be improved. Occasionally the assignable cause is jiggery-pokery on someone's part by which the defectives were prevented from getting into the sample for fear they would show up. The author once found *trouble* in the process when the lower limits were violated. The person responsible for the trouble had been *too* conscientious in concealing it! Lower limits can be read off from Fig. 55 in precisely the same way as the Upper Limits.

We then have one chance in a thousand that the Upper Action Limit will be violated and one chance in a thousand that the Lower Action Limit will be violated; 25 chances in 1,000 that the Upper Warning Limit will be violated and 25 chances in 1,000 that the Lower Warning Limit will be violated.

QUALITY CONTROL CHART FOR SAMPLING BY VARIABLES

The reader will see at once that cases of this sort require *two* charts to be kept simultaneously if we are to keep full control over the job. One chart will be for the average value recorded in our sample, the other will be a chart which takes care of the variability about the average. That is to say we shall want one chart for each of the two parameters of the Normal distribution, $\bar{x}$ and σ. The calculation of the average value of five items is very simple, but to calculate the standard deviation every time we took a sample, even of so small a number as five items, would be very laborious. For this reason, it is the usual practice to base the chart controlling variability on the sample *range* (i.e. the difference between the greatest and least values recorded in the sample). In doing this we throw away a little of the information available to us in our measurements, adopting the stand that small samples are only spot checks anyway, so that the moderate loss in information when we use the range instead of the standard deviation is more than compensated for by the time saved in routine calculation. The two charts are known as the Mean Chart and the Range Chart.

The second point on which we must be clear is that the limits for warning and action on our average chart have *absolutely no inherent connexion with the limits the designer sets* for the accuracy required. The limits on Control Charts are *statistical* limits, which depend on the inherent variability of the manufacturing process and on the size of the sample which is to be taken. Irrespective of the limits set by the designer, statistical control limits will widen if the job is made on a poor stability machine or by a poor operator (in so far as the operator has control over the accuracy of the product). Again, with the same design limits, with the same machine, and with the same operator, the statistical control limits on the average chart will close in if the number of items in the sample is increased. The average chart sets down limits of variability for the averages of samples of a given size drawn from a particular source. The range chart does the same for the sample ranges. The reader is asked to refer again to Fig. 51 which shows how the distribution of sample averages becomes more compact about the grand average value as the sample size is increased. It is very important that this idea should be clearly understood, not only by the people responsible for running the charts, but also by operatives on the machines, or there may be complaints that they are being made to work to tighter limits than shown on the drawing. Just as the limits on the average chart tighten in as the sample size is increased, so the limits on the range chart widen to take account of the fact that the larger the sample the more likely it will be to include extreme values, either way.

Fig. 57 shows how the distribution of individual values relates to the designer's limits. Since a total range of six standard deviations spans all but a negligible proportion of the individual values, it is evident that when the designer's tolerance (upper limit — lower limit) is greater than 6σ the job can be made by the process whose standard deviation is σ with a negligible proportion of defectives. If, on the other hand, the designer's tolerance is smaller than this value, 6σ, then a certain proportion of defectives will inevitably be made by the process in question. If these defectives are to be avoided, then the process must be modified, perhaps by using a more precise machine or – the designer must be less ambitious. Many design tolerances are set by conventional standards, and sometimes trouble is thereby occasioned. It happens on occasions that the machine set to do a particular job is extremely precise compared with the designer's tolerance. It would be foolish in many cases to 'take action' simply because the *statistical* limits indicated a significant shift in the values of the items being produced, irrespective of whether that shift was of practical importance. Common sense must never be forgotten. It should not be taken as a general rule, however, that we are always to take full advantage of the designer's tolerance. My dictionary defines toleration as 'allowing that which is not wholly approved'.

6

The nominal value specified by the designer is what he really wants. His tolerance is a concession to our inability to achieve absolute perfection. Particularly where complex assembly of components is to follow, trouble may arise in assemblies as a result of bias in piece parts. In the case of telephone exchange equipment, for example, unless the components are distributed about their nominal value without bias, assemblies of components all

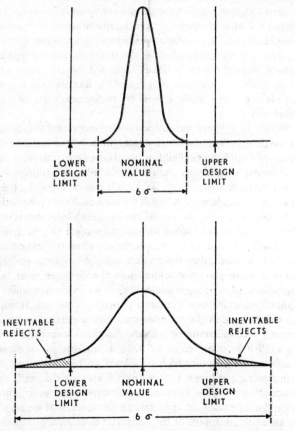

Fig. 57. Relationship between Design Limits and precision of a process

within limits, as components, give rise to a proportion of defectives, the systematic bias in one component being added to the systematic bias in another component.

The following tables of constants will be referred to in the subsequent discussion.

TABLE 1

CONVERSION OF MEAN SAMPLE RANGE TO STANDARD DEVIATION

Formula: Mean sample range $= d \times$ Population standard deviation where d has the value shown in the Table for different sample sizes.

Sample size n	d	Sample size n	d
2	1·128	7	2·704
3	1·693	8	2·847
4	2·059	9	2·970
5	2·326	10	3·078
6	2·534		

Example. If we know that the mean sample range calculated from a series of samples each containing $n = 3$ items has the value 8·4, then we can estimate the standard deviation for the distribution of *individual* items as $\sigma = \dfrac{8·4}{1·69} = 5·0$.

Or, again, if we knew that the distribution of individual items in a certain population had a standard deviation $\sigma = 7$, then we could use the table to estimate the mean sample range in samples of $n = 9$ items as:

Mean sample range $= 2·97 \times 7 = 20·79$

The range in samples is customarily denoted by the symbol w, and the mean range by $\bar{w}$ (spoken of as 'w-bar'), the addition of a bar to any symbol always signifying an average.

TABLE 2

CONTROL LIMIT FACTORS FOR THE AVERAGE CHART

The sample size, n, having been chosen, and the mean range for samples of that size being known, the four limits, Upper and Lower Action and Upper and Lower Warning, are calculated by multiplying the mean range, $\bar{w}$, by the appropriate Limit Factor, A, shown in the table, and adding the result to the Grand Average, $\bar{\bar{x}}$, in the case of Upper Limits and subtracting it from x in the case of Lower Limits. Thus,

$$\text{Upper Limits} = \bar{\bar{x}} + A\bar{w}$$
$$\text{Lower Limits} = \bar{\bar{x}} - A\bar{w}$$

(The symbol $\bar{\bar{x}}$, spoken of as 'x-double bar', is used to denote the average of the sample averages, viz. the Grand Average).

Sample size n	Warning factor A	Action factor A
2	1·229	1·937
3	0·668	1·054
4	0·476	0·750
5	0·377	0·594
6	0·316	0·498
7	0·274	0·432
8	0·244	0·384
9	0·220	0·347
10	0·202	0·317

Example. Set up control limits for the Average Chart, given that $\bar{\bar{x}} = 23$ and $\bar{w} = 4$, when the sample size is $n = 5$.

From the table we find that when $n = 5$ the Warning Factor is 0·377. Hence,

$$\text{Upper Warning} = \bar{\bar{x}} + A\bar{w} = 23 + 0·377 \times 4 = 24·5$$
$$\text{Lower Warning} = \bar{\bar{x}} - A\bar{w} = 23 - 0·377 \times 4 = 21·5$$

Similarly, we find the Action Factor to be 0·594, so that

$$\text{Upper Action} = \bar{\bar{x}} + A\bar{w} = 23 + 0·594 \times 4 = 25·4$$
$$\text{Lower Action} = \bar{\bar{x}} - A\bar{w} = 23 - 0·594 \times 4 = 20·6$$

It will be observed that the limits are symmetrically disposed about the Grand Average in the case of the Mean Chart.

TABLE 3

CONTROL LIMIT FACTORS FOR THE RANGE CHART

The sample size, n, and mean range in samples of that size, $\bar{w}$, being known, the four limits, Upper and Lower Warning and Upper and Lower Action, are calculated by multiplying the mean sample range, $\bar{w}$, by the limit factor, D, shown in the table for the value of n in question. Thus

$$\text{Limit} = D\bar{w}$$

Sample size n	Upper action factor D	Upper warning factor D	Lower warning factor D	Lower action factor D
2	4·12	2·81	0·04	0·00
3	2·98	2·17	0·18	0·04
4	2·57	1·93	0·29	0·10
5	2·34	1·81	0·37	0·16
6	2·21	1·72	0·42	0·21
7	2·11	1·66	0·46	0·26
8	2·04	1·62	0·50	0·29
9	1·99	1·58	0·52	0·32
10	1·93	1·56	0·54	0·35

Example. For sample of size $n=7$ the mean range is found to be $\bar{w}=6\cdot4$. Set up control limits for the Range Chart.

From the table we find that with $n=7$ the control limit factors are 2·11, 1·66, 0·46, and 0·35 for Upper Action, Upper Warning, Lower Warning, and Lower Action Limits respectively. Hence

$$\text{Upper Action} = D\bar{w} = 2\cdot11 \times 6\cdot4 = 13\cdot5$$
$$\text{Upper Warning} = D\bar{w} = 1\cdot66 \times 6\cdot4 = 10\cdot7$$
$$\text{Lower Warning} = D\bar{w} = 0\cdot46 \times 6\cdot4 = 2\cdot9$$
$$\text{Lower Action} = D\bar{w} = 0\cdot26 \times 6\cdot4 = 1\cdot7$$

It will be observed that in the Range Chart, unlike the Mean Chart, the Limits are *not* symmetrically disposed about the mean range.

Knowing how to use the tables the reader is now in a position to set up a control chart system for himself – of the straight-forward type.

The first step, in practice, is to collect results on about twenty samples. It is commonly most convenient to have samples of four or five items. As an illustration, let us suppose we are going to introduce quality control to the weights of medicinal tablets, whose nominal weight is 5 grains. We shall suppose that the weight of the tablet is equal to the weight of the medicament. We shall suppose that it is desired that these tablets shall not differ in any case from the nominal weight by more than 5% either way, i.e. we have an allowance of plus or minus 0·25 grains, to allow for lack of uniformity in the manufacturing process. We are going to do sampling inspection on the tablets, taking samples of five tablets at regular intervals.

Let us suppose that the first twenty samples gave the following results (the figures have been rounded off to ease the arithmetic in the example), the sample means and ranges being as shown.

5·1	5·0	5·1	4·8	4·9	5·0	5·0	4·7	4·9	5·0
5·0	4·8	4·9	5·2	4·9	5·0	5·1	4·9	4·8	5·2
5·0	4·9	5·1	5·0	5·0	5·1	4·4	5·2	5·0	5·0
5·1	5·2	4·9	4·9	5·0	5·0	5·0	5·0	5·1	4·7
5·3	5·0	5·1	4·9	5·0	5·1	5·2	4·8	4·8	5·0

Average	5·10	4·98	5·02	4·96	4·96	5·04	4·94	4·92	4·92	4·98
Range	0·3	0·4	0·2	0·4	0·1	0·1	0·8	0·5	0·3	0·5

4·9	5·0	5·0	5·1	4·9	4·5	5·0	5·0	5·2	5·2
5·0	5·1	4·9	4·8	4·9	5·0	5·1	5·1	5·1	5·1
5·3	5·0	4·8	4·8	4·9	5·0	5·0	5·1	5·0	4·6
5·2	4·9	4·8	4·8	4·9	4·8	4·9	5·0	5·1	5·0
5·1	5·3	4·8	4·9	5·0	4·9	4·9	4·8	5·3	5·1

Average	5·10	5·06	4·86	4·88	4·92	4·84	4·98	5·00	5·14	5·00
Range	0·4	0·4	0·2	0·3	0·1	0·5	0·2	0·3	0·3	0·6

Our next step would be to calculate the grand average, $\bar{\bar{x}}$, and the mean range, $\bar{w}$. We total the sample averages and divide by the number of samples to get the grand average as $\bar{\bar{x}} = \dfrac{99 \cdot 6}{20} = 4 \cdot 98$ grains. This may be accepted as being very close to the desired value of 5 grains. For the average sample range we find $\bar{w} = \dfrac{6 \cdot 9}{20} = 0 \cdot 345$ grains. The next sensible step would be to make use of Table 1, to estimate the standard deviation for the distribution of individual tablets, in order to check the inherent precision of the process against the required precision. We find that for $n = 5$, $d = 2 \cdot 326$, so our estimate of the population standard deviation is $\sigma = \dfrac{\bar{w}}{d} = \dfrac{0 \cdot 345}{2 \cdot 326} = 0 \cdot 15$ grains, approximately. Now we know that for a Normal distribution $99 \cdot 7 \%$ of the whole population lies within three standard deviations of the average. We may expect, therefore, that for all practical purposes the whole of our tablet population will differ from the average value, $4 \cdot 98$ grains, by no more than $3\sigma = 3 \times 0 \cdot 15 = 0 \cdot 45$ grains. But we are supposed to be making these tablets so that they differ by no more than $0 \cdot 25$ grains from the nominal value. We conclude, at once, that the present technique falls far short of our requirements. We may calculate the proportion of defective tablets this process must inevitably produce as follows. Our allowance of $0 \cdot 25$ grains either way is equal to $\dfrac{0 \cdot 25}{0 \cdot 15} = 1 \cdot 67$ standard deviations. If we enter the table of the Area of the Normal Curve in Chapter 9 with this value of t, we see that the probability of deviations greater than this value of t is (one tail), by rough interpolation, about $0 \cdot 05$, so that counting tablets that would be too large and tablets that would be too small we see that about 10% of them would be out of limits.

In order to continue with our illustration we shall (with profound apologies to the Pharmaceutical Society) change the limits so that our crude machine will count as satisfactory. We shall assume that we have a tolerance of 10%, i.e. $0 \cdot 5$ grains, either way, on these tablets. With such a tolerance we are in no difficulty.

Our next step is to plot the same results in chart form, to test whether there is any evidence of instability in the process as it stands. Fig. 58 shows the points plotted in the charts for mean and range, with the control limits drawn in. The computation of the control limits is as follows.

Mean Chart $\bar{x} = 4.98$ $\bar{w} = 0.345$ $n = 5$

(Use Table 2 for limit factors)

Upper Action $= \bar{x} + A\bar{w} = 4.98 + 0.594 \times 0.345 = 5.18$
Upper Warning $= \bar{x} + A\bar{w} = 4.98 + 0.377 \times 0.345 = 5.11$
Lower Warning $= \bar{x} - A\bar{w} = 4.98 - 0.377 \times 0.345 = 4.85$
Lower Action $= \bar{x} - A\bar{w} = 4.98 - 0.594 \times 0.345 = 4.78$

Range Chart $\bar{w} = 0.345$ $n = 5$

(Use Table 3 for limit factors)

Upper Action $= D\bar{w} = 2.34 \times 0.345 = 0.81$
Upper Warning $= D\bar{w} = 1.81 \times 0.345 = 0.62$
Lower Warning $= D\bar{w} = 0.37 \times 0.345 = 0.13$
Lower Action $= D\bar{w} = 0.25 \times 0.345 = 0.09$

The reader will note carefully that one point is plotted in each chart for each sample, the points representing any one sample being identifiable by the fact that they have the same sample number. It will be at once evident that the process is in anything but a state of statistical control. There is marked trouble in the range chart. Usually, when the range chart is in trouble, we also find signs of trouble in the average chart, since it will not invariably be the case that both a large and a small value will get into the same sample so as to keep the average of the sample at about the correct value. More usually, we shall have an odd large value or an odd small one in a sample, which will be reflected not only in the range chart but also in the average chart. Moreover, the range chart shows an unusual type of trouble, viz. abnormally *small* range as well as the customary excessive range. There would be value in investigating the cause of these disturbances. With the assignable causes found and removed, the process would enter a period of statistical control, something as shown in Fig. 59, the standard deviation having been reduced in the process of removing intrusive causes of variation.

A device often adopted is to plot, not the actual values, but deviations from the nominal value. This is a specially useful technique in engineering when dimensions are checked on a clock

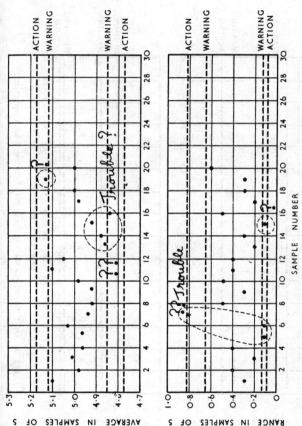

Fig. 58. Control chart for tablet weights, showing existence of trouble in the manufacturing process

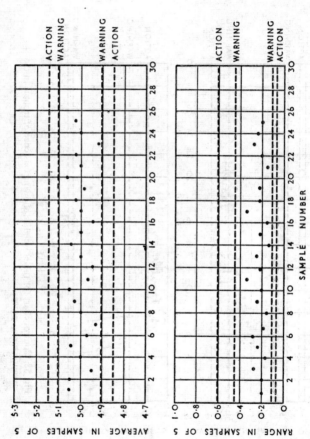

Fig. 59. Only variations such as these may be viewed with equanimity

gauge set to read zero when a test piece of the nominal dimension is inserted. The quality control charts might then be scaled in thousandths of an inch.

In cold print the system may look a little complex and time-consuming compared with the rough and ready methods frequently met with. In practice the schemes are simplicity itself to operate. The general management of the charts on a routine basis can well be left to assistants with intelligence but no more than elementary education. To the engineer in charge and the technical staff they are a real boon. When trouble occurs, the bell rings; when all goes well they are not troubled by red herrings. The psychological effect on operatives is very favourable, though it is a matter of obvious importance that schemes should not be pushed into operation in the full gaze of operatives until they are soundly based. Quality Control was killed in one organization because it was introduced with a flourish of trumpets by a dabbler who unfortunately 'got the formula wrong'. The best plan is for the scheme to be introduced, as an experiment, alongside the existing procedure. When this is done, confidence in the value and reliability of the scheme soon grows. Initial difficulties can be ironed out without the fate of the firm's good name being at stake. Sometimes there is a reduction in actual inspection costs. At other times it is found a profitable business to allow inspection costs to rise somewhat, this being true mostly in places where inspection, being previously very inefficient, allowed the existence of a high rejection rate. As a general rule, it may be said that statistical methods of inspection will lead to the most economic inspection technique *for the degree of protection demanded*. It not infrequently happens that people are aggrieved to be told that they will have to increase the inspection density to get the degree of protection they ask for. There is much confused thinking – by people who should know very much better from experience – on the question of inspection protection. It is a matter we shall be considering in some detail in the next chapter.

We shall now see what modifications are made in the statistical control scheme when the designer's tolerance is very wide compared with the inherent precision of the manufacturing process. Remembering that for a Normal Distribution virtually all the distribution lies within three standard deviations either side of the average, so that we may take the effective width of the distribution as 6σ, we see that, if the designer allows plus and minus a quantity T on either side of the nominal value, the ratio of 6σ to $2T$ will tell us at once whether the process is capable of meeting the design limits. If the ratio $\dfrac{6\sigma}{2T}$ is greater than unity, then rejects are inevitable, however careful the operator may be in adjusting his machine. It is as if we gave him a hack-saw and asked him to work to one-thousandth of an inch. Now usually in statistical quality control we use the mean sample range as our measure of dispersion instead of the standard deviation. We can of course use Table 1 to convert mean sample range to standard deviation. It is handy in practice, however, to be able to see the position at a glance using the mean sample range itself. Table 4 enables us to do this. We simply have to calculate the ratio of the designer's 'tolerance range', $2T$, to the mean sample range, $\bar{w}$, to get what is known as the *Tolerance Factor*. The result is compared with the minimum value of the factor quoted in Table 4 for the sample size in question. If the calculated value is less than the value quoted in the table we know that the process must produce reject material.

Example. Suppose in a particular case we had a mean sample range of 0·003 inch in samples of $n = 5$ items. Is the process capable of making to limits plus or minus 0·005 inch?

In this case we have $2T = 0·01$ inch and $\bar{w} = 0·003$ inch. Therefore

$$\text{Tolerance Factor} = \frac{2T}{\bar{w}} = \frac{0·01}{0·003} = 3·33$$

But the value quoted in Table 4 for $n = 5$ items is 2·580. We conclude that the process is capable of meeting the design limits quite comfortably.

There is obviously a simple relationship between the ratio of the calculated value of the Tolerance Factor to the Minimum value of the Factor and the minimum proportion of the product which will be outside limits. We have already shown how, having obtained the population standard deviation from the mean sample range, by using Table 1, we may use the table for the Areas of the

TABLE 4

MINIMUM VALUES OF THE TOLERANCE FACTOR

Tolerance factor

$$= \frac{2T}{\bar{w}}$$

Sample size n	Minimum value of factor
2	5·321
3	3·544
4	2·914
5	2·580
6	2·363
7	2·219
8	2·108
9	2·020

Normal Curve to estimate the proportion of the product which must be out of limits. Interested readers may like to follow up this clue and see for themselves the way in which the graph of Fig. 60 may be arrived at, which shows the minimum proportion of defectives for various values of the ratio.

$$\frac{\text{Calculated value of Tolerance Factor}}{\text{Minimum value of Tolerance Factor}}$$

(by minimum value in this context we mean, of course, not the minimum possible but the minimum necessary to ensure that the process is capable of meeting the design limits with virtually no rejections).

Suppose, now, we have a case where the calculated value of the Tolerance Factor is much greater than the minimum value indicated in Table 4, that is to say the design tolerance is very generous compared with the short-term precision of the process (as measured by the range chart). It might well be pernickety in practice to insist that the nominal value be held, provided only that we keep the product within the design tolerance limits. In such a case we shall naturally want to modify our chart for sample means so as to permit a certain instability in the process average.

A very sensible approach is to fix both the position of the control limit and the sample size by specifying Producer and Consumer Risks. In order to illustrate how this may be done, let us imagine that we have a process for which the range chart indicates that the short term standard deviation is only 1·5 units, while the design tolerance is plus and minus 10 units from the

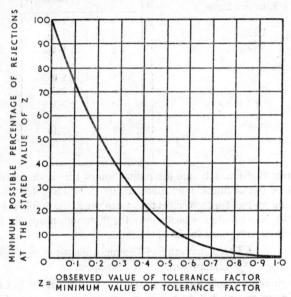

Fig. 60. Relationship between Rejection Rate and Tolerance Factor

nominal value (which we shall call zero). We shall determine the sample size and position of control limits to ensure that

(a) if the process is producing only 1% of product out of tolerance when the sample is taken, there will be a Producer Risk of 2% that the sample average will plot *outside* the control limit.

(b) if the process is producing 10% of product out of tolerance when the sample is taken, there will be a Consumer Risk of 5% that the sample average will plot *inside* the control limit.

To solve the problem, all we have to remember is that when we have individual values distributed with standard deviation σ the averages of n values will be distributed with standard deviation $\sigma_n = \sigma/\sqrt{n}$. The Table of Area of the Normal Curve on page 116 then enables us to find what we wish to know, as follows.

Let the proper position for the control limits be k *standard deviations* inside the tolerance limits and the appropriate sample size be n. Consider the Producer Risk condition illustrated in Figure 61. For 1% of product outside tolerance (one tail only need be bothered with), the Table of Area of the Normal Curve indicates a value of t equal to 2·25. That is to say the process average will have to be $2·25\sigma = 2·25 \times 1·5 = 3·37$ units inside the tolerance limit. With the process average in this position, we want 2% of sample averages expected outside the control limit. From the Table of Area we see that this implies that the control limit will have to be at a distance $2\sigma_n = 2\sigma/\sqrt{n} = 3·0/\sqrt{n}$ units away from the process average, in the direction of the tolerance limit. The reader will have no difficulty, now, in seeing from Figure 61 that the distance $k\sigma = 1·5k$ between the control limit and the tolerance limit will have to be such that

$$1·5k = 3·37 - 3·0/\sqrt{n} \quad . \quad . \quad . \quad . \quad (1)$$

If this equation is satisfied, the specified Producer Risk will obtain.

Turning now to the Consumer Risk condition, and using exactly the same form of argument, step by step, it will easily be deduced by the reader (if he has followed carefully) that the Consumer Risk condition illustrated in Figure 62 will obtain provided that

$$1·5k = 1·87 + 2·47/\sqrt{n} \quad . \quad . \quad . \quad . \quad (2)$$

Solving our two equations for n and k, we find that $n = 13·3$ and $k = 1·7$. Hence, the control limits should be placed at $1·7\sigma = 1·7 \times 1·5 = 2·5$ units inside the tolerance limits and the sample size should be $n = 13$. Figure 63 compares this solution with conventional control limits for $n = 13$ as well as with conventional control limits for the common arbitrary sample size of $n = 4$.

The reader will wish to have formulae for n and k. They are

$$n = \left(\frac{\tau_1 + \tau_2}{t_1 - t_2}\right)^2 \text{ and } k = \frac{\tau_1 t_2 + \tau_2 t_1}{\tau_1 + \tau_2}$$

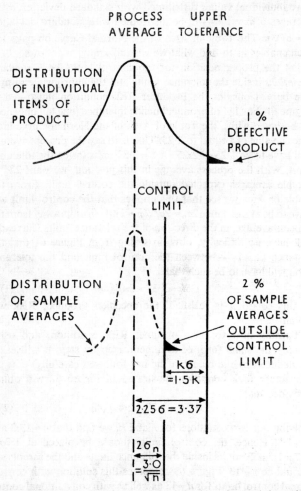

Fig. 61. Producer Risk Condition, showing behaviour of control chart when quality of product is acceptable (see Fig. 62)

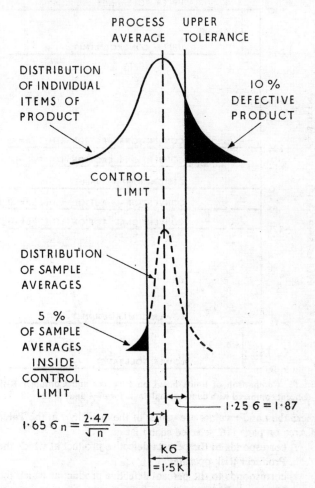

Fig. 62. Consumer Risk Condition, showing behaviour of control chart when quality of product is unacceptable (see Fig. 61)

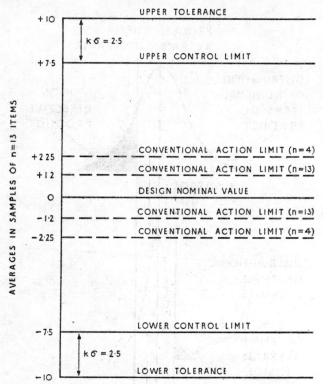

Fig. 63. Comparison of limits based on Producer and Consumer Risk concept compared with conventional limits for $n=4$ and $n=13$

where the t and τ values are values of the quantity t in the Table of Area on page 116, selected such that

t_1 corresponds to the percent defective product at which the Producer Risk operates

t_2 corresponds to the percent defective product at which the Consumer Risk operates

τ_1 corresponds to the Producer Risk

τ_2 corresponds to the Consumer Risk.

Thus, in the example just worked out $t_1=2\cdot25$, $t_2=1\cdot25$, $\tau_1=2\cdot0$ and $\tau_2=1\cdot65$. It is important to remember that when k is found the control limits are to be placed at $k\sigma$ units inside the tolerance limits. The reader may check the results for the example using the formulae.

Needless to say, when the machine drifts systematically in a predictable direction (e.g. owing to tool wear) we do not reset to the nominal but back to the safe side limit. If the average number of parts produced between resets is p and we inspect all the parts made since the last visit whenever the chart plots out of control, as a screening inspection, a rough rule for minimizing the total amount of inspection is to visit the machine at intervals long enough for the production of $\sqrt{np}$ pieces.

By considering a range of hypothetical percentages defective being made by the process the reader may care to try to deduce

(a) the probability of the chart plotting out of control for various conditions of the process (a plot of this is the Operating Characteristic)

(b) The expected amount of inspection as a total of (i) parts taken as samples and (ii) parts undergoing screening inspection, for various conditions of the process, assuming that $p = 130$, and hence arrive at a graph for the average Outgoing Quality.

(Part answer: Visit every 42 parts. A.O.Q.L. $= 1 \cdot 6 \%$ defective when the process is making 5% defective).

There remain only two practical points we should mention in this introductory discussion. The first is that the control limits need revising from time to time so as to be soundly based on recent experience. The second point is that these charts can be used with every confidence, even where the distribution of the individual items is extremely skew. The process of taking the average samples rapidly 'normalizes' skew distributions, the eccentricity of extreme values from the tail of the distribution being masked by averaging with values nearer the modal value.

NOW TRY YOUR HAND AT CONTROL CHARTS

1. Ten successive samples, each of 100 items, were taken from a production line in a factory and the number of items failing to pass a ring-gauge test in each sample was recorded as follows:

$$1, 2, 2, 4, 2, 1, 0, 1, 2, 0$$

Use these data to calculate the expected number of failures per sample of 100 items and use Fig. 55 to set up a control chart for this sampling arrangement.

2. Design a new control chart on the basis of the data in the above question to cover the case where 200 items were to be drawn in each sample.

3. A certain company has a quality control system on a tin-filling operation. Twenty successive samples, each of four tins, are weighed and the grand average weight found to be 2 lb with an average sample range of 3 drams (there are sixteen drams to an ounce). Use Table I to estimate the standard deviation, and hence estimate within what limits virtually all the tins lie.

4. What would you expect the mean sample range to be in samples of ten tins each? Use Tables 2 and 3 to set up control charts for mean and range in samples of ten tins, for the case mentioned in question 3.

5. The length of a certain dimension on a piece part to be used in vacuum cleaners is to be held within 1 thousandth of an inch of the nominal value. The job is put on to a certain machine and the average range in a series of samples of four items is found to be 1·4 thousandths of an inch. Estimate the standard deviation of the product from this machine, and so make use of tables of the area of the normal curve to estimate the minimum percentage of defective items which this machine would make. What standard deviation would be acceptable? What mean sample range in samples of four items does this correspond to? What is the minimum value for the tolerance factor (see Table 4)?

12

Safety in Sampling

' "No, no!" said the Queen. "Sentence first – verdict afterwards." ' LEWIS CARROLL

One of the main ideas behind sampling inspection is economy of
inspection effort, and considerable attention has been paid to the
problem of achieving the maximum economy of inspection effort
compatible with the degree of risk willingly faced. In order to
achieve this maximum economy, we shall have to make use of the
theory of probability which gives us knowledge of the behaviour
of sampling schemes. To introduce sampling schemes without
adequately considering how they will operate is the height of
foolishness.

We may summarize some of the fundamental principles already
dealt with as follows. Firstly, a small sample in isolation tells us
next to nothing about the quality of the batch from which it is
drawn. Thus a sampling scheme which says 'Deliver in batches of
50. Samples of 5 items to be taken. Allowable defect number = 0'
is pretty hopeless. In a pack of 52 playing cards there are 12 face
cards. As any card player knows, it is extremely common for a
hand of 5 cards to contain no face cards. In the same way it will
be very common for a sample of 5 items drawn from a batch
which is highly defective to contain no defective items. If, however, we accumulate sample results over a period, then we can use
the control chart technique to tell us whether the apparent differences between the samples may be ascribed to random sampling fluctuations, or whether there is evidence of real between
sample variation in quality. We may also use accumulated
samples to form an accurate estimate of the general quality level,
and with this knowledge at our disposal we can then use small
samples and a control chart technique to spot future departures from the quality level estimated from our previous
experience.

Inspection of batches may be by *Consignment Sampling*, in

which the onus rests primarily on the consumer, or it may be based on systematic records of the Quality Control type, kept by the manufacturer and checked by small samples taken by the consumer.

We said previously that the risk deliberately accepted in sampling inspection should be fairly divided between the producer and the consumer. The *Producer's Risk* in a sampling scheme is the risk that a batch of goods of acceptable quality will be rejected by the sampling scheme as a result of a pessimistic-looking sample being drawn. The *Consumer's Risk* is the chance that a batch of goods will be accepted by the sampling scheme as a result of an optimistic-looking sample being drawn from a batch which should properly be rejected. We have seen that there is a sharp distinction to be drawn between stringency and discrimination in a sampling scheme. Increased stringency does not bring increased discrimination. A further point is that every sampling scheme favours a particular quality level, so that increased stringency only has the effect of penalizing the producer without making any contribution to an equitable distribution of the risk.

Suppose, now, that you are a manufacturer, regularly receiving batches of goods and accepting or rejecting them on a sampling basis. The supplier may be some outside organization, or you may be receiving the consignments from a previous stage in your own organization. You ask the sampling scheme to give you protection. Immediately we ask: 'What sort of protection?'. You may want protection on every individual lot, so that you may be sure that the chance of any single lot being poorer than a certain quality level is small. You will want this *Lot Quality Protection* whenever the lots retain their individuality, not being mixed in store with other lots of similar items. But if the lots are passed into a store and mixed with other lots so that they lose their identity you will require *Average Quality Protection*. This is not to suggest that in either case you will be indifferent to one kind of protection. You will always want both – but there will be a natural emphasis. Either lot quality protection will have no significance for you, or it will be a matter of some importance. It will be clear that in guaranteeing one kind of protection we must automatically do something about the other. This distinction of practical importance is frequently not thought about. We vaguely realize that the two are closely related; that it is impossible for batches to be really bad in one respect and simultaneously really good in the other, and we leave it at that. A pity, for the distinction is worth making, and we can do something about it.

Suppose you say that you are interested in Lot Quality Protection. The statistician will then at once raise the unpleasant question of the Consumer's Risk. He will say that, since you want to sample, you must face squarely the question of this risk. When you specify the risk you are prepared to run, he will design for you the sampling scheme which gives you that level of guarantee with the minimum amount of inspection effort. If you are prepared to take big chances, the scheme will be very light on inspection costs, but if you are going to be very fussy, the cost will rise – but always the cost will be the minimum to ensure what you ask for. To specify your Consumer's Risk, you tell the statistician what you would consider to be a really bad lot in terms of percentage defective. If you wanted to be highly sure of rejecting by the time a batch was as poor as 5% defective, then it would be suggested that you took a chance of 10% of accepting such a batch. This would be your Consumer's Risk. The level 5% defective is then called the *Lot Tolerance Percent Defective*. This idea needs a little explaining in its psychological aspects. It does *not* mean that one batch out of every ten accepted would be 5% defective. It means that of all batches which are 5% defective, 90% will be returned as rejected batches. The reader with experience of industry will appreciate that a rejection rate of 90% is catastrophic. What we should picture is a supplier falling from grace, and his rejection rate rising so rapidly that it would reach 90% by the time his batches were 5% defective.

Suppose, on the other hand, you were interested in Average Quality Protection. In this case the statistician will ask what is the absolute upper limit to the percentage defective in the goods after inspection that you are prepared to accept in the long run. You may reply that you want to be absolutely sure that in the long run, no matter how bad the batches offered you, there will be no more than 4% defectives in the goods actually accepted by you. This value of 4% is called the *Average Outgoing Quality Limit*, i.e. the maximum percentage of defectives that will in the long run be left in the goods accepted and outgoing from the inspection process. Notice that it is an upper limit – in practice the outgoing percentage defective rarely exceeds half the limit value.

When we have told the statistician what we want, he will then have to consider the most economic way of achieving the result. The sizes of the batches to be inspected are not usually within his control – the most he can do is to recommend, in accordance with general principles, that for the sake of economy they should be as large as possible subject to the requirement of reasonable assurance of homogeneity. He will ask for one further bit of information, however. So far you will have told him what you want to be sure of in the way of quality after inspection. To give you the most economic sampling scheme he will need to know the pressure to which the sampling scheme will be subjected in the ordinary way. If the goods supplied normally contain a fairly high proportion of defectives, the pressure is great, and the sampling scheme will have to be made proportionally robust in the way of larger-sized samples, the real reason for this being that the quality of the goods supplied will be near to the rejection quality, so that a careful inspection will be required to decide whether or not to accept them. In statistical terminology, we shall be asked the value of the supplier's *Process Average Percent Defective*.

This whole problem has been carefully worked out and the results for all cases likely to arise in practice have been made available in the form of *Single and Double Sampling Tables*, by Dodge and Romig of the Bell Telephone Laboratories. We shall now explain these sampling schemes, which are characterized by provision for 100% inspection of all batches not accepted as a result of the drawing of a satisfactory sample. This 'screening inspection' plays a fundamental part in achieving the desired result, as will shortly appear. The reader will notice that the total amount of inspection performed in the long run under this system is made up of two distinct parts:

(a) the inspection of pieces drawn as samples;
(b) the inspection of the remainders of those batches which fail to be accepted by the sample results and so are detailed for 100% inspection.

It will be evident that in the event of the supplier's quality falling off, the amount of 100% inspection enforced by the schemes will rise. Thus we see increased risk resulting in greater protection costs, the normal insurance principle. Moreover, these increased inspection costs provide a compelling argument for action to be taken to stem the rot.

In the Single Sampling Schemes, whether for Lot Quality Protection or for Average Outgoing Quality Protection, each scheme will be represented by three numbers: N, the batch size, n, the sample size, and d, the allowable number of defectives. For a given value of the Process Average Percent Defective – which we shall in future refer to for convenience as the 'P.A.'– there will be a precise value for the probability of the allowable number of defectives being exceeded by chance. This probability is the chance that a lot which in fact is of acceptable quality will be rejected under the sampling plan. It is what we have learnt to call the Producer's Risk. Lots so rejected will be detailed for 100% inspection of their remainders.

We can calculate the average amount of inspection per lot for a given value of the P.A. as the number inspected in the sample *plus* the product of the remainder of the lot times the Producer's Risk. Mathematically, if we have lots of size N from which samples of n items are drawn, then the expected amount of inspection in the long run when the Producer's Risk has the probability R will be given by

$$I = n + (N - n)R$$

It is thus open to us to calculate this average amount of inspection for different sample sizes and different allowable defect numbers by the theory of probability, and so arrive at the scheme which gives the desired protection with the minimum amount of inspection on the average. In practice, of course, we have no need to do the work for ourselves; we can make use of the published tables already mentioned.

As an illustration of the way in which the calculations may be performed, let us design a sampling scheme for the following case. Batches of goods are to contain $N = 500$ items. We wish the scheme to ensure a Consumer's Risk of 10% of accepting batches which contain 5% defective, i.e. the scheme shall reject 90% of such batches. The scheme shall be the most economic possible for this degree of protection under the normal conditions, i.e. when the supplier is sending in batches of Process Average Quality. The P.A. is 1% defectives.

Our first job will be to make a list of sample size and allowable defective numbers which will give the required degree of protection when the supplier is submitting batches of Lot Tolerance Percent Defective, viz. 5%. We may do this very simply by making use of our Poisson Chart, which will be amply good as an approximation to the skew distribution of the relative Binomial $(0.95 + 0.05)^n$. Referring, then, to Fig. 39, we set up the following table.

Allowed defect number d	Expectation e	Sample size n
0	2·3	46
1	3·9	78
2	5·4	108
3	6·8	136
4	8·0	160
5	9·2	184

The first column shows allowable number of defectives, 0, 1, 2, etc. We use the Poisson Chart to read off the expected number of defectives per sample such that the probability of rejection, i.e. the probability of the number, d, being exceeded is 0·9. For example, when $d = 0$, we find the probability 0·9 on the left-hand vertical scale, run our finger out until we meet the curve $c = 1$ or more, and read off the expected number per sample for which these conditions hold on the bottom scale as equal to 2·3. Similarly, when $d = 1$, with the probability 0·9 and the curve $c = 2$ or more, we find that the expected number of defectives in our sample should be 3·9, and so on for other values of d. These numbers are entered in the second column. The third column is arrived at by asking ourselves what size of sample, n, would have the expectation given in the second column when the supplier is sending in batches containing the Lot Tolerance Percent Defective, 5%. Thus, with the value 5% defective in the bulk, we should have to have a sample of $n = 46$ to give us an expected number of defectives in the sample equal to 2·3. A sample of 78 would give us an expectation of 3·9, and so on. These sample sizes are entered in the third column. Any of the (n, d) combinations in this table will give us the protection we ask for.

The question which of them we shall use is an economic one. We argue that the supplier normally sends in lots of Process Average Quality, viz. 1% defective, and ask ourselves which of the schemes is most economic in inspection effort under these normal conditions.

We calculate the average amount of inspection using the formula previously quoted. The Producer's Risk, R, is different for each (n, d) combination. It is found from the Poisson Chart. The whole procedure for finding the minimum inspection scheme is shown in the following table. The third column, headed 'expec-

Sample size n	All. defects d	Expectation at P.A.	Prod. risk	Avg. inspected as remainders	Avg. Total inspected
46	0	0·46	3·37	168	214
78	1	0·78	0·19	80	158
→108	2	1·08	0·10	39	→147
136	3	1·36	0·06	22	158
160	4	1·6	0·03	10	170
184	5	1·84	0·01	3	187

tation at P.A.', is found by multiplying the sample size, n, by the P.A. expressed as *fraction defective*, in this case 0·01, since the P.A. is 1% defective. Knowing this value for the expected number of defectives in our sample, we can read from the Poisson paper the Producer's Risk for the scheme. Thus, for $n = 46$, the expected number of defectives in the sample under P.A. conditions is 0·46. The Producer's Risk is the probability that 1 or more defectives will be found in the sample when the allowable defect number is 0. We find the Producer's Risk $= 0·37$, i.e. with this scheme 37% of all batches at P.A. quality would be rejected by the sample result and have to go for 100% inspection of their remaining items. The average number of items inspected per batch on the 100% screening inspection is found by multiplying the remaining number of items in the batch by the Producer's Risk. The total amount of inspection expected on the average per batch is then easily found and the result entered in the last column. In our case the batch size is $N = 500$. Inspection of the last column shows that, as we pass down the table, the average amount of inspection at first falls, but then begins to rise again. The minimum amount of inspection occurs when we use the scheme ($n = 108$, $d = 2$). This is the required solution for our problem.

We shall next wish to draw for ourselves the Operating Characteristic for this scheme. We have already shown how this is done using Poisson paper, and assuming different values for the percent defective in the bulk. To avoid a lot of arithmetic, we may assume for this purpose that the sample size is $n = 100$; this will have a negligible effect on the Operating Characteristic. The calculation would then be as follows:

Assumed % defective in bulk	Defectives expected in sample $n = 100$	Probability of 3 or more defectives
0·5	0·5	0·015
1·0	1·0	0·08
1·5	1·5	0·20
3·0	3·0	0·57
6·0	6·0	0·94
10·0	10·0	0·996

The figures in the last column, multiplied by 100, are the percentages of batches which would be rejected by the samples at the stated percentage of defectives in the bulk. The results are shown graphically in Fig. 64. Figs. 65 and 66 show how the Producer's Risk and Consumer's Risk arise.

Now although the present scheme was designed specifically to give a certain Lot Quality protection, it is evident that it will also provide average quality protection, incidentally. We can investigate what the percentage of defective items left in the batches will be after inspection as follows. Let us suppose that defective items are either repaired or replaced whenever they are found, either in a sample or during screening inspection of remainders of

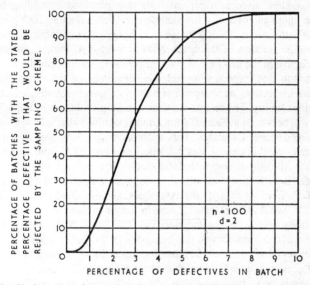

Fig. 64. Operating characteristic for samples of 100 items when the batch will be rejected whenever three or more defective items are found in the sample

batches rejected by their samples. Under these circumstances the proportion of the defectives in batches which will be removed will be in simple proportion to the fraction of the bulk inspected altogether. This fraction, as we have already seen, will vary as the percentage of defectives in the batch changes. The Operating Characteristic tells us at once what proportion of batches have 100% inspection at each possible value of the percent defective in the batch (Fig. 64). We calculate the average percent defective in the batches after inspection, as shown in the table on the adjoining page. For any given value of percent defective in the goods offered for acceptance we get the fraction of batches rejected by sample from the Operating Characteristic and enter it in column 2. Knowing this, and the size of batch remainders ($=400$ here), we can enter in column 3 the average number per batch which will be inspected as remainders. Column 5, the total average amount of inspection per batch, is then obtained by adding to the figure in column 3 the sample size (here taken as 100). But the batch size is $N=500$, so we can at once enter in column 6 the average fraction of the batch NOT inspected. If the percentage defective in the batches, as given in column 1, is multiplied by the fraction not inspected we get the percentage of defectives left after inspection, as shown in column 7. This is the Average Outgoing Quality. The results are shown in graphical form in Fig. 67. It will be seen that there is a maximum possible value for the Outgoing Percent Defective. This is the Average Outgoing Quality Limit. In this case it has a value just over $1 \cdot 1\%$, and occurs when the goods submitted for inspection contain about 2% defectives. Notice that, when the supplier is sending in goods at the P.A. value of 1%, the Average Outgoing Quality is about $0 \cdot 7\%$, and that if he started to send in batches at the Lot Tolerance Quality of 5% the goods passed on from inspection would only contain $0 \cdot 5\%$ defectives, this being due to the high proportion of batches detailed for 100% screening inspection (Consumer's Risk 10%, therefore 90% of batches get screening inspection).

We hope to have made the reader sufficiently at home by this example with the principles on which the Dodge and Romig Sampling Schemes are worked out, so that he may use the tables with understanding and appreciation of the very considerable care and hard work which went into their computation. We hope, too, that he will agree that rough guesses are not likely to give such good results in practice as use of the published tables. We emphasize yet again that sampling is a complex business in which decisions are best left to experts if we wish to know exactly what any scheme will really do in practice. It is easy to lay down the law; much less easy to know the meaning and effect of what you have said.

1	2	3	4	5	6	7
% defective in batches offered	Fraction of batches rejected by sample	Average number per batch inspected as 'remainders'	Number inspected as sample	Total average number inspected per batch	Fraction of batches NOT inspected	% defective in batches after inspection
0	0	0	100	100	0·8	0
0·5	0·015	6	100	106	0·79	0·4
1	0·08	32	100	132	0·74	0·74
1·5	0·20	80	100	180	0·64	0·96
2·0	0·30	120	100	220	0·56	1·1
2·5	0·45	180	100	280	0·44	1·1
3	0·57	228	100	328	0·34	1·0
6	0·94	376	100	476	0·05	0·3
10	0·996	398	100	498	0 (nearly)	0 (nearly)

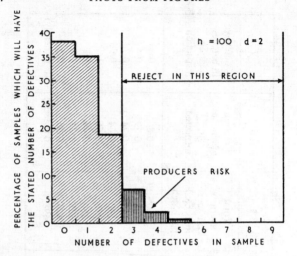

Fig. 65. Effect of sampling scheme when the supplier sends in his normal quality of 1% defectives

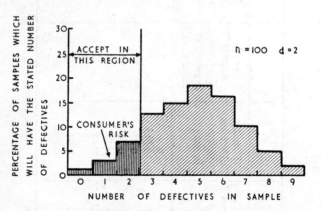

Fig. 66. Effect of sampling scheme when supplier is submitting batches of lot tolerance quality, viz. 5% defective

It remains now to give a description of the tables themselves. They are in two sets: one specifically designed for cases where the emphasis is on Lot Quality Protection, the other for Average Outgoing Quality Protection. The tables cover lot sizes from $N = 1$ to $N = 100,000$ for all practically useful values of Lot Tolerance Percent Defective and Average Outgoing Quality Limit up to 10%.

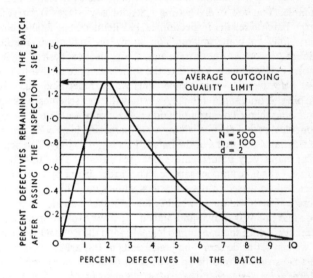

Fig. 67. How the average outgoing quality varies with the percentage defective in batches of 500 items from which samples of 100 items are taken with an allowable number of defects equal to two per sample. With the screening inspection there is a limit to the poorness of quality in the goods after sampling inspection

In the Lot Tolerance Tables, for each sample scheme we are given the A.O.Q.L. (Average Outgoing Quality Limit) corresponding to the scheme. In the Average Outgoing Quality Tables, for each scheme we are given the Lot Tolerance Percent Defective based on a Consumer's Risk of 10%. The general layout of the Single Sampling Tables is similar to that of the Double Sampling Tables illustrated on pages 190 and 191.

7

Our indebtedness to Messrs Dodge and Romig is not ended with the Single Sampling Tables, however. Imagine that you were inspecting a batch of $N = 5,000$ items, wishing to work to a Lot Tolerance Percent Defective of 2%, knowing that the supplier's P.A. ran at 0·1%. Consulting your Dodge and Romig Single Sampling Tables, you would be told to take a random sample of $n = 195$ from the batch and allow not more than 1 defective in the sample. You are really getting splendid advantages from your large batch size, the inspection of 195 items out of 5,000 being very jolly to contemplate. You know the scheme is mathematically worked out to give you the protection desired in the most economic way. You take the sample and are aghast to find *two* defectives in your sample. This would indeed be very disturbing. You cannot monkey about with the schemes without upsetting them. The strict position is that you should now roll up your sleeves and get busy doing 100% screening inspection on the remaining 4,805 items of the batch. This is not so jolly. The practical man's very natural and proper reaction is 'Blow this for a game. Let's take another sample.' The reader, being by now more than a little versed in these matters, while sympathizing with the practical man will query whether this is in fact a sensible thing to do. The line was drawn and agreed to; if we can rub it out and start again once there seems no logical end to the game. Obviously, if we can set aside sampling judgements in this arbitrary fashion just because we are ordered to do a bit of hard work in our own ultimate interests, then there is no point in having properly designed schemes at all. We just keep on taking samples until we get a favourable result. Yet surely the practical man is not being altogether silly? We feel that given circumstances of this sort, there should be some properly worked out system for taking a second sample. We shall of course insist that the result obtained on the unfortunate sample be not thrown away, that it shall be pooled in with any further sample result so as to have a fair say. We shall also probably feel that any second sample taken after an unfavourable first one should be strictly worked out in accordance with probability theory so that the protection we aim at from our sampling scheme shall not suffer as a result of this second chance.

The statistician agrees with all these points. They are common sense and so comfortably at home in statistics. He welcomes the idea for another reason: with this arrangement of the 'second chance' he can design his schemes even more economically in terms of average inspection. In fact, the more chances we have the more economic the scheme can be *in the long run*. We shall be discussing later in the chapter the schemes where we sample the batch *one item at a time*, and cease as soon as we can draw a conclusion. There is a drawback in practice to the use of multiple sampling schemes. Like the people who want to 'have a second shot', they are irresolute. Shilly-shallying of this sort would often be intolerable in a factory, where smooth running of the production machine depends as much on taking the bull by the horns as on being right in every detail. It all depends on the circumstances and each man must adopt the plan which best suits him in a particular case. This is not the affair of the statistician. His job is to give us the tools and let us choose from them as we think fit. Let us then look at the Double Sampling Schemes of Dodge and Romig.

In Fig. 68 the Double Sampling Scheme is made clear. As an actual case, if we enter the Dodge and Romig tables for a Double Sampling Scheme for inspecting a batch of size $N = 450$ when the P.A. of the supplier is 1% defective and we are prepared to accept a Consumer's Risk of a 10% chance of accepting a lot in which the percent defective is 3%, we find the scheme ($n_1 = 85$, $d_1 = 0$, $n_2 = 125$, $d_2 = 3$), i.e. we are to take a first sample of 85 items at random from the batch and accept the batch on the basis of this first sample provided no defectives at all are found in the sample. If more than three defectives are found in this first sample, the batch is to be rejected at once without any further sample being taken, but if the number of defectives in the first sample, while exceeding 0, is not more than 3, then we are to take a second sample of 125 items and may accept the batch provided the total number of defective items *for first and second samples combined* does not exceed 3.

The basic ideas behind the computation of these Double Sampling Schemes are precisely the same as those underlying the Single Sampling Schemes, though they are naturally rather more complex. The Consumer's Risk is now made up of two component parts, viz.

the probability of accepting a lot of Lot Tolerance Quality on the basis of the first sample *plus*

the probability of accepting such a lot on the basis of the combined first and second samples, after failure on the first sample.

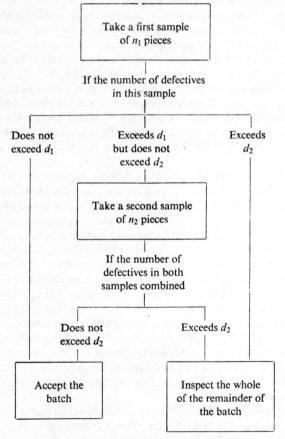

Fig. 68. Double Sampling Inspection Procedure

As for Single Sampling, tables are published covering the whole of the likely range of conditions, both for Lot Quality Protection and for Average Outgoing Quality Protection. Figs. 68 and 70 are excerpts from the two kinds of table, showing the layout.

When using the tables, we have to make an estimate of the supplier's process average percent defective. Sometimes we have little or no previous experience to guide us. In such cases it is better to *overestimate* the P.A. as the additional amount of inspection will then be less than if we underestimate the P.A. It should be clearly understood that the tables do *not* depend for safety on a well-controlled P.A. in the goods received from the supplier; the whole point is that, while quality submitted is good, acceptance will normally be by sample, but, as quality deteriorates in the goods supplied, 100% inspection will be forced more and more frequently. It will be appreciated that the plans are not only protective, but also corrective, in the sense that they create a back pressure whenever the quality starts to fall off.

It is a useful thing to add to the Single or Double Sampling Scheme a fraction defective control chart. The information for this chart is automatically to hand as a result of the sampling, so that it is simply a matter of plotting the results on the control chart. The control chart is set up by getting an estimate of the supplier's P.A. based on the first twenty or so samples drawn from consignments. If we denote the process average by p, then the Upper and Lower Warning Limits are set at $p \pm 2 \sqrt{\frac{p(1-p)}{n}}$ and the Upper and Lower Action Limits at $p \pm 3 \sqrt{\frac{p(1-p)}{n}}$ where n is the number of items in the sample. Where the samples drawn vary in size from batch to batch, it will be necessary to set the control limits separately for each batch. Under such conditions it is best to calculate the limits for several values in the likely range of n and plot them in a graph, so that the limits can be read off at once for any case. The assumed value of p should be revised from time to time as the variation in the supplier's P.A. demands.

The technique by which we build up our sample one item at a time, and after inspecting each item, ask ourselves: 'Can we be sure enough to accept or reject this batch on the information so

Lot Tolerance Percent Defective = 2.0%

Process Average%	0·21–0·40					0·41–0·60					0·61–0·80				
	Trial 1		Trial 2		A.O.Q.L.%	Trial 1		Trial 2		A.O.Q.L.%	Trial 1		Trial 2		A.O.Q.L.%
Lot size	n_1	d_1	n_2	d_2		n_1	d_1	n_2	d_2		n_1	d_1	n_2	d_2	
501–600	125	0	130	2	0·39	125	0	130	2	0·39	125	0	185	3	0·41
601–800	130	0	135	2	0·41	130	0	195	3	0·44	130	0	250	4	0·45
801–1,000	135	0	140	2	0·42	135	0	200	3	0·46	135	0	255	4	0·48

Fig. 69. Extract from Double Sampling Lot Inspection Tables for Quality Protection on Individual Lots based on Consumer's Risk = 10% [Dodge & Romig]

Average Outgoing Quality Limit = 2.0%

Process Average %	0·41–0·80							0·81–1·20							1·21–1·60						
	Trial 1		Trial 2			Lot tol. % def.		Trial 1		Trial 2			Lot tol. % def.		Trial 1		Trial 2			Lot. tol. % def.	
Lot size	n_1	d_1	n_2	d_2				n_1	d_1	n_2	d_2				n_1	d_1	n_2	d_2			
501–600	35	0	55	3		7·9		35	0	55	3		7·9		37	0	78	4		7·4	
601–800	35	0	60	3		7·7		38	0	82	4		7·3		38	0	82	4		7·3	
801–1,000	36	0	59	3		7·6		38	0	87	4		7·2		70	1	100	6		6·5	

Fig. 70. Extract from Double Sampling Lot Inspection Tables for Average Outgoing Quality Protection [Dodge & Romig]

far collected?' is the problem tackled in what is known as *Sequential Analysis*, a great deal of the work being done by the Statistical Research Group at Columbia University during the 1939–45 war, under the leadership of A. Wald, who had published in 1943 a report which gave the basic mathematical theory and showed how it could be applied to a variety of problems. The work on this subject was so much a team achievement that there was a reluctance in subsequent publications to assign credit to individuals. To quote from the publication *Sequential Analysis of Statistical Data: Applications*: 'Its value in enabling reliable conclusions to be wrung from a minimum of data was deemed sufficient to require that it be classified Restricted within the meaning of the Espionage Act. The Army, the Navy, and the Office of Scientific Research and Development, however, introduced it into several thousand manufacturing establishments as a basis for acceptance inspection, and this resulted in a widespread demand for access to information on the subject. In response to representations from the War Production Board, the Army, and the Navy, the Restricted classification was therefore removed in May 1945.' There can be no further need to emphasize the value of such techniques in industry, both in relation to process inspection and to research. We shall give a brief outline of some of the cases to which it may be applied.

Consider, first of all, the case where we are inspecting a batch of goods, classifying each item as 'O.K.' or 'Reject', that is to say we are inspecting in what is essentially a Binomial Distribution problem. How is this tackled by the Sequential technique? What we do is to lay down two values for the fraction defective, one of which we regard as good and the other which we regard as bad. Suppose, for example, we regarded 1% defectives as good and 5% defectives as bad quality in a consignment. Then our position would be that we should want the risk of rejecting a batch for which the percentage of defectives was less than 1% to be small, and the chance of accepting a batch for which the percent defective exceeded 5% to be small. The chance of a good batch being rejected is what we have learnt to call the Producer's Risk, and the chance of a bad batch being accepted is what we have called the Consumer's Risk. Now these four quantities, (1) a bad quality,

(2) a good quality, (3) the Producer's Risk, and (4) the Consumer's Risk, are sufficient to determine a sequential sampling plan. The following notation is used:

The acceptable quality, expressed as fraction defective $= p_1$

The probability of rejecting a lot of this acceptable
quality $= \alpha$

The unacceptable quality, expressed as fraction defective $= p_2$

The probability of accepting a lot of this unacceptable
quality $= \beta$

Given this demand $(p_1, \alpha, p_2, \beta)$, we then calculate three constants h_1, h_2, and s which characterize the control chart on which the inspection of batches will be based. The formulae for computing the three constants are:

$$h_1 = \frac{\log\left(\dfrac{1-\alpha}{\beta}\right)}{\log\dfrac{p_2}{p_1}\left(\dfrac{1-p_1}{1-p_2}\right)} \qquad h_2 = \frac{\log\left(\dfrac{1-\beta}{\alpha}\right)}{\log\dfrac{p_2}{p_1}\left(\dfrac{1-p_1}{1-p_2}\right)}$$

$$s = \frac{\log\left(\dfrac{1-p_1}{1-p_2}\right)}{\log\dfrac{p_2}{p_1}\left(\dfrac{1-p_1}{1-p_2}\right)}$$

The formulae look a little fearsome at first sight, but they are easy to handle as follows, and it should be borne in mind that these calculations are 'once and for all' efforts, which will enable us to inspect all future batches at once, without further calculation. Procedure: Calculate:

$$g_1 = \log\frac{p_2}{p_1}; \qquad g_2 = \log\left(\frac{1-p_1}{1-\mu_2}\right); \qquad a = \log\left(\frac{1-\beta}{\alpha}\right);$$

$$b = \log\left(\frac{1-\alpha}{\beta}\right)$$

Then, we have:

$$h_1 = \frac{b}{g_1 + g_2}; \qquad h_2 = \frac{a}{g_1 + g_2}; \qquad s = \frac{g_2}{g_1 + g_2}$$

It is worth noticing that if $\alpha = \beta$ then h_1 is equal to h_2.

With our three characteristic constants calculated, we set up the inspection chart, as shown in Fig. 71.

Let us take an actual case and work through the necessary steps to set up a chart. Suppose we name our acceptable quality as being of fraction defective $p_1 = 0.01$ (i.e. 1% defective) and agree to a probability of 0·10 (a 10% chance) of rejecting a batch of this quality. Let us suppose, further, that we name as unacceptable quality a fraction defective 0·05, and agree to a Consumer's Risk of a probability of 0·10 (a 10% chance again) of

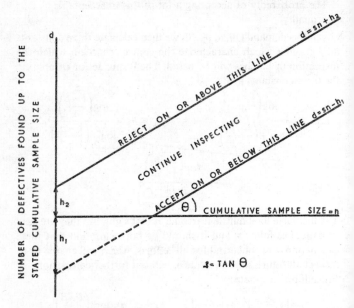

Fig. 71. Sequential sampling chart layout with meanings of the three characteristic constants of sequential schemes, h_1, h_2, and S

accepting a batch containing this fraction defective. We calculate h_1, h_2, and s, the characteristic constants of our sequential scheme as follows:

$$p_1 = 0.01 \qquad \alpha = 0.10 \qquad p_2 = 0.05 \qquad \beta = 0.10$$

Since $\alpha = \beta$, then $h_1 = h_2$ and we have:

$$g_1 = \log\frac{p_2}{p_1} = \log\frac{0.05}{0.01} = \log 5 = 0.699$$

$$g_2 = \log\left(\frac{1-p_1}{1-p_2}\right) = \log\frac{0.99}{0.95} = \log 1.04 = 0.017$$

$$a = \log\left(\frac{1-\beta}{\alpha}\right) = \log\frac{0.90}{0.10} = \log 9 = 0.954$$

And, since $\alpha = \beta$, we shall have $b = a = 0.954$

We then get:

$$h_1 = \frac{b}{g_1 + g_2} = \frac{0.954}{0.699 + 0.017} = \frac{0.954}{0.716} = 1.32$$

and

$$h_2 = h_1 = 1.32$$

$$s = \frac{g_2}{g_1 + g_2} = \frac{0.0170}{0.716} = 0.024$$

Characteristic Constants: $h_1 = h_2 = 1.32 \quad s = 0.024$

To fix the Acceptance and Rejection Lines in our Inspection Chart we need to have two known points on each. When n, 'the number of items inspected so far', is equal to zero, the Rejection Line is passing through the point h_2 on the axis for d, 'the number of defectives found so far', and the Acceptance Line is passing through the point $-h_1$ on that axis. A further point on each line may be found by substituting any convenient value for n in the equations of the lines. Thus, putting $n = 100$, we find that the corresponding value for d, the number of defectives found so far, is

For the Rejection Line $\quad d_2 = sn + h_2$
$$= 100 \times 0.024 + 1.32$$
$$= 3.7$$
For the Acceptance Line $d_1 = sn - h_1$
$$= 100 \times 0.024 - 1.32$$
$$= 1.1$$

Our Acceptance and Rejection Lines may thus be drawn, and the Inspection Chart is as shown in Fig. 72. The Acceptance Line below the axis of n is shown dotted, since it has no practical meaning, a negative number of defectives being quite impossible in practice.

The reader will see from the Inspection Chart, Fig. 72, that in this case, while a decision to reject can be made almost from the beginning, it would not be possible to accept until about sixty items had been inspected.

There will be certain points on which the reader will wish for further information about the scheme. Firstly, he will want to know how this scheme *operates*, that is to say he will want to know the probability of accepting batches of different quality. For this he will expect an Operating Characteristic. Secondly, he will want to know what the average percentage of defectives is

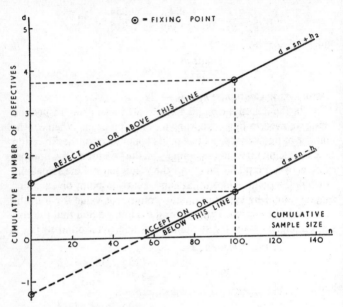

Fig. 72. An actual Sequential Inspections Chart showing the four fixing points computed in the text

after inspection, under different conditions of the supplier's process average. Thirdly, as a supplementary query to the previous demand, he will want to know the Average Outgoing Quality Limit of the scheme. Finally, he will want some idea as to the average sample size which will be required in order to reach a decision, since this is an economic matter of importance which in these schemes is not predetermined. All these questions are easily answered before any scheme is put into operation by the doing of some very simple calculations. We thus have at our disposal an inspection scheme which we can easily design for ourselves and whose nature we can thoroughly understand.

Let us take, first of all, the question of the Operating Characteristic. Five points on the Operating Characteristic (commonly known, aptly enough, as the O.C.) can be plotted at once. Thus:

Lot fraction defective	Probability of acceptance
0	1
p_1	$1 - \alpha$
s	$\dfrac{h_2}{h_1 + h_2}$
p_2	β
1	0

In the scheme we have just designed, we had

$$\alpha = 0\cdot10 \qquad \beta = 0\cdot10 \qquad h_1 = 1\cdot32 \qquad h_2 = 1\cdot32$$
$$p_1 = 0\cdot01 \qquad p_2 = 0\cdot05 \qquad s = 0\cdot024$$

We have five points on our O.C., then, as:

Lot fraction defective	0	$p_1 = 0\cdot01$	$s = 0\cdot0238$	$p_2 = 0\cdot05$	1
Probability of acceptance	1	$(1-\alpha) = 0\cdot90$	$\dfrac{h_2}{h_1 + h_2} = 0\cdot50$	$\beta = 0\cdot10$	0
i.e. Percentage of batches accepted is	100	90	50	10	0
When % defectives in the lot is	0	1	2·38	5	100

The O.C. is shown in Fig. 73.

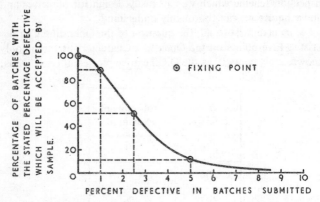

Fig. 73. Operating characteristic of the sequential plan computed in the text

We may similarly plot an Average Outgoing Quality Curve (A.O.Q.) from the following five points:

Lot fraction defective	0	p_1	s	p_2	1
A.O.Q. fraction defective	0	$(1-\alpha)p_1$	$\dfrac{sh_2}{h_1+h_2}$	βp_2	0

Substituting our own particular values, we get:

Lot fraction defective	0	0·01	0·0238	0·05	1
A.O.Q. fraction defective	0	0·009	0·0119	0·005	0
i.e. lot percent defective	0	1	2·38	5·0	100
gives A.O.Q. % defective	0	0·9	1·19	0·5	0

These results are plotted in Fig. 74 and a smooth curve put through them by eye tells us all we want to know about A.O.Q., as practical men. It will be observed that the A.O.Q. Curve has a maximum value for the Average Outgoing Quality Percent Defective. This, of course, is the Average Outgoing Quality Limit.

There remains the question of the average amount of inspection required to reach a decision under different circumstances. Again, we are able to plot a simple five-point curve, called the Average Sample Number Curve (A.S.N.), by using the following table:

Lot fraction defective	0	p_1	s	p_2	1
Average sample number	$\dfrac{h_1}{s}$	$\dfrac{h_1-\alpha(h_1+h_2)}{s-p_1}$	$\dfrac{h_1 h_2}{s(1-s)}$	$\dfrac{h_2-\beta(h_1+h_2)}{p_2-s}$	$\dfrac{h_2}{1-s}$

Substituting our own particular values, we get:

Lot fraction defective	0	0·01	0·024	0·05	1
Average sample number	55	75	74	41	1·3
% defective in the lot	0	1	2·4	5	100

The Average Sample Curve is shown plotted in Fig. 75.

Special tables have been published which eliminate the labour of calculation. Sequential Analysis is of particular value in conducting tests which are by their nature destructive, or in which the inspection cost per unit item is great. In cases where it is desired to classify defects into major and minor, separate inspection charts are kept for the two types, each having its own suitable values of $(p_1, \alpha, p_2, \beta)$. It will be possible, on occasion, for the test to proceed in such a way that though a considerable number of items have been inspected no decision is arrived at. Special provisions exist for truncating tests in such cases.

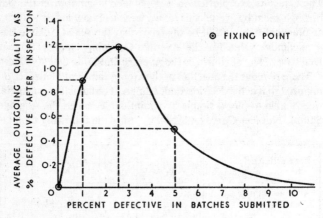

Fig. 74. A.O.Q. curve of the sequential plan computed in the text

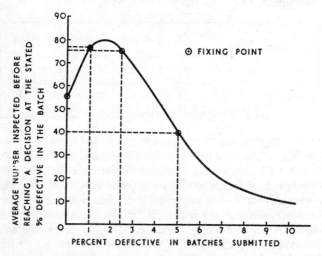

Fig. 75. Average sample number curve for the sequential plan computed in the text

In the case just discussed we were trying to decide whether a single batch should be regarded as of acceptable quality. Frequently we are faced with making a choice between two sources of supply and we wish to choose the source which is likely to contain the smallest proportion of defective items. We may, for example, receive samples from two competing suppliers. Alternatively, in a research laboratory, we may be trying to decide which of two possible processes for doing a job yields the best result. We are then dealing with what the statistician calls a 'double dichotomy', i.e. a double division, the two divisions referred to being (a) a division into source or product type and (b) a division into good and bad quality. Thus a double dichotomy gives us a fourfold classification of the type shown:

	O.K. items	Defectives
Product A	462	24
Product B	148	7

and it is our purpose to decide between the two sources. If we are presented with all the inspection completed, the decision would be made using the χ^2 test (see Chapter 15). But in cases where inspection is costly, or where it is a long and slow business to acquire information (e.g. as in many branches of medical research), then we shall want to review the situation continuously as the evidence piles up, so that a decision may be made at the earliest possible moment. We may be starting from scratch with no particular bias in favour of either process, or we may, for example, already be using one technique and wish to decide whether an alternative suggestion is sufficiently superior to warrant scrapping of the existing process in favour of the new one. In the latter case, considerations of cost involved in scrapping the old process may demand a marked superiority in the new process before we would be prepared to change over.

What is the underlying approach to such a problem in Sequential Analysis? We say that a pair of trials in which both the Standard and the Experimental process score either failure or success yields no information about the superiority of one process over the other. Only when we test one item from each source and get one a success and the other a failure do we learn anything positive about the relative merits of the processes. Pairs of this type are known as *pairs favourable* to one or the other process. We meet then Pairs Favourable (P.F.) to the Experimental process and

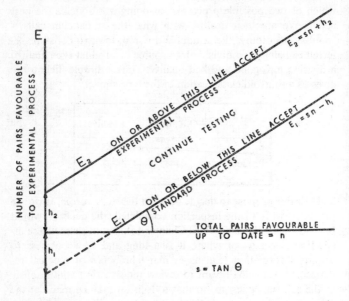

Fig. 76. Inspection Chart for sequential analysis on 'pairs favourable' basis to decide between two processes or materials

P.F. to the Standard process, and the Inspection Chart is arranged very much as in the previous example, as is shown in Fig. 76. As before, the Inspection Chart is characterized by three constants, h_1, h_2, and s, which we must now consider how to calculate.

To get at this, we must now introduce the idea of the *Odds Ratio*. Considering only a single process, the effectiveness of that process may be described satisfactorily by the proportion, p, of successes or O.K. items which it produces. Alternatively, we may describe it in terms of the number of successes per failure, i.e. by the odds on a success. Since the odds are a simple mathematical function of the proportion of successes, namely: odds $= \dfrac{p}{1-p}$, it matters little which method we use. If, now, we come to compare the relative merits of two different processes, we might think of using the difference between the values of p, the proportion of successes for the two processes, i.e. basing our comparison of Experimental and Standard processes on the difference $p_E - p_S$. This would be a poor measure of relative merit, since its significance is not independent of the magnitudes of p_E and p_S. A difference of $0 \cdot 02$ would matter little if p_E and p_S were large, but would be very important if they were small. A more likely measure would seem to be the ratio of the proportions of successes for the two processes, viz. $\dfrac{p_E}{p_S}$, but even here the meaning of the ratio is still dependent on the values of p_E and p_S. Thus, if we had $\dfrac{p_E}{p_S} = \dfrac{2}{1}$, this would indicate a difference $(p_E - p)_S = 0 \cdot 1$ if the value of p_S were $0 \cdot 1$, and a difference $(p_E - p_S)$ of only $0 \cdot 01$ if p_S had the value $0 \cdot 01$. Moreover, the ratio $\dfrac{p_E}{p_S} = \dfrac{2}{1}$ could not even exist if p_S were greater than $0 \cdot 5$, since this would require for p_E a value greater than unity. The best method of comparing the relative merits of the two processes is as the ratio of the odds in favour of a success for the two processes. The odds for the Experimental process are $\dfrac{p_E}{1-p_E}$ and the odds for the Standard process are $\dfrac{p_S}{1-p_S}$, and the *odds ratio* is therefore defined as

$$u = \frac{\left(\dfrac{p_E}{1-p_E}\right)}{\left(\dfrac{p_S}{1-p_S}\right)} = \frac{p_E(1-p_S)}{p_S(1-p_E)}$$

Interchanging the designations 'success' and 'failure', or 'standard' and 'experimental' has the effect of converting the odds ratio from u to $\dfrac{1}{u}$.

The three quantities, h_1, h_2, and s, which characterize a Sequential Plan are essentially arrived at by choosing two points on the Operating Characteristic, viz:.

u_1 the odds ratio below which the standard process is taken as superior;

u_2 the odds ratio above which the experimental process is taken as superior.

α the maximum risk of accepting the experimental process when the standard is superior;

β the maximum risk of accepting the standard process when the experimental is superior.

If, now, we let L represent the probability that sample evidence will lead to a decision in favour of the standard when the *true* odds ratio is u, then the Operating Characteristic will be a graph of L against u, and when $u = u_1$ we shall have $L = 1 - \alpha$, and when $u = u_2$ we shall have $L = \beta$.

To set up the testing chart, we perform the following calculations:

$$h_1 = \frac{\log\left(\frac{1-\alpha}{\beta}\right)}{\log\left(\frac{u_2}{u_1}\right)} \qquad h_2 = \frac{\log\left(\frac{1-\beta}{\alpha}\right)}{\log\left(\frac{u_2}{u_1}\right)}$$

$$s = \frac{\log\left(\frac{1+u_2}{1+u_1}\right)}{\log\left(\frac{u_2}{u_1}\right)}$$

Then letting $n = $ 'total pairs favourable up to date'

and $E = $ 'pairs favourable to experimental process up to date',

we calculate the equations for the control limit lines on our chart as

$$E_2 = sn + h_2 \text{ (upper line)}$$
and $$E_1 = sn - h_1 \text{ (lower line)}$$

The inspection chart then looks as shown in Fig. 76. If at any stage the line E_1 is equalled or fallen short of, we accept the Standard Process. If E_2 is equalled or exceeded, we accept the Experimental Process. Failing either of these decisions, we continue testing.

It will be apparent that, as we only make use of 'pairs favourable', the average amount of data will be less than the average amount of actual testing. To reach a decision, the average number of pairs favourable depends only on the difference between the two processes as measured by the odds ratio, but the amount of actual testing to be expected depends on the actual probabilities of successes of the two processes, p_E and p_S.

Formulae for computing the Operating Characteristic:

(1) When $u = 0$ $\qquad\qquad$ $L = 1$

(2) $\quad$,, $\quad u = u_1$ $\qquad\qquad$ $L = 1 - \alpha$

(3) $\quad$,, $\quad u = \left(\dfrac{s}{1-s}\right)$ $\qquad$ $L = \left(\dfrac{h_2}{h_1 + h_2}\right)$

(4) $\quad$,, $\quad u = u_2$ $\qquad\qquad$ $L = \beta$

(5) $\quad$,, $\quad u = \infty$ $\qquad\qquad$ $L = 0$

$\quad$ (N.B. The sign ∞ is used to denote 'infinitely great'.)

Formulae for Average Sample Number Curve (Average Number of Favourable Pairs):

(1) When $\quad u = 0$ $\qquad\qquad$ $\bar{n} = \dfrac{h_1}{s}$

(2) $\quad$,, $\quad u = u_1$ $\qquad\qquad$ $\bar{n} = \dfrac{h_1 - \alpha(h_1 + h_2)}{s - \left(\dfrac{u_1}{1 + u_1}\right)}$

(3) $\quad$,, $\quad u = \dfrac{s}{1-s}$ $\qquad\quad$ $\bar{n} = \dfrac{h_1 h_2}{s(1-s)}$

(4) $\quad$,, $\quad u = u_2$ $\qquad\qquad$ $\bar{n} = \dfrac{h_2 - \beta(h_1 + h_2)}{\left(\dfrac{u_2}{1 + u_2}\right) - s}$

(5) $\quad$,, $\quad u = \infty$ $\qquad\qquad$ $\bar{n} = \dfrac{h_2}{1-s}$

(N.B. This A.S.N. Curve tells us the average number of pairs favourable required to reach a decision, NOT the average amount of testing.)

The average number of *tests*, $\bar{N}$, required to reach a decision, is obtained by multiplying the average number of favourable pairs required, $\bar{n}$, by the factor

$$k = \frac{1}{p_E + p_S - 2p_E p_S}$$

where p_E and p_S are the probabilities of successes for the experimental and standard processes, respectively. It will normally be the case that we have from experience a good knowledge of the value of p_S for the standard process. In such a case the factor k may be written as a function of u and it becomes possible to calculate $\bar{N}$ for each value of u, using the following formula:

$$k = \frac{1 \times p_S(u-1)}{p_S(1-p_S)(u+1)}$$

On occasion it is possible to change the level of p_S by changing the severity of the test conditions, i.e. to make a change in the absolute effectiveness of both experimental and standard processes, without disturbing their comparative effectiveness. If we do this so as to make $p_S = \frac{1}{2}$ then k will be equal to 2 irrespective of the value of u or p_S, as may readily be seen by writing $p_S = \frac{1}{2}$ in the last formula given for k.

On other occasions a reasonably fair estimate of the odds ratio will be known before the experiment starts. In such cases the value of k may be made a minimum by adjusting the test conditions so that

$$p_S = \frac{1}{1 \times \sqrt{u}}$$

Special provision is also made for performing the tests in *groups* of unequal sizes or equal size, instead of in single pairs at a time, which is not always convenient in practice. Details of the procedures will be found in the literature quoted in the bibliography.

The following is an example of the method quoted in *Sequential Analysis: Applications*, published by the Research Group of Columbia University.

Example. A standard gun is to be compared with an experimental gun on the basis of hits on a designated target under specified conditions.

An odds ratio, u, of three or more is set as the criterion of superiority for the experimental gun, and an odds ratio of $1\cdot2$ or less as the criterion of superiority for the standard gun. That is, if the ratio of hits to misses for the experimental gun is three or more times as large as for the standard gun, it is important to decide in favour of the experimental gun; but if the ratio is $1\cdot2$ or less times as large for the experimental as for the standard gun, it is important to decide in favour of the standard. It is regarded as more serious to decide erroneously in favour of the experimental gun than to make an erroneous decision in favour of the standard. For this reason it is decided to accept a risk $\alpha = 0.02$ of deciding that the experimental is superior when in fact the standard is superior, but a risk of $\beta = 0.05$ of deciding that the standard is superior when in fact the experimental is superior.

We leave the reader to work out this inspection chart for himself. Calculate, first, the values of h_1, h_2, and s, by substituting in the formulae

$$u_1 = 1.2 \qquad \alpha = 0.02 \qquad u_2 = 3 \qquad \beta = 0.05$$

to obtain the results

$$h_1 = 3.247 \qquad h_2 = 4.215 \qquad s = 0.653$$

Then compute the equations of the two control limit lines as

Upper Line $E_2 = sn + h_2 = 0.653n + 4.215$ and
Lower Line $E_1 = sn - h_1 = 0.653n - 3.247$

where $n = $ 'total pairs favourable to date',
The testing chart should then be drawn as shown in Fig. 77.

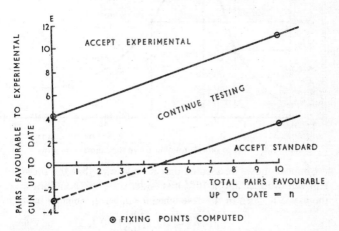

Fig. 77. Sequential Testing Chart computed in the text for choosing between two guns

The next step is to compute the A.S.N. for the average number of favourable pairs required, by substituting in the formulae given to obtain

When $u = 0$ $\bar{n} = \dfrac{h_1}{s} = 5$

  ,, $u = u_1 = 1\cdot2$ $\bar{n} = \dfrac{h_1 - \alpha(h_1 + h_2)}{s - \left(\dfrac{u_1}{1 + u_1}\right)} = 29$

  ,, $u = \dfrac{s}{1 - s} = 1\cdot9$ $\bar{n} = \dfrac{h_1 h_2}{s(1 - s)} = 60$

  ,, $u = u_2 = 3$ $\bar{n} = \dfrac{h_2 - \beta(h_1 + h_2)}{\left(\dfrac{u_2}{1 + u_2}\right) - s} = 40$

  ,, $u = \infty$ $\bar{n} = \dfrac{h_2}{1 - s} = 12$

The A.S.N. Curve may then be plotted as in Fig. 78.

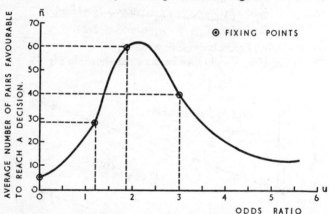

Fig. 78. Average sample number curve for example on guns

Suppose, now, we assume that it be known that the standard gun will produce about 10% hits under the given conditions, i.e. the $p_S = 0\cdot1$. Then in the case when $u = u_1 = 1\cdot2$, we shall have:

$$\frac{p_E}{1 - p_E} = u\left(\frac{p_S}{1 - p_S}\right) = 1\cdot2\left(\frac{0\cdot1}{0\cdot9}\right) = 0\cdot1333$$

from which we find $p_E = 0\cdot1176$

We then find

$$k = \frac{1}{p_E + p_S - 2p_E p_S} = 5 \cdot 15$$

and so learn that when $u = 1 \cdot 2$ the average number of trials $\bar{N} = 148$.

In similar manner, for $u = 3$, we find the average number of trials as $\bar{N} = 132$.

The Operating Characteristic, which tells us the probability of deciding in favour of the standard process when u has different values, is found by substituting in the formulae given. Thus:

When	$u = 0$	$L = 1$
,,	$u = u_1 = 1 \cdot 2$	$L = 1 - \alpha = 1 - 0 \cdot 02 = 0 \cdot 98$
,,	$u = \dfrac{s}{1-s} = 1 \cdot 877$	$L = \dfrac{h_2}{h_1 + h_2} = 0 \cdot 565$
,,	$u = u_2 = 3$	$L = \beta = 0 \cdot 05$
,,	$u = \infty$	$L = 0$

The Operating Characteristic may then be plotted as shown in Fig. 79.

In the two cases so far considered we have been dealing with inspection by dichotomy, that is on an 'O.K.–defective' basis. But the sequential technique is also applicable to cases where we make actual measurements on the articles tested. A common type of problem is where we wish to know whether a specified standard is exceeded or fallen short of. Thus, for example, a firm purchasing electrical condensers from an outside supplier may wish to satisfy themselves that the average value for the loss angle of the condensers did not exceed a specified value. Alternatively, if the firm were purchasing valves they might wish to be sure that the average life was not less than a specified value. The reader will observe that we are concerned in such cases with a one-sided condition. We do not care how much smaller the loss angle is than the specified value, nor how much longer the life of the valves than the specified value. Let it be supposed that in a case of this sort we have a reasonable knowledge of the standard deviation likely to be found in the product offered for acceptance. Then on the further assumption that the distribution of the measured quantity is reasonably approximated by the Normal or Gaussian

Distribution, we can set up a sequential testing scheme in the following manner.

As always in sampling inspection, we shall have to face a double risk: accepting a lot which ought properly to be rejected and rejecting a lot which should be accepted. Having stated what risks we are prepared to take, a sequential scheme can be drawn up which will do our inspection in the most economic fashion. As in

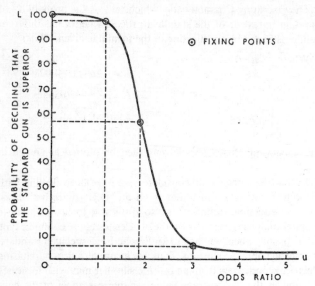

Fig. 79. Operating characteristic for sequential testing scheme computed in the text for example on guns (Probability quoted as percentage)

all sequential schemes, the sample size required to make a decision on a given lot will not be known beforehand.

We lay down two values for the average of the quantity to be measured corresponding to unacceptable quality, m_1, and acceptable quality, m_2. We denote the risk of accepting a batch when the quality has the average value m_1 by α, and the risk of rejecting a batch of average quality m_2 by β. The sequential scheme is completely determined by the four quantities m_1, α, m_2, β.

Let us assume that m_1 is the smaller quantity, and that the standard deviation will be some value σ. Call the value recorded on a given item inspected x, and let n denote the number of observations. We may then denote the sum of the values found in the first n observations by Σx.

The first step in this type of problem is to get an idea of the amount of inspection likely to be incurred by a given scheme. To do this we calculate $a = 2\cdot3 \log\left(\dfrac{1-\beta}{\alpha}\right)$ and $b = 2\cdot3 \log\left(\dfrac{1-\alpha}{\beta}\right)$. Then the average sample size $\bar{n}$ when the average value of the measured variable in the batch is at the level m_1 is given by

$$\bar{n} = \frac{(1-\alpha)\,b - \alpha a}{\dfrac{(m_2 - m_1)^2}{2\sigma^2}}$$

And the average sample size when the average value of the measured variable is at the level m_2 is given by

$$\bar{n} = \frac{(1-\beta)\,a - \beta b}{\dfrac{(m_2 - m_1)^2}{2\sigma^2}}$$

We adjust m_1, m_2, α, and β until the amount of inspection likely to be required, as indicated by the above check calculations, seems reasonable.

The next step is to calculate our three basic quantities, h_1, h_2, and s, which tell us how to draw our inspection chart. They are found as:

$$h_1 = \frac{b\sigma^2}{m_2 - m_1} \qquad\qquad h_2 = \frac{a\sigma^2}{m_2 - m_1}$$

$$s = \frac{m_1 + m_2}{2}$$

The equations to the control limit lines on our inspection chart are then:

Upper Line $\quad \Sigma x = sn + h_2$
Lower Line $\quad \Sigma x = sn - h_1$

and the inspection chart is drawn up as indicated in Fig. 80. The reader will note that the criterion in this test is the *sum* of the values obtained – not their average.

Operating Characteristic and Average Sample Number Curves may be drawn for this case.

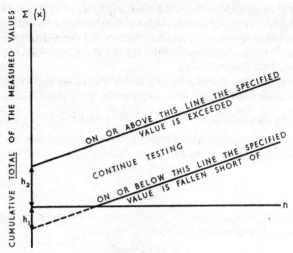

Fig. 80. Sequential Testing Chart for testing whether the average value of some numerical characteristic exceeds or falls short of a specified value

Operating Characteristic. The probability of accepting the lot, L, when the average value of the measured variable for the lot is at the level m is given by

$$L = \frac{e^p - 1}{e^q - 1}$$

where e is the base of the Natural logarithms ($e = 2 \cdot 718$) and $p = h_1 k$ and $q = (h_1 + h_2)k$, the value of k being given by the equation $k = \frac{2(s - m)}{\sigma^2}$ and s, as we have already noted, has the value $\frac{m_1 + m_2}{2}$. When $m = s$, this formula for L becomes indeterminate, having the value $\frac{0}{0}$, but it may be shown that the value of L is then $\frac{h_1}{h_1 + h_2}$. By applying the above formula for L, the O.C. is easily computed.

Average Sample Number Curve. Points for this curve may easily be computed using the formula:

$$\bar{n} = \frac{L(h_1 + h_2) - h_1}{m - s}$$

where L is the probability of accepting a lot whose average value is m, as computed for the O.C. above. When $m = s$, it may be shown that $\bar{n} = \dfrac{h_1 h_2}{\sigma^2}$. The reader will find in the questions at the end of this chapter an example of this type for him to work for himself.

There are occasions when a departure *either way* from the specified average value is equally undesirable, as, for example, when a rubber is desired to have a certain modulus of elasticity, or a solution a specified viscosity or specific gravity. Sequential schemes similar to those already outlined have been designed for such cases. Yet again, we may be more concerned with uniformity than with the average value, i.e. we shall want to be sure that the standard deviation for the distribution of the measured quantity shall not exceed a certain value. Such a case has already been quoted, namely the life of street lamps. A different case is illustrated in shrinkage testing of hosiery. Different testing procedures not only differ in the figure they yield for the average percent shrinkage, but also vary very considerably in the standard deviation of the results obtained. The difference is inherent in the testing method. Clearly, a test that gives uniform results has something to be said in its favour as against a test which gives less consistent results. In hosiery testing, one test specification is used in England and another in America. They differ considerably in assessing shrinkage. Clearly for exporters and importers it is desirable that comparable tests be used by them both.

We have outlined in this chapter some of the ways in which the statistician, by applying the mathematical theory of probability, introduces maximum economy into sampling inspection – without needlessly sacrificing safety. We have shown how he not only gives us a scheme but also tells us how that scheme may be expected to operate as the stresses to which it is subjected vary. We are not given a pig in a poke or a blind guess – but a scientific system to do the particular job required. There are of course other schemes which it is not possible to include in this book. Simon's Grand Lot Schemes, for example, where we use our experience of a supplier to adjust the amount of inspection done on consignments of goods received – treating him with confidence so long as he deserves it, and putting him on probation when he falls from grace, until such time as he proves once more that he may be trusted with a lighter inspection.

At this point we shall be taking our leave of industrial inspection. Before we do so, let us reiterate that in our belief the inspector's main tools are not micrometers and microscopes, but statistical techniques to which all the rest are subservient, in the inspector's real job of stepping up and maintaining quality in the manufacturing organization. It would be a very great step forward if heads of inspection departments who may be too old or too busy to take a course in the statistical principles of inspection themselves would encourage those who are to succeed them to do so. These are new techniques, and in the drive to maintain a larger export market than ever before in our history we cannot afford to ignore applications of mathematics and science which other countries like America are so quick to introduce. In the mathematical field this country has done more than its share of pioneering in the modern statistics. The results are practical. Let them be practised.

NOW SEE IF YOU CAN DESIGN SAMPLING SCHEMES

1. It is desired to set up a sampling scheme to cover the case where a supplier whose Process Average Percent Defective is known from experience to be 2% is sending in batches of 1,000 items at a time. It is considered that the Consumer Risk should be set at 10% for a Lot Tolerance Percent Defective of 4% (i.e. 90% of batches containing 4% defective should fail to pass the sampling test). Failure to pass the sampling test would entail 100% inspection of the remainder of the batch. Design the most economic single sampling scheme to give this degree of protection.

2. Plot the Operating Characteristic for your scheme and the Average Outgoing Quality Curve.

3. Consult Fig. 69 to find a Double Sampling Scheme for a Lot Tolerance Percent Defective of 2% for a supplier whose Process Average Percent Defective is known from experience to be 0·7%, assuming the goods delivered in batches of 550 items. What is the A.O.Q.L. for the scheme?

4. Consult Fig. 70 to find a Double Sampling Scheme for the case of a supplier whose Process Average is known to be $1 \cdot 1\%$ if the goods are delivered in batches of 500 and the consumer wishes to be assured that in the long run the product accepted after inspection will not contain more than $1 \cdot 5\%$ ($=$A.O.Q.L.).

5. From long experience it is estimated that goods from a particular supplier contain 2% defectives, and this is considered a satisfactory performance for the case in question. Design a quality control chart for percentage defective based on the assumption that the consignment will contain 400 items each.

6. Design a sequential sampling scheme to cover the following case. 2% defective is considered acceptable quality and the risk of rejecting a batch as good as this is to be $p=0 \cdot 1$. A batch of 5% defectives is considered so bad that the probability of its being accepted is to be only $p=0 \cdot 1$. Plot the Operating Characteristic, Outgoing Quality Curve (so getting the A.O.Q.L. of the scheme) and the Average Sample Number Curve of the Scheme.

7. A wholesaling firm does not consider it economic to do business with retailers more than 25 miles from the depot unless the weekly sales to be expected reach 40 dozen of the product in question. The standard deviation is known very roughly from experience to be of the order of 10 dozen. If the sales are to be of the order of 35 dozen a week, the wholesaler only wants a 10% chance ($p=0 \cdot 1$) of signing a contract for deliveries. On the other hand, if the sales will be of the order of 50 dozen a week then the wholesaler only wishes to run a 10% risk of refusing to enter into a contract. Deliveries are to be made for a trial period. Set up a sequential testing scheme by which the wholesaler might make his decision with the minimum expected delay for the degree of assurance he is asking. Plot the Operating Characteristic and the Average Sample Number Curve for the scheme you design.

13

How to be a Good Judge – Tests of Significance

'Omnis perfectio in hac vita quandam imperfectionem sibi
habet annexam: et omnis speculatio nostra quadam caligine
non caret.' THOMAS À KEMPIS

In the previous chapter we considered the type of problem where
we have to decide on sample evidence which – if either – of two products is the superior. It was assumed that sampling could be continued more or less indefinitely on a sequential basis until a
decision could be made with the risks of errors in judgement held
to predetermined levels. For a given degree of certainty, the
average amount of inspection required to reach a decision will
increase as the difference in quality between the two populations
from which the two samples are drawn gets smaller. But even with
extremely small differences between the populations we can make
the distinction to any required degree of certainty by sampling,
provided only that we are prepared – and able – to let the sampling continue long enough. The world of fact being a world of
limitations, however, particularly in the sense that life is short
and action often imperative at a level far short of certainty, we are
frequently compelled to make the best judgement possible with
the evidence at our disposal. By this we do not necessarily mean
that a decision one way or the other must always be made, for
even in the most pressing case there will be the possibility that
anything more than a blind guess is impossible. On such occasions
we must dig in our heels and refuse to be rushed into an un-
warranted pronouncement. Yet, often, we shall have to make
decisions and bury our mistakes. It is perhaps less fair to make
this jibe about burying mistakes against the doctor than against
the man of affairs and the engineer, who make mistakes no less
frequently than the medical man. Many of their decisions an-
nounced with a flourish of trumpets are mistakes – luckily, for the
most part, about matters short of life and death.

In everyday life we are constantly making judgements on the
basis of the evidence from small samples. Not only so, but there is

something wonderfully satisfying in making snap judgements with an air of omniscience which provokes the sense of worship and admiration in subordinates. When we prove lucky we are inclined to underline the fact with 'I knew in my bones, somehow' – for all the world as if we were possessed of a special grace of insight from on high. When the event proves us wrong, we keep a discreet silence. The fact is: it is all largely luck – and, fortunately, it rarely matters whether we are right or wrong. But this business of snap judgements on *prima facie* evidence is an insidious habit which we all too easily carry over into matters where it *does* matter whether we are right or wrong. The evidence of small samples, as we have seen, can be very treacherous, and inspired guesses are stupid in such circumstances, for even should they prove correct we are morally to blame for having trusted to guesswork instead of careful judgement.

The research worker, following up a bright idea, will often get small sample evidence which favours his hunch. A sensible and cautious man will at once try to put bias out of court by considering the possibility of the apparent value of his hunch being due to pure chance. Suppose he were asking whether a new process he had thought of were better than the existing process. Then he might sensibly adopt what the statistician calls a *Null Hypothesis*, i.e. he would assume that there was no real significant difference between his pet process and the standard. He would assume, provisionally, that the sample results obtained by his new process might well have come from the same population as results obtained by the standard process. The position then would be that his pet process had produced a sample of above average quality. His next step would be to calculate the probability that the standard process would give a sample as good as that obtained by the new process. If it proved that the chance of the standard process giving so good a sample were extremely low, then, although his sample were small, he would be justified in rejecting the Null Hypothesis, on the grounds that it seemed a very unlikely explanation. It would then be fair – and unbiased – to conclude that his new process could be accepted as having a real superiority to the standard process. On the other hand, if it proved that such a sample might arise with fair frequency from the standard

8

process, it would be rash or dishonest to claim the new process as superior to the standard process.

When we get a result which is very unlikely to have arisen by chance we say that the result is *statistically significant*. By this we mean simply that it would be rather fantastic to ascribe it to chance, that the difference must, in all common sense, be accepted as a real difference. Since the judgement is based on probability, falling short of absolute certainty, we indicate our degree of confidence in the reality of the difference by describing it as 'Probably Significant' or 'Significant' or 'Highly Significant' depending on the probability level associated with our judgement. Thus a result that would only arise in one trial in twenty on the basis of pure chance we should describe as 'Probably Significant'. A result that would arise on the basis of pure chance only once in a hundred trials we should describe as 'Significant'. A result that would arise by chance only once in a thousand trials we should describe as 'Highly Significant', and so on. The proper thing to do, of course, is not simply to use words of this kind but to quote the level of probability, $p = 0.05$, $p = 0.01$, or $p = 0.001$. When the results have to be assessed by people unversed in probability theory, say straight out in plain English: 'This result could arise by chance once in twenty trials', or whatever it is. There is no value in technical jargon. It is irritating to those who do not understand it, and is as likely to produce a bad effect as a good one.

What practical points arise out of all this? In the first place there can never be any question, in practice, of making a decision *purely* on the basis of a statistical significance test. Practical considerations must always be paramount. We must never lose sight of commonsense and all those other relevant factors which cannot possibly be taken care of statistically. An engineer doing a statistical test must remain an engineer, an economist must remain an economist, a pharmacologist must remain a pharmacologist. Practical statistics is only one tool among many. The importance of non-statistical considerations will be apparent if we consider a hypothetical case. Suppose I did a fancy bit of research and found that my new process gave results which were highly significant, $p = 0.001$, i.e. there was only one chance in a thousand of the result arising by chance. I am naturally very pleased. But there are a lot of matters to be considered before I should be justified in putting the new process forward to replace the standard process. Firstly, the high statistical significance relates only to the *reality* of the difference between my process and the standard. Now a very real difference may yet be very small. Atoms are no less real because they are invisible to the unaided eye. I should have to show not only that my process is statistically significant, but also that the difference is of practical importance in magnitude. How great the difference will have to be in this respect will depend on how costly and how disturbing a change-over in process will be. There is a lot of bunk talked about large companies suppressing the practical use of new developments and inventions. It would be possible only in a lunatic asylum for every invention to be put straight into production just because it proved a little better than what was already being done. Economically, we must wait until the standard process has had its run; that is, until newer methods are so superior that the changeover can be made without punishing the customer with a savage rise in price for an incommensurate improvement in what he buys. The inventor is only one of many people with a say in how business shall be run. If we could start from scratch, we could have a much better telephone system than we have. But total scrapping is too fantastic to consider. We sensibly wait for growth rather than shout for revolution. Thus, the choice of significance levels involves taking into account not only our degree of certainty but also the question of economic and practical feasibility. Logically, we have first to establish the reality of the difference, and then to estimate its magnitude and practical importance.

The reader should be clear that there can be no possibility of attaining absolute certainty in any statistical test of significance. We shall always have the two risks of sampling, viz. deciding that a real difference exists when in fact there is none; or deciding that no difference really exists when it does. Using the Null Hypothesis, if the result proves non-significant it is equivalent to a verdict of 'not proven' – we are still open to consider further evidence which may be offered. We work on the principle that what is inherently unlikely is not likely to have happened to us on the basis of chance. We argue, in fact, that the 'exception proves the rule', in the original meaning of the word prove, i.e. tests the validity of the rule.

There exists a great variety of tests of significance in statistical method. In this book we shall only be able to consider some of the more commonly used tests. One of these, the χ^2 test, will be separately considered in a special chapter. Others, not dealt with here, will be introduced more appropriately in various chapters where the need for them arises naturally, e.g. tests of the significance of correlation coefficients, of ranking, and so forth.

A result of fundamental importance in the theory of significance testing is the following.

The variance of the sum or difference of two independent* random variables is equal to the sum of their variances.

Now we already know that the variance of the average of samples of n items drawn from a population whose standard deviation is equal to σ is given by $\dfrac{\sigma^2}{n}$ (it will be remembered that the standard deviation is the square root of the variance). If, then, we have a sample of n_1 items drawn from a population whose standard deviation is σ_1 and a sample of n_2 items drawn from a population whose standard deviation is σ_2, the variance for the distribution of the difference of sample means such as $\bar{x}_1$ and $\bar{x}_2$ will be given by

$$\text{Var}\,(\bar{x}_1 - \bar{x}_2) = \frac{\sigma_1^2}{n_1} + \frac{\sigma_2^2}{n_2}$$

Since we know that departures greater than two standard deviations occur relatively rarely (of the order of once in twenty trials on the basis of random sampling), it is apparent that we have here a means of testing the statistical significance of the difference between sample means. The standard deviation for the distribution of sample means is usually referred to as the *standard error of the difference*, and we regard a difference of more than two standard errors between the sample means as probably significant, i.e. not very likely to have arisen by chance and therefore suggestive of a real difference in the mean values of the two populations from which the samples were respectively drawn. A difference of three

---

* Provided the variables are not correlated.

or more standard errors is regarded as definitely significant, the associated probability being of the order of less than one-half of one per cent that so great a difference should arise by chance in random sampling.

Example. In the *Physique of Young Males*, by W. J. Martin, previously referred to, we find that the average chest girth in 74,459 males classed as Grade I at medical inspection for military service was 35·8 inches with a standard deviation for the group of 1·94 inch. For 2,146 males classified as Grade IV the average girth was 34·8 inches with a standard deviation for the group of 2·01 inches. Is there a significant difference in chest girth between the two Grades?

We have

$$n_1 = 74,459 \qquad \bar{x}_1 = 35·8 \qquad \sigma_1 = 1·94 \qquad \therefore \sigma_1^2 = 3·764$$
$$n_2 = 2,146 \qquad \bar{x}_2 = 34·8 \qquad \sigma_2 = 2·01 \qquad \therefore \sigma_2^2 = 4·040$$

The difference between the sample means is

$$\bar{x}_1 - \bar{x}_2 = 35·8 - 34·8 = 1·0 \text{ inch}$$

Also
$$\text{Var}\,(\bar{x}_1 - \bar{x}_2) = \frac{\sigma_1^2}{n_1} + \frac{\sigma_2^2}{n_2} = \frac{3·764}{74,459} + \frac{4·040}{2,146}$$
$$= 0·00005 + 0·00187 = 0·00192$$

The standard error of the difference is the square root of the variance of the difference,

i.e. $\qquad$ Std. Error of Diff. $= \sqrt{0·00192} = 0·044$

Hence, the observed difference between the sample means, 1 inch, although not large, is very highly significant indeed, being of the order of more than twenty times its standard error.

Consider, now, a similar type of problem where, instead of having actual measured quantities, we have the Binomial type of distribution. To make the case concrete let us suppose that we were trying to assess the effectiveness of some particular inoculation. We shall suppose that n_1 persons received the inoculation and of these x_1 subsequently developed the infection which the inoculation was supposed to guard against, and that a further group of n_2 persons, of whom x_2 were infected, did not receive the inoculation. The problem will then be to try to assess the effectiveness of the inoculation by comparing the proportion of inoculated persons who were infected, $\dfrac{x_1}{n_1}$, with the proportion of those not inoculated who were infected, $\dfrac{x_2}{n_2}$.

It would be the part of wisdom in such a matter to make the Null Hypothesis that the inoculation was without effect, and then see how likely the observed difference was to arise by chance in random sampling. On our Null Hypothesis there is no reason why we should not pool the two sample results together, so as to get a better estimate of the proportion of persons likely to be infected, assuming the inoculation to be neither good nor bad. This estimate for the proportion infected would then be

$$p = \frac{x_1 + x_2}{n_1 + n_2} = \frac{\text{total infected}}{\text{total exposed to infection}}$$

This value, p, is of course the *probability* that an exposed person will be infected. The probability that an exposed person will *not* be infected is $q = 1 - p$. Now we know that the standard deviation for a Binomial *frequency* distribution for samples of n items is given by $\sqrt{pqn}$. Hence, the standard deviation for the Binomial *probability* distribution will be $\sqrt{pq}$ (n being put equal to unity). The variance for the distribution of proportion defective in a sample of n items will therefore be $\dfrac{pq}{n}$. It follows that the variance for the difference in proportion defective in two samples of n_1 and n_2 items both drawn from a population whose proportion infected is equal to p will be given by

$$\text{Var. (Diff. in proportions)} = \frac{pq}{n_1} + \frac{pq}{n_2}$$

Evidently then the standard error of the difference will be

$$\sigma_w = \sqrt{\frac{pq}{n_1} + \frac{pq}{n_2}}$$

and it is against this standard error that we shall have to judge the significance of the observed difference in proportions

$$w = \left| \frac{x_1}{n_1} - \frac{x_2}{n_2} \right|$$

The vertical lines enclosing the difference in proportions are meant to indicate that we consider only the absolute value of the difference, ignoring whether it is positive or negative for the purpose of establishing significance (though not, of course, in considering the practical meaning of the difference).

Example. The figures for antitoxin treatment in the City of Toronto Hospital for the first decade of this century in the treatment of diphtheria were:

	Cases	Deaths
Antitoxin treatment	228	37
Ordinary treatment	337	28

Are we to conclude that death was significantly more frequent in the group treated by antitoxin?

Adopting the Null Hypothesis that the antitoxin was without effect, we calculate the proportion of deaths for the combined samples as

$$p = \frac{\text{total deaths}}{\text{total cases}} = \frac{65}{565} = 0 \cdot 115$$

The standard error of the difference in proportions between two samples of $n_1 = 228$ and $n_2 = 337$ cases will then be

$$\sigma_w = \sqrt{pq\left(\frac{1}{n_1} + \frac{1}{n_2}\right)} = \sqrt{0 \cdot 115 \times 0 \cdot 885(\tfrac{1}{228} + \tfrac{1}{337})}$$
$$= \sqrt{0 \cdot 115 \times 0 \cdot 885 \times 0 \cdot 00736} = \underline{0 \cdot 027}$$

The proportion of deaths in the group receiving antitoxin treatment was

$$\tfrac{37}{228} = 0 \cdot 163$$

and among those who received ordinary treatment was

$$\tfrac{28}{337} = 0 \cdot 083$$

Hence the difference in proportions was $0 \cdot 163 - 0 \cdot 083 = 0 \cdot 08$. The observed difference in proportions is thus extremely significant indeed, being equal to *three* standard errors. The chance of so great a difference is infinitesimally small on the basis of pure chance, and we are bound to conclude that antitoxin treatment was undoubtedly positively associated with greater mortality.

At this point we must forget statistics, as such, and start to do some commonsense thinking. Are we *necessarily* to conclude from this evidence that antitoxin treatment was a bad thing? It must at once be conceded that this is the sort of fact which the protagonists of antitoxin treatment are going to keep discreetly quiet about, while those who set their face against this form of treatment on principle will shout it from the housetops. We must not draw general conclusions from particular instances without realizing the inherent dangers of such a proceeding. That is not to say, of course, that such instances may be ignored. The first thing we should ask is whether the two groups were exposed to the same risk. Was it perhaps the case that those who received the antitoxin treatment were those most seriously ill? In all such cases unless the two groups were exposed to the same risk and had equal treatment in other respects we are not likely to be able to draw any valid conclusion – however significant the difference in mortality rate may be. The statistical significance will in such cases merely reflect the unequal exposure to risk. No statement on the practical significance of the figures is possible until such questions have satisfactorily been answered. Precisely the same precautions have to be observed when the figures favour a particular treatment. It might well be, for example – as Anti-vivisectionists are quick to tell us – that the part of the population which comes forward for immunizations on a voluntary basis are the very group which are exposed to the lesser risk by virtue of the fact that they are more educated, better fed, better clothed, and better housed. There is no matter fraught with greater pitfalls for the unwary than the making of deductions from medical statistics. It is the exception rather than the rule for the groups being compared to be identical in other material respects than the one under consideration. Every statistician who has ever played about with medical statistics knows how frequently he is thwarted because the groups offered for comparison are not strictly – or even at all – comparable. Our faith in treatments of the immunization and antitoxin variety is very largely based on experiments on animals – and it is not infrequently questionable how far such conclusions are completely referable to human beings. Undoubtedly it is true that the greatest medical advance in the fight against infectious diseases has been the improved standard of living. As overcrowding is eliminated, as sewage is disposed of in more civilized fashion, as soap is plentifully used, and as children are fed and protected from exploitation as cheap labour, we may well not be surprised that infectious disease vanishes from our midst whether we have prophylactic treatment or not. The sanitary inspector and dustman play perhaps an even more vital part in society than the medical man – on considerably less pay and with considerably less glamour. Those who oppose prophylactic treatment, arguing that our aim should be improvement of the standard of living, argue in a good cause from a social point of view, but the doctor must consider the individual who cannot help his poor environment and who needs protection from it – if such protection is to be found.

The problem of significant differences in proportions may also be tackled by the χ^2 test, dealt with in Chapter 15.

Of particular importance are problems where we have small samples and wish to make valid significance tests as to differences in dispersion or differences in mean value. Development of an adequate theory to deal with such cases is the work of the present century, being associated especially with the names of W. S. Gosset, who published his researches under the pseudonym 'Student', and of R. A. Fisher. Readers desirous of a detailed knowledge of the mathematical foundations of what is to follow must refer to textbooks referred to in the bibliography. Here we can only indicate the analytical methods which should be adopted.

We have already mentioned that, while the mean value of a sample of n items is an unbiased estimate of the mean value in the population from which the sample is drawn, the standard deviation is biased, tending to underestimate the population value. This bias is especially marked in small samples. It may be shown that the expected value of the variance in a sample of n items, s^2, is related to the population variance, σ^2, in accordance with the equation

$$E(s^2) = \left(\frac{n-1}{n}\right)\sigma^2$$

where the symbol $E(s^2)$ denotes the expected value for the variance of the sample. The factor $\left(\dfrac{n-1}{n}\right)$ is referred to as *Bessel's correction*. It will be necessary, from this point onwards, for the reader to make a clear distinction in his mind between the following three terms:

Population variance, denoted by the symbol σ^2;

Sample variance, denoted by s^2; and

Best estimate of the population variance, denoted by the symbol $\hat{\sigma}^2$, which is obtained from the sample variance, s^2, by applying Bessel's correction, thus

$$\hat{\sigma}^2 = \left(\frac{n}{n-1}\right)s^2$$

(The circumflex accent over any symbol is always used to denote that the quantity is a 'best estimate' of some parameter.) The real reason why the sample variance tends to underestimate the true variance in the population is that the sum of the squares of the deviations of the values in a sample has a minimum value when the deviations are taken as deviations about the sample mean. In general, the sample mean will not coincide exactly with the true population mean, so that the sum of the squares of the deviations of the sample values from the population mean will normally be greater than the sum of the squares of the deviations measured from the sample mean. Bessel's correction makes an adjustment for the discrepancy which may be expected to arise in samples of given numbers of items. The reader will observe that, as n increases, Bessel's correction $\left(\dfrac{n}{n-1}\right)$ approaches closer and closer to unity, so that when n is large it becomes a matter of trivial importance whether the correction is applied or not.

As an extension to the above it may be shown that if we have several independent samples drawn from the same population, whose variance is σ^2, the samples being of $n_1, n_2, n_3, \ldots n_k$ items respectively which have sample variances $s_1^2, s_2^2, s_3^2, \ldots s_k^2$, then the best estimate of the population variance which we can make by pooling all the sample information is

$$\hat{\sigma}^2 = \frac{T}{N-k}$$

where $\qquad T = n_1 s_1^2 + n_2 s_2^2 + n_3 s_3^2 + \ldots + n_k s_k^2$

and $\qquad N = n_1 + n_2 + n_3 + \ldots + n_k$

k being the number of samples.

Example. Four samples drawn from the same parent population had the following numbers of items and gave the stated sample variances. Make a best estimate of the variance of the parent population.

$$n_1 = 7 \qquad s_1^2 = 24 \qquad n_2 = 10 \qquad s_2^2 = 37$$
$$n_3 = 13 \qquad s_3^2 = 27 \qquad n_4 = 22 \qquad s_4^2 = 32$$

We calculate $\qquad T = n_1 s_1^2 + n_2 s_2^2 + n_3 s_3^2 + n_4 s_4^2$
$$= 168 + 370 + 351 + 704 = 1,593$$

and $\qquad N = n_1 + n_2 + n_3 + n_4$
$$= 7 + 10 + 13 + 22 = 52$$

We then have the best estimate of the population variance as

$$\hat{\sigma}^2 = \frac{T}{N-4} = \frac{1593}{48} = 33$$

The divisor $(N - k)$ is usually referred to as the number of *degrees of freedom* – an important term which the reader will do well to note carefully, as he will hear a great deal of it a little later.

'STUDENT'S' t DISTRIBUTION

If we wish to test the hypothesis that a sample whose mean value is $\bar{x}$ could have come from a population whose mean value is $\bar{X}$ and whose standard deviation is σ, we calculate the ratio

$$t = \frac{\text{Error in Mean}}{\text{Standard Error of Mean}} = \frac{|\bar{X} - \bar{x}|}{\left(\dfrac{\sigma}{\sqrt{n}}\right)} = \frac{|\bar{X} - \bar{x}|\sqrt{n}}{\sigma}$$

which is called Student's t. The vertical lines enclosing the difference between the means of the sample and the population $|\bar{X} - \bar{x}|$ denote that the difference is to be taken as positive irrespective of whether it is positive or negative. In practice, when we apply this formula, we do not as a rule know the value of σ, and are forced to estimate it from the sample data. If the sample has a standard deviation s, then the best estimate we can make of σ will be $\sigma = s\sqrt{\dfrac{n}{n-1}}$. Writing this best estimate in our formula for Student's t, we get:

$$t = \frac{|\bar{X} - \bar{x}|\sqrt{n-1}}{s}$$

Evidently the larger the discrepancy between the means of sample and population the greater will be the value of t. Now t will have its own probability distribution – any specified value for t being exceeded with a calculable probability. Special tables have been drawn up showing the value t may reach for given probability levels, and so we have a simple method for testing whether any sample mean differs significantly (in the statistical sense) from any proposed hypothetical population mean. To make the approach clear, let us take an example.

Example. Two laboratories carry out independent estimates of fat content for ice-cream made by a certain manufacturer. A sample is taken from each batch, halved, and the separate halves sent to the respective laboratories. The results obtained on 10 batches were as follows:

PERCENTAGE FAT CONTENT IN SAMPLES OF ICE-CREAM

Batch number	1	2	3	4	5	6	7	8	9	10
Laboratory A	7·2	8·5	7·4	3·2	8·9	6·7	9·4	4·6	7·7	6·9
Laboratory B	9·1	8·5	7·9	4·3	8·4	7·7	9·3	6·6	6·8	6·7

The laboratories differ in their assessments. Moreover, it appears that the manufacturer made an ice-cream of varying fat content, both labs agreeing in finding a marked fluctuation. The manufacturer points to the discrepancies between the findings of the two labs, and suggests that the testing is not too reliable. The question arises as to whether the discrepancies between the two laboratories are such that laboratory A tends to return a lower estimate of the fat content than laboratory B.

This problem might well be tackled as follows. It is the difference in estimates on the same batch which is in dispute. Moreover, since there seems to be some agreement about the variation in the manufacturer's fat content from batch to batch, it will be best to conduct the analysis in terms of the discrepancies between the labs on the several batches. We subtract the estimate of laboratory A from the estimate of laboratory B, and obtain the following table.

BETWEEN LABORATORY DISCREPANCIES –
LAB. B MINUS LAB. A

Batch Number	1	2	3	4	6	6	7	8	9	10
Discrepancy	1·9	0·0	0·5	1·1	−0·5	1·0	−0·1	2·0	−0·9	−0·2

The average discrepancy is found by calculation to be $+0.48\%$ fat content. If there were no bias between the labs we should expect that this discrepancy will not differ significantly from zero. Our first step is to calculate the sample variance of the ten discrepancies, using the formula:

$$s^2 = \frac{\Sigma x^2}{n} - \bar{x}^2$$

for which we already know $n = 10$ and $\bar{x} = 0.48$. We get

$s^2 = \frac{1}{10}[(1\cdot9)^2 + (0\cdot5)^2 + (1\cdot1)^2 + \ldots\ldots + (0\cdot9)^2 + (0\cdot2)^2] - (0\cdot48)^2$

i.e. $s^2 = 0.89$; $s = 0.94$

We now apply Bessel's correction to obtain a best estimate of the population standard deviation of the discrepancies:

$$\hat{\sigma} = s\sqrt{\frac{n}{n-1}} = 0.94\sqrt{\tfrac{10}{9}} = 0.99$$

The assumed value of the population mean discrepancy $\bar{X} = 0$.
We now calculate Student's t as:

$$t = \frac{|\bar{X} - \bar{x}|\sqrt{n-1}}{s} \text{ or } \frac{|\bar{X} - \bar{x}|\sqrt{n}}{\sigma}$$

$$= \frac{0.48\sqrt{9}}{0.94} \text{ or } \frac{0.48\sqrt{10}}{0.99}$$

$\underline{t = 1.53}$

The graph shown in Fig. 81 indicates the value of t which will be exceeded by chance (a) only once in twenty trials, (b) only once in a hundred trials, (c) only once in a thousand trials. If the calculated value of t exceeds the value given by the 5% probability level curve for the number of *degrees of freedom* in question, we conclude that the result is probably significant. If the 1% probability level is exceeded, we conclude that the result is definitely

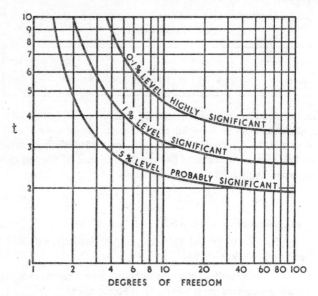

Fig. 81. Graphs of Student's t for 5%, 1%, and 0·1% significance level. If the calculated value for t is greater than the value shown above for the appropriate number of degrees of freedom, the indicated level of significance is reached*

significant, and if the 0·1% probability level is exceeded the difference is regarded as highly significant – in the statistical sense. The number of degrees of freedom, $N - k$, for a single sample of n items will be seen to be equal to 9. Referring to the graph of Student's t we find that the difference between the laboratories is not significant. We conclude that it is reasonable to ascribe it to

* See acknowledgements, p. viii

chance, arising out of experimental error in the test. (By 'experimental error' we do not mean 'mistakes' but the inevitable lack of accuracy to which any experiment is subject.)

The reader will recall that the result 'not significant' from a statistical significance test is not so much a complete acquittal as a verdict of 'not proven'. There may be bias between these labs, but the evidence so far is insufficient to create doubt in the mind of an unbiased observer – as distinct from a suspicious one, such as our manufacturer might conceivably be. With more evidence it might ultimately be that a significant difference could be established. There is obviously some point, therefore, in asking what degree of uncertainty remains in the figure of 0.48% difference found between the labs. This point will be taken up in Chapter 14 when we come to deal with the problem of estimation and confidence limits, as they are called.

Besides the problem where we wish to consider whether a single sample has a mean value differing significantly from some hypothetical value, there is the similar – and in some fields much more common – type where we have to decide whether the difference between the mean values of two samples drawn from different sources is significant of a real difference between the parent sources. Let us take an actual example.

Example. Lea strength tests carried out on samples of two yarns spun to the same count gave the following results:

	Number in sample	Sample mean	Sample variance
Yarn A	9	42	56
Yarn B	4	50	42

The strengths are expressed in pounds. Is the difference in mean strengths significant of a real difference in the mean strengths of the sources from which the samples were drawn?

We have previously investigated the significance of the difference in chest girth of Grade I and Grade IV army candidates, where the samples were very large. In this case the method there used is not valid because of the small size of the present samples. To illustrate the very different result obtained using the refinement of the Student's t distribution, we shall first work out the present problem by the method valid for large samples, and then repeat the analysis using the correct procedure for small samples.

Large sample method (*invalid*). We assume (a) that the sample variance is an unbiased estimate of the population variance and (b) refer the results to the Normal Probability distribution instead of to the distribution for Student's t.

Standard Error of difference of two means is equal to

$$\sigma_w = \sqrt{\tfrac{56}{9} + \tfrac{42}{4}} = \sqrt{16 \cdot 7} = 4 \cdot 08$$

Difference of means $= 50 - 42 = 8$

$$\therefore \quad t = \frac{\text{Difference of Means}}{\text{Standard Error of Difference}} = \frac{8}{4 \cdot 08} = 2$$

Referring this value of t to the Normal Distribution we find that the probability of so great a difference arising by chance is $4 \cdot 5 \%$.

Conclusion. The difference is probably significant.

Small sample method (*valid*). We take account of the bias in small samples, applying the Bessel correction, and refer the resultant ratio to Student's t distribution.

The first step is to make a pooled estimate of the variance – on the Null Hypothesis that the two samples are drawn from populations identical both as to mean and variance (see F test below for important remarks):

$$\hat{\sigma}^2 = \frac{n_1 s_1{}^2 + n_2 s_2{}^2}{n_1 + n_2 - 2} = \frac{9 \times 56 + 4 \times 42}{9 + 4 - 2} = 61$$

$$\therefore \quad \hat{\sigma} = \sqrt{61} = 7 \cdot 8$$

It follows that our best estimate of the standard error for the difference of the means of two samples of this size is

$$\hat{\sigma}_w = \hat{\sigma} \sqrt{\frac{1}{n_1} + \frac{1}{n_2}} = 7 \cdot 8 \sqrt{\tfrac{1}{9} + \tfrac{1}{4}} = 4 \cdot 67$$

The observed difference between the means of the samples is, as already found, equal to 8. We calculate Student's t as:

$$t = \frac{\text{Difference of Means}}{\text{Standard Error of Difference}} = \frac{8}{4 \cdot 67} = 1 \cdot 7$$

The number of degrees of freedom for Student's $t = 9 + 4 - 2 = 11$. Referring the calculated value of t to tables of Student's t, with 11 degrees of freedom, we find that the observed difference could arise by chance in rather more than 10% of trials.

Conclusion. Significance of difference not established.

Comparing the results, the reader will not fail to notice the very marked difference between the two assessments of the probability that the observed difference might arise by chance. Student's t shows a probability twice as great as that obtained in the large sample method that the difference might have occurred by chance. The use of the refinement is therefore imperative.

The reader will have noticed that in testing the significance of the difference of the sample means we not only included in our Null Hypothesis the assumption that the means of the parent population were identical but a further assumption: that the variances of the parent populations were also identical. The reason for this extra assumption is that we pooled the two sample variances to get the best estimate of a population variance which the Student's t test assumes is the same for both populations. This being the case, it will be evident that *before doing Student's t test to investigate the difference between the sample means, we should logically do a prior test to investigate whether the sample variances are sufficiently alike to warrant our assuming that they are independent estimates of the same population variance*. We test the significance of the difference between sample variances by the Variance Ratio test. This test depends mathematically on Fisher's z distribution, an extremely general and fundamental distribution which includes the Normal distribution, the χ^2 distribution, and Student's t distribution as special cases. The Variance Ratio test is often referred to as Snedecor's F test, since Snedecor computed tables for the variance ratio distribution, and named the ratio F, in honour of R. A. Fisher.

Variance Ratio test. The variance ratio is defined as

$$F = \frac{\text{greater estimate of the variance of the population}}{\text{lesser estimate of the variance of the population}}$$

What population? The assumed common parent population postulated by the Null Hypothesis. The estimates are best estimates arrived at by applying Bessel's correction to the sample variances. It is clear that the greater the variance ratio the less likely it is that the Null Hypothesis is a valid one. But it will be no less clear that the magnitude of the ratio alone will not decide the matter. We shall not be surprised if two small samples give a variance ratio appreciably different from the expected value of unity. Large samples, if the Null Hypothesis is true, should give a value of F which differs little from unity. Thus, in our significance test we shall have to consider (a) the calculated value of F and (b) the numbers of items in the two samples whose variances are being compared. Tables have been drawn up showing the value of F which will be exceeded with a given degree of probability for various sample sizes. The number of degrees of freedom for a sample of n items will, according to the rule already given, be equal to $n-1$. The tables are drawn up, for reasons later apparent, in terms of degrees of freedom instead of sample sizes.

The following is an abbreviated version of Snedecor's Table for the Variance Ratio, sufficient to give the reader an idea of how the tables are laid out and how they are made use of.

5% LEVEL OF VARIANCE RATIO*

		Number of degrees of freedom in the greater variance estimate							
		1	2	3	4	5	10	20	∞
Number of degrees of freedom in lesser variance estimate	1	161	200	216	225	230	242	248	254
	2	18·5	19	19·2	19·2	19·3	19·4	19·4	19·5
	3	10·1	9·6	9·3	9·1	9·0	8·8	8·7	8·5
	4	7·7	6·9	6·6	6·4	6·3	6·0	5·8	5·6
	5	6·6	5·8	5·4	5·2	5·0	4·7	4·6	4·4
	10	5·0	4·1	3·7	3·5	3·3	3·0	2·8	2·5
	20	4·3	3·5	3·1	2·9	2·7	2·3	2·1	1·8
	∞	3·8	3·0	2·6	2·4	2·2	1·8	1·6	1·0

* See acknowledgements, p. viii.

1% LEVEL OF VARIANCE RATIO*

		Number of degrees of freedom in the greater variance estimate							
		1	2	3	4	5	10	20	∞
Number of degrees of freedom in lesser variance estimate	1	4,100	5,000	5,400	5,600	5,800	6,000	6,200	6,400
	2	98	99	99	99	99	99	99	99
	3	34	31	29	29	28	27	27	26
	4	21	18	17	16	16	15	14	13
	5	16	13	12	11	11	10	9·6	9·0
	10	10	7·6	6·6	6·0	5·6	4·8	4·4	3·9
	20	8·1	5·8	4·9	4·4	4·1	3·4	2·9	2·4
	∞	6·6	4·6	3·8	3·3	3·0	2·3	1·9	1·0

N.B. The symbol ∞ denotes 'infinitely great', i.e., in practice, 'very large'.

Example. A sample of $n_1 = 11$ items has a standard deviation $s_1 = 5·0$ and a second sample of $n_2 = 6$ items has a standard deviation $s_2 = 8·0$. Do these sample standard deviations differ significantly?

For the first sample we have a sample variance of $5^2 = 25$ based on $11 - 1 = 10$ degrees of freedom. Applying Bessel's correction, $\hat{\sigma}_1^2 = \left(\dfrac{n_1}{n_1 - 1}\right)s_1^2 = (\tfrac{11}{10})25 = 27·5$. In like manner, for the second sample $\hat{\sigma}_2^2 = \left(\dfrac{n_2}{n_2 - 1}\right)s_2^2 = (\tfrac{6}{5})64 = 77$ with $6 - 1 = 5$ d.f.

Hence, the variance ratio:

$$F = \frac{\text{Greater Var. Est.}}{\text{Lesser Var. Est.}} = \frac{77}{27·5} = 2·8$$

The number of degrees of freedom is 5 for the greater variance estimate, 10 for the lesser variance estimate. Entering the tables for the variance ratio with these degrees of freedom, we find

5% level of $F = 3·3$ and 1% level of $F = 5·6$

Since the observed value for F is less than the 5% level, we conclude that the difference between the standard deviations is not significant.

In the case of large samples we can test the significance of a difference in standard deviations by using the straightforward

* See acknowledgements, p. viii.

standard error of a difference method, and the fact that the variance for the distribution of sample standard deviations is $\frac{\sigma^2}{2n}$ (see Chapter 10, page 137), and the fact that the variance of a difference is equal to the sum of the variances.

Example. W. J. Martin, in *The Physique of Young Males* previously quoted, found a mean weight of 136·4 lb. with standard deviation 16·1 lb. for 74,429 males classified as Grade I at medical examination, and a mean weight 129·2 lb. with standard deviation 20·6 lb. for 2,183 males classified as Grade IV. Is the difference in standard deviations significant?

Adopting the Null Hypothesis that the observed difference could have arisen by chance, we calculate a pooled estimate of the assumed common variance.

$$\hat{\sigma}^2 = \frac{n_1 s_1{}^2 + n_2 s_2{}^2}{n_1 + n_2} = \frac{74,429(16·6)^2 + 2,183(20·6)^2}{74,429 + 2,183}$$

(Bessel's correction being ignored in so large samples.) This leads to $\hat{\sigma}^2 = 263$, and the standard error of the difference of standard deviations of samples is

$$\sigma_w = \sqrt{\hat{\sigma}^2 \left(\frac{1}{2n_1} + \frac{1}{2n_2} \right)} = \sqrt{263 \left(\frac{1}{148,858} + \frac{1}{4,366} \right)}$$

$$= \sqrt{263 \times 0·000237} = 0·25$$

The observed difference in standard deviations is $w = 20·6 - 16·1 = 4·5$. Hence, the observed difference is equal to no less than 18 times its standard error, and must be regarded as extremely significant. This result will not surprise the reader, who will have spotted that the extremely puny and the extremely corpulent will not have been allocated to Grade I but most probably to Grade IV.

We shall show later that we may test the significance of the difference between sample averages using the F test instead of the t test, using the technique known as Analysis of Variance (Chapter 19).

NOW SEE IF YOU ARE A GOOD JUDGE

1. Two people are having a chat and you are told the difference in their I.Q. is 90 units. Is it likely that they are a random sample from the population as a whole? Who might they conceivably be (especially as there is someone to tell you the range in I.Q.)? (Take the standard deviation of I.Q. as 13 units.)

2. Fifty children are given a special diet for a certain period and a control group of fifty other children have normal meals. The two groups are of similar background and physique. Their gains in weight are recorded:

Special 7·2 lb. average   Controls 5·7 lb. average

The standard deviation for weight gains may be taken as 2 lb. Is the evidence sufficiently strong for us to assert that the special diet really promotes weight?

3. Taking the standard deviation for pulse rate in adults as 8, would you say a high pulse rate was diagnostic if in a group of fifty people suffering from a certain disease the average pulse rate were 75 as against a normal rate of 70? Supposing this were to prove significant statistically, how significant would it be clinically to the doctor in practice?

4. Two types of aircraft are on the same route and both fly all the year round, so that there is no question of weather affecting the results in such a way as to be indistinguishable from differences between the aircraft. One type develops minor troubles four times in 100 flights, the other nineteen times in 150 flights. Investigate and comment on these data.

5. The important thing about a navigator's watch is not whether it gains or loses but whether it makes a uniform gain or loss regularly. If the rate of gain or loss is consistent, it is easy to allow for. If it is irregular, the watch is useless for the job. The following show the daily losses and gains for two watches. Is one significantly more variable than the other?

WATCH A GAINS

(sec/day)   54   63   49   50   62   54   58   57   60   61

WATCH B LOSSES

(sec/day)   116   108   116   122   112   118   123   114   111   117

14

How to be Precise though Vague – Estimation and Confidence Limits

'There is nothing more frightful than ignorance in action.'
GOETHE

Whenever we take a sample, we do so with the idea of learning something about the population from which the sample is drawn. Provided that the sample is drawn in an unbiased manner we believe that it may be taken as representative of the parent population. But representatives are not all equally authoritative. Spokesmen – even official spokesmen – do not always tell a reliable tale, and it is very necessary in retailing a story secondhand from such a source that we indicate the degree of confidence which may be placed in what the spokesman has said. Just as the journalist tries to emphasize for his readers the difference between rumour and 'usually well informed sources', so too the statistician has to attempt a similar thing.

The degree of confidence which we can rest in estimates of population parameters such as means, standard deviations, proportions, and so on is clearly tied up very closely with the size of the sample taken and with the standard error of the statistic in question. Since the average value of a sample, for example, will in general differ more or less from the true value for the population, we can see that our estimate for the latter should properly be quoted, not as a single figure, but rather as *a range within which we are confident that the value lies*. The reader will at once ask: How confident? Since the answer to this can only be in terms of probability, we see that our answer will have to be in terms of a *range together with an associated probability* which expresses the confidence we have that the value lies within the range.

Given large samples, the problem is easily enough disposed of intuitively. An average, standard deviation, or proportion based on a large sample will be an unbiased estimate – a best estimate, needing no correction of the type of Bessel's correction for the standard deviation of small samples. But, when the samples are small, we have to face not only the possibility of bias but also the fact that the average, standard deviation, or proportion found in the sample may differ quite appreciably from the population parameter it is sought to estimate through the sample. It is evident that there can be no possibility of finding a method of estimation which will guarantee us a close estimate under all conditions. All we can hope for is a method which will be the best possible in the sense that it will have a high probability of being correct in the long run. The formula we use to make our estimate we shall call the Estimator and the value reached by using the formula the Estimate. In general, the accuracy of an estimator increases with n the number of items in the sample data. A good estimator will be unbiased and will converge more and more closely (in the long run) on the true value as the sample size increases. Such estimators are known as *consistent*.

But consistency is not all we can ask of an estimator. In estimating the central tendency of a distribution, we are not confined to using the arithmetic mean; we might just as well use the median. Given a choice of possible estimators, all consistent in the sense just defined, we can see whether there is anything which recommends the choice of one rather than another. The thing which at once suggests itself is the sampling variance of the different estimators, since an estimator with a small sampling variance will be less likely to differ from the true value by a large amount than an estimator whose sampling variance is large. In Chapter 10 we stated that the standard error of the means of samples drawn from a population σ is given by $\frac{\sigma}{\sqrt{n}}$ where n is the number of items in the sample, whereas the standard error of the median is given by $\frac{1 \cdot 25\sigma}{\sqrt{n}}$. There is obvious meaning, therefore, in saying that the mean is a more *efficient* estimator of central tendency than is the median. The formula given for the standard error of the median is strictly true only for large values of n, but it may be shown that even when n is small the efficiency of the mean as against the median still holds. The estimator which has a smaller sampling variance than other estimators is called the *most efficient estimator*, and the efficiency of other estimators is expressed by taking the ratio of the sampling variance of the most efficient estimator to the sampling variance of the estimator in question. For example, since it may be shown that the arithmetic mean is the most efficient estimator of central tendency for Normal distributions, the efficiency of the median as an estimator is given by

$$\text{Efficiency of Median} = \frac{\text{Sampling Var. of Mean}}{\text{Sampling Var. of Median}}$$

$$= \frac{\left(\dfrac{\sigma^2}{n}\right)}{\left(\dfrac{1\cdot25^2\sigma^2}{n}\right)} = \frac{1}{1\cdot25^2} = 0\cdot64$$

What is the practical significance of this? It means that if we use the mean as our estimator, our sample need only be 64% as large as the sample required using the median as estimator, in order to have the same sampling variance. Putting it the other way round: if we decide to use the median as estimator, it is equivalent to throwing away 36% of our data from the point of view of accuracy of estimation. Given a very large set of data we might well be only too happy to throw some of them away in order to save ourselves the trouble of calculating the mean. Interpolation of the median from a grouped frequency table might give us ample accuracy for our purpose. The search for most efficient estimators is the intriguing task of the mathematical statistician and cannot be entered into here in detail.

We now come to the more specific part of our problem, namely, the specification of the interval within which the true value we are estimating may be said to lie with a specified probability. We shall not enter here into the differentiation between *Fiducial Limits* and *Confidence Intervals*, the former associated with the name of R. A. Fisher and the latter with that of E. S. Pearson. There are matters of great interest in the arguments of the two schools of thought on the question of statistical inference. M. G. Kendall in the Preface of Volume II of his *Advanced Statistics* says: 'Some day I hope to show that this disagreement is more apparent than real, and that all the existing theories of inference in probability differ essentially only in matters of taste in the choice of postulates'. Such discussions are mainly matters for the professional statistician and would be out of place in the present introductory sketch of the subject. There are cases where the two theories lead to different results. It is most likely that in such cases the two methods are asking and answering questions that are different, but difficult to distinguish. The reader must be satisfied that in the majority of practical cases the results are identical.

We shall now deal with the method for getting what we shall call (*pace* both schools of thought!) *confidence intervals*, using this as a convenient term for our present purpose, without reference to the family squabbles of the statistical logicians. Let us take, first of all, the case of large samples. The simplest method is to take the unbiased estimate of the parameter, as given by our sample, and say that the population value lies within one standard error fairly probably, or within two standard errors probably, or within three standard errors very probably. One or two examples will suffice to illustrate.

Example. A sample of 400 items yields a mean $\bar{x} = 47$ with standard deviation $s = 7$. Find confidence intervals for the population mean.

With so large a sample the sample standard deviation may be taken as the standard deviation of the population. The standard error of the mean of samples of n items is $\frac{\sigma}{\sqrt{n}}$, and we may regard this as our *standard error of estimate*. In this case

$$\frac{\sigma}{\sqrt{n}} = \frac{7}{\sqrt{400}} = 0 \cdot 35.$$

Referring the distribution to the Normal scale, the probability of a deviation of up to one standard deviation either way is 68%. We may therefore say that the population mean lies in the range 47 plus or minus 0·35, i.e. in the range 46·65 to 47·35, and express our confidence in this claim by saying that in a long series of estimates of this type, if we were to use exactly the same kind of argument, we should expect to be correct 68% of the time.

If it were suggested that this was not a very high proportion of successes, we could modify our claim by stating that the population mean lies in the range 46·3 to 47·7, i.e. by allowing two standard errors on either side of the sample mean. Clearly with this more cautious estimate, we shall have greater confidence of being correct. Referring to the Normal scale, we find that a deviation of up to two standard deviations from the mean can occur with frequency about 95%, i.e. we could now hope that by arguing in this revised way, we should be correct in 95 out of every 100 such predictions.

Confidence intervals of this type are said to be symmetrical about the mean value. But we do not always want symmetrical confidence intervals. Suppose, for example, we were estimating the toxicity of some substance to be used for medicinal purposes – we should be less interested in overestimates of the toxicity than in underestimates. What we should want, in fact, is a confidence interval based on the upper limit of toxicity, a statement that we could be 99% sure that the toxicity did not exceed some specified value. On the other hand, if we were estimating the proportion of viable seeds in a sample, we should be mainly concerned with the lower limit which could with confidence be assigned to the proportion. Such confidence intervals we may refer to as *asymmetric*.

Example. A sample of 100 items gave a mean value 32 with standard deviation 5. Calculate (a) symmetric confidence limits within which we may have 95·5% confidence that the true population mean lies and (b) an upper confidence limit which we may have a 99% confidence will not be exceeded and (c) a lower limit above which we may be 96% sure that the population mean lies. (See Table of the Area of the Normal Curve, Chapter 9, page 116.)

The standard error of the mean of samples of 100 items drawn from a population whose standard deviation may be taken as 5 is $\frac{\sigma}{\sqrt{n}} = \frac{5}{\sqrt{100}} = 0·5$. With a large sample, we may take this as the standard error of estimate.

(a) *Symmetric Confidence Interval.* We may have 95·5% confidence that the population mean is not more than two standard errors away from the mean of our large sample on either side. Our confidence interval is therefore $32 \pm 2(0·5)$, i.e. the range 31·0 to 33·0.

(b) *Upper Confidence Limit.* Assuming symmetry, we may take it that the population mean has a 50% chance of being less than the sample mean. Our problem reduces, therefore, to finding that number of standard errors which has a 1% chance of being exceeded. Referring to the Table of Areas of the Normal Curve, we find that the appropriate number of standard errors is 2·25, and so may say that we have 99% confidence that the population mean value does not exceed the sample mean value by more than $2·25 \times 0·5 = 1·125$. Our 99% upper confidence limit is therefore $32 + 1·125 = 33·125$.

(c) *Lower Confidence Limit.* Assuming symmetry, as before, we argue that there is a 50% probability that the population mean will exceed the sample mean, and this time our problem reduces to finding that number of standard errors by which the sample mean may differ from the population mean with a probability of 4%. Consulting the Table of Areas of the Normal Curve we find this number of standard errors to be 1·75, and set our lower confidence limit at $32 - 1·75(0·5) = 31·125$.

Turning, now, to small samples, the method is very little more difficult, the main difference being that we have to use the Student's *t* distribution instead of the Normal distribution. The method is best illustrated by an example. In Chapter 13 we discussed the problem of two laboratories where it was alleged that a significant difference existed between their findings of fat content in ice-cream. The average discrepancy between the lab analyses was 0·48% and the standard deviation of the discrepancies, using Bessel's correction to get a best estimate, was 0·99%. Suppose now we wished to lay down a symmetrical confidence interval for the discrepancy, using a method which will satisfy us if it gives the correct result for the confidence interval in 95% of cases. In this case the number of degrees of freedom for Student's *t* is 9 and tables of Student's *t* show that for this number of degrees of freedom the value of *t* is 2·26 and the population mean will only differ by more than this number of standard errors with a probability of 5%. We therefore lay down our confidence interval as

$$\bar{x} \pm \frac{t\sigma}{\sqrt{n}} = 0·48 \pm \frac{2·26 \times 0·99}{\sqrt{10}}$$
$$= 0·48 \pm 0·70$$

For all practical purposes, therefore, we may say that the discrepancy between the labs in the long run may lie anywhere in the range -0.2% to $+1.2\%$. The minus result indicates that, while laboratory B seems so far to give the higher result, it might well prove in the long run that laboratory A tended to give the more favourable verdict as to fat content.

We may round off this ice-cream problem now, by asking how many paired analyses would be required to establish a significant difference on the basis of an average discrepancy of 0.48%. Referring to Chapter 13, the significance of the difference was based on the value of t given by the formula

$$t = \frac{|X - \bar{x}| \sqrt{n}}{\sigma}$$

where $|\bar{X} - \bar{x}| = 0.48$ and $\sigma = 0.99$. So we may write:

$$t = \left(\frac{0.48}{0.99}\right) \sqrt{n} = 0.48 \sqrt{n}$$

If we are prepared to work at the 5% level of t, the problem boils down to finding the value of n which substituted in this formula will give a value for t which is significant at the 5% level with $(n-1)$ degrees of freedom. If the reader will consult the graph of Student's t (page 230) he will see that we may immediately get the required value of n by writing $t = 2$, since as n increases t rapidly approaches this value. We get

$$0.48\sqrt{n} = 2 \quad \text{i.e. } n = \left(\frac{2}{0.48}\right)^2 = 17 \text{ approximately.}$$

Thus, if the apparent discrepancy were maintained (and we have no guarantee at all that it will be), some 17 parallel analyses would be required to establish the significance of the difference between the laboratories at the 95% confidence level. The reader may care as an exercise to investigate for himself what number of samples would be required for various average discrepancies within the confidence interval we have calculated to establish a significant difference, asking himself, on commonsense grounds, how he would expect the number of samples required to change as the average discrepancy grew larger or smaller.

The problem of laying down confidence intervals for the standard deviation of the population when we have an estimate based on *large* samples may be tackled in a manner precisely analogous to that for the mean, using the standard error of the standard deviation $\frac{\sigma}{\sqrt{2n}}$ as our standard error of estimate. We may take it that we may be 95% sure that the population standard deviation will not differ from the large sample standard deviation by more than two standard errors.

Example. Strength tests on 200 leas of yarn gave a standard deviation of 5·8 lb. Find the symmetrical 95% confidence interval for the standard deviation.

The standard error of the standard deviation is

$$\frac{\sigma}{\sqrt{2n}} = \frac{5·8}{\sqrt{400}} = 0·29$$

We may be 95% sure that the population standard deviation lies in the range $5·8 \pm 2 \times 0·29$, i.e. in the range 5·22 to 6·38. The problem of assigning confidence intervals to the standard deviation from small sample results we defer to the next chapter where we deal with the χ^2 distribution.

NOW TRY YOUR HAND AT ESTIMATION

1. Out of a large consignment of screws you take a random sample of 200 and find two of them have not had the head slotted. Use Fig. 39 to find a value for the percentage of screws in the consignment which have this fault such that there is only a 1% chance that your estimate is below the true value. (Hint: The probability of three or more taken at $p = 0·99$ means just the same as the probability of two or less $= 0·01$. Hence, using $p = 0·99$ find the expectation, z, corresponding to the curve $c = 3$. Then ask yourself what percentage defective will give this expectation in a sample of 200 screws.)

2. For the same data of example 1, find a lower limit for the percentage defective in the consignment such that there is only a 10% chance of the true value being less than the one you state. (Hint: Find the expectation, z, corresponding to $c = 2$ at $p = 0·1$)

3. Repeat analyses for the percentage of impurity in a chemical compound gave the results 3·4%, 3·7%, 3·5%. Set up a 95% confidence interval (symmetrical) for the percentage of impurity. (For 2 degrees of freedom Student's $t = 4·3$.)

4. A test on 100 ice-cream portions shows that the machine has been cutting with a standard deviation of 0·1 fluid ounces. Set up 95% confidence limits for the standard deviation (two sigma limits).

Association, Contingency, and Goodness of Fit –
The χ^2 Distribution

'Entia non sunt multiplicanda praeter necessitatem.'
WILLIAM OF OCCAM

It very rarely happens that an effect is brought about by a single cause – rather do we find that a certain combination of circumstances is necessary, and the absence of even one of them is enough to prevent the occurrence of the event. Take a very simple example: the case of a child contracting diphtheria. What causes this disease to develop? A much too simple answer would be that the child 'caught the germ'. It is too simple because, in the first place, there are many people who carry the bacillus without having the disease at all. It follows that there must also be another cause. If we assume that the bacillus is the specific cause of the disease, we must also acknowledge that the bacillus must find in some but not all persons, at some not not at all times, suitable conditions for the success of its evil purpose. A person who is 'run down' will be more likely to succumb to an invasion than a person in good condition. Yet 'run down' is very vague. Some people in poor condition may escape, whilst others who seem in excellent condition will be overcome. This suggests that the catching of the disease is even more complex. How, then, did we get the idea that specific germs are the causative agents of certain diseases? The answer to this is that we find the germ in question *associated* with the particular disease. That is to say, we find the germ more frequently in people with the disease than in those not suffering from it.

The careful reader will have noticed that we said the germ is found more frequently in people who suffer than in those who do not, implying not only that some people having the germ do not have the disease, but that some people having the disease do not have the germ. To the non-medical reader, relying on commonsense, this will seem a very queer kettle of fish. The German bacteriologist, Robert Koch (1843–1910), who was awarded a Nobel prize for his pioneer work, enunciated certain postulates, one of which was that the organism must always be found in cases of the disorder. The difficulty of problems of association will be appreciated when it is realized that in a notable proportion of cases of diphtheria it is not possible to find the bacillus, although, clinically, there is no possible doubt that the patient is suffering from the disease. The physician has to think of many more things than bacteriological findings. It will be appreciated that, however great the difficulties, the research worker has to press on with his task of trying to piece together the whole story. Association and the theory of Dependence are at once great assets to him and dangerous pitfalls, especially when he is dealing with small samples. In this chapter we shall try to show how the statistician goes about the job of steering a course through dangerous straits.

In December 1897 there was an outbreak of plague in a jail in Bombay. Of 127 persons who were uninoculated, 10 contracted plague, 6 of them dying. Of 147 persons who had been inoculated, 3 contracted the plague and there were no deaths. These data may be set up in the following way to show

(a) the association between inoculation and contracting the disease and

(b) the association between inoculation and mortality among persons who have contracted the disease.

	Infected	Not infected
Uninoculated	10	117
Inoculated	3	144

	Died	Recovered
Uninoculated	6	4
Inoculated	0	3

Considering the first table, if inoculation is of no avail we should expect that the proportion of infected persons among the inoculated $\frac{3}{147}$ would not differ significantly from the proportion of infected persons among the uninoculated $\frac{10}{127}$. Since the proportion of infected persons among the inoculated is less than the proportion among the uninoculated, we may say that inoculation and infection are negatively associated. Had there been more infected persons among the inoculated than among the uninoculated, we should have said inoculation and infection were positively associated. Our second table suggests a negative association between inoculation and death once the disease has been contracted. Overall, therefore, the impression is given that inoculated persons are (a) less likely to get the plague and (b) less likely to die if they do contract it.

It will, of course, happen but rarely that the proportions will be identical, even if no real association exists. Evidently, therefore, we need a significance test to reassure ourselves that the observed difference of proportion is greater than could reasonably be attributed to chance. The significance test will test the *reality* of the association, without telling us anything about the *intensity* of association. It will be apparent that we need two distinct things: (a) a test of significance, to be used on the data first of all, and (b) some measure of the intensity of the association, which we shall only be justified in using if the significance test confirms that the association is real. Before we go on to deal with these, there is one point on which the reader should be very clear, as it is absolutely fundamental to understanding what exactly we mean when we talk about association in Statistics. The word has a rather more restricted meaning in statistical methodology than in ordinary speech. The crux of the matter is that in statistics when we speak of association, there is always a comparison implied. In common speech, the simple fact that two things are found frequently together justifies us in saying that they are associated. In this sense, as a trivial example, we might say that drinking beer is associated with men. True enough, it is. But the statistician would be little interested in such an isolated statement. He takes an interest only when the statement is extended so as to make a comparison; if, for example, we say that beer drinking is associated with maleness rather than femaleness. Cancer of the stomach is associated with men – and also with women. The statistician, however, finds that men are more liable to get this disease than women, and when he says that cancer of the stomach is associated with men, he is implying that men – rather than women – get the disease; that is, that the disease, while attacking both sexes, has a preference for men.

The danger of drawing the obvious conclusion from association has already been pointed out. The association between two things might be due, not to any direct causal relation between them, but to their joint association with a third factor. Cold weather in England is associated with high sales of blankets in Canada. It is not that the Canadians buy blankets because English people feel cold in the winter. They buy the blankets because they feel cold themselves at the same time as we do. There is the linking factor of a common hemisphere. Pseudo-associations of this sort are very common. The number of wireless licences purchased over the last twenty years or so correlates extremely highly with the numbers of people certified insane in the same years. They show a parallel growth. Who will be so bold as to say that the one phenomenon is the cause of the other? These cases, where the association is obviously not due to a cause and effect relationship subsisting between the two phenomena, should warn us against the too hasty assumption of a cause and effect relationship in cases where the idea is not so preposterous. A man who stands on the river bank while someone else rescues a drowning man can be said to be associated with the rescue, but he is not the cause of the effect.

χ^{2*} TEST

The reality of associations of this sort is tested by using the χ^2 test. The χ^2 distribution is one of the most versatile in statistical theory. We cannot enter here into the mathematical theory which underlies this test, but shall have to confine ourselves to a description of how χ^2 is calculated in given cases and how its significance is tested using the published tables. χ^2 tests essentially whether the observed frequencies in a distribution differ significantly from the frequencies which might be expected according to some assumed

---

* Pronounced 'Keye square' (rhyming with 'eye'). Also written, sometimes: 'Chi-square'. χ is a Greek letter.

hypothesis. Corresponding to each frequency predicted by our hypothesis there will be an observed frequency. If we denote the expected frequency by E and the observed frequency by O, then χ^2 is calculated as the sum of terms like $\frac{(O-E)^2}{E}$, that is to say, we may write

$$\chi^2 = \sum \frac{(O-E)^2}{E}$$

As the simplest possible example, suppose that a coin were tossed 50 times and that heads occurred only 15 times, should we be justified in asserting without more ado that the coin was biased or the man doing the tossing not as honest as he looked?

In this case, we have an *a priori* theory as to what the relative frequencies for head and tail should be. We expect roughly 25 heads and 25 tails, and 25 is our best estimate of the expected frequency. We calculate

$$\chi^2 = \frac{(O-E)^2}{E} + \frac{(O-E)^2}{E}$$
$$= \frac{(35-25)^2}{25} + \frac{(15-25)^2}{25}$$
$$\text{(for tails)} \quad \text{for heads)}$$
$$= \tfrac{100}{25} + \tfrac{100}{25} = 8$$

It will be evident to the reader that the expected value for χ^2 is zero, and the question now is whether the calculated value of χ^2 is sufficiently great to refute a Null Hypothesis that the observed discrepancy between the frequency of head and tail could have arisen by chance. To answer this question we have to decide the appropriate number of *degrees of freedom* with which the tables for χ^2 should be entered. The number of degrees of freedom is obtained as the number of classes whose frequency may be assigned arbitrarily. In this example, for instance, we could arbitrarily make the frequency of heads what we liked. But, this having been done, the frequency of tails would then be automatically settled for a given number of throws of the coin. We may say, then, that the Goddess of Chance had only one degree of freedom in fixing the frequencies. Accordingly, we have to enter the table of χ^2 with one degree of freedom.* Doing this, we find that the 5%

* The reader may check what follows by using the chart of χ^2 in Fig. 82.

level of χ^2 appropriate for our problem is 3·84 and the 1% level 6·64. Since our calculated value for χ^2 exceeds the value given in the table for the 1% level, we should be on strong ground in asserting that the coin-spinning experiment was not free from bias. Suppose, however, that it was vitally important that such a claim of bias should not be made short of an extremely high degree of confidence, as, for example, if a false claim of this kind would result in our being prosecuted, we might test it at the 0·1% level, i.e. demand a value of χ^2 so large that it would be exceeded by chance only once in a thousand similar experiments. This value of χ^2 is 10·83, so that under these circumstances while we should have our own opinion we should have to keep it to ourselves, not daring to make it public without further confirmation.

Now the agreement between the expected and observed frequencies may be too good as well as too bad for it to have been a matter of chance. That is to say, we may come across values of χ^2 that would almost certainly be exceeded by chance. Cases of this sort make us suspect that possibly the data have been 'cooked' by someone with a very good idea of what the answer should be. For this reason, the published tables of χ^2 show not only the 5%, 1%, and 0·1% levels but also the 95%, 99%, and 99·9% levels.

Consider, next, the following data, due to Coll and Jones of the Central Middlesex Hospital. They interviewed 4,871 men at random. The following table shows the numbers interviewed by age groups, and the numbers in each age group estimated to have, or have had in the past, peptic ulcers.

Age group	14–	20–	25–	35–	45–	55–	65–
Number seen	199	300	1,128	1,375	1,089	625	155
P.U. cases	1	8	38	96	105	56	12

Suppose that we wished to ask whether these figures are such as might have been observed by chance on the hypothesis that equal proportions would be found in each age group. The following table compares the numbers of cases found in each age group with the numbers which were to be expected on our hypothesis, the expectations for each age group being based on the fact that a total of 316 cases were found in 4,871 persons interviewed, i.e. on an expectation of 6·5% constant for each age group.

Age group	14–	20–	25–	35–	45–	55–	65–
Cases expected	13	19·5	73	89	71	40·4	10
Cases seen	1	8	38	96	105	56	12

The total of the cases expected should be equal, of course, to the total of the cases seen. The value of χ^2 is then given by

$$\chi^2 = \frac{12^2}{13} + \frac{11 \cdot 5^2}{19 \cdot 5} + \frac{35^2}{73} + \frac{7^2}{89} + \frac{34^2}{71} + \frac{15 \cdot 5^2}{40 \cdot 5} + \frac{2^2}{10}$$

i.e. $\chi^2 = 57 \cdot 6$

There are 7 age groups, the frequencies for 6 of which could be assigned arbitrarily, so that we enter the table of χ^2 with 6 degrees of freedom. We find that even the 0·1% level of χ^2 is 22·5 only, compared with our calculated value of 57·6, and conclude, therefore, as we ought to expect in this particular case, that the observed frequencies in the several age groups are not compatible with the hypothesis that the finding of peptic ulcer or a history of peptic ulcer is constant from age group to age group.

But the obvious conclusion is not always the correct one necessarily. Consider, for example, the following table which shows the number of accidents occurring in a particular period of time on each of three eight-hour shifts in a factory, the working conditions and numbers of people exposed to risk being assumed similar for all shifts (example due to K. A. Brownlee).

Shift	Accidents in the period
A	1
B	7
C	7

If we test the hypothesis that there is no significant difference between shift and number of accidents the result obtained is quite unexpected. The expectation per shift is taken as 5, and we find

$$\chi^2 = \frac{4^2}{5} + \frac{2^2}{5} + \frac{2^2}{5} = 4 \cdot 8$$

If the reader refers to the graph of χ^2 given in Fig. 82 he will see that with two degrees of freedom (one less than the number of shifts), even to reach the 5% probability level we should need

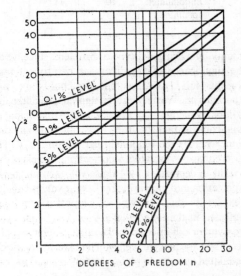

Fig. 82.* Graphs of χ^2. The 0·1%, 1% and 5% levels indicate suspiciously *bad* fit. The 95% and 99% levels are used to indicate suspiciously *good* fit. For degrees of freedom greater than 30, $\sqrt{2\chi^2}$ is normally distributed with unit standard deviation about a mean value $\sqrt{2n-1}$

$\chi^2 = 6$. As a matter of fact, such a distribution of the frequencies – or worse – might occur with a 10% probability. While we cannot deny that a difference between the shifts may exist, we are bound to say that the evidence scarcely justifies us in regarding the existence of a difference as established. We should adopt a wait and

* See acknowledgements, p. viii.

see attitude until further experience enables the matter to be settled.

Consider, now, a somewhat different problem, namely the inoculation data already quoted earlier in this chapter.

	Infected	Not infected
Uninoculated	10	117
Inoculated	3	144

This is essentially a Binomial type of problem, since we are comparing the significance of the difference of proportions in two samples on the Null Hypothesis that they could have come from the same population. We may test the significance of the difference in proportions by using the χ^2 distribution. A mathematical difficulty arises from the fact that the χ^2 distribution is a continuous distribution, whereas the Binomial distribution is not. This difficulty is overcome by applying a correction suggested by Yates which consists in decreasing by $\frac{1}{2}$ those values in our table which exceed expectation and increasing by $\frac{1}{2}$ those values which are less than the expected value. On our Null Hypothesis the number of persons infected in the uninoculated group exceeds expectation, so that the number not infected in the same group must obviously be less than the expected frequency. The reverse conditions hold in the inoculated group. Applying Yates' correction, our table becomes:

	Infected	Not infected	Totals
Uninoculated	$9\frac{1}{2}$	$117\frac{1}{2}$	127
Inoculated	$3\frac{1}{2}$	$143\frac{1}{2}$	147
Totals	13	261	274

Tables of this type may be represented symbolically, as follows:

	Infected	Not infected	Totals
Group 1	a	c	e
Group 2	b	d	f
Totals	g	h	k

We could, of course, calculate the expected frequencies in the usual way, but it may be shown that χ^2 is given by the formula

$$\chi^2 = \frac{(bc - ad)^2 k}{efgh}$$

Applying this to our table, after Yates' correction has been applied, we find

$$\chi^2 = \frac{(3\frac{1}{2} \times 117\frac{1}{2} - 9\frac{1}{2} \times 143\frac{1}{2})^2 \times 274}{127 \times 147 \times 13 \times 261} = 3 \cdot 9$$

We now need to know how many degrees of freedom are appropriate for entering the tables (in our case, graph) of χ^2. The number of degrees of freedom, as before, is equal to the number of frequencies which could arbitrarily be entered into the table, without disturbing the totals. If the reader will consider the table of frequencies for a moment he will soon see that there is only one degree of freedom. Once any frequency is arbitrarily fixed, the rest are determined by this frequency and the marginal totals in the table. Thus, if we were to assign the frequency 7 for the number of uninoculated persons infected, then the number of uninoculated who were not infected must be $127 - 7 = 120$, the number of inoculated who were infected must be $13 - 7 = 6$, and the number of inoculated who were not infected must be $147 - 6 = 141$. Consulting our graph for χ^2 we find that with 1 degree of freedom the 5% level of $\chi^2 = 3 \cdot 8$ and the 1% level $6 \cdot 6$. The calculated value for χ^2 just reaches the 5% level therefore, and we may conclude that the observed discrepancy is probably significant, i.e. that it is probably true that the inoculated are less likely to contract plague than the uninoculated. The reader may care to confirm for himself that the application of Yates' correction makes a considerable difference to the value of χ^2 arrived at. Without the correction we find $\chi^2 = 5 \cdot 0$ approximately. In cases of this type, where the sample sizes are relatively small and the Binomial distribution very skew, we should use Yates' correction and the χ^2 test rather than test the significance of the difference in proportions by the standard error method which can only give a crude guide as to the probability of the observed difference being due to chance.

Frequency tables of this sort may be more complex. Consider, for example, the following table which shows fractional test meal results in a series of pathologically verified cases of ulcer and cancer of the stomach.

	Achlor-hydria	Hypo-chlorhydria	Normal	Hyper-chlorhydria
Chronic ulcer	3	7	35	9
Cancer	22	2	6	0

These data are due to Stewart of Leeds University. The first matter to be considered is how the expected frequencies are to be calculated for each cell of the table. This is best shown schematically as follows.

	a	b	c	d	e	Totals
A						P
B			$\dfrac{Qs}{N}$			Q
C						R
D						S
Totals	p	q	r	s	t	N

In the table, the grand total frequency for the whole table is N. The row totals are denoted by P, Q, R, and S. The column totals are denoted by p, q, r, s, and t. We have, therefore, that $p+q+r+s+t=P+Q+R+S=N$. The several cells in the table can be indicated by quoting the 'map reference', e.g. Aa, Cd, Be, etc. The expected frequencies are derived from the marginal totals, by asking ourselves: What is the probability that a given patient will fall simultaneously in a given row and column? Thus, for example, the probability that a patient will occur in the row B is given by $\frac{Q}{N}$. In like manner, the probability that a patient will occur in column d is given by $\frac{s}{N}$. Now, the probability for the joint occurrence of two events is obtained by multiplying together the probabilities for their individual occurrence. Hence, the probability that an individual will occur in the cell Bd of the table is given by $\frac{Q}{N} \cdot \frac{s}{N} = \frac{Qs}{N^2}$. The probability of the occurrence of a patient in other cells may be arrived at in similar fashion. Now, for our χ^2 test, we do not want probabilities but expected frequencies. These latter will, of course, be obtained from the cell probabilities by multiplying by the total number of patients dealt with in the table, viz. N. The expected frequency for the cell Bd is thus $\frac{Qs}{N^2} \times N = \frac{Qs}{N}$. We see, therefore, that the expected frequency in a given cell is obtained by taking the product of the row and column totals appropriate to the cell and dividing this product by N, the total frequency for the whole table.

If, then, we let A and B denote chronic ulcer and cancer respectively, and a, b, c, and d represent achlorhydria, hypochlorhydria, normal and hyperchlorhydria, our table of observed frequencies with marginal totals becomes:

	a	b	c	d	Totals
A	3	7	35	9	54
B	22	2	6	0	30
Totals	25	9	41	9	84

And our table of expected frequencies will be

	a	b	c	d	Totals
A	16	5·8	26·4	5·8	54
B	9	3·2	14·6	3·2	30
Totals	25	9	41	9	84

We then calculate the total value of χ^2 for the whole table by squaring the difference between each observed frequency and our calculated expected frequency, and dividing the result by the expectation. The contribution of the cell Aa to χ^2 is $\dfrac{(16-3)^2}{16} = 10·5$, and totalling the contribution of all the cells we find $\chi^2 = 42·9$.

Now in order to decide whether the observed difference in acidity conditions as between cancer and chronic ulcer cases might be due to chance, we have to know how many degrees of freedom to use in entering the tables for χ^2. The table we have been considering is called a 4×2 table, since there are 4 columns and 2 rows. If, in the general case, we let n_1 and n_2 represent the number of rows and columns in our table, then the number of degrees of freedom is given by $(n_1 - 1)(n_2 - 1)$. In our case, therefore, the number of degrees is $3 \times 1 = 3$. As the reader may confirm from the graph of χ^2 the 5% level with 3 degrees of freedom is 8, the 1% level 12. The full tables show that the 0·1 level is only 17. We conclude then that beyond all reasonable doubt there is a significant difference in acidity conditions as between chronic ulcer and cancer of the stomach.

In analysing the above case we deliberately avoided mention of an important fact, so as not to burden the reader with too many things at a time. The χ^2 test cannot safely be applied when the expected frequency in any cell is less than 5. In our table there were two cells, Bb and Bd, which did not satisfy this criterion. In an actual case in practice we should get over this difficulty by pooling together columns a and b, and columns c and d, so that the contrast would be the less detailed one between hypochlor-hydria and its extreme case achlorhydria, on the one hand, and normal or hyperacidity on the other hand. Our table, in this case, would then degenerate into a 2×2 table of the kind met with in the inoculation data. Thus:

	$(a+b)$	$(c+d)$	Totals
A	10	44	54
B	24	6	30
Totals	34	50	84

The reader may check for himself that the expected frequency in all cells is then greater than 5 by the method already indicated. We calculate the value for χ^2 using the method illustrated in the inoculation data as:

$$\chi^2 = \frac{(24 \times 44 - 10 \times 6)^2 \times 84}{34 \times 50 \times 54 \times 30} = 30 \text{ approximately.}$$

The appropriate number of degrees of freedom in this case is 1. The reader will find that the 1 % level of χ^2 from the graph is 6·6, and tables show that the 0·1 % level is only 10·8, so the conclusion previously reached is confirmed.

Other exercises for the reader to try for himself are given at the end of this chapter.

This distribution is also used for testing the goodness of fit of theoretical distribution and observed data. To some extent, test-ing the mean and standard deviation using the t test and the F test does the same thing, but the χ^2 test provides us with a much more detailed approach since it considers, not simply a couple of para-meters, but the overall shape of the distribution. As an illustration of the use of the χ^2 test as a 'goodness of fit test', let us take the data given in Chapter 8 for the number of goals scored per team per match at football. We there calculated the expected frequency for the different scores (a) using the Poisson distribution and (b) a modified form which allowed for fluctuation in the expectation.

Consider, first of all, the predicted frequencies given by the Poisson.

Goals per match	0	1	2	3	4	5	6	7
Predicted by Poisson	88	150	126	72	30	10	3	1
Observed frequency	95	158	108	63	40	9	5	2

We calculate χ^2 as the sum of terms such as $\dfrac{(95-88)^2}{88}$ and find $\chi^2 = 8 \cdot 25$. (The last three cells, for 5, 6, and 7 goals, have to be pooled together to ensure that the expected frequency is greater than 5 for all cells.) The appropriate number of degrees of freedom here is one less than the number of cells, after the pooling of the last three cells, viz. 5. The 5% level of χ^2 for 5 degrees of freedom is 11·1. We cannot, therefore, say with confidence that the Poisson distribution is a poor fit. However, the tables of χ^2 show that with 5 degrees of freedom the 10% level is 9·24 and our calculated value for χ^2, though still less than this value, is getting near to it. If, therefore, we wished to be doubting Thomases, we might still keep our fingers crossed against the possibility that the Poisson distribution might prove a bad fit, given further evidence.

Let us now consider the prediction we obtained using the modified distribution which allowed for fluctuations in the expected value for the number of goals per team per match. Pooling the last three cells again, we get:

Goals per match	0	1	2	3	4	5, 6, and 7
Predicted frequency	96	147	119	69	32	17
Observed frequency	95	158	108	63	40	16

And the reader may check for himself that $\chi^2 = 4 \cdot 4$ with 5 degrees of freedom. This is almost exactly the 50% level of χ^2, i.e. that value which is as likely as not to be exceeded, so there is absolutely no reason why we should not be pleased with the fit and attribute any variations between predicted and observed values to pure chance in random sampling. This is a suitable point to comment on a matter which is sometimes puzzling to the novice. We have seen that either the Poisson or the modified distribution fits the observed frequencies sufficiently well for us to be able to regard them as workable forecasters. Which is correct? It is important to be clear that, although the modified distribution fits better apparently than the Poisson, there is as yet no really cogent proof of this. Probably there never is a mathematical function which fits a practical case absolutely perfectly. Nor is it at all necessary that there should be. What we seek is not a *perfect* description of a distribution but an *adequate* one; that is to say, one which is good enough for the purpose we have in view. A simple mathematical distribution may well be chosen for its simplicity, although it fits the facts rather less well than a more complex distribution, provided it fits well enough for our purpose. We should not ask: which is correct? but rather: Which is adequate? A man going on a journey may prefer a sketch map to an Ordnance Survey map on the grounds that it suits his purpose better, being sufficiently accurate and simpler to follow. On precisely the same grounds of adequacy and simplicity do we choose mathematical distributions.

We have shown how the χ^2 test may be used to test the reality of association. Before passing on to measures of intensity of association we shall here mention how the χ^2 distribution is used to establish confidence intervals for the variance of a population from which a sample of n items had a sample variance s^2, a matter which we left over from Chapter 14 as it could not be dealt with until we had introduced the χ^2 distribution. Suppose, for example, that a sample of 8 items gave a sample variance of 37. Let us say at once that the appropriate number of degrees of freedom for χ^2 in what follows is always one less than the number of items in the sample – in this case 7. There are various questions about confidence limits that we might wish to ask, and we shall consider them in turn.

(1) What is our estimate of the value of the population variance which has only a 5% chance of being exceeded by the true population variance?

To find this we look up the 95% level of χ^2 with 7 degrees of freedom, viz. 2·2, and our upper confidence limit is then given by

$$\hat{\sigma}^2\text{max} = \frac{ns^2}{\chi^2} = \frac{8 \times 37}{2 \cdot 2} = 134$$

(2) What estimate of the population variance has only a 5% chance of being in excess of the true value?

To answer this we look up the 5% value of χ^2 with 7 degrees of freedom, viz. 14·1, and our lower confidence limit is then given by

$$\hat{\sigma}^2\text{min} = \frac{ns^2}{\chi^2} = \frac{8 \times 37}{14 \cdot 1} = 21$$

It is evident that we shall have a 90% probability of being correct if we make the claim that the population variance lies in the range 21 to 134, i.e. that the population standard deviation lies in the range $\sqrt{21} = 4\cdot6$ to $\sqrt{134} = 11\cdot6$.

This is only one out of an infinite number of confidence intervals all having a 90% probability of being correct. We could, for example, have got another 90% confidence interval by choosing the 98% and 8% levels of χ^2 to calculate $\hat{\sigma}^2\text{max}$ and $\hat{\sigma}^2\text{min}$. Alternatively, we could calculate the value of σ^2 which has only a 10% chance of being exceeded, using the 90% level of $\chi^2 = 2\cdot8$, and we could then say that we were 90% sure that σ^2 lay in the range 0 to $\frac{ns^2}{\chi^2} = \frac{8 \times 37}{2 \cdot 8} = 106$, i.e that the standard deviation did not exceed $\sqrt{106} = 10\cdot3$.

The questions asked so far have enabled us to lay down a range for the variance for a given degree of confidence. We might well wish to know what confidence to place in a claim that the variance lay between certain specified limits.

(1) What confidence may we have that the population variance lies in the range 25 to 235?

To answer this, we calculate

$$\chi^2 = \frac{ns^2}{\hat{\sigma}^2} = \frac{8 \times 37}{25} = 11\cdot8$$

and also

$$\chi^2 = \frac{ns^2}{\sigma^2} = \frac{8 \times 37}{235} = 1\cdot25$$

Reference to tables of χ^2 for 7 degrees of freedom show that 11·9 is almost exactly the 10% level (=12) and 1·25 is almost exactly the 99% level (=1·24). The probability that the variance lies in the range 25 to 235 is therefore 99% − 10% = 89%.

The reader will find exercises to try for himself at the end of the chapter. It is well to remember that for samples with n greater than 30 we can use the standard error of estimate method, the standard error of the standard deviation being given by $\frac{\sigma}{\sqrt{2n}}$.

Consider, now, the problem of finding measures of the intensity of association in our inoculation problem, where we had:

	Infected	Not infected
Uninoculated	10	117
Inoculated	3	144

Total frequency for the table = N = 274

All tables of this type may be typified by the schematic layout:

	A	not A
B	a	b
not B	c	d

Total frequency for the table = $a + b + c + d = N$

A coefficient of association, due to Yule, is then given by

$$Q = \frac{ad - bc}{ad + bc}$$

for which the standard error is $\left(\dfrac{1 - Q^2}{2}\right)\sqrt{\dfrac{1}{a} + \dfrac{1}{b} + \dfrac{1}{c} + \dfrac{1}{d}}$

For our inoculation data we find

$$Q = \frac{10 \times 144 - 3 \times 117}{10 \times 144 + 3 \times 117} = 0 \cdot 61$$

with a standard error

$$1 - \frac{(0 \cdot 61)^2}{2}\sqrt{\tfrac{1}{10} + \tfrac{1}{117} + \tfrac{1}{3} + \tfrac{1}{444}} = 0 \cdot 21$$

If we take it as reasonably certain (roughly 95 % probability) that the true value lies within two standard errors of the calculated value, we may claim with fair confidence that the coefficient of association lies in the range 0·61 plus or minus 0·42, i.e. between 0·19 and 1·03. The latter value, as we shall in a moment show, is impossible, since that coefficient cannot exceed the value unity. All we can say, then, is that the true value probably lies between 0·19 and 1·0. Let us consider how the coefficient is to be interpreted. This will best be done by numerical examples, specially invented.

Consider, first of all, the case where the proportions of persons infected are exactly the same for the inoculated as for the un-inoculated, as in the following table:

	Infected	Not infected
Uninoculated	2	5
Inoculated	20	50

It is evident that in all such cases the term $ad - bc$ must be zero, so that the coefficient will be zero. Hence, a zero coefficient occurs if the proportions are the same in the inoculated as in the un-inoculated. Next consider what happens to the coefficient if one of the observed frequencies in the table happens to be zero, i.e. if one of the combinations does not occur at all. Suppose, for example, that we had the following table:

	Infected	Not infected
Uninoculated	0	5
Inoculated	2	12

Then the term ad in the formula for the coefficient would be zero and we should have

$$Q = \frac{ad - bc}{ad + bc} = \frac{-bc}{bc} = -1$$

This is the maximum negative value the coefficient can attain. It indicates that the incidence of infection is completely dis-associated from the uninoculated, i.e. that infection is found only in people who have been inoculated. A value such as minus 0·6 would indicate that while infection was found among the un-inoculated, it was less prevalent there than among the inoculated.

Next consider the following table:

	Infected	Not infected
Uninoculated	3	10
Inoculated	2	0

Here again the term ad is zero and the coefficient has the value minus 1. This time the value minus 1 indicates that while some of the uninoculated were infected, there were none of the inoculated who escaped infection. Thus the value minus 1 may indicate either that none of the uninoculated were infected or that none of the inoculated escaped infection – a totality in either case.

The reader should satisfy himself that, if a zero frequency occurs either as the frequency b or the frequency c in our typical table, a similar pair of totalities arises, associated with the coefficient plus

1, which indicates either that none of the inoculated were infected or none of the uninoculated escaped infection. Thus, the sign, plus or minus, of the coefficient indicates the sense of the association, i.e. the direction in which it operates. The magnitude of the coefficient can never be greater than plus 1 or less than minus 1.

A second coefficient of association, also due to Yule, is the so-called coefficient of colligation, defined by

$$Y = \frac{1 - \sqrt{\dfrac{bc}{ad}}}{1 + \sqrt{\dfrac{bc}{ad}}}$$

whose standard error is given by

$$\frac{1 - Y^2}{4} \sqrt{\frac{1}{a} + \frac{1}{b} + \frac{1}{c} + \frac{1}{d}}$$

If the reader cares to make the necessary substitutions he will find that for the inoculation data the coefficient of colligation comes out to $Y = 0.33$, with a standard error of 0.15, approximately. The reader will possibly be surprised that the two coefficients give such different values, although they are both supposed to measure the same degree of association. He will be more surprised when he learns – as he may easily check for himself along the lines followed for the coefficient of association – that the coefficient of colligation also has maximum and minimum values of plus and minus 1, with similar significance to those shown in the first coefficient. He will remember, then, that the two coefficients are not comparable. All comparisons should be made in terms of the same coefficient.

We held forth at some length earlier on the danger of drawing the obvious conclusion of cause and effect from association. In 1941 there was one death from diphtheria among 766,000 immunized children in Scotland, whereas 418 children died out of the 389,000 not immunized. The obvious conclusion is indeed obvious. Yet the National Anti-Vaccination League was far from satisfied. Their reply might be summarized as follows:

(1) The great majority of these children were not immunized until after November 1940, when the immunization drive was commenced.

(2) In 1940 there were 675 deaths, as against 419 in 1941, so that evidently diphtheria was quite a menace before the introduction of immunization, this, presumably, being the reason for its introduction.

(3) What saved the 766,000 children before they were immunized?

(4) The uninoculated are the very young, the very poor and undernourished, those living in overcrowded homes, and those who have been weakly since birth with heart trouble or some other physical defect. Any disease is likely to be more frequently fatal in a class weighed down by these disabilities.

(5) The bulk of the deaths occur in the large towns such as Glasgow.

(6) Even in Glasgow the risk of death from diphtheria is not worth all the heavy expenditure of time and energy which was put into the campaign. 'What are 158 deaths in a child population of something like 200,000?'

(This argument is summarized from a pamphlet copy of a letter sent by the Secretary of the League to the principal newspapers in Scotland.) It is elsewhere suggested that the method of immunization is the cheap way to avoid the cost of sanitation reform.

The reader will find it a useful exercise to go through the above argument critically. Where are the points fair, if they are substantiated? Where does emotion come in? Is there evidence here on which a reasonable person might reject immunization? The next step is to get information from your Local Medical Officer. Why does he recommend immunization? Is it because the Ministry of Health has adopted it as a policy? What are the chances that immunization will finish up the same miserable fiasco as vaccination? It is especially important that intelligent members of the community should have access to more than propaganda leaflets from the Ministry of Health. Can you get it? What evidence can you find that the valid points suggested by the Anti-Vaccination League are seriously considered by the medical profession? How much of the basic research is in the hands of private commercial enterprise? It is an interesting topic and excellent exercise in solid thinking.

The reader will see that where we can split data into rational subgroups corresponding to possible differences, this should be done. Techniques are available for so many different possibilities that it is impossible to deal with them all here. The reader should refer to the texts quoted in the bibliography for further details. There are, however, two further points with which the reader may be acquainted. The first is the additive nature of independent estimates of χ^2 and, what is often associated with additions of χ^2 estimates, the method of deciding whether a value of χ^2 based on a large number of degrees of freedom is significant, the published tables going no higher than 30 degrees of freedom. We shall illustrate both points in one example. Suppose that 41 investigators try out a drug with a view to establishing its curative properties, each investigator arriving at a table something as shown.

	Treated	Not treated
Cured	24	57
Not cured	53	257

Then each investigator could, independently, assess his own results using the χ^2 test with 1 degree of freedom. These independent values for χ^2 may be added together and the overall significance of the results judged by entering the tables for χ^2 with the total degrees of freedom. Suppose, for example, that the values for χ^2 obtained by 41 investigators totalled 72. Then, since there was 1 degree of freedom for each investigator, there were altogether 41 degrees of freedom, which is beyond the range of the tables. Now, it has been shown by Fisher that for more than 30 degrees of freedom $\sqrt{2\chi^2}$ forms a normal distribution whose mean value is $\sqrt{2n-1}$, where n is the number of degrees of freedom (provided n be large) and whose standard deviation is unity.

In our case, the mean is $\sqrt{2n-1} = \sqrt{81} = 9$

And for $\sqrt{2\chi^2}$ we find $\sqrt{2 \times 72} = \sqrt{144} = 12$

Hence, the deviation of our observed value for $\sqrt{2\chi^2}$ from its mean value $\sqrt{2n-1}$ is given by $12 - 9 = 3$, i.e. since the standard error is equal to unity the discrepancy is equal to three standard errors, which is undoubtedly significant.

As a check on the accuracy of this approximation when the number of degrees of freedom is large, we may work out the value of χ^2 which has a probability of only 5% of being exceeded. Tables of the Normal distribution tell us that a deviation of more than 1·65 standard deviation *on the high side only* occurs with a probability of 5%. Hence, since the standard deviation of this approximate distribution is equal to unity, the value of $\sqrt{2\chi^2}$ will be 1·65 greater than the mean value of the distribution,

$$\sqrt{2n-1} = \sqrt{59} = 7·67$$

for 30 degrees of freedom. That is to say, the 5% level of χ^2 will be given by

$$\sqrt{2\chi^2} = \sqrt{2n-1} + t$$
$$= 7·67 + 1·65 = 9·32$$

so that
$$\chi^2 = \frac{9·32 \times 9·32}{2} = 43·5$$

The true value of the 5% level of χ^2 with 30 degrees of freedom, as may be checked from the graph of χ^2, is 43·8, so the approximation is very good even at $n = 30$. As the number of degrees of freedom increase, it gets even better.

NOW SEE IF YOU CAN APPLY χ^2 TO THESE PROBLEMS

1. In order to investigate whether hair colour was associated with culture among the females of the species, I did a little experiment. At a Bach concert I counted the number of blondes (real and artificial) and the number of brunettes. In the interests of science, I went to a Bebop session and did the same. The results were as shown in the table. The question is: Would it be fair of me, on the strength of this evidence, to state that blondes prefer Bebop to Bach?

	Blonde	Brunette
Bach	7	143
Bebop	14	108

2. Two treatments were tried out in the control of a certain type of plant infestation, with the following results. May we conclude that

Treatment B is superior to Treatment A in controlling this type of infestation?

> Treatment A: 200 plants examined and 24 found infested
> Treatment B: 200 plants examined and 9 found infested

3. The following data on vaccination are purely imaginary. They are data such as might be collected in a hospital over a period of years and – if they were genuine – would serve to indicate whether vaccination, apart altogether from whether it has any prophylactic effect, mitigates the severity of any actual attack of smallpox.

	Haemorrhagic or Confluent	Abundant	Sparse
Vaccinated within 10 years of attack	10	150	240
Never vaccinated	60	30	10

Use χ^2 to test the significance of the association.

16

Correlation, Cause and Effect

'There is no more common error than to assume that, because prolonged and accurate mathematical calculations have been made, the application of the result to some fact of nature is absolutely certain.' A. N. WHITEHEAD

When the mathematician speaks of the existence of a 'functional relation' between two variable quantities, he means that they are connected by a simple 'formula', that is to say, if we are told the value of one of the variable quantities we can find the value of the second quantity by substituting in the formula which tells us how they are related. As a simple illustration, let us suppose that bananas cost 2s. per dozen. We can then write down a formula which will enable us to calculate the cost in shillings of any number of dozens:

Cost in shillings $= 2 \times$ number of dozens

If we let C represent the cost, and n the number of dozens, the mathematical formula would take the form

$$C = 2n$$

This formula would apply only as long as the price per dozen remained fixed at 2s. The reader will see that, if the price rose to 3s. per dozen, the formula would have to be changed to

$$C = 3n$$

We can generalize this formula to make it apply to any price per dozen as follows. Let p be the price per dozen, then

$$C = pn$$

The formula is now in its most general condition – all numerical values have been replaced by letters. In a given problem all we have to do is to replace the letters by the appropriate numerical quantities. The price may now be given in pence, shillings, or pounds for a single article, a dozen articles, or a gross of articles, and commonsense will then tell us whether n is to be stated as single articles, dozens, or grosses, and whether the value obtained for C, after substitution for p and n, will be in pence, shillings, or pounds.

Each of the equations $C=n$, $C=2n$, $C=3n$, $C=4n$, and so on, could be plotted as graph of C against n. If the reader cares to try it he will find that each of the graphs is a straight line, but that as the value of p rises the slope of the line increases. All this means, of course, is that the cost rises more steeply as the price is increased. The quantity p of our equation, which is a constant numerical value in any given problem, is called, for obvious reasons, the 'slope' of the line. Constants of this kind are called parameters. Fig. 83 shows examples of the straight line $C=pn$,

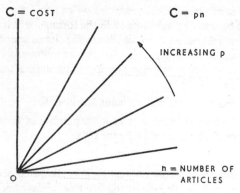

Fig. 83. The parameter p fixes the slope of the line. In our example p is the price per article

with the parameter p set at different values. It will be noticed that in every case when n is equal to zero C is also equal to zero. When a graph is drawn showing both scales with their zero points coinciding, the common zero point is called the origin – because it is the point from which our scales begin. We see then that the equation $C=pn$ really represents a whole 'family' of straight lines, all of which pass through the origin. Mathematicians call it the equation of straight lines through the origin.

Now of course there is no real reason why a straight line should always pass through the origin. Consider a practical example. Our equation $C=pn$ might well represent the amount of money it costs a manufacturer to produce n articles when the manufacturing cost per article is p. We may properly consider that the cost of manufacturing a number of articles is directly proportional to the number of articles. But not all of a manufacturer's costs are direct costs of this kind. He has to bear certain overhead costs of a fixed nature whether he produces any articles in his factory or not. He must pay out rents and other fixed charges. These charges simply push up his total costs by a fixed amount

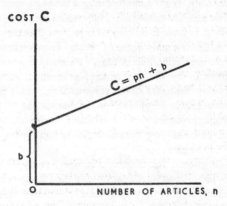

Fig. 84. The parameter b fixes the point at which the line will cut the axis of C. In our example b is overhead costs

irrespective of the number of articles produced. There is a fixed burden to be carried, which we may denote by the symbol b. The effect of this burden of fixed overheads on the business will be very great if the volume of production is small (resulting in a high overall cost per article produced) and relatively small if the volume of production is large (since in this case the fixed overhead is spread over a large number of articles, thereby making for a lower overall cost per article). This is the fundamental idea which led to mass production. Fig. 84 shows the appearance of the cost of production graph when the burden, b, is allowed for. It will be seen that the straight line now cuts the Cost axis in the value b, thereby indicating that even if there are no articles produced there is still this expense to be met. It is evident that our equation for this straight line will be of the form

$$C = pn + b$$

The magnitude of the fixed burden, b, will vary from manufacturer to manufacturer. Like p, the unit cost of production, it will be characteristic of a particular organization, and is the second parameter of the straight line. Parameters p and b, then, are characteristic constants, peculiar to a particular case.

Quite generally, from a mathematical point of view, p and b may be either positive or negative, depending on the problem. In the illustration we have been using it is evident that they will both be positive in the normal course of events. The overburden, b, in these modern and enlightened days, is sometimes made into a negative quantity by the government granting a subsidy. The result of this will be to make the value of b markedly positive in the taxpayer's graph of operations. Someone has to carry the burden. Problems often occur in scientific research where one quantity decreases as the others increase. In such cases, the value of p would be negative.

Not all functional relationships between two quantities are straight line laws, however. Most usually they are curves of some sort, and then the equations (formulae) connecting the varying quantities tend to become more complex. The equation which tells us the height of the Normal Curve, for example, has to describe a fairly tricky shape, and we are not surprised that it is rather complex. We met this curve in Chapter 9 and learnt there that its equation is

$$y = \frac{1}{\sigma\sqrt{2\pi}} e^{\frac{-(x-\bar{x})^2}{2\sigma^2}}$$

The characteristic constants or parameters of this equation are $\bar{x}$ and σ, which, as we know, represent the mean and standard deviation of the distribution being considered in any particular problem. We also learnt that the equation could be stated in a simpler form:

$$y = \frac{1}{\sqrt{2\pi}} e^{\frac{-t^2}{2}}$$

by shifting the origin of measurement for the variable, x, to the mean value, $\bar{x}$, and by measuring deviations, not in terms of the original units, but in terms of the standard deviation. This trick of simplifying calculations by a change of origin to the mean value, $\bar{x}$, is a common one and we shall meet it again. The reader should notice that the constant 2π in the above equation is *not* a parameter. It is always the same in every problem, and so is not characteristic of the data being dealt with -- which is the criterion for a parameter.

The mathematician is interested in functional relationships for their own sake. But he is also interested in them practically since very often these functional relationships form a good enough approximation to practical cases. We have seen how the Binomial, Poisson, Normal, χ^2, Student's t, Snedecor's F, and other mathematical functions derived from mathematical theory enable us to deal with practical problems in a very satisfactory way. We do not claim that a mathematical function will give a perfect description of the behaviour of naturally occurring variable quantities; nevertheless, we are in a very powerful position when we find one that is a good approximation. Problems that could only be tackled by sheer guesswork may be dealt with swiftly and confidently. The thing to be clear about before we proceed further is that a functional relationship in mathematics means an exact and predictable relationship, with no ifs or buts about it. It is useful in practice so long as the ifs and buts are only tiny voices which even the most ardent protagonist of proportional representation can ignore with a clear conscience.

In cases where there are many factors which have a notable bearing on a problem, we find that for research to be tolerable at all we have to restrict our investigation to the observation of relatively few of the factors. We shut our eyes to the rest, either deliberately because we just cannot cope with everything, or unconsciously because we just cannot name all the factors anyway. But the fact that we shut our eyes to factors does not mean that they cease to exist and to exert an influence. When we can name a factor which we are going deliberately to ignore, we can often do something to minimize the disturbing effect of its existence on our results by experimental design before the experiment is put under way. We can arrange for the factor to be held constant during the course of the experiment, or, failing this, we take steps, such as randomization or paired comparisons (see Chapter 18 and elsewhere), to ensure that such a factor shall not introduce bias into our data which would lead to misleading conclusions. When we are ignorant of the nature of disturbing factors we just have to let them do their worst and hope that they will not introduce such confusion into our data that we can never find anything significant in them. In a word, we shall have to expect a large experimental error.

When an investigation is carried out in the presence of many disturbing factors, we find that there is no simple relation between the factors on which the experiment was based. We plot graphs of one thing against another and find that, instead of the nice functional relationships so dear to the heart of the mathematician and the student at college, instead of nice straight lines and elegant-looking curves, we get plum puddings, the points in our graph being scattered very much at random. This is always a bad sign. It means that the disturbing factors have been more important than we had hoped. The student will either shrug his shoulders and say: 'It doesn't make sense', or he will try to draw in a trend line, if there is any suggestion of a relationship between the factors plotted against each other in the graph. The mathematician, however, looks on this as a challenge. His attitude is that we are undoubtedly in a pretty bad position on the face of it. He takes the view, however, that since we have gone to a lot of trouble collecting the data in a fairly sensible way, there should be some conclusions which are possible. These conclusions will be surrounded by a halo of greater or lesser uncertainty. He sees what he can do to extract those conclusions with an indication of the degree of confidence which may be placed in them. He looks at the graphs of the experimental results. This one suggests that, in the absence of disturbing factors, it might have been a straight line of the form $C = pn + b$. This other suggests to him (possibly because he has some *a priori* notions as to the form of the relationship which is likely between the two quantities in the graph) that there may be an underlying law of the type $y = ax^2 + bx + c$, and so on. In other words he will try to form some idea of the type of underlying mathematical law – if there should be such a thing. For reasons both theoretical and practical, when the problem is one in plum puddings he most commonly thinks of trying to get a straight line law out of it. The straight line law is the easiest to deal with of all possible laws – so much so that if we cannot get a straight line without jiggery pokery we have special mathematical dodges which enable us to throw a set of data into an approximately straight line trend. We might, for example, plot the logarithms of one set of values, or the square roots. These are professional tricks which must be got from textbooks by those who are interested. For our present purpose it is sufficient if the reader will take it that analysis of straight line trends is the commonest problem. It is this basic type of problem which we shall cover in this chapter.

If two quantities, y and x, are related by a straight line law, the equation expressing the relationship will be of the form

$$y = mx + c$$

where m is the parameter expressing the slope of the line, and c is the parameter which tells us at what value the straight line cuts the axis of x. The slope, m, tells us by how much y increases for an increase of unity in the value of x. Whenever there is a straight line trend between two quantities, y and x, we shall be able to find values for the two parameters m and c, which give us the equation of the straight line which is the best fit to the points in our graph. The best fit may be a good or bad one, but there always will be some straight line which is a better fit than all other straight lines. In Fig. 85, for example, it is clear that, while the line is a good fit with regard to slope, it is a poor one with regard to the intercept on the y axis. On the other hand, in Fig. 86 we have a straight line which seems to get the intercept on the y axis fairly well, but is obviously hopeless as regards slope. Our problem is to get the best slope and best intercept. What do we mean by best?

There are many criteria by which we might define what we mean by a best fit. The generally accepted criterion is the 'least squares' one. What do we mean by 'least squares'? There are three least squares criteria, each of which leads to a different straight line, as we shall now see. To illustrate the procedure of fitting a line by the method of least squares, we shall take an example.

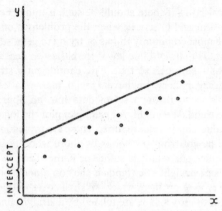

Fig. 85. A good fit for slope. A bad fit for intercept on *y* axis

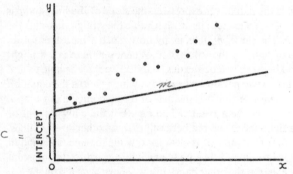

Fig. 86. A good fit for intercept on the *y* axis. A bad fit for slope

Suppose an investigation were made into the relationship between two quantities *y* and *x*. Let the following table represent the values of *y* observed for several values of *x*.

y =	5	8	9	10
x =	1	2	3	4

A graph of these data is shown in Fig. 87. Although the points do not lie on a straight line exactly, they do suggest that such *might have been* the case were it not that some disturbing factors had entered in. We may therefore take it as a reasonable proposition that the relationship between y and x can be expressed in the form of a straight line $y = mx + c$. Our problem is to determine the values of m and c which will enable us, given a value of x, to make the best possible prediction of the value of y. If the law is of this type, then when x is equal to 1 our formula predicts that we shall have $y = m + c$. When $x = 2$ our formula predicts that we shall

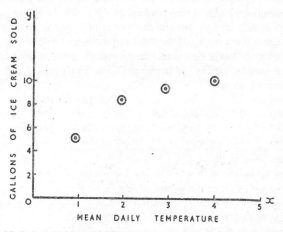

Fig. 87. Points which might have lain on a straight line had not some disturbing element been present

have $y = 2m + c$. When $x = 3$ the formula predicts $y = 3m + c$, and when $x = 4$ we should expect $y = 4m + c$, and so on. Of course, we could draw in a straight line on our graph of the data and make our predictions that way. Fair enough in the present case, where the points lie reasonably well on a pretty obvious line. Not much use, however, if the points were roughly scattered. Remember that what we are after is a technique to give us the best prediction even when the points are crudely scattered, so that fitting a line by eye is a chancy affair.

Let us now draw up a table of predicted values for y and actual values observed, and see what the discrepancies are.

Value of x	Predicted y	Observed y	Discrepancy
1	$m+c$	5	$m+c-5$
2	$2m+c$	8	$2m+c-8$
3	$3m+c$	9	$3m+c-9$
4	$4m+c$	10	$4m+c-10$

The discrepancies shown in the last column are the differences between predicted and observed values for y. On the least squares criterion of a best fit, we find the values of m and c which make the sum of the *squares* of these discrepancies as small as possible, There must always be a discrepancy overall, unless the points of our graph lie exactly on a straight line. Squaring out the discrepancies, we get:

$$(m+c-5)^2 = m^2 + c^2 + 25 + 2mc - 10m - 10c$$
$$(2m+c-8)^2 = 4m^2 + c^2 + 64 + 4mc - 32m - 16c$$
$$(3m+c-9)^2 = 9m^2 + c^2 + 81 + 6mc - 54m - 18c$$
$$(4m+c-10)^2 = 16m^2 + c^2 + 100 + 8mc - 80m - 20c$$

Total of squared
discrepancies $= 30m^2 + 4c^2 + 270 + 20mc - 176m - 64c$

If now we can find the values of m and c which make this algebraic expression have the minimum value possible, our problem will be solved. We could do this very clumsily by trial and error, choosing values for m and c and working out for each case the value of the sums of the squares of the discrepancies from the long formula we have just calculated. No one will be very keen to do this, for the simple reason that it is unsystematic, and we should never be sure that we had got the real minimum value. More systematic would be to set m at some value suggested by our graph of y against x. Inspection of the graph shows that m, which is actually the amount by which y increases for unit increase in x, must certainly be approximately equal to 2. We can also make a fairly decent guess that c, which is the value of y at which the line cuts the axis of y (the y intercept) must be about equal to 3. We might then try a more systematic investigation by trying values of

x and y in these regions. Such a method could not be mathematically exact, however. Moreover, trial and error would be very crude if the points were badly scattered in the graph, since then we could only make very rough guesses at the values of m and c. This difficulty has been overcome by the mathematicians, who have found a simple and exact way of determining the values of m and c, by the so-called differential calculus.

Suppose we have an expression of the type

$$S = pm^2 + qm + c$$

where p and q are numbers, e.g. 6, -8. If we wish to determine what value of m makes S a minimum, we proceed as follows. Put

$$2pm = -q$$

so that

$$m = \frac{-q}{2p}$$

Then this is the value of m for which S is a minimum. Take a simple example.

Let

$$S = 7m^2 - 21m + 4$$

In this case we have $p = 7$ and $q = -21$. So that the minimum value of S occurs when

$$m = \frac{-q}{2p} = \frac{-(-21)}{14} = \frac{21}{14} = \frac{3}{2}$$

The minimum value of S will then be found by substituting this value of m in our equation for S, thus:

$$S = 7m^2 - 21m + 4$$

and Minimum S is given by

$$S = 7(\tfrac{3}{2})^2 - 21(\tfrac{3}{2}) + = -11\tfrac{3}{4}$$

No matter what value we try for m, we shall never get S less than $-11\tfrac{3}{4}$.

Let us now return to our least squares problem. The sum of the squares of the discrepancies between observed and predicted values of y is given by

$$S = 30m^2 + 4c^2 + 270 + 20mc - 176m - 64c$$

10

Consider, first of all, m. The equation for S may be arranged as follows:

$$S = 30m^2 + (20c - 176)m + (270 - 64c + 4c^2)$$

which is exactly similar in form to

$$S = pm^2 + qm + c$$

where $\qquad p = 30$ and $q = (20c - 176)$

From this point of view, therefore, we shall expect S to attain its minimum value when

$$m = \frac{-q}{2p}$$

i.e. when $\qquad m = \dfrac{-(20c - 176)}{60}$

This reduces to the condition that we must have

$$\underline{60m + 20c - 176 = 0}$$

This is our first condition.

But the expression for S may also be arranged as an equation in c thus:

$$S = 4c^2 + (20m - 64)c + (270 - 176m + 30m^2)$$

This is exactly the same sort of thing as we had before with c replacing m and now we have

$$p = 4 \text{ and } q = (20m - 64)$$

From this point of view, therefore, we shall expect that S will attain its minimum value when

$$c = \frac{-q}{2p}$$

i.e. when $\qquad c = \dfrac{-(20m - 64)}{8}$

This reduces to the condition that we must have

$$\underline{20m + 8c - 64 = 0}$$

In addition, as we have already seen, we must have

$$\underline{60m + 20c - 176 = 0}$$

All we have to do then is to find values of m and c which satisfy these two conditions simultaneously. Let us make the coefficient of m equal to 60 in both equations by multiplying through by 3 in the equation where the coefficient of m is equal to 20. Our two conditions then are

$$60m + 24c - 192 = 0$$

and

$$60m + 20c - 176 = 0$$

by subtraction, it is clear that we must have

$$4c - 16 = 0, \quad \text{i.e. } \underline{c = 4}$$

We may then find the value of m by substituting this value for c in one of the equations. We get

$$60m + 80 - 176 = 0$$

$$\therefore \qquad 60m - 96 = 0, \quad \text{i.e. } \underline{m = 1 \cdot 6}$$

The equation of the line which best fits our points is therefore

$$y = mx + c$$

i.e.

$$\underline{y = 1 \cdot 6x + 4}$$

Most things in this life are harder to explain than do. There is always with us the efficiency expert, who finds quick and uninteresting ways of doing what was previously slow but interesting. So it is with this matter. We have two alternative procedures, which are as follows.

First Procedure. Draw up the following table, working from the original values of x and y

x	y	xy	x^2	
1	5	5	1	Number of pairs
2	8	16	4	of x, y values =
3	9	27	9	$N = 4$
4	10	40	16	
Totals 10	32	88	30	
Symbols for totals Σx	Σy	Σxy	Σx^2	

The values of m and c are then given by

$$m = \frac{\Sigma xy - \frac{(\Sigma x)(\Sigma y)}{N}}{\Sigma x^2 - \frac{(\Sigma x)^2}{N}}$$

which gives, on substitution,

$$m = \frac{88 - \frac{10 \times 32}{4}}{30 - \frac{10 \times 10}{4}} = \frac{88 - 80}{30 - 25} = \tfrac{8}{5} = 1 \cdot 6$$

and

$$c = \frac{(\Sigma x)(\Sigma xy) - (\Sigma y)(\Sigma x^2)}{(\Sigma x)^2 - N(\Sigma x^2)}$$

which gives, on substitution,

$$c = \frac{10 \times 88 - 32 \times 30}{100 - 4 \times 30} = 4$$

So the required equation for the best fitting straight line is

$$y = mx + c$$

i.e.
$$y = 1 \cdot 6x + 4$$

Which is the same result as before, obtained much more rapidly.

Second Procedure. This is done in three steps as follows.

Step 1. In the equation $y = mx + c$, substitute each of the observed pairs of values for x and y. Then add the resulting equations.

Step 2. Form a second similar set of equations, by multiplying through each of the equations of step 1 by its coefficient of m. Add this set of equations.

Step 3. Steps 1 and 2 will each have produced an equation in m and c. Solve these simultaneous equations for m and c.

Applying the method to our data, we get:

$5 = m + c$	multiply through by 1 and get	$5 = m + c$
$8 = 2m + c$	multiply through by 2 and get	$16 = 4m + 2c$
$9 = 3m + c$	multiply through by 3 and get	$27 = 9m + 3c$
$10 = 4m + c$	multiply through by 4 and get	$40 = 16m + 4c$
$\overline{32 = 10m + 4c}$		$\overline{88 = 30m + 10c}$

We then solve simultaneously the two equations

$$30m + 10c = 88$$

and
$$10m + 4c = 32$$

and again find that $m = 1 \cdot 6$ with $c = 4$, i.e. $y = 1 \cdot 6x + 4$

Since $\Sigma x = 10$ and $\Sigma y = 32$ for $N = 4$ we have

$$\bar{x} = \frac{\Sigma x}{N} = \frac{10}{4} = 2\cdot5$$

$$\bar{y} = \frac{\Sigma y}{N} = \frac{32}{4} = 8\cdot0$$

If we substitute these values in the regression equation we get

$$8\cdot0 = 1\cdot6 \times 2\cdot5 + 4$$

which proves that our regression line passes through the point $(\bar{x}, \bar{y})$. This is a very useful rule for which we shall find use later. Its value lies in the fact that, having calculated $\bar{x}$ and $\bar{y}$, we only need to calculate m, the slope, and our regression line is completely determined.

The reader will be wondering how certain we may be of the prediction given by a trend line. He will say that, since the predicted value is almost certain to be wrong, it is important to have some idea of just how wrong it is likely to be. In a given case, in fact, is the trend line of any use whatsoever for making predictions? It is to such questions that we must now turn our attention. We must get some clear ideas as to what we mean by correlation and how it may be measured.

As a preliminary we must introduce the reader to the very simple idea of the Cartesian co-ordinate method of plotting curves and points, so as to have a graphical representation of the relation between two quantities. The main idea will be familiar already under the name 'graphs'. All we have to do is to make clear how negative quantities are plotted. In graphs most frequently met with, all the quantities are positive. We deal with negative quantities by extending the axes beyond the origin, as shown in Fig. 88. Any point falling to the right of the vertical line YY^1 has a positive x value. If it falls to the left of the line YY^1 it has a negative x value. In similar fashion, any point falling above the horizontal line XX^1 has a positive y value, while if it falls below the line it has a negative y value. We may indicate any point by quoting its 'co-ordinates', just as in giving a map reference. The co-ordinates are the value of x and the value of y which correspond to the point, expressed in that order. The general symbol for a point in the xy plane is therefore reasonably taken as (x, y). In the figure several points are plotted, their co-ordinates being quoted beside them. If now we have a set of points (x, y) plotted and we find that they show a trend, we say that the variable quantities x and y are correlated. By this we mean that, although there is not a strictly functional relation between them, we are able to make some sort of prediction of the value of y, given a knowledge

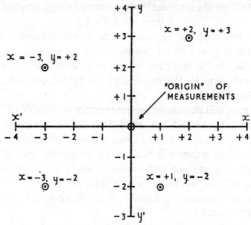

Fig. 88. Cartesian co-ordinates

of the value of x. When, as in Fig. 89, increasing y is associated with increasing x, we say that the two variables are positively correlated. When, as in Fig. 90, an increase in x results in a decrease in y, the variables are said to be negatively correlated. Crude scattering of the points about the trend line is indicative of low correlation, while a set of points none of which is far from the trend line is highly correlated.

The degree of correlation is measured by the so-called *product moment correlation coefficient*, which is defined as

$$r = \frac{\frac{1}{N}\Sigma(x - \bar{x})(y - \bar{y})}{\sigma_x \sigma_y}$$

where $\bar{x}$ and $\bar{y}$ are respectively the mean of all the x values and the mean of all the y values, and σ_x and σ_y are respectively the standard deviations of all the x values and all the y values. The product term $\frac{1}{N}\Sigma(x - \bar{x})(y - \bar{y})$ is called the *covariance* of x and y.

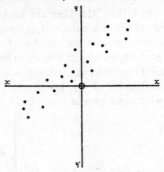

Fig. 89. Positive correlation. An increase in y is associated with an increase in x

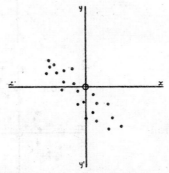

Fig. 90. Negative correlation. A decrease in y is associated with an increase in x

Since, therefore, σ_x^2 and σ_y^2 are the variances of x and y, we may remember this formula as

$$r = \frac{\text{covariance of } x \text{ and } y}{\sqrt{[\text{Var}(x)] \times [\text{Var}(y)]}}$$

It may be shown that the correlation coefficient, r, cannot exceed $+1$ or be less than -1 in value. A value of $+1$ denotes perfect functional relationship between y and x, an increasing x being associated with an increasing y. When r is equal to -1, we again have a perfect functional relationship, but this time an increasing x is associated with a decreasing y. When $r = 0$, there is no relation at all between x and y (Fig. 91). They are not correlated. Other intermediate values of r indicate that, while there is not a strictly functional relationship between the variables, there is a trend. If the coefficient is positive, increasing x tends to be associated with increasing y, while, if the coefficient is negative, increasing x tends to be associated with decreasing y. It may also be shown that it does not matter what value of x or y we choose as our origins of

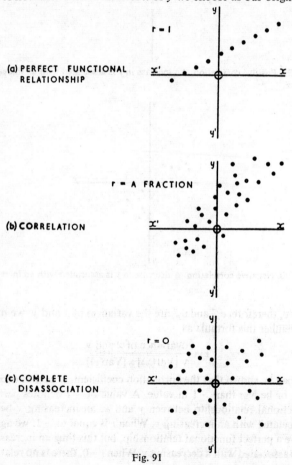

(a) PERFECT FUNCTIONAL RELATIONSHIP

(b) CORRELATION

(c) COMPLETE DISASSOCIATION

Fig. 91

measurement, nor what units the quantities x and y are measured in. The value of r remains constant for a given distribution throughout all changes of this type. These properties enable considerable savings to be made in the labour of calculation.

To illustrate the way in which the origin and units of measurement may be fixed arbitrarily for the calculation of the product moment correlation coefficient, we shall use the following data, quoted by W. W. Sawyer in his excellent popular book *Mathematics in Theory and Practice* (Odhams Press) whose attention was drawn to the figures by A. B. Lowndes, Head of the School of Commerce, College of Technology, Leicester.

District	Proportion of open spaces % = x	Proportion of accidents to children as percentage of all accidents = y
Bermondsey	5·0	46·3
Deptford	2·2	43·4
Islington	1·3	42·9
Fulham	4·2	42·2
Shoreditch	1·4	40·0
Finsbury	2·0	38·8
Woolwich	7·0	38·2
Stepney	2·5	37·4
Poplar	4·5	37·0
Southwark	3·1	33·3
Camberwell	5·2	33·6
Paddington	7·2	33·6
Stoke Newington	6·3	30·8
Hammersmith	12·2	28·3
Wandsworth	14·6	23·8
Marylebone	23·6	17·8
Hampstead	14·8	17·1
Westminster	27·5	10·8

Let us choose as an arbitrary origin for the percentage of all accidents which are accidents to children, the figure 35%. To each district there will then be a plus or minus figure which tells us how that district stands in relation to the arbitrary origin. Bermondsey will be +11·3% and Westminster −24·2. To cut out decimals, we multiply all these differences by 10, and enter them in the following table, under the heading v. In like manner, we choose an arbitrary origin 5% for the proportion of open spaces and again find for each district a plus or minus figure which tells us how the district compares with this arbitrary origin. These differences, multiplied by 10 to eliminate decimals, are entered in our table under the heading u. Thus u is a 'transformed' version of the values x of our original table, and v is a transformed version of the

	u	v	uv +	uv −	u^2 +	v^2 +
	− 9	+113		0	0	12,769
	− 28	+ 84	2,352		784	7,056
	− 37	+ 79	2,923		1,369	6,241
	− 8	+ 72	576		64	5,184
	− 36	+ 50	1,800		1,296	2,500
	− 30	+ 38	1,140		900	1,444
	+ 20	+ 32		640	400	1,024
	− 25	+ 24	600		625	576
	− 5	+ 20	100		25	400
	− 19	+ 3	57		361	9
	+ 2	− 14	28		4	196
	+ 22	− 14	308		484	196
	+ 13	− 42	546		169	1,764
	+ 72	− 67	4,824		5,184	4,489
	+ 96	−112	10,752		9,216	12,544
	+186	−172	31,992		34,596	29,584
	+ 98	−179	17,542		9,604	32,041
	+225	−242	54,450		50,625	58,564
Sums	+546	−327	−129,350		+115,706	+176,581
	Σu	Σv	Σuv		Σu^2	Σv^2

values y. For calculating the correlation coefficient we need not record the names of the districts, though for convenience we have put them in the same order as in the first table.

The correlation coefficient between x and y is then given by

$$r = \frac{\frac{1}{N}\Sigma uv - \bar{u}\bar{v}}{\sigma_u \sigma_v}$$

where $N = 18 =$ the number of (x, y) pairs in our original table. We have

$$\bar{u} = \frac{\Sigma u}{N} = \frac{546}{18} = 30 \cdot 3 \text{ and } \bar{v} = \frac{\Sigma v}{N} = \frac{-327}{18} = -18 \cdot 2$$

so that $\bar{u}\bar{v} = 30 \cdot 3(-18 \cdot 2) = -550$

$$\frac{1}{N}\Sigma uv = \frac{-129,350}{18} = -7,180$$

$$\sigma_u^2 = \frac{1}{N}\Sigma u^2 - (\bar{u})^2 = \frac{115,706}{18} - (30 \cdot 3)^2 = 5,500$$

$$\therefore \quad \sigma_u = \sqrt{5,500} = 74$$

$$\sigma_v^2 = \frac{1}{N}\Sigma v^2 - (\bar{v})^2 = \frac{176,581}{18} - (-18 \cdot 2)^2 = 9,490$$

$$\therefore \quad \sigma_v = 97.4$$

We get, therefore,

$$r = \frac{\frac{1}{N}\Sigma uv - \bar{u}\bar{v}}{\sigma_u \sigma_v}$$

$$= \frac{-7,180 - (-550)}{74 \times 97 \cdot 4} = \frac{-6,630}{7,200} = -0 \cdot 92$$

$$r = -0 \cdot 92$$

This is a high degree of negative correlation. The negative sign indicates that as the percentage of park space increases, the proportion of all accidents which are accidents to children decreases.

As always, there is the question of the significance of the correlation coefficient. We must ask ourselves whether so high a value of the correlation coefficient could easily have arisen by chance. This is a matter we shall take up a little further on. Yet again, having established the significance of the coefficient, we have to discuss its relevance to what action should be taken. As Sawyer points out, the objection might be raised that the existence of much park space in the areas where there are few accidents to children may be unrelated in a causative sense with that happy condition. In well parked areas there may be relatively fewer children in the population and a high proportion of nursemaids. It is right that such objections should be raised before money is spent. It is important that the statistician foresee them and be prepared to counter them with concrete evidence, if there is danger of false economy in matters of vital importance.

Suppose, now, having calculated our correlation coefficient, we wished to set up the equation of the regression line for the problem, that is to calculate an equation between y, the proportion of accidents to children as a percentage of all accidents, and x, the proportion of open spaces. This is quite easy if we think carefully of the meaning of our u and v units. If the reader will consider how the u and v values were arrived at he will find that

$$u = 10(x - 5) \qquad \text{and} \qquad v = 10(y - 35)$$

A little rearrangement of these equations gives us

$$x = \frac{u + 50}{10} \qquad\qquad y = \frac{v + 350}{10}$$

so that the averages are related by the equations

$$\bar{x} = \frac{\bar{u} + 50}{10} = \frac{30 \cdot 3 + 50}{10} = 8 \text{ (very nearly)}$$

$$\bar{y} = \frac{\bar{v} + 350}{10} = \frac{-18 \cdot 2 + 350}{10} = 33 \text{ (very nearly)}$$

We also have that

$$\sigma_x = \frac{\sigma_u}{10} = \frac{74}{10} = 7 \cdot 4$$

$$\sigma_y = \frac{\sigma_v}{10} = \frac{97 \cdot 4}{10} = 9 \cdot 7$$

(It will be recalled that the x and y values were each multiplied by 10 to get into the scale of u and v.)

With this information we can at once write down the equation for the regression equation for y on x as

$$y - \bar{y} = r\left(\frac{\sigma_y}{\sigma_x}\right)(x - \bar{x})$$

that is:

$$y - 33 = -0 \cdot 92 \left(\frac{9 \cdot 7}{7 \cdot 4}\right)(x - 8)$$

$$y - 33 = -1 \cdot 21(x - 8) = -1 \cdot 21x + 9 \cdot 2$$

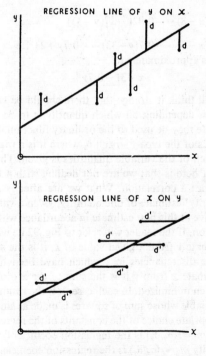

REGRESSION LINE OF y ON x

REGRESSION LINE OF x ON y

Fig. 92. Estimating y from x is not just the reverse of estimating x from y
    When we estimate y from x using the regression equation we make the sum of the squares of the quantities d a minimum
    When we estimate x from y using the regression equation we make the sum of the squares of the quantities d' a minimum

Which reduces approximately to

$$y = 43 - 1\cdot21x$$

This is the appropriate equation to use if we wish to estimate the accident percentage from the open space percentage. The problem might, of course, be stated the other way round: Given the accident percentage, to estimate the open space percentage. In this case the appropriate regression equation is

$$(x - \bar{x}) = r\left(\frac{\sigma_x}{\sigma_y}\right)(y - \bar{y}) \quad \text{GIVEN: } y \text{ - FIND: } x$$

$$(x - 8) = -0\cdot92\left(\frac{7\cdot4}{9\cdot7}\right)(y - 33)$$

$$(x - 8) = -0\cdot7(y - 33) = -0\cdot7y + 23\cdot1$$

Which reduces approximately to

$$x = 31 - 0\cdot7y$$

The reader will think it strange that there should be two regression equations, depending on which quantity is to be estimated from which. He may be used to the ordinary functional equation of mathematics of the type $y = mx + b$, where it is a matter of indifference which of the variable quantities is given. The thing to be clear about here is that we are not dealing with a functional relationship, but a correlation. What we are after is the 'minimum uncertainty' estimate of one quantity, given a value for the other. We arrive at this best estimate in accordance with the least squares criterion. If the reader will refer to Fig. 92 he will see that when we estimate y from a given value of x, it is the sum of the squares of the discrepancies in y which have been minimized. When we estimate x from y it is the sum of the x discrepancies which have been minimized. In each case, it is the residuals in the dependent variable whose sum of squares is made as small as possible by appropriate choice of the constants of the regression line. The quantity $m_1 = r(\sigma_y/\sigma_x)$ is the regression coefficient of y on x, and the quantity $m_2 = r(\sigma_x/\sigma_y)$ is the regression coefficient of x on y. It will be seen that the correlation coefficient r is the geometric mean $\sqrt{m_1 m_2}$ of the regression coefficients, and that the two regression lines intersect at the point $(\bar{x}, \bar{y})$, i.e. (8, 33) in our example. This example, too, brings out clearly that extrapolation can be nonsensical. If we were to ask what the percentage of open space would be to make accidents to children 50% of all accidents, we find that we get a negative value for the percentage of open spaces. The regression applies within the range of the observed data, and we extrapolate at our peril, always.

The regression line gives only a 'best estimate' of the value of the quantity in question. We may assess the degree of uncertainty

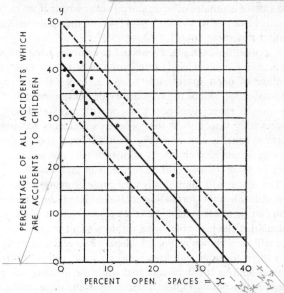

Fig. 93. Regression of y on x with control limits placed at two standard errors of estimate, S_y, on either side of the regression line.

in this estimate by calculating a quantity known as the Standard Error of Estimate, given by

$$S_y = \sigma_y \sqrt{1 - r^2}$$

or

$$S_x = \sigma_x \sqrt{1 - r^2}$$

according as we are estimating y or x. We may explain the meaning of the standard error of estimate from our example. We have

$$S_y = \sigma_y \sqrt{1 - r^2} = 9 \cdot 7 \sqrt{1 - (0 \cdot 92)^2} = 9 \cdot 7 \sqrt{0 \cdot 154} = 3 \cdot 8\%$$
$$S_x = \sigma_x \sqrt{1 - r^2} = 7 \cdot 4 \sqrt{1 - (0 \cdot 92)^2} = 7 \cdot 4 \sqrt{0 \cdot 154} = 2 \cdot 9\%$$

In about 95% of the cases, the actual values will lie within plus or minus two standard errors of the estimate values given by the regression equation; and almost without exception actual values will be found to depart from the estimated value by not more than three standard errors. Thus we should be correct 95 times out of 100 in making the claim that actual values lay within $2 \times 3\cdot8 = 7\cdot6\%$ of the estimated value given by the regression equation in the case of estimates of y; or scarcely ever wrong if we claim that actual values lie within $3 \times 3\cdot8 = 11\cdot4\%$ of the estimated value. A similar statement holds for estimates of x.

Suppose, for example, we wished to estimate what proportion of accidents are accidents to children in an area where the percentage of open spaces is 10%. We have $y = 43 - 1\cdot21x = 30\%$ approximately. Since the standard error of estimate is $S_y = 3\cdot8\%$, we should expect that of all places with the stated 10% open spaces 95% would show that children's accidents accounted for between roughly 22% and 38% of all accidents, and we should be almost certain that children's accidents were not less than about 18% or more than 42% of all accidents in that place.

The reader will think this is very crude estimation. He is right. It is only when the correlation coefficient is very high that estimation can be at all precise. Yet the reasonableness of the rule for calculating the probable range within which the estimated quantity will lie is shown in Fig. 93 where we have the regression line of y on x, together with lines set at plus and minus $2S_y$ from the regression line. It will be seen that while the limits thus indicated contain the points plotted reasonably well, there could be no question of narrowing the limits.

Very often correlation analyses have to be carried out on very large samples. In such cases we may considerably lighten the work by an extension of the grouped frequency table which we met in Chapter 6, that is to say, by working with a grouped frequency correlation table. Since the method of correlation analysis is primarily used in cases where it is not possible to control the experimental conditions, but we have to analyse such data as we can collect as they occur – the usual condition in biometry and economic analysis, we shall illustrate the correlation table method by an example from the field of biometry. To simplify illustration of the computational procedure, the figures given are quite imaginary.

Suppose the question were whether there is a correlation between the height of girls and the height of their fathers. The following table might then show the numbers of girls whose heights fall within the stated ranges, for the stated heights of the fathers. To simplify the arithmetic, we now make the following changes. We choose arbitrary origins at 67·5 inches for the heights of fathers, and 63·5 inches for the heights of daughters. The reader should note that in this example the class interval for heights of both fathers and daughters is 1 inch. We then have:

$$u = \text{Height of father} - 67\cdot5 \quad = x - 67\cdot5$$
$$v = \text{Height of daughter} - 63\cdot5 = y - 63\cdot5$$

Working in the u, v units, the correlation coefficient is given by an expression which involves the sum of uv products, $\bar{u}$, $\bar{v}$, σ_u, σ_y, and N as before. But whereas previously we had our data given as individual (x, y) pairs, now we have a grouped table and the computational formulae have to be modified to allow for this. The following table shows the customary layout.

The square section, in the upper left-hand portion of the table, will be seen to be our original table with u and v replacing x and y. The column and row labelled f_v and f_u are respectively the columns showing marginal totals, as in the original table. It will be seen that the lower extension corresponds exactly to the right-handed extension to the table, with u and v interchanged. It will therefore suffice if we explain the meaning of the remaining columns at the right of the table, since the reader will then be able to follow the meaning of the bottom of the table for himself along the same lines.

The values in the column headed $v.f_v$ are obtained by multiplying the values in the f_v column by the value of v to which they correspond. The values in the $v^2.f_v$ column are obtained by multiplying the values in the $v.f_v$ column again by the value of v to which they correspond. The reader will recognize this as essentially the same procedure as was adopted in Chapter 6 for the grouped frequency table for a single variable, and will see that from the totals of these columns we shall be able to compute $\bar{v}$

x = Height of father in inches

y = Height of daughter in inches

y \ x	61·5	62·5	63·5	64·5	65·5	66·5	67·5	68·5	69·5	70·5	71·5	72·5	73·5	Total
58·5		1	1											2
59·5	1	2	1	2	1	1				1				9
60·5			1	2	2	2	1	1						9
61·5			1	2	5	2	2							12
62·5		1	1		2	5	6	3		1				18
63·5				1	2	4	7	2	1					17
64·5						1	5	2						8
65·5					1		2	2	4	2	1			13
66·5							1		2	1	2	1	1	6
67·5										2	1			5
68·5													1	1
Total	1	4	5	7	13	15	24	10	7	7	4	1	2	100

Values of u

v	v.U	U	v²fᵥ	vᵥfᵥ	fᵥ	6	5	4	3	2	1	0	−1	−2	−3	−4	−5	−6
−5	45	−9	50	−10	2												1	
−4	104	−26	144	−36	9						1	1	1	1	2	1	2	1
−3	45	−15	81	−27	9							2	2	2	2	1		
−2	44	−22	48	−24	12							2	2	5	2	1		
−1	8	−8	18	−18	18					1	2	8	5	2			1	
0	0	−7	0	0	17			1	1	1	3	6	4	2	1			
1	1	−1	8	8	8			1	1	2	2	2	1					
2	28	14	52	26	13			1	2	3	2	3		1		1		
3	63	21	54	18	6	1		2	2	1								
4	60	15	80	20	5		1	1	2		1							
5	30	6	25	5	1	1												
Totals	428	−30	560	−38	100	2	1	4	7	7	10	24	15	13	7	5	4	1
fᵤ	100					2	1	4	7	7	10	24	15	13	7	5	4	1
u.fᵤ	−30					12	5	16	21	14	10	0	−15	−26	−21	−20	−20	−6
u².fᵤ	608					72	25	64	63	28	10	0	15	52	63	80	100	36
V	−38					8	4	12	10	14	0	0	−18	−20	−18	−12	−14	−4
u.V	428					48	20	48	30	28	0	0	18	40	54	48	70	24

Values of v

and σ_v – two of the quantities which enter into the computation of the correlation coefficient. From the corresponding row totals at the foot of the table we shall be able to compute $\bar{u}$ and σ_u, which are also needed to get r. The value of N, the total number of original x,y pairs, will be given by the total of either the f_u row or the f_v column, in this case 100. All we now need is the term involving the sum of the uv products.

It is for this purpose that the columns headed U and $v.U$ are used. The corresponding rows V and $u.V$ at the foot of the table do exactly the same job by a different route, and so lead to a check of numerical accuracy. Each value in the U column is obtained by multiplying each frequency entry in that row by the value of u to which it corresponds and adding together all these products. Thus, the first entry in the U column is obtained as $1.(-5) + 1.(-4) = -9$. The second entry as $1.(-6) + 2.(-5) + 1.(-4) + 2.(-3) + 1.(-2) + 1.(-1) + 1.(+3) = -26$. These entries multiplied by the value of v to which they correspond give us the entries for the $v.U$ column. All the columns at the right of the table, with the exception of the U column, are totalled as shown. When the same procedure has been gone through for the rows at the foot of the table, all the necessary quantities for the computation of the correlation coefficient are at the bottom right-hand of the table. We now extract and label them.

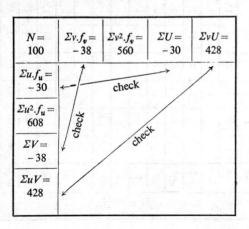

$N =$ 100	$\Sigma v.f_v =$ -38	$\Sigma v^2.f_v =$ 560	$\Sigma U =$ -30	$\Sigma vU =$ 428
$\Sigma u.f_u =$ -30				
$\Sigma u^2.f_u =$ 608				
$\Sigma V =$ -38				
$\Sigma uV =$ 428				

We then get:
$$\bar{u} = \frac{\Sigma u.f_u}{N} = \frac{-30}{100} = -0.30$$

$$\bar{v} = \frac{\Sigma v.f_v}{N} = \frac{-38}{100} = -0.38$$

Since our arbitrary origin is chosen at $x_0 = 67.5$, $y_0 = 63.5$, and since the class interval, c, is equal to unity for both x and y variables, we get

$$\bar{x} = c\bar{u} + x_0 = 1.(-0.30) + 67.5 = 67.2$$
$$\bar{y} = c\bar{v} + y_0 = 1.(-0.38) + 63.5 = 63.12$$

Also $\sigma^2_u = \dfrac{\Sigma u^2.f_u}{N} - \bar{u}^2 = \frac{608}{100} - (-0.3)^2 = 5.99$

Whence $\sigma_u = 2.45$

so that $\sigma_x = c.\sigma_u = 1.(2.45) = 2.45$

And $\sigma_v^2 = \dfrac{\Sigma v^2.f_v}{N} - \bar{v}^2 = \frac{560}{100} - (-0.38)^2 = 5.46$

Whence $\sigma_v = 2.34$

so that $\sigma_y = c.\sigma_v = 1.(2.34) = 2.34$

The correlation coefficient may be calculated

either as
$$r = \frac{\frac{1}{N}\Sigma v.U - \bar{u}.\bar{v}}{\sigma_u \sigma_v}$$

or as
$$r = \frac{\frac{1}{N}\Sigma u.V - \bar{u}.\bar{v}}{\sigma_u \sigma_v}$$

In either case we get
$$r = \frac{\frac{428}{100} - (-0.30)(-0.38)}{2.45 \times 2.34} = +0.73 \text{ approx.}$$

As before, the regression of y on x may be expressed by the equation
$$(y - \bar{y}) = r\left(\frac{\sigma_y}{\sigma_x}\right)(x - \bar{x})$$

that is $(y - 63.1) = 0.73\left(\dfrac{2.34}{2.45}\right)(x - 67.2)$

which reduces to
$$y = 16.9 + 0.69x$$

And the Standard Error of Estimate of y will be
$$S_y = \sigma_y \sqrt{1 - r^2} = 2 \cdot 34 \sqrt{1 - (0 \cdot 73)^2} = 1 \cdot 6 \text{ inch}$$

The total variability of the y values is measured by the quantity $\sigma_y = 2 \cdot 34$. The standard error of estimate S_y is a measure of the variability in the y values which remains unexplained by the fact that there is a true regression between y and x. In other words, if the correlation coefficient were not significant, then, whatever value of x we were given, our best estimate of y would always be $\bar{y}$ with a standard error of estimate σ_y, since with r not proved significantly different from zero $S_y = \sigma_y$. But if the correlation is established by testing the significance of r, we can account for some of the variability in height of the daughters on the grounds that their fathers were not all of the same height, and the taller fathers tend to have taller daughters. We have here a case of the partitioning of the total variance into two parts, (1) the variance component due to regression and (2) a component of variance which, not being explained by the regression, is due to other causes. Other causes in this case would include, for example, the height of the mothers and environmental factors by which inherent tendencies might be assisted or thwarted. It is variance, not standard deviation, which is the additive parameter. So we may write:

$$\text{Total variance} = \begin{array}{c} \text{Variance due to} \\ \text{regression} \end{array} + \begin{array}{c} \text{Variance not explained} \\ \text{by regression} \end{array}$$
$$\sigma_y^2 = \sigma_y^2 . r^2 + \sigma_y^2 (1 - r^2)$$

The critical reader will have noticed that through all this we make the assumption that the regression is a straight line type. He will ask whether we ought not to test whether an actual regression departs significantly from this assumption. There is a rough test which we may do from the correlation table: namely, to calculate the average value of v for each of the columns and see whether these column averages lie reasonably well on a straight line. There is a more exact test, depending on the calculation of the quantity known as the *correlation ratio*. It should be remembered, always, that unless the means of the columns lie reasonably on a straight line, the use of the correlation coefficient may be very misleading, for the reason that a value $r = 0$ indicates that there is an absence of linear correlation. There may, however, be correlation of a high order without the straight line regression which is fundamental to the methods described in this chapter. The correlation ratio referred to not only leads to a criterion for the testing of linearity of regression, but also to a measure of non-linear regression. Readers interested in non-linear regression should refer to standard textbooks quoted in the bibliography.

Before introducing the reader to more complex cases of regression analysis, we wish to emphasize that at no point are statistical methods more of a sausage machine than in correlation analysis. The problem of interpretation is always very much more difficult to deal with than the statistical manipulations, and for this side of the work there is no substitute for detailed practical acquaintance with every aspect of the problem. The statistician can only help out the specialist in the field, not replace him. The man who plays carelessly with sharp tools is asking to be cut.

In the fields where controlled experimentation is usually more or less impossible, such as economics or social research, it is also true, unfortunately, that in any problem under discussion we have to take account of several factors at the same time. Under these conditions we may calculate the correlation coefficient between any pair of the variables. But the obvious conclusion is not always the correct one, as is clearly seen in a very interesting investigation by Ogburn in the United States. He found a correlation of – 0·14 between crime rate as measured by the number of known offences per thousand inhabitants and church membership as measured by the percentage of church members among the age group 13 years and over. Taking this at face value, we should infer that religious belief makes a person less liable to commit crimes. There seems nothing inherently unlikely about this, but a more detailed analysis which took account of other factors showed the obvious conclusion to be incorrect. It was found that when the effect of the proportion of young children was excluded the correlation between crime and church membership was positive. Moreover, when the effect of the proportion of foreign immigrants was excluded, the correlation between crime and church membership was again positive. Since both foreign immigrants and large families are associated with the Catholic faith, a crude correlation coefficient between church membership and crime showed up as negative. It appears that if we look for a low crime rate we should look for law-abiding foreigners with large families, rather than churchmen. In the rest of the population church-going and crime seem to be positively associated. Is this a happy or sad thing? It is probably a good thing. Certainly a church that can only attract the respectable is failing to get at the people most in need of assistance. A reasonable case may be made out that the church should be the place where sinners feel at home, in accordance with the well-known story of the hard-bitten sinner who dropped into church just in time to hear the parson saying: 'We have done those things which we ought not to have done, and left undone those things which we ought to have done' – and said: 'Thank God. I've found my crowd at last.' The best advice that we can give to the man who finds a correlation and starts to say 'It's obvious' is: Think again. Ten to one there's a catch in it. The reader has been well enough warned by now unless he is 'invincibly ignorant', as the theologians have it. We shall therefore explain, briefly, the routine for analysis with several factors, making at once the proviso that it is usually profitless to apply the methods to cases involving more than four variables.

As an example, consider the following figures which show the marks scored during the year, the Intelligence Quotient, and the marks obtained in the final examination by each of ten students.

Student	Exam % x_1	I.Q. x_2	Year's % x_3
A	35	100	35
B	40	100	50
C	25	110	30
D	55	140	75
E	85	150	80
F	90	130	90
G	65	100	75
H	55	120	50
J	45	140	35
K	50	110	50

It will be evident that we can calculate simple correlation coefficients between the pairs of these three variables, viz. for x_1 and x_2, for x_1 and x_3, and for x_2 and x_3, ignoring in each case the third variable. As a result of these three correlation analyses, we should be able to set up six regression equations enabling us to predict x_1 from x_2, x_1 from x_3, and x_2 from x_3, respectively, or vice versa.

Suppose we were predicting x_1, the examination percentage, from x_2, the intelligence quotient, then anyone with any sense would feel that a more reliable prediction could be made if the student's preparation for the examination, as measured by x_3, were included. Teachers have got on very well without I.Q.'s, using the student's class marks as their basis for prognostication. Hard work goes a long way towards overcoming deficiency in native genius. Brilliance without application shows little profit in examinations. Nevertheless, it is undoubtedly true that the bright child often gets away in the examination, even if he has slacked during the year. We feel that the optimum system of prediction would include both the year's mark and the I.Q. Most people will agree that by and large the year's mark is likely to prove a better prophet than the I.Q. This means that we shall wish to give more weight to the year's mark than to the I.Q. They could be weighted by guesswork, but this is not very satisfactory. The old-fashioned, but excellent teacher, who regards I.Q.'s as a lot of tommy-rot, might think his assessment on the basis of the year's mark to be fifty times as reliable as any fancy psychological test. The young teacher, just out of college, might think the scientifically standardized I.Q. test every bit as reliable as his amateur judgement based on inexperienced marking. Both views, in their respective circumstances, might well be right. It follows that the weighting will depend on the circumstances of the particular case – what suits an experienced teacher could well be a poor weighting system applied to the circumstances of a novice.

This should be a warning against the mixing of non-homogeneous data for correlation analysis. The results of this type of analysis always apply to a particular set of circumstances. Once these are materially changed, a fresh analysis becomes necessary. In our case, we may suppose that our ten students have been assessed, both for I.Q. and for year's mark under the same conditions. Our regression analysis will tell us how – so long as these conditions remain substantially the same – to make a best estimate of the students' examination marks. The first step is to put the magnitudes into 'code' form.

Let us write $u_1 = x_1 - 50$ $u_2 = x_2 - 120$ $u_3 = x_3 - 50$

For $n = 10$ students

u_1	u_2	u_3	u_1^2	u_2^2	u_3^2	u_1u_2	u_1u_3	u_2u_3
−15	−20	−15	225	400	225	300	225	300
−10	−20	0	100	400	0	200	0	0
−25	−10	−20	625	100	400	250	500	200
5	20	25	25	400	625	100	125	500
35	30	30	1,225	900	900	1,050	1,050	900
40	10	40	1,600	100	1,600	400	1,600	400
15	−20	25	225	400	625	−300	375	−500
5	0	0	25	0	0	0	0	0
−5	20	−15	25	400	225	−100	75	−300
0	−10	0	0	100	0	0	0	0
+45	0	+70	+4,075	+3,200	+4,600	+1,900	+3,950	+1,500
Σu_1	Σu_2	Σu_3	Σu_1^2	Σu_2^2	Σu_3^2	Σu_1u_2	Σu_1u_3	Σu_2u_3

Our first calculation from the table of coded data is to get the means and corrected sums of squares and products. It will be convenient to introduce the symbol Σ' to denote a corrected sum. We find:

$$\left. \begin{array}{l} \bar{u}_1 = \dfrac{\Sigma u_1}{n} = \dfrac{45}{10} = 4\cdot5 \\[2mm] \bar{u}_2 = \dfrac{\Sigma u_2}{n} = \dfrac{0}{10} = 0 \\[2mm] \bar{u}_3 = \dfrac{\Sigma u_3}{n} = \dfrac{70}{10} = 7\cdot0 \end{array} \right\} \text{Means}$$

$$\Sigma'u_1{}^2 = \Sigma u_1{}^2 - \frac{(\Sigma u_1)^2}{n} = 4{,}075 - \frac{45 \times 45}{10} = 3{,}875$$

$$\Sigma'u_2{}^2 = \Sigma u_2{}^2 - \frac{(\Sigma u_2)^2}{n} = 3{,}200 - \frac{0 \times 0}{10} = 3{,}200 \quad \rbrace \text{Squares}$$

$$\Sigma'u_3{}^2 = \Sigma u_3{}^2 - \frac{(\Sigma u_3)^2}{n} = 4{,}600 - \frac{70 \times 70}{10} = 4{,}110$$

$$\Sigma'u_1u_2 = \Sigma u_1u_2 - \frac{(\Sigma u_1)(\Sigma u_2)}{n} = 1{,}900 - \frac{45 \times 0}{10} = 1{,}900$$

$$\Sigma'u_1u_3 = \Sigma u_1u_3 - \frac{(\Sigma u_1)(\Sigma u_3)}{n} = 3{,}950 - \frac{45 \times 70}{10} = 3{,}635 \quad \rbrace \text{Products}$$

$$\Sigma'u_2u_3 = \Sigma u_2u_3 - \frac{(\Sigma u_2)(\Sigma u_3)}{n} = 1{,}500 - \frac{0 \times 70}{10} = 1{,}500$$

Let us now suppose that u_1 is best predicted from u_2 and u_3 by a formula of the type

$$(u_1 - \bar{u}_1) = a(u_2 - \bar{u}_2) + b(u_3 - \bar{u}_3)$$

This is known as a partial regression equation, and it is now our problem to determine the partial regression coefficients a and b. The constant a tells us how much u_1 increases when u_2 increases by one unit, u_3 being held constant meanwhile. Likewise, if u_2 is held constant, b tells us the amount by which u_1 is expected to increase for each unit increase in u_3. The two unknowns a and b are found by solving two simultaneous equations, and there is a simple dodge by which we may find out what these two equations are.

Step 1. Call $\bar{u}_1$, $\bar{u}_2$, and $\bar{u}_3$ each zero and write the regression equation as

$$u_1 = au_2 + bu_3$$

Step 2. Multiply right through by u_2, and we have

$$u_1u_2 = au_2{}^2 + bu_2u_3$$

Then insert the sign Σ' before the u squares and products to get the first of our simultaneous equations:

$$\Sigma'u_1u_2 = a\Sigma'u_2{}^2 + b\Sigma'u_2u_3 \qquad (1)$$

which, when we put in numerical values for the Σ's, becomes

$$1{,}900 = 3{,}200a + 1{,}500b \qquad (1)$$

Step 3. Next, multiply through the regression equation of step 1 by u_3, getting

$$u_1u_3 = au_2u_3 + bu_3{}^2$$

Then insert the sign Σ' before the u squares and products to get the second equation:

$$\Sigma'u_1u_3 = a\Sigma'u_2u_3 + b\Sigma'u_3{}^2 \tag{2}$$

We next insert numerical values for the Σ's, for simplicity in this illustration correct to two significant figures, and find

$$3{,}600 = 1{,}500a + 4{,}100b \tag{2}$$

Dividing right through each equation by 100, we get:

$$32a + 15b = 19 \tag{1}$$
$$15a + 41b = 36 \tag{2}$$

Equate the coefficients of a by multiplying through the first equation by 15 and through the second by 32, thus:

$$480a + 225b = 285 \tag{1}$$
$$480a + 1312b = 1152 \tag{2}$$

Subtract $1087b = 867$ $\therefore\ b = 0 \cdot 8$ approx.

and it follows by substitution of this value: $a = 0 \cdot 24$ approx.

Our regression equation is therefore

$$(u_1 - \bar{u}_1) = 0\cdot 24(u_2 - \bar{u}_2) + 0\cdot 8(u_3 - \bar{u}_3)$$

i.e. $(u_1 - 4\cdot 5) = 0\cdot 24(u_2 - 0) + 0\cdot 8(u_3 - 7\cdot 0)$

which reduces to

$$u_1 = 0\cdot 24u_2 + 0\cdot 8u_3 - 1\cdot 1$$

We now translate the code regression equation to the original units by writing

$$\bar{u}_1 = (x_1 - 50) \qquad u_2 = (x_2 - 120) \qquad u_3 = (x_3 - 50)$$

and find

$$(x_1 - 50) = 0\cdot 24(x_2 - 120) + 0\cdot 8(x_3 - 50) - 1\cdot 1$$

which reduces to

$$x_1 = 0\cdot 24x_2 + 0\cdot 8x_3 - 20$$

This is the equation to be used in predicting final examination results from I.Q. and the students' marks during the year.* As an exercise (and a check on our working) let us try to predict one of

---

* The question of testing significance in partial regression is referred to at the end of the chapter.

the examination results in the original data. Student A had I.Q. = 100 and a mark for the year of 35. We predict his examination result as

$$x_1 = (0\cdot24)(100) + (0\cdot8)(35) - 20$$
$$= \quad 24 \quad + \quad 28 \quad - 20 = 32$$

His actual score was 35.

Again, Student E had I.Q.—150 with year's mark = 80, and we predict

$$x_1 = (0\cdot24)(150) + (0\cdot8)(80) - 20$$
$$= \quad 36 \quad + \quad 64 \quad - 20 = 80$$

His actual score was 85.

The reader should be clear that this *partial regression equation* is suitable only for predicting examination results. If we wished, for example, to estimate I.Q. from a knowledge of year's mark and examination mark, we would have to calculate the most appropriate equation for this entirely different job. We would assume

$$(u_2 - \bar{u}_2) = a(u_1 - \bar{u}_1) + b(u_3 - \bar{u}_3)$$

and go through the whole process again to find the best values for a and b in this situation.

It will be evident to the reader that, since the values predicted from a partial regression equation – while approximating actual values – differ somewhat from them, we should find a correlation existing between actual and predicted values. Such a correlation coefficient is called a *Multiple Correlation* coefficient, and we shall now calculate it for the case where examination scores are predicted from our partial regression equation.

Student	Actual x	Predicted y
A	35	32
B	40	44
C	25	30
D	55	74
E	85	80
F	90	83
G	65	64
H	55	49
J	45	42
K	50	46

It will be convenient to work with the data in a coded form by writing $u = x - 55$, $v = y - 55$. The correlation coefficient is, of course, unaffected by coding. The calculation is as follows:

u	v	u^2	v^2	uv
−20	−23	400	529	460
−15	−11	225	121	165
−30	−25	900	625	750
0	19	0	361	0
30	25	900	625	750
35	28	1,225	784	980
10	9	100	81	90
0	−6	0	36	0
−10	−13	100	169	130
−5	−9	25	81	45
Sums −5	−6	3,875	3,412	3,370
Σu	Σv	Σu^2	Σv^2	Σuv

$N = 10$

Covariance of u and v

$$\frac{1}{N}\Sigma' uv = \frac{1}{N}\Sigma uv - \frac{(\Sigma u)}{N}\frac{(\Sigma v)}{N} = \frac{3,370}{10} - \frac{(-5)}{10}\cdot\frac{(-6)}{10} = 337 \text{ approx.}$$

Variance of u

$$\frac{1}{N}\Sigma' u^2 = \frac{1}{N}\Sigma u^2 - \left(\frac{\Sigma u}{N}\right)^2 = \frac{3,875}{10} - \left(\frac{-5}{10}\right)^2 = 387 \text{ approx.}$$

Variance of v

$$\frac{1}{N}\Sigma' v^2 = \frac{1}{N}\Sigma v^2 - \left(\frac{\Sigma v}{N}\right)^2 = \frac{3,412}{10} - \left(\frac{-6}{10}\right)^2 = 341 \text{ approx.}$$

Correlation Coefficient $= \dfrac{\text{Covar }(u, v)}{\sqrt{\text{Var}(u).\text{Var}(v)}}$

$$= \frac{337}{\sqrt{341 \times 387}} = 0\cdot 9 \text{ approx.}$$

Armed with a knowledge of the Multiple Correlation Coefficient, we may compute a standard error of estimate, exactly as in the case of simple correlation. It is given by

$$S_{x_1} = \sigma_{x_1}\sqrt{1-r^2}$$

We know that $r = 0.9$ and that the variance of u is 387. Since, in getting u, we simply changed the origin of reference without introducing any scale factor, the variance of x_1 is also 387. Hence $\sigma_{x_1} = \sqrt{387} = 19$ approx. It follows that the standard error of estimate is

$$S_{x_1} = 19\sqrt{1-(0.9)^2} = 10\sqrt{0.19} = \underline{8.5 \text{ approx.}}$$

Whenever we make a prediction, therefore, we shall be correct 95 times out of 100 if we say the examination score will be within $2 \times 8.5 = 17$ on either side of the value arrived at by using the partial regression equation. Evidently, there is a considerable margin of uncertainty in predicting from these data. We shall now deal with methods for testing the significance of correlation coefficients, and ways of pooling independent estimates of correlation.

Most commonly we wish to know whether the observed correlation coefficient could have arisen by chance with fair probability in a sample of the size dealt with. This may conveniently be tested using tables of the distribution of Student's t, by calculating

$$t = \frac{r\sqrt{N-2}}{\sqrt{1-r^2}}$$

and entering the tables with $N-2$ degrees of freedom.

Example. In our problem of accidents to children in relation to park space, we found $r = -0.92$, based on $N = 18$ districts. So far as the significance, as distinct from the meaning, of the correlation coefficient is concerned, we may ignore the minus sign. We find

$$t = \frac{0.92\sqrt{16}}{\sqrt{1-(0.92)^2}} = 9.32$$

with $N = 18 - 2 = 16$ degrees of freedom. The tables show that at the 5% level $t = 2.12$, and at the 1% level $t = 2.92$. We conclude, therefore, that the observed value of the correlation coefficient is extremely significant.

Provided that the value of N is large (say, not less than 100), and provided also that the value of r is small, we may regard the standard error of the correlation coefficient as

$$\text{S. E. of } r = \frac{1 - r^2}{\sqrt{N}}$$

Suppose, for example, in a particular case, we found $r = 0 \cdot 2$ with $N = 400$. Then the standard error of r is obtained as $0 \cdot 048$. Thus, the observed value of the coefficient is four times its standard error, and so definitely significant. We could always use the Student's t method, however. The labour is little more.

When we have independent estimates, and can show them not to differ significantly, we shall want to pool them together, so as to get a pooled estimate based on the whole available information. It is not permissible to add all the independent estimates together and divide by the number of them to get an average correlation coefficient. A special procedure has to be followed which takes proper account of the number of items used in computing each of the estimates.

It is at this point that we introduce Fisher's z transformation, by which we write

$$z = 1 \cdot 15 \, \log_{10}\left(\frac{1 + r}{1 - r}\right)$$

Whatever the sign, plus or minus, of our correlation coefficient, we first of all calculate z calling r positive. Then if our r was originally negative, we prefix the negative sign to the final value of z; but if r was positive originally, we leave z positive. In order to pool several independent estimates of r, we first of all transform them to z values. Each z is then multiplied by $(N - 3)$ where N is the original number of pairs in the corresponding value of r. The products are then summed and divided by the total of the $(N - 3)$ terms, to give us a mean value of z, which is then transformed back to give us our pooled r.

Example. Three independent estimates of r were $0 \cdot 25$ with $N = 23$, $-0 \cdot 14$ with $N = 28$, $+0 \cdot 17$ with $N = 43$. Find a pooled estimate

$$r = 0 \cdot 25 \text{ gives } z = 1 \cdot 15 \, \log_{10}\left(\frac{1 \cdot 25}{0 \cdot 75}\right) = 0 \cdot 255$$

$$r = -0.14 \text{ gives } z = -1.15 \log_{10}\left(\frac{1.14}{0.86}\right) = -0.141$$

$$r = 0.17 \text{ gives } z = 1.15 \log_{10}\left(\frac{1.17}{0.83}\right) = 0.172$$

and we then get the following table:

r	N	z	$(N-3)$	$z(N-3)$
0.25	23	0.255	20	5.100
−0.14	28	−0.141	25	−3.525
0.17	43	0.172	40	6.880
			85	8.455
			$\Sigma(N-3)$	$\Sigma z(N-3)$

$$\text{Pooled } z = \frac{8.455}{85} = 0.1 \text{ (very nearly)}$$

Now, since

$$z = 1.15 \log_{10}\left(\frac{1+r}{1-r}\right)$$

we have

$$\log_{10}\left(\frac{1+r}{1-r}\right) = \frac{z}{1.15} = \frac{0.1}{1.15} = 0.087$$

$$\therefore \qquad \frac{1+r}{1-r} = 1.222$$

$$\therefore \qquad 1.222 - 1.222r = 1 + r, \text{ i.e. } 2.222r = 0.222$$

$$\therefore \qquad r = \frac{0.222}{2.222} = 0.10$$

and this is the required pooled value of r. The reader should notice that, if the pooled value of z had been negative, the minus sign would have been ignored in decoding z back into r, and the value of r would finally have been given the negative sign.

This transformation may also be used for testing the significance of a correlation coefficient. It may be shown that z is distributed with a standard error $\dfrac{1}{\sqrt{N-3}}$. As an example, the accidents to children problem gave us $r = -0.92$, with $N = 18$. The reader may easily check for himself that this leads us to $z = 1.6$, apart from sign. Now the standard error is $\dfrac{1}{\sqrt{15}} = 0.26$, so the observed value of z is about six times its standard error, and therefore highly significant, as we found previously.

11

We may use the z transformation to test the hypothesis that the observed sample was drawn from a population with a specified value of r. Suppose we had other grounds for believing that the correlation coefficient for accidents to children in relation to provision of park space were -0.5, and it was desired to know whether the London figures differed significantly from -0.5. On the assumption that the figure 0.5 is based on a very large sample, we proceed as follows. The value of z corresponding to the postulated value -0.5 for r is computed as $z = -0.549$. The difference between this postulated value and the London figures (since both z values are negative, and we may ignore sign) $1.6 - 0.55 = 1.05$. But the standard error of z is, for the London figures, 0.26. Since the difference between the hypothetical value and the London value for z is four standard errors, we should have to conclude that the London case showed a significantly higher correlation than that indicated by the figure $r = -0.5$.

If we have two independent estimates of a correlation coefficient, and wish to test whether they differ significantly, it is absolutely asking for trouble in the case of small samples to rely on using the standard error of the correlation coefficient itself. The distribution of r is very far from the Normal distribution which is tacitly assumed as a good approximation when we use the standard error approach. It is, however, safe for most practical cases to transform to z values, and refer the difference of these values to the standard error of their difference, namely

$$\sqrt{\frac{1}{N_1 - 3} + \frac{1}{N_2 - 3}}$$

Suppose, for example, we have two independent estimates of a correlation coefficient $r = 0.39$ with $N = 23$ and $r = 0.47$ with $N = 53$. Is the difference significant? When $r = 0.39$, we get $z = 0.412$, and when $r = 0.47$ we find $z = 0.511$. The difference between the z values is therefore $0.511 - 0.412 = 0.099$. The standard error of the difference is

$$\sqrt{\frac{1}{N_1 - 3} + \frac{1}{N_2 - 3}} = \sqrt{\tfrac{1}{20} + \tfrac{1}{50}} = \sqrt{0.07} = 0.265$$

Since the difference is much less than one standard error, it is not significant.

Fisher's z transformation may be used in testing the significance of partial regression coefficients, illustrating the method by using the data obtained earlier in this chapter on the prediction of examination marks from I.Q. and year's marks. It will be recalled that, in coded form, the regression equation was

$$u_1 = 0·24u_2 + 0·8u_3 - 1·1$$

where u_1 = examination score, u_2 = I.Q., and u_3 = year's marks. Consider, first, the partial regression coefficient for u_1 and u_2. We may convert it to the corresponding partial correlation coefficient as follows:

$$r = a\sqrt{\frac{\Sigma' u_2{}^2}{\Sigma' u_1{}^2}} = 0·24\sqrt{\frac{3,200}{3,900}} = 0·2 \text{ approx.}$$

Hence $z = 1·15 \log\left(\frac{1+r}{1-r}\right) = 1·15 \log\left(\frac{1·2}{0·8}\right) = 0·2 \text{ approx.}$

There were $N = 10$ pairs of u_1, u_2 values and we have eliminated $m = 1$ variable, viz. u_3. Hence the standard error of z is

$$\sigma = \frac{1}{\sqrt{N-m-3}} = \frac{1}{\sqrt{10-1-3}} = \frac{1}{\sqrt{6}} = 0·4 \text{ approx.}$$

Since z is only half its own standard error, it has not been proved significant by these data and it appears that I.Q. is of very little value for prediction purposes.

Considering next the partial regression coefficient for u_1 and u_3, we get

$$r = b\sqrt{\frac{\Sigma^1 u_3{}^2}{\Sigma^1 u_1{}^2}} = 0·8\sqrt{\frac{4,100}{3,900}} = 0·8 \text{ approx.}$$

and $z = 1·15 \log\left(\frac{1+r}{1-r}\right) = 1·15 \log\left(\frac{1·8}{0·2}\right) = 1·1 \text{ approx.}$

As before, the standard error of z is 0·4. In this case, since z is almost three times its standard error, we may consider its significance well established and conclude that a student's year's marks have been demonstrated to be of value in predicting his examination performance in this case.

It is a remarkable fact that many apparently quite different problems all have the same best computing technique and lead to Snedecor's F for a significance test. Discriminatory Analysis affords one example where the computations follow those of correlation. Consider, for example, the case of the archaeologist who wishes to determine the particular race of men to which a skull or portion of a skull probably belongs. It is well known that the skull configuration is broadly characteristic of race; but within each race any length or angle we measure will be a variable quantity, so that the individual skull, while conforming as a whole to its family shape, will have individual measurements such as are commonly observed in skulls of other families. Since it is not the individual measurements but the *set* which is the basis of discrimination, the problem of weighting and combining the individual measurements to get a single figure which will give the most sensitive diagnosis naturally arises. Problems of this type are common in technology. For example, rubber cements are easily recognizable in use as good, bad, or indifferent. There is no defined unit for the measurement of adhesion, which is too complex a phenomenon to be forced into a simple definition. All we can say is that it is recognizable and that certain tests can be carried out whose results correlate with it. It might well be useful for such tests to be assembled in a statistical discriminant function to forecast the operational quality of various manufactured batches.

Yet another example of computations following the correlation model is Hotelling's T^2 test, which we now illustrate by means of an example. Suppose a certain examination is taken by two types of student attending a technical college: part-time day release students and evening students. Suppose that the marks received by students in the three subjects of the examination are as shown in the following table, where X, Y, and Z denote scores in the different subjects. To keep the arithmetic simple, we have made the marks out of ten instead of out of the customary hundred. It will be seen that in the table we have calculated sums of squares and products as already explained for regression analysis.

Our first step is to pool together the 'within set' corrected sums of squares, for each of the three subjects, X, Y and Z, in turn. Thus for X we get

$$\Sigma x^2 = \Sigma_1 x^2 + \Sigma_2 x^2 = \left(308 - \frac{42^2}{6}\right) + \left(86 - \frac{18^2}{4}\right) = 19$$

In similar manner we find:

$$\Sigma y^2 = 30 \qquad \text{and} \qquad \Sigma z^2 = 18$$

	X	Y	Z	X²	Y²	Z²	XY	XZ	YZ
Part-time Release	7	9	8	49	81	64	63	56	72
	9	8	7	81	64	49	72	63	56
	4	10	5	16	100	25	40	20	50
	7	7	7	49	49	49	49	49	49
$N_1 = 6$	8	5	5	64	25	25	40	40	25
	7	9	4	49	81	16	63	28	36
Totals	42	48	36	308	400	228	327	256	288
Evening	5	6	6	25	36	36	30	30	36
$N_2 = 4$	6	8	3	36	64	9	48	18	24
	4	3	6	16	9	36	12	24	18
	3	7	5	9	49	25	21	15	35
Totals	18	24	20	86	158	106	111	87	113

Our next step is to do the same thing for the 'within set' sums of products:

$$\Sigma xy = \Sigma_1 xy + \Sigma_2 xy = \left(327 - \frac{42 \times 48}{6}\right) + \left(111 - \frac{18 \times 24}{4}\right) = -6$$

And likewise:

$$\Sigma xz = 1 \text{ and } \Sigma yz = -7$$

Suppose, now, we wished to test the hypothesis that the marks for the two sets of candidates are samples from the same population. The group averages by subjects are

	X	Y	Z
Part-time Release	7	8	6
Evening	4·5	6	5
Differences	2·5	2	1

The true values of these differences, which we shall call d_x, d_y and d_z, are by hypothesis zero. A departure from hypothesis due, for example, to part-time release students having a better performance than evening students would mean that the subject differences were not zero. A test of the hypothesis may be obtained by working out a certain function, known as Hotelling's T^2, of the differences d_x, d_y and d_t, and finding whether this exceeds some critical value which would be obtained, at a chosen probability level, were the hypothesis true. Our next task is to describe a convenient way of calculating T^2. We first set up three linear equations in three unknowns, the multipliers on the left being the sums of squares and products, while the right-hand members are the differences, d_x, d_y and d_t, multiplied by $(N_1 + N_2 - 2) = (N - 2)$ $= (10 - 2) = 8$. Thus:

$$a\Sigma x^2 + b\Sigma xy + c\Sigma xz = (N-2)d_x$$
$$a\Sigma xy + b\Sigma y^2 + c\Sigma yz = (N-2)d_y$$
$$a\Sigma xz + b\Sigma yz + c\Sigma z^2 = (N-2)d_t$$

Substituting, we get

$$19a - 6b + c = 20$$
$$-6a + 30b - 7c = 16$$
$$a - 7b + 18c = 8$$

Solving these equations gives us

$$a = 1 \cdot 320, \ b = 0 \cdot 972, \ c = 0 \cdot 749$$

Hotelling's T^2 is then obtained as

$$T^2 = \frac{N_1 N_2}{N_1 + N_2} (ad_x + bd_y + cd_t)$$

$$= \frac{6 \times 4}{10}\left[1 \cdot 320(2 \cdot 5) + 0 \cdot 972(2) + 0 \cdot 749(1)\right]$$

$$= 2 \cdot 4 \times 5 \cdot 993 = 14 \cdot 38$$

To test for the significance of T^2 we must convert it into a quantity F following Snedecor's F distribution. To do this we multiply T^2 in general by

$$\frac{N - p - 1}{p(N - 2)}$$

where p is the number of separate tests in the examination, in this case, 3. For $N = 10$ the multiplier becomes

$$\frac{10 - 3 - 1}{3 \times 8} = \frac{6}{3 \times 8} = \frac{1}{4}$$

so that F is $14 \cdot 38/4 = 3 \cdot 60$. We enter the tables of F with degrees of freedom p and $N - p - 1$, i.e. 3 and 6, and find that the value corresponding to a probability $P = 0.05$ is 4.76. We conclude that T^2 is not significant, so that either the data are compatible with the hypothesis that both sets of students have equal performance as judged by these three tests, or the samples are too small to demonstrate the significance of the differences which exist here in favour of the part-time release students.

There seems to be very little application in industry of Discriminatory Analysis; yet one would imagine that it should prove extremely useful in many situations. Quite apart from possible technological applications, there seems to be a case for trying it in personnel selection for the pooling of selection test results. In the hope that some readers may be tempted to try practical applications (if only to stimulate the theoretical statisticians not to lose interest!), we shall indicate briefly how the process works, though anyone interested in application would be well advised to take advice from a statistician or at least get a more detailed account from one of the standard textbooks.

In the example just considered, we concluded that the evidence was insufficient to establish a difference between our two groups of students. Obviously, then, we have no real grounds for bothering with a discriminant function except for the purposes of illustration. If, however, we had found persuasive evidence that the two groups of students were characterized by different examination results and if we wished to play the role of Sherlock Holmes and find from a student's examination marks whether he was a Part-time Day Release student or an Evening student, we should proceed as follows.

First, it would be necessary to have average scores in the three subjects for representative groups of the two kinds of student. In our example, the averages by subjects were:

	X	Y	Z
Part-time Release	7	8	6
Evening	4·5	6	5

We should also need to know the values of a, b and c, found by solving our three linear equations, which were:

$$a = 1.320 \qquad b = 0.972 \qquad c = 0.749$$

The typical value for the Discriminant Function is then easily found as

$$D = a\bar{X} + b\bar{Y} + c\bar{Z}$$

Thus, for the Part-time Release students, the typical value is

$$D_P = 1 \cdot 320(7) + 0 \cdot 970(8) + 0 \cdot 749(6) = 21 \cdot 494$$

and for the Evening students it is

$$D_E = 1 \cdot 320(4 \cdot 5) + 0 \cdot 970(6) + 0 \cdot 749(5) = 15 \cdot 505$$

Now let us suppose that we are told that a certain student scored as follows:

$$X = 6 \quad Y = 6 \quad Z = 7$$

Is he most likely to be a part-time or an evening student? We calculate the value of the Discriminant Function for his scores:

$$D = 1 \cdot 320(6) + 0 \cdot 970(6) + 0 \cdot 749(7) = 18 \cdot 983$$

Since this is nearer to the typical value for Part-time students, we should conclude that he belonged to that group. It should be noticed that this system does not rely on simple averaging of the students' marks, but applies weighting in the form of the coefficients a, b and c so as to get the maximum discrimination.

SEE IF YOU HAVE LEARNED ANYTHING ABOUT CORRELATION

1. In an experiment to measure the stiffness of a spring, the length of the spring under different loads was measured as follows:

X = Load (lb.)	0	1	2	3	4
Y = Length (in.)	8	$8\frac{3}{4}$	10	$10\frac{1}{2}$	$11\frac{3}{4}$

Find regression equations appropriate for predicting (a) the length, given the weight on the spring; (b) the weight, given the length. Draw these regression lines on a graph showing the original readings.

2. Find the correlation coefficient for the data of question 1 and use Student's t to test whether it is significant.

17

Time Series and Fortune Telling

'It is never possible to step twice into the same river.'
HERACLITUS

Fashions change in nonsense and superstition no less than in ladies' hats. There was a time when popes and kings had astrologers at court to help them plan for the future. Nowadays government departments have statisticians for the same purpose. One day they will be relegated to the Sunday newspapers to displace the astrologers from their last refuge. I can well understand the cult of the astrologer at court. After all, the astrologer was an astronomer, and if a man has success in predicting eclipses by star-gazing why should he not have equal success in predicting the course of more mundane matters by taking cognizance of the disposition of the heavenly bodies? But for much of the statistical work that is done by government departments I can see little excuse.* It is a vile superstition beyond anything imaginable in the middle ages. Whereas astrology at least encouraged men to look at the beauty of the heavens and be glad, this later mumbo jumbo encourages men to look at themselves and be miserable. It simply cannot be chance that the gentlemen engaged on this work are always making gloomy forecasts with never the slightest suggestion that things will grow better. Never, never has the Registrar-General spoken of the future of an individual child, promising it fame and riches and the affection of the poor when it grows up. It is a very sad thing.

The reader will guess that my views on time series are as biased and unsympathetic as they were in the case of index numbers. When I think of these curses on modern civilization I feel in me the spirit of St George and I long to dash into battle with this dragon of superstition which ensnares so many young maidens in the pit of idle computation. All you can hope for is a bald account of the obvious mechanics. There are many who believe in the

* Measuring exports of machinery by the ton weight, irrespective of its value.

efficacy of these things who have written about them at great
length. You may read their books. I hope you do – provided you
constantly test the value of what they preach by asking: Is this
really any good? Read them for fun and I promise you a jolly
time. Read them for practical profit and I promise you a loss.
What a sad thing it is that the popular superstition in any age is
so popular! I tremble to think of the hordes of students of commerce and economics who at preliminary, intermediate, and
final examinations are tested in their proficiency at sorting out the
seasonal variation and long-term trend. This is the sort of thing
that any competent ice-cream manufacturer does in a flash without statistics. Only where the effect is very marked is it worth the
doing. In that case it is so obvious that there is no need to do it
statistically.

I can think of no better illustration of the ideas in time series
analysis than the ice-cream business. There we have a seasonal
effect with a vengeance. Moreover, being a luxury trade, it is very
sensitive to changes in the general level of prosperity. Given a full
pocket of money people will often treat themselves to an ice-
cream. But as soon as money begins to get tight they will cut down
on ice-cream consumption. From a time of boom to a time of
slump there will be a steady downward fall in the takings of an
ice-cream manufacturer year by year. He will go higher in the
boom and lower in the slump than any other business man. He
is, in fact, an ideal barometer for the others to watch if they wish
to detect the beginning of harder times to come. But, since he will
be one of the last to climb out of distress, he will look to other
more basic industries to spot when better times are coming.
Superimposed on the long term up or down trend, there will be a
seasonal fluctuation, high in each summer, low in each winter.
The reason is, of course, that in summer ice-cream advances to
the position of a near necessity, but in winter it rapidly recedes to
the status of a luxury. In winter, the people's spending pattern
changes in favour of something hot like fish and chips.

Now the avowed purpose of time series in the commercial
world is to predict what is possible in the coming year. Unfortunately, no one ever really foresees the beginning of a slump.
This may sound a foolish remark when we have an army of

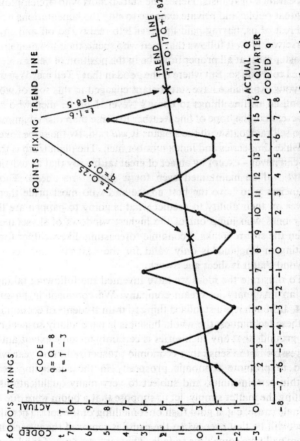

Fig. 94. Ice-cream sales £000's by quarters over four years. Regression of sales on time

statisticians chanting the lamentations of Jeremiah, but it is true. Do you remember the story of the shepherd boy who kept crying wolf? No one wants to believe in hardship. Yet we like to have the appearance of realists. Hence the statisticians who are employed at great public and private expense to sing the lamentations while the rest of us, having paid lip service to reality, go off and enjoy ourselves. Now it follows that men who spend their life predicting disaster must at all proper times be in the position of being able to say: I told you so. But where is the good in that? Tell me: When in all your experience have statisticians engaged in this sort of work promised us fine things to come? Never. I prefer men who sell ice-cream in the hope of fine weather to come than dismal jimmies who sell raincoats with the slogan: It *will* rain. By the same token, I dislike time series and index number men. The plain truth is that we can never – except by an act of great faith – say that an existing trend will be maintained even for a short time ahead. Those financiers who have the best advice and who most pride themselves on their ability to predict what is going to happen are the very ones who jump out of the highest windows of skyscrapers when the storm breaks. Economic forecasting, like weather forecasting in England, is only valid for the next six hours or so. Beyond that it is sheer guesswork.

To illustrate the ideas we have invented the following takings for an imaginary ice-cream company. We comment in passing that, although it is a standard thing to train students of economics in these techniques, the whole business is particularly suspect on the grounds that any such series is certainly to some extent auto-regressive in the sense that economic prosperity in one year will tend to promote economic prosperity in the succeeding year (within certain limits, and subject to very many qualifications). Putting the matter simply, let us suppose that a boom were due to a single cause, e.g. a gold rush or something of the sort. Then the effect will be that even when the cause is removed the prosperity boom will take some time to fade. There is a tendency for a boom to be self-supporting, as it were. There is an equal tendency for a depression to support itself, since trade can, to some extent, only get going when people have the money to order goods – which they won't have until they already have jobs making the goods.

What a pity that politicians see this and think they can do something about it without taking away people's freedom to starve.

Example. An ice-cream manufacturer divides his year into four quarters as follows:

1st quarter: December, January, and February (worst quarter)

2nd quarter: March, April, and May (trade picking up)

3rd quarter: June, July, and August (peak months)

4th quarter: September, October, and November (trade falling off)

Over a period of four successive years his takings (in thousands of pounds) were:

	1st quarter	2nd quarter	3rd quarter	4th quarter
Year 1	1	2	5	2
Year 2	1	3	6	2
Year 3	1	3	6	4
Year 4	2	2	8	4

The data are shown plotted in a graph in Fig. 94. For the purpose of analysis, we shall number the sixteen quarters in order and regard quarter number as our independent variable (Q). The takings we shall denote by the symbol T. For ease in computation we shall code the data according to

$$q = Q - 8 \qquad t = T - 3$$

The first seven columns in the next table are concerned with fitting a regression line to the data by the method of least squares with which we are already familiar. The remaining columns are for a purpose which we shall explain after we have the trend line.

Q	T	q	t	q^2	t^2	qt	t'	$(T-T')=$ $(t-t')$	T'	$\left(\dfrac{T-T'}{T'}\right)100$
1	1	−7	−2	49	4	14	−1·22	−0·78	1·78	−44%
2	2	−6	−1	36	1	6	−1·04	+0·04	1·96	+2%
3	5	−5	2	25	4	−10	−0·87	+2·87	2·13	+134%
4	2	−4	−1	16	1	4	−0·70	−0·30	2·30	−13%
5	1	−3	−2	9	4	6	−0·52	−1·48	2·48	−60%
6	3	−2	0	4	0	0	−0·35	+0·35	2·65	+13%
7	6	−1	3	1	9	−3	−0·17	+3·17	2·83	+112%
8	2	0	−1	0	1	0	0·00	−1·00	3·00	−33%
9	1	1	−2	1	4	−2	0·17	−2·17	3·17	−67%
10	3	2	0	4	0	0	0·25	−0·35	3·35	−10%
11	6	3	3	9	9	9	0·52	+2·48	3·52	+70%
12	4	4	1	16	1	4	0·70	+0·30	3·70	+8%
13	2	5	−1	25	1	−5	0·87	−1·87	3·87	−48%
14	2	6	−1	36	1	−6	1·04	−2·04	4·04	−51%
15	8	7	5	49	25	35	1·22	+3·78	4·22	+90%
16	4	8	1	64	1	8	1·40	−0·40	4·40	−9%
Totals		8	4	344	66	60 for $n=16$ quarters				

Computation for trend line in coded values

$$\bar{t} = \frac{\Sigma t}{n} = \frac{4}{16} = 0·25 \qquad\qquad \bar{q} = \frac{\Sigma q}{n} = \frac{8}{16} = 0·5$$

The trend line passes through the point $(\bar{q}, \bar{t})$ so this point may at once be marked in on our graph (Fig. 94) by using the coded scales on that graph. The regression coefficient of t on q is

$$b = \frac{\Sigma qt - \dfrac{\Sigma q . \Sigma t}{n}}{\Sigma q^2 - \dfrac{(\Sigma q)^2}{n}} = \frac{60 - \dfrac{8 \times 4}{16}}{344 - \dfrac{8 \times 8}{16}} = \frac{58}{340} = 0·17$$

Hence, for unit increase in q we expect t to increase by $0·17$. If, then, we let q have the value $\bar{q} + 8 = 8·5$, the new value of t predicted by the trend (regression) like will be $\bar{t} + (0·17)8 = 1·6$. This gives us a second point on our trend line which we can mark in the graph: When $q = 8·5$, $t = 1·6$. The trend line may then be drawn, as shown in the figure.

In coded units, the equation of the trend line is

$$(t' - \bar{t}) = b(q - \bar{q})$$

(We write t' to denote *predicted* takings based on the trend line.)

i.e.
$$(t' - 0·25) = 0·17(q - 0·5)$$

or
$$t' = 0·17q + 0·165$$

In the original units, since $t' = T' - 3$ and $q = Q - 8$, we get

$$T' - 3 = 0.17(Q - 8) + 0.165$$

or
$$\underline{T' = 0.17Q + 1.80}$$

Given our trend equation, it is a simple matter to insert the values in the eighth column of our table, which shows the trend values corresponding to each value of q (working in the coded values). The ninth column of our table shows the difference between the actual takings T and the takings predicted by the trend line T'. The last but one column shows the trend takings in actual units,

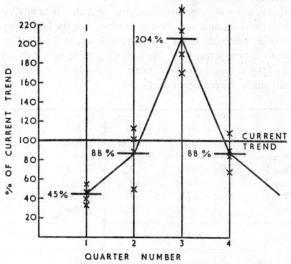

Fig. 95. Takings by quarter within the year as percentage of the current trend value

and the final column shows the difference between the trend and actual takings expression as a percentage of the trend value in the original units.

There is very good reason for showing the seasonal effect in the last column as a percentage of the trend, as the reader will soon spot for himself if he is anything of a business man, namely that the seasonal effect is not likely to be a constant number of thousands of pounds, but dependent on the general volume of takings at the period in question – roughly speaking at any rate. The last column measures not simply the seasonal effect but includes other causes of variation, such as good and bad weather in different seasons (using 'season' in the sense of a trading year – a common way of speaking in trades which are largely confined to one of the four seasons of the year). It would also include other irregular effects of a non-regular type, such as the holding of a special festival or a Trades Union conference by which sales were increased because of an abnormally large population temporarily in the trading area.

Having got our long term trend, our next step is to analyse the seasonal and residual variation as contained in the last column of our table. The cycle has a yearly periodicity, and we collect the relevant data together as in the following table which shows the data of the last column of our table laid out in a way suitable for investigating the periodic effect.

	1st quarter	2nd quarter	3rd quarter	4th quarter
Year 1	– 44%	+ 2%	+134%	–13%
Year 2	– 60%	+13%	+112%	–33%
Year 3	– 67%	–10%	+ 70%	+ 8%
Year 4	– 48%	–51%	+ 90%	– 9%
Totals	–219	– 46	+416	–47
Quarterly Averages	– 55%	–12%	+104%	–12%

The first quarter, on average, is 55% below the trend value. It may therefore be calculated as 45% of the trend value. Likewise, the other three quarters, in order, may be calculated as 88%, 204%, and 88% respectively of their trend values in the year in question. Fig. 95 shows the pure seasonal effect as represented by these percentages, taking the trend value as constant from season to season at 100. We have plotted in the same graph the takings for each of the four years covered by our data, so that the discrepancy caused by residual sources of variation may be seen. Provided that economic conditions affecting ice-cream were to remain stable, we should now be in a very happy position to predict future sales, allowing both for seasonal and long term trend effects. It is precisely because it is all so easy to do, and so nice to contemplate when it is done, that this sort of thing is done so often. Particularly when the trend is upwards, I am prepared to bet that in times of boom this kind of forecasting is very much more indulged in than in times when the long term trend is downwards. It is a gorgeous way of counting one's chickens before they are hatched – a basic characteristic without which you have no chance of prospering in business. It is often called 'insight' or 'acumen' and all sorts of other things which show how close it is in spirit to astrology.

Within any one quarter, each year will have takings which differ from the average for that quarter. These 'within quarters' differences enable the forecaster to get an idea of the uncertainty which attaches to any prediction he makes for the future, i.e. the uncertainty which will still be present even if there is no change in the general trend and seasonal pattern of trade as represented by the four years considered in the analysis. It is convenient again to work in percentages of the trend value. Looking back to the last table where we calculated the seasonal effect as a percentage of the trend, we find that in the first quarter the worst year showed takings which were 67% below trend and the best year only 44% below trend. Thus a sample of four years gave us a range of $67 - 44 = 23\%$ of trend. The other quarters gave us 64%, 64%, and 41% of trend as the range in samples of four. The average range in samples of four is thus found to be $\frac{1}{4}(23 + 64 + 64 + 41) = 48$. Now we learnt in the chapter on Control Charts how we might estimate standard deviation from mean range. We leave it as an exercise to the reader to satisfy himself that our mean range suggests a standard deviation of 24%. Provided, then, that there is no serious change in conditions, we are not likely to be more than two standard deviations (say 50% of the trend value) in error if we use our regression equation to find the trend, and then multiply the trend value by the seasonal factor. This is a very

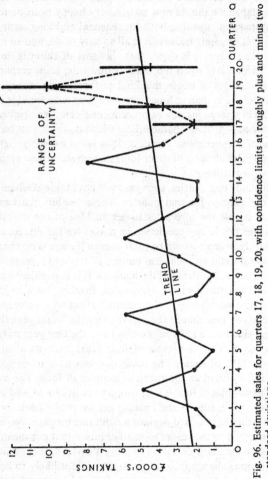

Fig. 96. Estimated sales for quarters 17, 18, 19, 20, with confidence limits at roughly plus and minus two standard deviations

considerable margin of possible error. In practice there is very real danger that we could be very much further out.

As an illustration of the technique of prediction, we shall show how we might go about predicting the takings for the four seasons in the year immediately following the four years on which the analysis is based. Our quarters would have the numbers 17, 18,

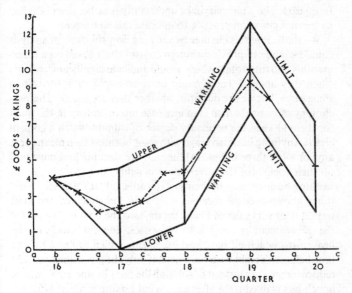

Fig. 97. Graph of three monthly moving takings total, moving within predicted confidence belt based on regression analysis

19, and 20 respectively. The regression equation for getting the trend is

$$T' = 0.17Q + 1.80$$

Substituting the Q values in turn gives us

Q	17	18	19	20
T'	4.69	4.86	5.03	5.20

The seasonal factors are 45%, 88%, 204%, and 88% of trend value respectively. The uncertainty is in each case measured by

50% of trend. Applying these, we get the following (takings in thousands of pounds):

Quarter	17	18	19	20
Estimated takings	2·1	4·1	10·3	4·6
Plus or minus	2·3	2·4	2·5	2·6

Fig. 96 shows these predictions following on the data of the first four years. The wide margin of uncertainty is rather discouraging, so it is not common practice to indicate this so brazenly.

We shall close this chapter by showing how this type of analysis could be made to provide a rough control chart based on a three-monthly moving total, which would indicate significant changes when they appear. There might be some application for this in some cases, but we are doubtful whether they are many. The psychology of business men is in any case too predatory in the main for them to keep the necessary degree of calm to watch a control chart. Anything under average with most business men means one, any, or all of three things: (a) the staff are slacking and must pull up their socks, (b) the government is deliberately robbing hard-working business men of their just rewards, (c) 'It's a devil'. Anything above average means (a) now is the time for the staff to pull their socks up and back up the lead the boss has given, (b) the government is coming to its senses, and (c) 'God's in His heaven (to which all hardworking business men go) and for the time being all's right with the world, if only the government would reduce income tax instead of robbing the poor businessman whose hunch has proved right after all'. What hokum it all is! Now for our control chart.

Suppose the actual takings for the months in the stated quarters were as shown below.

Quarter	16			17			18			19		
Month in quarter	a	b	c	a	b	c	a	b	c	a	b	c
Monthly takings	1·4	1·4	1·2	0·7	0·2	1·4	1·1	1·7	1·6	2·5	4·0	3·0
3-monthly total		4·0	3·3	2·1	2·3	2·7	4·2	4·4	5·8	8·1	9·5	

These three monthly totals could then be plotted in our rough control chart as shown in Fig. 97. The technique is rough – but so is the whole business.

NOW TRY YOUR HAND AT TIME SERIES ANALYSIS

The following table shows the death rate per thousand living persons as given in the Registrar General's Statistical Review for England and Wales.

	Quarter ended			
	March	June	September	December
1841/50	24·7	22·0	21·0	21·7
1851/60	24·7	22·1	20·3	21·9
1861/70	25·2	21·8	21·0	22·1
1871/80	23·7	20·9	19·6	21·3
1881/90	21·6	18·7	17·3	19·1
1891/1900	20·7	17·6	17·0	17·7
1901/10	17·7	14·6	13·8	15·4
1911/20	17·2	13·6	11·8	14·9
1921/30	15·5	11·7	9·5	11·8
1931/40	15·8	11·6	9·8	12·0

Fit a trend line suitable for estimating the annual death rate from the date of the decade. Make a seasonal analysis and so get seasonal factors expressed as a percentage of the current trend death rate and, finally, estimate the uncertainty of prediction under stable conditions as a percentage of the current trend value. See if you can set up a rough control chart for the quarters of the year in the decade 1941/50, which would indicate any significant changes in the trend of the death rate.

18

Ranking Methods

'You have only to take in what you please and leave out what you please; to select your own conditions of time and place; to multiply and divide at discretion; and you can pay the National Debt in half an hour. Calculation is nothing but cookery.' LORD BROUGHAM, 1849

Very frequently we are interested in being able to draw conclusions from the order in which things occur. There are several types of problem of this kind, and we shall deal with them in this chapter. They are usually problems in which we can place things in an order of merit, without necessarily being able to give a numerical measure of the intrinsic worth of each individual. A teacher, for example, might rank ten children in order of merit without assigning an actual mark to each child. A judge in a beauty contest might rank the contestants in order of merit without committing himself to any indication of how much better the winner is than the runners up. Ranking arises naturally in cases where for lack of time, money, instruments, or reasonably defined units, measurement of the characteristic being judged is impossible. We sometimes have recourse to ranking methods even where measurements have been made in order to reduce the labour of computation or to get a rapid result.*

The best known technique in this field is Spearman's Rank Correlation Coefficient. Suppose we have ten pupils ranked in order of ability by two schoolmasters. Let us suppose that the ten pupils are denoted by the letters A, B, C, ... L, and that the two teachers are denoted by X and Y. The ranking results were as follows:

Student	A	B	C	D	E	F	G	H	K	L
Ranked by X	2	1	3	4	6	5	8	7	10	9
Ranked by Y	3	2	1	4	6	7	5	9	10	8
Rank difference $= d$	1	1	-2	0	0	2	-3	2	0	-1
Square of difference $= d^2$	1	1	4	0	0	4	9	4	0	

* Special mention should be made of Friedmann, who first developed much of the theory of ranking.

The problem is: do the teachers show evidence of agreement among themselves in regard to ranking? We solve this problem by calculating Spearman's Rank Correlation Coefficient which is defined by

$$R = 1 - \frac{6\Sigma d^2}{n^3 - n}$$

where Σd^2 is the sum of the squares of the rank differences, and n is the number of students ranked, viz. 10 in our example. We find Σd^2 equal to 24 with n equal to 10, so that the rank correlation coefficient is

$$R = 1 - \frac{6 \times 24}{1,000 - 10} = 1 - \tfrac{144}{990} = 0.85$$

The rank correlation coefficient has been designed so that when the two rankings are identical the rank correlation has the value plus 1; when the rankings are as greatly in disagreement as possible, i.e. when one ranking is exactly the reverse of the other, the rank correlation coefficient is equal to minus 1. Apparently, then, our teachers show a fair agreement between one another as to the order of merit of the students. How may we be sure that this measure of agreement could not arise by chance? In other words, how do we test the significance of the rank correlation coefficient? Provided that n, the number of items ranked, is not less than 10, we may calculate

$$\text{Student's } t = R\sqrt{\frac{n-2}{1 - R^2}}$$

with $n - 2$ degrees of freedom. Making the necessary substitutions in the formula we find

$$\text{Student's } t = 0.85\sqrt{\frac{8}{1 - 0.72}} = 0.85\sqrt{\frac{8}{0.28}}$$
$$= 4.55$$

and this is greater than the 1% level of t with 8 degrees of freedom, so that we conclude that the degree of agreement between the two observers is significant.

This does not of course mean that the two observers are really placing the students in the correct order approximately. It is possible that though they both agree they are both wrong. They might, for example, be pulling our legs and calling the duffers the bright boys and vice versa.

If we have other exact means of knowing the correct ranking we can use Spearman's rank correlation coefficient to test whether an individual is a good judge. Suppose we have ten weights, very finely graded, and we wish to test how good a judge a man is of weight. The ranking he gives might be as follows:

Weight	A	B	C	D	E	F	G	H	J	K
True rank	1	2	3	4	5	6	7	8	9	10
Given as	3	2	4	1	7	5	10	6	9	8
$d^2 =$	4	0	1	9	4	1	9	4	0	4

which gives us $\Sigma d^2 = 36$ with $n = 10$

$$R = 1 - \frac{6\Sigma d^2}{n^3 - n} = 1 - \tfrac{216}{990} = 0.78$$

from which we get

$$\text{Student's } t = R\sqrt{\frac{n-2}{1-R^2}} = 0.78\sqrt{\frac{8}{0.4}} = 3.5$$

The 1% level of Student's t with $n - 2 = 8$ degrees of freedom is 3.36, so we conclude that the man's ranking correlates significantly with the true ranking.

Spearman's rank correlation coefficient may also be used as a test of efficiency in the shuffling of cards. Each card is given a rank number for its position in the pack. The pack is then shuffled and the new rank of each card recorded. The calculated value of the rank correlation coefficient should not be significantly high if the shuffling is adequate.

Very often, we are not concerned simply with the agreement between two judges, but have several judges and wish to know whether there is a significant measure of agreement between the judges as a whole. Suppose, for example, there were $m = 5$ judges tasting $n = 7$ makes of ice-cream, as might be the case where a large cinema circuit carries out palatability tests on ice-cream from several suppliers. Let us suppose that the judges assign the following rankings to the different makes and it is desired to test whether there is evidence of overall agreement between the judges.

Make of ice-cream	A	B	C	D	E	F	G
Ranked by judge P	2	4	3	7	5	1	6
Ranked by judge Q	4	5	2	3	6	1	7
Ranked by judge R	1	3	2	4	6	5	7
Ranked by judge S	3	1	4	2	7	6	5
Ranked by judge T	1	3	5	7	6	2	4
Total of ranks	11	16	16	23	30	15	29

The total of the ranks for each judge is $1+2+3+4+5+6+7=28$ and, in general, when there are n items to be ranked, the total of the ranks for each judge will be the sum of the first n natural numbers, which is given by the formula $\frac{n(n+1)}{2}$. Clearly, if there are m judges the grand total of the ranks will be m times this quantity, viz. $\frac{mn(n+1)}{2}$. In our case with $m=5$ and $n=7$, the grand total of the ranks will be 140, and this figure may be checked by adding the rank totals in the bottom of the table.

Now, if the judges were able to exert no real discrimination, we should expect each make of ice-cream to have a rank total of one-seventh of the grand total of ranks, viz, in general, $\frac{m(n+1)}{2}=20$.

On the other hand, if our judges were in perfect agreement as to the order of merit, we should expect the rank totals to form the series 5, 10, 15, 20, 25, 30, and 35 (though not necessarily in that order), i.e. in general the rank totals would form the series

$$m, 2m, 3m, 4m, 5m, 6m, \ldots nm$$

in the case where there were n kinds of ice-cream and m judges. It is natural to regard the difference between the observed rank totals and the expected rank totals as a measure of the agreement between the judges. Now it can be shown that when the expected rank totals, on the hypothesis that the judges have no agreement at all, are $\frac{m(n+1)}{2}$, the sum of the squares of the differences between observed and expected rank totals is given by

$$S_{max} = \frac{m^2(n^3 - n)}{12}$$

This is the maximum possible sum of squares, since when the judges are in complete agreement we shall have the maximum discrepancy between observed rank totals and their expectation on the Null Hypothesis of no agreement between judges. In any case where the judges show only partial agreement, the sum of squares will be less than this amount. It is convenient to use the ratio

$$W = \frac{S}{S_{max}} = \frac{S}{\left[\frac{m^2(n^3 - n)}{12}\right]} = \frac{12S}{m^2(n^3 - n)}$$

as a measure of the degree of agreement between the judges. This ratio is known as the Coefficient of Concordance.

In our example, the rank totals were 11, 16, 16, 23, 30, 15, and 29. On the Null Hypothesis, the expected value was 20. We get then the sum of squared differences between observed and expected rank totals as

$$S = 9^2 + 4^2 + 4^2 + 3^2 + 10^2 + 5^2 + 9^2$$
$$= 81 + 16 + 16 + 9 + 100 + 25 + 81 = 328$$

and since $m = 5$ and $n = 7$, the coefficient of concordance is

$$W = \frac{12S}{m^2(n^3 - n)} = \frac{12 \times 328}{25(343 - 7)} = 0 \cdot 47$$

The coefficient is designed so that it can vary from 0 signifying complete randomness in the allocation of rankings to 1 signifying complete agreement among the judges. (A little reflection will convince the reader that there can be no such thing as complete *dis*-agreement between more than two judges.) The calculated value for W in our example appears high. The question arises: Could so high a value arise by chance with anything but a remote probability?

It may be shown that W may be tested for significance, using Snedecor's distribution for F, as follows.

Step 1. A 'continuity correction' must be applied in the calculation of W:

(a) subtract unity from the calculated value of S

(b) increase the divisor $\dfrac{m^2(n^3 - n)}{12}$ by 2.

Then calculate W.

Step 2. Calculate Snedecor's F as $F = \dfrac{(m-1)W}{1-W}$ and enter the tables of F with:

Degrees of freedom for the greater estimate

$$= (n-1) - \frac{2}{m}$$

Degrees of freedom for the lesser estimate

$$= (m-1)\left[(n-1) - \frac{2}{m}\right]$$

In general the numbers of degrees of freedom will not be whole numbers and we have to estimate the value of F by interpolation. This test is good at the 1% level, better at the 5% level, but of doubtful reliability at the 0·1% level.

Consider, now, our example. We found $S = 328$, so the corrected value will be $328 - 1 = 327$. For $\dfrac{m^2(n^3 - n)}{12}$ we got $\dfrac{25(343 - 7)}{12} = 700$. The corrected value then becomes $700 + 2 = 702$, so that we have, finally, the correction here being negligible,

$$W = \tfrac{327}{702} = 0 \cdot 47$$

We then calculate Snedecor's F as

$$F = \frac{(m-1)W}{1-W} = \frac{4 \times 0 \cdot 47}{0 \cdot 53} = 3 \cdot 5$$

Greater estimate degrees of freedom

$$= (n-1) - \frac{2}{m} = 6 - \tfrac{2}{3} = 5 \cdot 6$$

Lesser estimate degrees of freedom

$$= (m-1)\left[(n-1) - \frac{2}{m}\right] = 4 \times 5 \cdot 6 = 22 \cdot 4$$

Entering Snedecor's tables for F with these degrees of freedom, we estimate

$$5\% \text{ level of } F = 2 \cdot 7 \quad 1\% \text{ level of } F = 4 \cdot 1$$

We are thus left with fair confidence that our judges do exhibit a notable degree of agreement in their judgements of the palatability of the ice-cream from the different manufacturers – notwithstanding that individual judges disagree very markedly in the ranking assigned to the different makes, as inspection of the original table of rankings makes plain.

It will have occurred to the reader that we might have used Spearman's rank correlation coefficient between every possible pair of judges, and then have averaged the values of R. The number of ways of picking two judges from five, to do a rank correlation test, is $5C2 = \dfrac{5 \times 4}{2} = 10$. This would have been a lengthy procedure, then. As a matter of fact, there is a simple relationship between W and R_{avg}, namely

$$R_{avg} = \frac{mW - 1}{m - 1}$$

In our example, therefore,

$$R_{avg} = \frac{5 \times 0 \cdot 47 - 1}{5 - 1} = \frac{1 \cdot 35}{4} = 0 \cdot 34$$

Having established that there is a significant measure of agreement between our judges, we are at liberty to estimate a 'true ranking' which is based on the combined estimates of the judges. To do this, we use the obvious method of ranking the makes in order of the rank totals, thus getting the following result:

Make of ice-cream	A	B	C	D	E	F	G
Rank totals	11	16	16	23	30	15	29
Final Rank	1	3 =	3 =	5	7	2	6

The example just dealt with leads us nicely into the next point we wish to make, namely, that it is often questionable whether

ranking is a legitimate procedure at all. It can often be the case
that we sensibly have a preference for one item rather than another
without being able to show logical justification for a ranking procedure. In our ice-cream example there were many factors which
might influence the several judges differently. One man may be
influenced by taste, another by colour, another by the attractive-
ness of the wrapper or a fancy for the maker's name, and so on.
We call judgements of this sort 'multidimensional'. Characteristic of all such cases is inconsistency of judgements expressed
by the same observer. The problem is seen clearly in the following.
We might say to a man: Which do you prefer, orange or apple?
The man will reply: apple. We then ask him: Which do you prefer, orange or banana? The man replies: orange. We then ask
him: Which do you prefer, apple or banana? Illogically, he replies:
banana. What has happened is that the 'dimension' in which he
makes his judgement has changed. Appearance, for example, has
become less important than taste. There is no reason at all why he
should not make this switch over if we have not specified the
dimension in which judgements are to be made – and, even if we
have, it is not always easy for the man to know what complex of
factors and what balance of them is operating at any given instant.
Many products in industry are judged by their customers on this
basis. A man will open a tin of rubber cement, for example, and
after a most cursory test announce that he likes it or that it isn't
quite up to scratch. He claims, possibly with some right, that this
is experience. Not infrequently it is nothing more than the result
of uncontrolled psychological factors. A tin which is looked at
askance today, tomorrow may be accepted without a murmur.
The truth is that in multi-dimensional judgements of this sort we
are always more or less out of our depth. To ask a man to arrange
a set of items in a ranked list under such circumstances is artificial
and inappropriate. We are asking the impossible.

It is well known that direct comparison between two items is
far more sensitive and discerning than actual measurement on a
scale of values. We can tackle the problem of multi-dimensional
judgements on the basis of paired comparisons, rather than
straight ranking. We present the judge with every possible combination of two items from the set to be evaluated, and leave him

scope for inconsistent judgements, where formal ranking would obscure them.

In general, given n items, we can choose pairs for comparison in $nC2$ ways, i.e. $\frac{n(n-1)}{2}$ ways. Suppose we have 7 items, A, B, C, D, E, F, and G, then we can compare the following 21 pairs:

$$
\begin{array}{cccccc}
AB & AC & AD & AE & AF & AG \\
   & BC & BD & BE & BF & BG \\
   &   & CD & CE & CF & CG \\
   &   &   & DE & DF & DG \\
   &   &   &   & EF & EG \\
   &   &   &   &   & FG
\end{array}
$$

In the theory, as so far developed, the judge is not allowed to declare himself unable to decide between one item of a pair and another. He must decide either way, at least to the extent of saying which he will choose, even if he thinks the other just as good. He will have the sympathy of women who like four hats equally well but can only afford to buy one. We might record his choices as between the 21 pairs in the form of a table:

	A	B	C	D	E	F	G
A		1	1	0	0	1	1
B			0	1	1	0	1
C				0	1	1	1
D					0	0	1
E		0					0
F							1

The notation used in this table is as follows. The result of the comparison of A with B was that A was chosen as superior. This is denoted by the symbol 1. On the other hand, A was rejected in favour of D. This is denoted by the symbol 0. Thus, in general, the symbol 1 indicates that the item denoting the row of the table was preferred to the item denoting the column. The symbol 0 indicates that the item denoting the row of the table was rejected in favour of the item denoting the column. It is evident that, since no item is compared with itself, the diagonal of the table will be blank, and that the lower left-hand side of the table can be filled in from the results recorded in the upper right-hand section of the table. We have shown only one complementary record of this kind. Since B was preferred to E (denoted by entry 1 in upper right of table) it follows that E was rejected in favour of B (denoted by 0 in the lower left of table).

We must now do a little thinking. Let us denote the fact that A is preferred to B by the notation $A \rightarrow B$, or alternatively by $B \leftarrow A$, that is to say, the direction of the arrow indicates the direction of decreasing preference. Then, if the judge makes the choices $A \rightarrow B$ and $B \rightarrow C$ when presented in turn with the pairs AB and BC, we should logically expect that when presented with the pair AC he would make the choice $A \rightarrow C$, and would regard the choice $A \leftarrow C$ as inconsistent with his previous two choices. We may illustrate these two possibilities diagrammatically in the form of preference triads, as follows:

Consistent choices give   Inconsistent choices give
a Resultant Triad   a Circular Triad

Consider, first of all, the consistent choices illustrated in the left-hand part of the diagram. Starting at A, we read off that A was preferred to B, and proceeding we find that B was preferred to C. So far, the arrows have led us in a clockwise direction. The consistent choice, namely A preferred to C is denoted by the arrow head in the anticlockwise direction.

Next consider the inconsistent choices illustrated in the right-hand part of the diagram. It will be seen that in this case all the arrows have the same clockwise sense. We have called this type of diagram a Circular Triad. Thus, Resultant Triads denote consistent choices, while Circular Triads denote inconsistent choices.

Complex cases are dealt with as polyads broken into their component triads. The results of our original table, for example, could be shown in the following form.

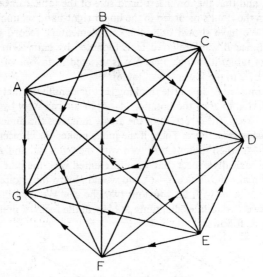

Fig. 98. Preference polyad

Two important facts may be shown by mathematical analysis:

(1) With n items under consideration, the maximum number of circular triads which can possibly occur is given by

$$\frac{n^3 - n}{24} \quad \text{if } n \text{ is an odd number}$$

or

$$\frac{n^3 - 4n}{24} \quad \text{if } n \text{ is an even number}$$

The minimum number of circular triads is of course zero, this being the case when all the judgements are consistent, so that we then have the equivalent of ordinary ranking.

(2) There is always some set-up of preferences which will attain the theoretical maximum number of circular triads.

We test the consistency of the judge by calculating the Coefficient of Consistency, as follows:

$$K = 1 - \frac{24d}{n^3 - n} \quad \text{for } n \text{ an odd number}$$

or
$$K = 1 - \frac{24d}{n^3 - 4n} \quad \text{for } n \text{ an even number}$$

where d is the number of circular triads observed in a given set-up of choices. The coefficient of consistency, K, attains the value 1 if there are no inconsistent triads of judgement, otherwise it is less than 1. When $K = 1$, we are justified, of course, in setting up an ordinary ranking for the items, but not otherwise. The coefficient becomes zero when the number of inconsistent triads of judgement reaches the maximum possible for the number of items being compared.

How is the value of d, the number of inconsistent triads, arrived at? We can, of course, draw out all the triads from our data and count up the number of circular triads obtained. In a complex case this might prove tedious – though possibly interesting, if it were important to investigate where the inconsistencies arose. There is, however, a rapid method of computing the value of d from the original table of results, which we now indicate.

The first step is to complete the table by filling in the complementary results. We then calculate the row totals for the symbol 1. Now, if we make no assumption as to how the symbols 1 and 0 will be spread over the table, or rather assume that they are distributed at random, there will be an expected number of occurrences of the symbol 1 in each row. The judge is presented with
$$nC2 = \frac{n(n-1)}{2} \text{ pairs for judgement. It follows that this will be the}$$
total number of times the symbol 1 will appear in the table. Since there are n rows in the table, it follows again that the expected number of times the symbol 1 should appear in each row will be
$$\frac{n(n-1)}{2n} = \frac{n-1}{2}. \text{ We denote this expectation by } E. \text{ Each row sum is}$$
subtracted from the expectation, E, and squared. Finally, the sum of these squared differences is obtained, and this is denoted by T. The maximum possible value for T can be shown to be

12

$T_{max} = \dfrac{n^3 - n}{12}$, and it may be demonstrated that the value of d, the number of inconsistent triads for the table, is given by

$$d = \frac{T_{max} - T}{2}$$

Knowing d, we can at once get the coefficient of consistency, K, using the formula already given. We shall now take an actual example and work it through.

Example. In an experiment to determine whether a judge exercised significant discrimination in sorting leathers according to a particular quality which was, in fact, a complex of several factors, he was presented in turn with every possible pair from seven samples and asked to choose between them. His judgements were recorded in the following table. Calculate his coefficient of consistency and comment on the significance of the results.

	A	B	C	D	E	F	G	Row sum s	$(s - E)^2$
A	–	1	1	1	0	1	1	5	4
B	0	–	0	1	1	0	1	3	0
C	0	1	–	0	1	0	1	3	0
D	0	0	1	–	1	1	1	4	1
E	1	0	0	0	–	1	1	3	0
F	0	1	1	0	0	–	0	2	1
G	0	0	0	0	0	1	–	1	4
								Total $= T = 10$	

With $n = 7$ items to be compared, the expected frequency of the symbol 1 per row is $E = \dfrac{n - 1}{2} = 3$. This is used in the last column of the table. Now the maximum possible value of T is given by

$$T_{max} = \frac{n^3 - n}{12} = \frac{7^3 - 7}{12} = \frac{343 - 7}{12} = 28$$

and the number of circular triads (inconsistent judgements) is then given by

$$d = \frac{T_{max} - T}{2} = \frac{28 - 10}{2} = 9$$

(N.B. As a check on the arithmetic, the number of inconsistent judgements must obviously be a whole number, even though, as will sometimes happen, the arithmetic in the table involves us in fractions.)

To calculate the coefficient of consistency, since $n = 7$, we use the formula for $n =$ an odd number, and get

$$K = 1 - \frac{24d}{n^3 - n} = 1 - \frac{24 \times 9}{7^3 - 7} = 1 - \tfrac{216}{336}$$

i.e. $K = 0{\cdot}36$

This certainly indicates a measure of consistency, but we shall expect, as usual, to have a significance test to determine whether so great a value is likely to have arisen by chance. The reader might think we could use the χ^2 test to compare the observed and expected frequencies in our rows, but since the row totals are not independent of each other (nor, for the mathematicians, linearly dependent on each other), the χ^2 test is not applicable. The problem of a significance test for the coefficient of consistency is not yet completely solved, nothing having been done beyond the case $n = 7$. This is not very satisfactory, since for $n = 5$ even $d = 0$ is not sufficient for us to be really sure that the observed degree of consistency could not have arisen by chance. For $n = 6$ the chance of getting $d = 0$ is only one in fifty, and the probability of getting d not greater than 1 is about one in twenty. When we come to the case of $n = 7$, $d = 4$ or less is probably significant of real consistency, the chance of getting such a result by chance being about 7%. The chance of getting 2 or less for d is about one in fifty, of getting 1 or less, less than 1%, and of getting $d = 0$ by chance only about one in five hundred. In our example we found $d = 9$, so there is a very good chance that the degree of consistency observed could have arisen by chance, so that, while the judge may in fact show significant consistency in his judgements, it is not so marked as to have shown up in this experiment. Until such time as tables are published for higher cases, we can of course take it that, for n greater than 7, if the value of d is sufficient to reach significance in the case of $n = 7$, then it will have even higher significance for the greater value of n.

We should note that the existence of significant consistency in an observer does not necessarily guarantee that his judgement is sound. A man may well be consistently wrong. Even a group of observers may be consistently and jointly wrong. Such is often the case where we are dealing with what the writer calls the mythology of industry. Anyone with experience of industry knows how many fairy tales keep in circulation year after year, until some independent spirit establishes by careful research that they are fairy tales. It may be believed, for example, that a certain material must not be used if it exhibits a certain appearance. Once the myth gets a hold it has little chance of being exposed, since no one will take the chance of using such material. The dog has been given a bad name, and the bad name sticks. Shortage of materials in war time often forces the use of inferior materials, and sometimes the existence of myths is thus brought to light.

An obvious extension to the previous case is to increase the number of judges doing our paired comparison test. It is felt, naturally, that a panel of judges will do a better job than a single judge, other things being equal. The question then arises as to the degree of agreement between the judges (whether or not they are right in an absolute sense). Suppose we have m judges doing the paired tests. Then in our table of results we could record, square by square, the number of judges stating the preference in question. In this way each cell in our table might contain any number from m (when all the judges state the preference $A \rightarrow B$) to zero (when all the judges state the preference $B \rightarrow A$). When some judges prefer A and some prefer B, the number entered into the cell will take some intermediate value between 0 and m. Given n items to be compared, there will be $nC2$ paired comparisons. If all the judges are in perfect agreement, there will thus be $nC2$ cells in our table containing the score m, and $nC2$ cells containing the score 0.

The next point to consider is the number of agreements between pairs of judges. Suppose, for example, that a particular cell in the table contained the score j, to indicate that j judges had agreed in making that particular choice. These j judges could be arranged in $jC2$ pairs all agreeing about the judgement in question. We could carry out the same calculation for the number of agreements between pairs of judges for every cell in the table, getting for each cell a term of the type $jC2$, where j is the number of judges in the several cells. Adding up all these $jC2$ terms for the whole table, we should have the total number of agreements between pairs of judges for the whole experiment as

$$J = \Sigma jC2$$

With n items to be compared, there would be $n(n-1)$ cells in the table (the diagonal being ignored, of course). With m judges and n items being compared, we then define a Coefficient of Agreement as

$$A = \frac{2J}{mC2.nC2} - 1$$

It will be noted that the maximum number of agreements occurs when $nC2$ cells each contain the number m, and that the maximum possible number of agreements between judges will then be $mC2.nC2$. Only in this case will the coefficient of agreement reach the value 1. As J, the number of agreements between pairs of judges, decreases, so also the value for A, the coefficient of agreement, decreases. Again, we have the condition that between more than two judges there cannot possibly be complete *dis*-agreement in paired judgements. With only two judges, complete disagreement is possible, and in this case the coefficient can attain the value minus 1. In general, with m judges, the minimum possible value for the coefficient of agreement, A, is

$$A_{min} = \frac{-1}{m-1} \quad \text{for } m \text{ an even number of judges}$$

or $\quad A_{min} = \frac{-1}{m} \quad$ for m an odd number of judges.

Example. Five judges were presented with every possible pair from a series of six dogs and asked to say which dog of the pair was the better.

The following table shows the numbers of judges expressing the various preferences:

	A	B	C	D	E	F
A	–	3	2	3	1	0
B	2	–	3	2	2	1
C	3	2	–	2	0	0
D	2	3	3	–	0	0
E	4	3	5	5	–	0
F	5	4	5	5	5	–

How to read the table

←Two judges said they preferred dog B to dog D, So it follows that:

←Three judges preferred dog D to dog B

The number of cells in the table is $n(n-1) = 6 \times 5 = 30$. (Check by counting). Our next step is to calculate the number of agreements between pairs of judges about a given judgement, i.e. to calculate the value of $jC2$ for each cell, where j is the number of judges recorded in the cell as having given that judgement. Thus, for the top row in the table the results are $3C2 = 3$, $2C2 = 1$, $3C2 = 3$, $1C2 = 0$ (since with only one judge expressing this opinion there cannot be any agreements between pairs of judges), and $0C2 = 0$ (for the reason just given). The number of agreements between pairs of judges for the whole table may itself be laid out in tabular form as follows:

	A	B	C	D	E	F
A	–	3	1	3	0	0
B	1	–	3	1	1	0
C	3	1	–	1	0	0
D	1	3	3	–	0	0
E	6	3	10	10	–	0
F	10	6	10	10	10	–

Note:

$$jC2 = \frac{j(j-1)}{2}$$

Adding up over the whole table, we find the total number of agreements between pairs of judges for the whole investigation to be $J = \Sigma jC2 = 100$.

We then calculate the coefficient of agreement as

$$A = \frac{2J}{mC2 . nC2} - 1 = \frac{2 \times 100}{5C2 \times 6C2} - 1$$
$$= \frac{2 \times 100}{10 \times 15} - 1 = 1 \cdot 33 - 1 = 0 \cdot 33$$

This suggests a measure of agreement between the judges. Could this value of the coefficient of agreement have arisen by chance with fair probability? The answer depends on the number of items being judged and the number of judges expressing an opinion. Tables for small values of m and n appear in M. G. Kendall's *Advanced Statistics*, from which it appears that in our example, where $n=6$ with $m=5$, we are outside the range of the published tables. In such cases, the expression

$$Z = \left[\left(\frac{4J}{m-2} \right) \frac{-m(m-1)(m-3)n(n-1)}{2(m-2)^2} \right]$$

is distributed as χ^2 with degrees of freedom equal to

$$\frac{m(m-1)n(n-1)}{2(m-2)^2}$$

In our case, we have $m=5$, $n=6$, and $J=100$, so we find

$$Z = \frac{4 \times 100}{5-2} - \frac{5 \times 4 \times 2 \times 6 \times 5}{2(5-2)^2}$$

$$= \tfrac{400}{3} - \tfrac{1200}{18} = 133 \cdot 3 - 66 \cdot 7$$

i.e. $\qquad Z = 66 \cdot 6$

with $\qquad \dfrac{5 \times 4 \times 6 \times 5}{2(5-2)^2} = 33 \cdot 3$ degrees of freedom.

The tables for χ^2 do not extend beyond 30 degrees of freedom, but we know that $\sqrt{2\chi^2}$ is distributed about a mean value $\sqrt{2n-1}$ with unit standard deviation, when the number of degrees of freedom is n. (N.B. This n, for the number of degrees of freedom, should not be confused with the n in the problem we are discussing, which stands for the number of items being compared.)

For $33 \cdot 3$ degrees of freedom for χ^2 we then have a mean value $\sqrt{2n-1} = \sqrt{65 \cdot 6} = 8 \cdot 1$. With a calculated value for $\chi^2 = Z = 66 \cdot 6$ we have $\sqrt{2\chi^2} = \sqrt{2Z} = \sqrt{133 \cdot 2} = 11 \cdot 6$. The difference $11 \cdot 6 - 8 \cdot 1 = 3 \cdot 5$, being equal to $3 \cdot 5$ standard errors, is highly significant, and we conclude that our judges show a degree of agreement between themselves which is extremely unlikely to have arisen by chance. With the significance established we may now set up an estimated ranking based on the overall opinion of the judges. Two alternatives are open to us here. We may base our estimation either on the rows or on the columns of the original table. The dog with the largest row total will have won in the greatest number of paired comparisons, and so will be the best dog. The dog with the second highest score will be ranked the second best dog, and so on. Alternatively, we may establish the ranking on the basis of the column totals, in which case, since the column total tells us the number of times a dog was rejected in a paired comparison, the dog with the least column total will be the winner, and so on. It is evident that the row total plus the column total must come to 25, the number of judgements passed on each dog, being comparisons with each of $(n - 1)$ other dogs at the hands of m judges, i.e. $m(n - 1) = 5 \times 5 = 25$ judgements. Either method will lead to the same ranking. The reader may confirm for himself that the ranking in order of decreasing merit is F, E, B, A, D, and C.

Yet, again, we may argue that the merit of a particular dog might be estimated by the number of times there was agreement between pairs of judges that it should be accepted minus the number of times there was agreement between pairs of judges that it should be rejected. We can get this from the row and column totals of the table of $jC2$ values (page 350). We leave it to the reader to confirm the following results of doing this:

Dog	Row total	Column total	Row minus column	Rank
A	7	21	-14	4
B	6	16	-10	3
C	5	27	-22	6
D	7	25	-18	5
E	29	11	$+18$	2
F	46	0	$+46$	1

The ranking comes out the same as before.

The levels of probable significance (corresponding to a probability of about 5%) may be calculated for low values of m and n, using the following expressions which give the values of J which will be exceeded in only about 5% of trials by chance.

For m = 3, and n ranging from 3 to 8

    J is probably significant if it equals or exceeds $n^2 - \dfrac{5n}{2} + 6$

For m = 4, and n ranging from 3 to 6

    J is probably significant if it equals or exceeds $n^2 + 3n - 4$

For m = 5, and n ranging from 2 to 5

    J is probably significant if it equals or exceeds $n^2 + 10n - 15$

For m = 6, and n ranging from 2 to 4

    J is probably significant if it equals or exceeds $n^2 + 15n - 20$

The following expressions may be used to get a rough guide as to the 1% levels.

Form m = 3, and n ranging from 3 to 8

    J may be taken as significant if it equals or exceeds $n^2 - 2n + 8$

For m = 4, and n ranging from 3 to 6

    J may be taken as significant if it equals or exceeds $n^2 + 5n - 8$

For m = 5, and n ranging from 3 to 5

    J may be taken as significant if it equals or exceeds $n^2 + 12n - 21$

For m = 6, and n equals 3 or 4

    With $n = 3$, take J significant at 34. With $n = 4$, take J significant at 59.

For cases of m or n outside these ranges, use the χ^2 distribution, as explained in the example.

We now turn to other applications of ranking, with particular attention to the rapid evaluation of experimental results. Such preliminary evaluations are often extremely useful. True, they do not utilize all the information in the data collected, yet they are surprisingly accurate and give a very good guide as to whether full scale analysis by more detailed methods will be worth embarking on, as well as giving a good picture of the main conclusions which are likely to result from the full scale analysis. Moreover, the procedures do not require an assumption that the data follow the Normal distribution, as is the case in Analysis of Variance which we shall be considering in the next chapter.

A common type of problem is the one where we are comparing two sets of data and wish to know whether the difference between the sets is such as to warrant a conclusion that the difference is significant of a real difference in the sources from which the data were drawn. We have already met this kind of problem in our consideration of Student's *t* test. Let us now tackle it from the point of view of ranking. We shall take an actual example, so as to make the ideas concrete.

Example. Two blocks of land were each divided up into ten plots of equal areas and sown with corn. The two blocks were in every way treated identically, except for the amount of phosphate applied as fertilizer. Is there a significant difference between the mean yields of the blocks?

YIELDS IN BUSHELS PER ACRE

Plot	1	2	3	4	5	6	7	8	9	10	Mean
Block A	5·8	6·0	6·0	5·7	5·8	6·2	5·7	6·5	6·0	6·3	6·0
Block B	5·5	5·7	5·5	6·0	5·7	5·8	5·6	5·9	5·6	5·7	5·7

There is, of course, no reason for comparing similar plot numbers of the two blocks, since it is assumed that all the plots within a block are *replicates*, i.e. repeats under the same controlled conditions, so that any between-plot differences within a block are to be attributed to those random factors which constitute experimental error.

To test the significance of the difference by ranking technique, we assign to each yield a rank number, tied values being given a mean rank. The lowest rank number is given to the highest yield, and the ranks are assigned from 1 to 20, i.e. ignoring the block differentiation.

The 20 plot yields may be arranged in order of size, thus:

```
 1    2    3    4    5    6    7    8    9    10   11
6·5  6·3  6·2         6·0         5·9       5·8
           12   13   14   15   16   17   18   19   20
                      5·7              5·6       5·5
```

Thus the plots with a yield of 6·0 bushels per acre are given a ranking $\frac{4+5+6+7}{4} = 5 \cdot 5$, and similarly for other ties. We then set up the following table showing the rankings within blocks:

Plot	1	2	3	4	5	6	6	8	9	10	Rank totals
Block A	10	5·5	5·5	14	10	3	14	1	5·5	2	70·5
Block B	19·5	14	19·5	5·5	14	10	17·5	8	17·5	14	139·5

Check Grand Total = 210

The grand total of the ranks should, of course, be equal to the sum of the numbers 1 to 20. The sum of the first n natural numbers is given by the formula $\frac{n(n+1)}{2}$. In this case, $n=20$, so we have $\frac{20 \times 21}{2} = 210$; thus we may have confidence in the arithmetic so far.

Now we may make the lower rank total the basis of a significance test. The question is what is the probability of getting a rank total as low as the observed value 70·5, when the expected rank total is $\frac{210}{2} = 105$ on a Null Hypothesis that the ranks are randomly distributed between the two blocks (= treatments)? It may be shown that, for a problem of this type, where we have N replicates (the number of replicates in our data is 10 since there were 10 repeats in each block), there is a probability of approximately 5% of getting a lower rank total (70·5) as small as or smaller than

$$\frac{9N^2}{10} - \frac{3N}{2} + 3$$

and roughly a 1% chance of getting a lower rank total as small as or smaller than

$$\frac{4N^2}{5} - 9$$

These expressions, then, enable us to calculate the 5% and 1% significance levels for the lower rank total in any problem of this kind. In our case, with $N=10$, we have:

5% level for lower rank total $= \frac{9N^2}{10} - \frac{3N}{2} + 3 = 90 - 15 + 3 = 78$

1% level for lower rank total $= \frac{4N^2}{5} - 9 = 80 - 9 = 71$

Since our observed lower rank total is 70·5, we conclude that it is significant at the 1% level, so that there is a real difference between the blocks (treatments). The reader may care to repeat the analysis, using Student's t test, so as to confirm that the same conclusion is arrived at, with the same degree of confidence, as indicated by the probability level.

We now propose to give the reader a simple account of the way in which the significance levels for problems of the above type are arrived at, so that he will appreciate the nature of the test more fully. We shall illustrate the ideas by taking a very simple case. The reader may then care to amuse and instruct himself by taking successively harder cases, with a view to trying to spot how the system grows.

Suppose we had two blocks in our experiment, with only three replications in each plot. Then the six yields would be ranked with numbers 1 to 6. Each plot would contain three rank numbers, and the basis of the significance test is the total of the rank numbers within one plot. The grand total of all the rank numbers would be the sum of the numbers 1 to 6, i.e. $\frac{n(n+1)}{2} = \frac{6 \times 7}{2} = 21$,

so, on the hypothesis that the rank numbers were assigned at random to the plots, we should expect the rank total for each plot to be $\frac{21}{2} = 10·5$. A chosen block would have three rank numbers and each of the ranks from 1 to 6 would be equally likely to appear in that plot. How many ways are there of selecting a combination of three rank numbers from 6 to appear in the chosen plot? The answer is $6C3 = \frac{6 \times 5 \times 4}{3 \times 2 \times 1} = 20$. Let us list them out:

```
    123  124  125  126
              134  135  136
                        145  146
                                  156
    ────────────────────────────────────
              234  235  236
                        245  246
                                  256
    ────────────────────────────────────
                        345  346
                                  356
    ────────────────────────────────────
                                       456
```

The above layout may strike the reader, at first sight, as a little eccentric. But there is method in the madness. The top section contains all the combinations which contain the rank 1, the first line showing all the combinations that include 1 and 2, the second line all the combinations that contain 1 and 3, the third line all the combinations that contain 1 and 4, and the last line the only possible combination containing 1 and 5. By 'contain' in this connection we mean 'contain as the leading or first terms of the combination' without prejudice to the fact that other combinations may contain the two terms named in other positions than the first two. The reader may check for himself by counting that (a) the table does show the proper number, 20, of combinations, and (b) no combination is repeated twice. It should be kept clearly in mind that we are here concerned with combinations as distinct from permutations. From the point of view of the rank total for the treatment block, the arrangement of the ranks in the block is immaterial, i.e. 123, 321, 213, etc., are all equivalent, in giving the same total. The major eccentricity of the table lies in the way the entries are staggered. The reason for this arrangement is that we have put all combinations giving the same rank total in the same column, and the rank total characteristic of the columns increases by one unit as we pass from the left to the right of the table. Thus in the fourth column from the left of the table we have the entries 126, 135, 234, all of which have a rank total equal to 9.

We may now draw up the following table which shows the frequency with which each rank total might occur on the basis of pure chance, by finding the rank total for each column and the number of combinations recorded in that column. Thus in the fourth column from the left we learn that the frequency of occurrence of rank total 9 is 3.

Rank total	6	7	8	9	10	11	12	13	14	15
Frequency	1	1	2	3	3	3	3	2	1	1
Probability %	5	5	10	15	15	15	15	10	5	5

The probabilities shown in the bottom line are easily arrived at by noticing that the total frequency of occurrence, i.e. the total number of combinations of 3 ranks chosen from 6, is equal to 20. Of these 20 combinations, one gives a rank total 6, one a rank total 7, two a rank total 8, three a rank total 9, and so on. Since all combinations are equally likely, the probability of the occurrence of a given rank total is obviously the value shown for that rank total in the last line.

The reader will notice that with only three replications, even the lowest rank total possible, 6, can occur by chance with a probability of 5%, so that at very best we could not draw a conclusion of more than 'probably significant' with so few replications. If the reader will work out the case of four replicates for himself he will get the following table. In this case the ranks for the two blocks will range from 1 to 8, and the number of ways of choosing a combination of four ranks from 8 to appear in a chosen block will be $8C4 = \dfrac{8 \times 7 \times 6 \times 5}{4 \times 3 \times 2 \times 1} = 70$. This figure may be checked by doing a cross tot of the line labelled Frequency. The probabilities in this case are obtained by dividing each frequency by 70.

Rank total	10	11	12	13	14	15	16	17	18	19	20	21	22	23	24	25	26
Frequency	1	1	2	3	5	5	7	7	8	7	7	5	5	3	2	1	1

Here we are better off. True, even the lowest rank total of 10 can occur with a probability of 1 in 70, but this almost reaches the 1% level. The 5% probability level corresponds to a frequency of occurrence of 3·5 in 70. From the table we see that a rank total of 12 or less occurs with a frequency of 4 in 70, i.e. 5·7%. We could therefore take this value as our level of probable significance. The reader whose mathematical equipment does not extend much further than commonsense and arithmetic of the simplest variety will find in this problem a source of great fun, as he builds up the cases of four, five, and so on replicates. The amount of work rapidly increases as we proceed, but there is in it all the fun that mathematicians get from their work. He will find that there are patterns of behaviour, so that very soon he will be able to write down whole sections of his tables at a time without having to think out every entry. It is the sort of problem we might suggest for a hobby over the winter, to be picked up and laid down at leisure. That is how the mathematician joins work to pleasure, making no distinction between what is highbrow or lowbrow, toil or frolic. We should, in fairness, advise readers that all cases up to $n = 20$ have been worked out already. It is on this basis that we were able to give formulae for calculating the 5% and 1% significance levels. Given a set of values we can find a formula for calculating them, approximately at any rate. The formula replaces a set of tables, by summarizing their essence, as it were.

In the previous problem we had the case of 'unpaired replicates', that is to say there was no point in contrasting the plots of the two blocks which had the same plot number. All plots within a block were undifferentiated. Very frequently, however, the replicates are paired. This is done deliberately in experimental design, so as to eliminate certain disturbing factors. Suppose, for example, it were decided to make a pilot survey to find out whether a particular manurial treatment increased yield of corn. The experiment, we shall suppose, is carried out on one farm in two blocks of land. Suppose that an analysis of the results showed block A to give a significantly higher yield than block B. What have we established about the treatment? Nothing for certain. Several criticisms of the design of the investigation may be made. For example: the difference established is a difference between blocks. Who is to say that there were not other differences between the blocks apart from our manurial treatment? One block might be more fertile than the other, even if we had never applied our manurial treatment to it. It is notoriously difficult to get two patches of ground, even in the same field, which are equally good. Again, even supposing that our two blocks in absence of the manurial treatment are equally good, they might both be abnormally deficient in the substances we have added as manure, so that a repeat of the experiment in another locality where the deficiency was not so pronounced would produce an entirely negative result!

To overcome the possibility of such criticism, we should have to replicate our experiment, i.e. repeat it several times at different places. At each place there would be two plots chosen, and the manurial treatment would be applied to one of the plots only. How should we choose the block to receive the manurial treatment? To avoid bias, the best procedure would be to toss a penny. In this way, over the whole of our investigation, we might reasonably expect that differences in natural fertility of the soil between plots would be averaged out. Our criterion of the value of the manurial treatment in question would then sensibly be the excess yield obtained from the manured plots over the yield from the untreated plots. The significance of the excess would have to be decided in terms of the probability of getting an excess as great as that observed. We shall see how this type of experiment is tackled by exact methods when we come to the chapter on the Analysis of Variance. Meantime, we can show how the problem might be tackled on a ranking approach.

The essential of the method of experimentation we have just indicated is that we should be making comparisons between pairs of replicates. If the experiment were tried out at 10 different localities, we should have two plots at each locality and the comparison would lie between the 10 pairs of plots. Let the following table represent yields in bushels per acre.

Site	1	2	3	4	5	6	7	8	9	10	Mean
Treated plot	6·3	5·8	4·3	6·4	7·3	5·5	5·8	6·0	5·4	5·8	5·86
Control	4·9	5·9	5·2	5·4	4·8	5·4	6·1	5·7	5·7	5·7	5·48
Difference	1·4	−0·1	−0·9	1·0	2·5	0·1	−0·3	0·3	−0·3	0·1	
Rank of diff.	9	−2	−7	8	10	2	−5	5	−5	2	
	Lower Rank Total = 19										

The line labelled Difference is obtained by subtracting from the yield of the treated plot the yield of the control plot. Then, ignoring the signs of the differences, we assign rank numbers to them as in the last line, giving ties a mean rank in the way explained in the previous example. Finally, these ranks are given signs corresponding to the signs of the original differences. We then total the positive ranks, total the negative ranks, and see which gives the smaller total. In our example the negative ranks have the smaller total. The question then is: could so small a total of ranks have arisen by chance with fair probability, or must we accept the differences in yields as indicating that the manurial treatment is of definite value?

We may calculate the approximate significance levels for the lower rank total by using the following formulae:

5% level for lower rank total is given by $\dfrac{N^2 - 7N + 10}{5}$

1% level for lower rank total is given by $\dfrac{11N^2}{60} - 2N + 5$

Where N is the number of replications.

In our example there were $N = 10$ replications, so we have

$$5\% \text{ level for lower rank total} = \frac{100 - 70 + 10}{5} = 8$$

It is at once evident that our lower rank total is too large even for the 5% level, being equal to 19. There is no point, therefore, in computing the 1% level. We conclude that the treatment has not been proved to have any effect. As usual, in all significance tests, the verdict is 'not proven' rather than 'not guilty'. Further evidence might suffice to establish the significance of the difference.

It may sometimes occur that the treatment and the control have the same value. In this case the difference will be zero, and if this result were included in the ranking we should assign to it the rank 1. The question would then arise: What sign should we give to the rank, positive or negative? Obviously, we cannot properly give it any sign, without upsetting our test. The best plan in such cases is to exclude ties as contributing nothing to our decision. The test will then be carried out as usual, but, of course, in calculating our significance level we shall have to reduce the number of replications in the actual experiment by the number of excluded ties.

Even more common in practice is the type of experiment where comparisons of treatments are made under several different conditions, but with several replications within each condition, instead of simply one comparison under each set of conditions. An actual example will make this clear.

Suppose we wished to investigate whether there were any difference in reading ability between children having a poor home background and children with a good home background. We might set about investigating the matter as follows. On the basis that one swallow does not make a summer we should consider it important to test more than one child with each type of background. If the children of good background were drawn from one school and the children with a poor background from another, the experimental design would be poor, on the grounds that any observed difference might as well be due to a difference between schools as a difference between home backgrounds. As the statistician would say: 'the between background difference would be confounded with the between schools difference', the two being inextricably together. (*Confounded* is used in the root meaning of the word: blended or mingled.) To eliminate this confounding, the comparison would have to be within a school – better still within a class, children being chosen who have travelled the educational road together as far as possible. In a word, the children should be as like as is reasonably possible, except in the matter of home background.

If the experiment were confined to one particular school, however, the criticism might be made that the results of the experiment apply only to children with that kind of educational background, and it is certainly reasonable *prima facie* that the effect of home background might well 'interact' with the school background. Such questions have always to be met before experiments are embarked on. Let us in this case cut a long story short and suppose that the experimental design finally chosen was as follows.

Four schools of different type to be chosen. In each school ten children of similar background educationally to be chosen – five with a good home background (probably defined as better than average for the school in question) and five children with poor background at home. The ten children in each school to be given the same reading test under the same conditions, the marking to be in accordance with a standard scale. Suppose the scores to be as shown in the table on next page.

The reader will see that what we have done is to assign to each reading score a rank number within its own school. Since there are ten children tested in each school, the total of the rank numbers for each school will be the sum of the first ten natural

	Good home	Rank	Poor home	Rank
School A	85	1	47	7·5
	63	5	65	4
	47	7·5	52	6
	76	2	42	9
	70	3	41	10
	Total	18·5	Total	36·5
School B	57	5	84	1
	72	2	67	4
	43	9·5	45	8
	52	6	43	9·5
	68	3	48	7
	Total	25·5	Total	29·5
School C	97	1	54	6
	53	7·5	67	2
	64	4	65	3
	57	5	48	9
	19	10	53	7·5
	Total	27·5	Total	27·5
School D	59	5	45	9
	68	3	34	10
	72	1	69	2
	56	7	64	4
	47	8	57	6
	Total	24	Total	31
Grand totals of ranks		95·5		124·5

numbers, viz. $\dfrac{n(n+1)}{2} = \dfrac{10 \times 11}{2} = 55$. This fact we may use as a check on the calculations within each school. With four schools, the grand total of all the ranks will be $4 \times 55 = 220$, and this again constitutes a check on the final rank additions. The question to be put now is whether so small a rank total as that observed for the Good Home Background group could easily have arisen by chance, or whether it is so small that we can regard the effect of good home background as established. The general answer to this question will clearly depend on both the number of groups (schools) and the number of replications within the group. Tables have been calculated for the various probability levels. The following formula enables us to check roughly whether significance is attained. If the lower rank total in an experiment in n groups with N replicates in each group is less than or equal to

$$\frac{(2n-1)N^2 + N - 4}{2}$$

we may take it that the 1% level of significance has been reached. And if the lower rank total is less than or equal to

$$\frac{(2n-1)N^2 + 3N - 4}{2}$$

we may take it that the 5% significance level has been reached.

In our example, we had $n = 4$ groups, with $N = 5$ replicates in each group. Substituting in the above formulae, we find:

$$1\% \text{ significance level} \quad \frac{7 \times 25 + 5 - 4}{2} = 88$$

$$5\% \text{ significance level} \quad \frac{7 \times 25 + 15 - 4}{2} = 93$$

We found a lower rank total of 95·5 in our experiment. This value is just about on the 5% level, so we conclude that the effect of home background is probably significant. The reader should bear in mind that the formulae we have given for calculating significance levels are substitutes for the tables only for rough working. For this purpose they are amply good, as the approximations they give are on the whole quite good. Anyone doing careful work should, of course, make use of proper tables.

So far, we have seen what may be done in the way of comparing two treatments only. In practice, experiments are often designed in which several treatments are compared simultaneously. Suppose, for example, that the number of articles a workman could complete in a given period of time depended on some physical characteristic of the material with which he were working. Suppose further, that research were in progress to find methods whereby this characteristic (itself possibly a complex of characteristics, rather than a simple one) might be modified so as to make the job more easy for the operative. (Readers in the Boot and Shoe industry may be reminded of 'mulling'.) Let us suppose that the research workers had produced four suggestions, as possible improvements. An experiment might then be designed to see whether there was any chance of any of these proving helpful. We have here a typical case of process research, that is research at the factory level rather than in a laboratory. It is well known that many things work wonderfully well in the controlled conditions of the laboratory, only to prove a failure in the much less stable conditions of the manufacturing organization. Processes, to be suitable for manufacturing, have to be robust. For this reason there is a growing tendency amongst industrial statisticians (who are usually chemists or physicists, primarily – and statisticians only because they find it pays good dividends) to carry out a great deal of their research in the production unit as such, in so far as this may reasonably be arranged without disturbance to the flow of production. It is well to remember that the ultimate experiment is in the shops, anyway.

Let us suppose, then, that the investigator decided to have an experiment on the following lines. Five operators would be chosen, each operator to be regarded as a block (i.e. a source of supply). The four suggestions as to treatment of the material would be added to the current method (i.e. the one with which dissatisfaction has been expressed), making five treatments in all to be compared. To eliminate between operator effect, each operator would have a trial run with each of the five treatments of the material. In this way the treatment effects would not be confounded with the operators. In addition, the order in which each operator would take the experimental materials would be assigned at random. Thus, each operator would work through the specimen materials in a different order. This would eliminate any systematic time factor, such as might arise if the operator's productivity varied from time to time during the day – e.g. slowing down before 'knocking off time'! The relative merits of the material treatments would sensibly be measured by the number of articles completed in a standard time, say one hour. Naturally, every precaution would be taken to ensure that during his test periods the workman was not held up or disturbed for any extraneous reasons. The following table might then represent the number of articles produced in the standard time by the several workmen with the various treatments of the working material.

Work-man	Treatments of working material				
	Control	A	B	C	D
1	72	65	37	57	64
2	24	42	25	62	83
3	49	20	42	24	44
4	52	33	27	72	35
5	38	17	45	44	40

Our next step is to set up a table showing how each workman ranks the various treatments, as indicated by his productivity.

Workman	Control	A	B	C	D
1	1	2	5	4	3
2	5	3	4	2	1
3	1	5	3	4	2
4	2	4	5	1	3
5	4	5	1	2	3
Rank totals	13	19	18	12	12

Since a low rank total is the hall-mark of a successful modification of the material, it is evident that we have no improvement offered to us. (Often the case, unfortunately!) This need not deter us, for our present purpose, however. We have simply to interchange the column headings 'Control' and '*A*' to get a set of data in which the experiment looks promising, for in that case there would be four treatments apparently better than the Control. Our statistical problem now is to decide whether the treatments as a whole differ among themselves. This is still a sensible question even if no treatment looks better than the control. If we find that the treatments do differ significantly one from another, then we shall be justified in making comparisons between individual treatments. But if the treatments cannot be shown to differ significantly from each other, as a whole, then we should be very cautious in making claims about differences between individuals.

We test the results for lack of homogeneity as follows. If the number of blocks (workmen in this case) is equal to n, and number of treatments (including the control, if there is one in the experiment) is equal to p, then we can calculate the 'rank difference' χ^2 as

$$\chi^2_r = \frac{12}{np(p+1)}\left[\begin{array}{c}\text{Sum of Squares of}\\\text{Treatment Rank Totals}\end{array}\right] - 3n(p+1)$$

The appropriate number of degrees of freedom being $(p-1)$. In our example we had $n=5$ operators and $p=5$ treatments. The sum of the squares of the treatment rank totals is

$$13^2 + 19^2 + 18^2 + 13^2 + 12^2 = 1,167$$

We find, then, that

$$\chi^2_r = \frac{12}{5 \times 5 \times 6}[1,167] - 3 \times 5 \times 6 = 3\cdot36$$

with $(p-1)$ degrees of freedom, i.e. 4 degrees of freedom. From tables of χ^2 (the reader may check on his graph), we find that the 5% level of χ^2 is 9·5. It is evident that there is no evidence here that the treatments have any real effect – either as improving productivity or as retarding it. The 'backroom boys' must go away and have another think.

It may possibly have occurred to some readers that the same technique and the same data could be made the basis of a test for significant differences between the operators with regard to productivity. In this case we should look upon the treatments as blocks, and the operators as treatments. Our ranking would then be within treatments, instead of within operators. Instead of saying: How does this operator get on with the various materials? we should say: How does this material get on with the various operators? The rankings, instead of running across the rows of our table, would then run down the columns, and instead of getting a rank total for each material we should get one for each workman. The reader may care to work through this case for himself, and see whether there is evidence of a significant difference in productivity between the workmen. Would this be a fair test of the between workman differences or is there a possibility that each workman might find particular trouble with a particular kind of material? Does this apply to the previous analysis? What we are asking is whether there might not possibly be an 'interaction' between workman and material, so that we get a special boost or set back in production when a particular workman is teamed up with a particular material. This type of problem will receive our attention when we come to the Analysis of Variance.

We close this section of our review of statistical ranking methods by going back to our first example in this chapter. We there had the case of two teachers ranking ten students in order of estimated ability, and we found, by using Spearman's rank correlation coefficient, that there was a significant correlation between their rankings. The same conclusion might be reached by means of the rank difference χ^2_r we have just introduced. In this case our teachers become our operators, and our students become our treatments. We form the following table:

Student	A	B	C	D	E	F	G	H	K	L
Ranked by X	2	1	3	4	6	5	8	7	10	9
Ranked by Y	3	2	1	4	6	7	5	9	10	8
Rank totals	5	3	4	8	12	12	13	16	20	17

In this case $n = 2$ and $p = 10$, so we get on substitution in

$$\chi^2_r = \frac{12}{np(p+1)} \left[\begin{array}{c} \text{Sum of squares of} \\ \text{student rank totals} \end{array} \right] - 3n(p+1)$$

since the sum of the squares of the student rank totals is

$$5^2 + 3^2 + 4^2 + 8^2 + 12^2 + 12^2 + 13^2 + 16^2 + 20^2 + 17^2 = 1,516$$

$$\chi^2_r = \frac{12}{2 \times 10 \times 11}[1,516] - 3 \times 2 \times 11 = 16\cdot7$$

With $p - 1 = 10 - 1 = 9$ degrees of freedom, the 5% level of χ^2 is $16\cdot9$.

We may take it, therefore, that there is probably a significant correlation between the rankings of the teachers. If the reader will compare this conclusion with the one reached at the beginning of the chapter he will see that we are not quite so confident this time. He should remember that these significance tests are approximate, and be satisfied that they line up as well as they do. In practice, we are not concerned so much with the exact probability level reached, as with an indication as to what judgement we should pass. On the whole, these approximate tests serve this purpose excellently. Properly applied, they will never lead us astray in our broad purpose.

The quantity χ^2_r is simply related to Spearman's rank correlation coefficient by the following formula:

$$R = \left(\frac{\chi^2_r}{p-1}\right) - 1$$

In the present case, with $p = 10$ and $\chi^2_r = 16\cdot7$, we estimate R as

$$R = \frac{16\cdot7}{9} - 1 = 0\cdot85$$

a value which agrees with that calculated by the direct method at the beginning of the chapter. The value $R = 0\cdot85$ may also be tested by comparing it with its standard error. The standard error of R is $\frac{1}{\sqrt{p-1}} = \frac{1}{\sqrt{9}} = 0\cdot333$. The ratio of R to its standard error is therefore

$$t = \frac{0\cdot85}{0\cdot333} = 2\cdot55$$

Since this lies between 2 and 3 standard errors, we again conclude that the correlation is probably significant.

As the reader will by now see, there is almost no end to the types of problem which can successfully be tackled by the technique of ranking. Other techniques will be found in the books referred to in the bibliography. For the man who is not a professional statistician there is great value in simple techniques of this kind. It is true that they do not utilize to the full all the information in a set of data, and are to that extent inefficient. On the other side of the ledger, however, there must be made a substantial credit entry in view of their time-saving nature and splendid approximations.

NOW SEE WHAT YOU MAKE OF THESE

1. In a painting competition the various entries are ranked by two judges. Use Spearman's Rank Correlation Coefficient to test whether there is significant agreement among the judges.

Entry	A	B	C	D	E	F	G	H	K	L
Judge X	5	2	6	8	1	7	4	9	3	10
Judge Y	1	7	6	10	4	5	3	8	2	9

2. Do the ladies show a real measure of agreement as to the features they like best in popular magazines? Calculate the coefficient of concordance-

Feature	A	B	C	D	E	F
Miss P's rank	3	1	6	2	5	4
Miss Q's rank	4	3	2	5	1	6
Miss R's rank	2	1	6	5	4	3
Miss S's rank	5	4	2	6	1	3

3. Mr. Robinson considered the six people A, B, C, D, E and F two at a time and made up his mind which he liked best of each pair. His judgments are as in the following table. For instance he preferred, Mr A to Mr B, but Mr E to Mr A.

	B	C	D	E	F
A	1	1	1	0	0
B		1	0	0	1
C			0	0	1
D				1	1
E					1

Calculate the coefficient of consistency for Mr Robinson's judgements.

4. Two drugs are tested for their soporific effect, each on a group of ten people, the number of hours sleep induced being stated. Is it reasonable to claim that one drug is superior to the other in inducing sleep?

Drug A	$7\frac{1}{4}$	$6\frac{1}{2}$	$5\frac{3}{4}$	$7\frac{1}{2}$	$8\frac{1}{2}$	$7\frac{1}{4}$	$8\frac{3}{4}$	9	$7\frac{1}{2}$	8
Drug B	9	$8\frac{1}{2}$	7	$6\frac{1}{2}$	$8\frac{3}{4}$	$9\frac{3}{4}$	$9\frac{1}{2}$	$8\frac{1}{2}$	$9\frac{1}{4}$	$7\frac{3}{4}$

19

The Analysis of Variation and Co-variation

> 'After two years Pharaoh had a dream. He thought he stood
> by the river out of which came up seven kine, very beautiful
> and fat.'

Undoubtedly one of the most elegant, powerful, and useful techniques in modern statistical method is that of the Analysis of Variation and Co-variation by which the total variation in a set of data may be reduced to components associated with possible sources of variability whose relative importance we wish to assess. The precise form which any given analysis will take is intimately connected with the structure of the investigation from which the data are obtained. A simple structure will lead to a simple analysis; a complex structure to a complex analysis. In this chapter we shall consider some of the more common types of analysis so that the reader may get hold of the basic principles and appreciate the beauty of the technique.*

It will be recalled that we calculate the variance of a set of data as the mean square deviation of the several items from their grand average. Thus, if the individual items be denoted by x, their grand average by $\bar{x}$, and the number of items by N, then the variance will be

$$V = \sigma^2 = \frac{1}{N} \Sigma (x - \bar{x})^2$$

This will be the sample variance. But we also know that a small sample tends to underestimate the variance of the parent population and that a better estimate of the population variance is obtained by dividing the 'Sum of Squares', $\Sigma(x - \bar{x})^2$ by the number of 'degrees of freedom', $(N-1)$. We have then that the 'Population Variance Estimate' is

$$\hat{V} = \sigma^2 = \frac{\Sigma(x - \bar{x})^2}{N-1}$$

We shall show, in a moment, by way of example, how the total variation may be resolved into components in suitable cases.

* Introduced by R. A. Fisher.

First, however, the reader should have it clearly in his mind that in the Analysis of Variance we compute for each source of variability in turn:

(a) the sum of squares, (b) the number of degrees of freedom. Consider, then, the following table of data which shows the values of 20 items which have been collected in four samples of 5 items each. Even if the data were collected at random from a perfectly homogeneous population, we should not expect each sample to have the same average value, since even sample averages must reflect the variance in the parent population. What we should expect in these circumstances is that the variation between sample averages should be commensurate with the population variance as indicated by the variation within the individual samples. If it should prove that the 'between sample variation' were significantly greater than the 'within sample variation', then we should suspect that the samples were not, in fact, drawn from the same population, but from populations whose average values differed, so that on top of the 'within population variation' there existed also a 'between population variation'.

	Sample 1	Sample 2	Sample 3	Sample 4
	2	3	6	5
	3	4	8	5
	1	3	7	5
	3	5	4	3
	1	0	10	2
Sample totals	10	15	35	20
Sample means	2	3	7	4

Total number of items $= N = 20$

Grand Total of all items $= T = 80$

Grand Average of all items $= \dfrac{T}{N} = \dfrac{80}{20} = 4$

The table on next page shows the squares of the deviations of the 20 items from their grand average value of 4.

The number of degrees of freedom on which this total sum of squares was computed is found as one less than the number of items on which the calculation was made. We had 20 items and so

Total Degrees of Freedom $= 19$

	Sample 1	Sample 2	Sample 3	Sample 4
	4	1	4	1
	1	0	16	1
	9	1	9	1
	1	1	0	1
	9	16	36	4
Totals	24	19	65	8

Grand Total of Squared Deviations from the Grand Average
$$= \text{Total Sum of Squares} = 24 + 19 + 65 + 8 = \underline{116}$$

Let us now try to partition the total sum of squares and the total degrees of freedom into components corresponding to 'between sample averages' and 'within samples' respectively. In order to get the between sample effect, we must eliminate the within sample effect. We can do this by replacing each item by its own sample average. Doing this, we obtain the following table:

Sample 1	Sample 2	Sample 3	Sample 4
2	3	7	4
2	3	7	4
2	3	7	4
2	3	7	4
2	3	7	4

For which the Grand Total is still $T = 80$, of course

In order to get the between sample sum of squares, we now proceed exactly as we did when we were calculating the total sums of squares. We set up the following table which shows the squares of the deviations of the entries in our new table from their grand average, thus:

	Sample 1	Sample 2	Sample 3	Sample 4
	4	1	9	0
	4	1	9	0
	4	1	9	0
	4	1	9	0
	4	1	9	0
Totals	20	5	45	0

Between sample sum of squares $= 20 + 5 + 45 = 70$.
To get the relevant degrees of freedom, we take one less than the number of sample averages on which the computation was based. Hence:
Between sample degrees of freedom $= 4 - 1 = 3$

It now remains for us to get the sum of squares and the degrees of freedom which correspond to within sample variation. In order to do this, we must remove the between sample average effect. We are now concerned only with the variability within the individual samples. To get this, we subtract from each item in our original table of data its own sample average. The result is shown in the following table:

	Sample 1	Sample 2	Sample 3	Sample 4
	0	0	−1	1
	1	1	1	1
	−1	0	0	1
	1	2	−3	−1
	−1	−3	3	−2
Totals	0	0	0	0

The grand average of the items in this new table is, of course, zero, and the sum of squares for the within sample source of variation is obtained by finding the sum of the squares of the deviations of the items in this table from their grand average, zero. All we have to do, then, is to square the items as they stand. The result is:

	Sample 1	Sample 2	Sample 3	Sample 4
	0	0	1	1
	1	1	1	1
	1	0	0	1
	1	4	9	1
	1	9	9	4
Totals	4	14	20	8

Within Sample Sum of Squares $= 4 + 14 + 20 + 8 = 46$.

In order to get the within sample degrees of freedom, we argue as follows: each sample consists of five items. For each sample the number of degrees of freedom within that sample will be one less than the number of items within that sample, viz. 4. However, there are four such samples, so the total degrees of freedom within samples will be $4 \times 4 = 16$.

Let us now collect our results together in a Table of the Analysis of Variance.

TABLE OF ANALYSIS OF VARIANCE

Source of variation	Sums of squares	Degrees of freedom	Variance estimate
Between samples	70	3	$\frac{70}{3} = 23 \cdot 3$
Within samples	46	16	$\frac{46}{16} = 2 \cdot 9$
Total	116	19	

It will be seen that our procedure has neatly divided the total sum of squares and the total degrees of freedom into two independent components, which correspond to between sample and within sample variation.

Now let us think a little, and see if we can turn this device to practical account. When we divide a sum of squares by the corresponding number of degrees of freedom on which the sum of squares is based, we are estimating a variance. In our example, the Table of the Analysis of Variance shows this done for the two components of our variation. If we set up the Null Hypothesis that the between sample variation is only a reflexion of the variation of the items in the common parent population from which the items were drawn, the two Variance estimates are estimates of the same variance. What we are saying, in effect, is this: it does not matter whether we estimate the population variance on the basis of the variation between sample averages or on the basis of the variation of the items about their own sample average. Both are completely determined by the variance of the items in the common parent population. Since the two estimates are independent of each other, we shall not expect them to be identical in value. But we shall expect them not to differ more than is to be expected taking into account the number of degrees of freedom on which they are based. Now we already have a simple test for the mutual compatibility of two variance estimates, namely Snedecor's Variance Ratio Test which we dealt with in Chapter 13. If our Null Hypothesis is correct, and there is no specific between sample effect other than that introduced by the variance of the common parent population, then we should expect Snedecor's Test to yield a non-significant result.

On the face of it, judging from our Table of Analysis of Variance, there is a specific between sample effect, i.e. in addition to the between sample variation to be expected on our Null Hypothesis, there is an extra variation between the samples which is unaccounted for by the Null Hypothesis. Applying Snedecor's Test we get

$$F = \frac{23 \cdot 3}{2 \cdot 9} = 8 \cdot 1$$

For the greater variance estimate there are 3 degrees of freedom and for the lesser variance estimate there are 13 degrees of freedom.

Consulting the Table for Snedecor's F given in Chapter 13, we find that the 1% level of F is about 5·3. The 0·1% level is about 9. Our observed value of 8·1 is therefore well above the 1% level and very nearly at the 0·1% level. We conclude that the observed variance ratio is too great for the Null Hypothesis to be maintained and that there is a specific between sample variation. The implication is that, whatever we may have hoped or thought to the contrary, if we are wise we shall act on the assumption that the samples were, in fact, drawn from sources whose average values differed from each other. If for our purpose it were desirable to have the average value as large as possible, then we should do our business with the source which gave us Sample 3 for which the average value came out at 7. We should then have to remember that, although this particular sample gave an average value of 7, it might have been an optimistic-looking sample from a population with a rather lower average, and we should therefore be interested in setting up confidence limits for the mean value in the population from which the sample was drawn. This is a matter which the reader can follow up for himself along the lines laid down in Chapter 14.

Unless the reader is of a different psychological make-up from the author, he will feel that while this is a very useful device, there ought to be some quick method of arriving at the same result. This is not just slothfulness on our part. Decisions of the kind for which this technique would be useful have to be made speedily in many cases. Moreover, it is inelegant to use crude methods of computing when there are more speedy approaches. There is, of course, a better method. To illustrate it, we shall re-work the analysis of the previous data so that the reader can cross check and satisfy himself that the speedy method is absolutely accurate.

We first of all find the sample totals and the grand total for the original data, as in the following table:

	Sample 1	Sample 2	Sample 3	Sample 4
	2	3	6	5
	3	4	8	5
	1	3	7	5
	3	5	4	3
	1	0	10	2
Totals	10	15	35	20

Grand total $T = 80$ Number of items $= N$

We next compute a very important quantity known as the 'Correction Factor':

$$\text{Correction Factor} = \frac{T^2}{N} = \frac{80 \times 80}{20} = \underline{320}$$

This Correction Factor enters into the computation of all further sums of squares that are directly computed.

The next step is to set up a table showing the squares of the original items, thus:

	Sample 1	Sample 2	Sample 3	Sample 4
	4	9	36	25
	9	16	64	25
	1	9	49	25
	9	25	16	9
	1	0	100	4
Totals	24	59	265	88

The Total Sum of Squares is then obtained by subtracting the

13

Correction Factor from the grand total of the square items in this table, thus:

$$\text{Total Sum of Squares} = (24 + 59 + 265 + 88) - 320$$
$$= 436 - 320 = \underline{116}$$

This agrees with what we obtained when we did the calculation by the first method.

In order to get the Between Sample Sum of Squares, we find the sum of the squares of the sample totals and divide this sum by the number of items which went to make up each sample total. Finally, we subtract the Correction Factor. In this way we obtain the following:

$$\text{Between Sample Sum of Squares} = \tfrac{1}{5}(10^2 + 15^2 + 35^2 + 20^2) - 320$$
$$= \frac{100 + 225 + 1,225 + 400}{5} - 320$$
$$= \tfrac{1950}{5} - 320 = 390 - 320 = \underline{70}$$

The Within Sample Sum of Squares is then found by subtracting the Between Sample Sum of Squares from the Total Sum of Squares, and we find:

$$\text{Within Sample Sum of Squares} = 116 - 70 = 46$$

Both the Between Sample Sum of Squares and the Within Sample Sum of Squares agree with the values found previously.

The Degrees of Freedom are found as follows:

Total number of items $= 20$, hence Total d.f. $= 20 - 1 = 19$

Total number of samples $= 4$, hence Between Sample d.f.
$$= 4 - 1 = 3.$$

Within Sample d.f. $=$ Total d.f. minus Between Sample d.f.
$$= 19 - 3 = 16.$$

We are now in a position to draw up the Table of Analysis of Variance as before. The saving in time is considerable. The reader is advised to master the procedure just outlined before proceeding further. He should invent a similar example for himself and work it out both ways. He will be well advised to keep the values of the items small. The procedure is exactly the same however many items we have in each sample, or however many samples we have. The first method will work even when there are unequal numbers of items in each sample. The second method is applicable exactly as we have given it only if the samples all have the same number of items. If the number of items in the samples varies, then we have to get the Between Sample Sum of Squares by the following method:

(a) Square each sample total;
(b) Divide the square of each sample total by the number of items which went to make it up;
(c) Find the totals of the items thus obtained for the individual samples;
(d) Subtract the Correction Factor.

The Total Sum of Squares and the Within Sample Sum of Squares are found exactly as previously explained.

We advised the reader to keep the values of the items small when making up his own sample. If the reader had a calculating machine handy, this warning was not needed. We were thinking of the poor fellow who had to struggle with his arithmetic unaided. In practice, of course, we cannot control the magnitude of the items in the samples. They come to us already fixed in magnitude, and we have to make do and mend. How do we make do and mend if the items are large and we have no machine to help us with the arithmetic?

The reader will quickly get the idea once he sees that a set of data whose smallest item is 117 and whose largest item is 124 is no more and no less variable than a set whose greatest item is 16 and whose smallest is 9. In both cases the range (maximum minus minimum value) is equal to seven. It follows that:

The variance is unchanged by the subtraction (or addition) of a constant amount from every item.

To illustrate this useful trick we shall take an example from market research. A manufacturer is about to put a certain product on the market. He has four packages in mind which he thinks will appeal to different price markets. Would the purchasing public, seeing the same product in different packages, fix different prices as reasonable? This is one aspect of a total problem in which the manufacturer would have to consider the possibilities of smaller sales volume in a higher priced market as well as the extra cost of the more appealing carton. To settle whether the four packages suggest different price levels in the customer's mind, he shows each package to six members of the shopping public, choosing a different (but comparable) set of customers for each package so that the customers do not feel that they are expected to grade the packages in any way. Let us suppose (what is perhaps rather unlikely) that the possible customers quote their estimates to the nearest penny in this case and that we receive the following results for analysis.

CUSTOMER'S VALUATION IN PENCE

Pack 1	Pack 2	Pack 3	Pack 4
66	42	54	78
82	66	90	54
60	30	60	60
50	60	81	42
60	36	60	71
90	48	51	49

The variation within packages is a reflexion of the fact that customers tend to value by the price ticket and find themselves rather at sea without the shopkeeper's assistance in deciding how much the article is worth. In this example, the within package variability is sufficiently great to make us confident that the customers questioned must have been ladies.

Getting back to our sheep, as the French say, it is clear that if we had to square the items in the table as they stand, we should soon have quite a lot of arithmetic on our hands. To avoid this as far as possible we decide to subtract from each item a constant amount so as to make the figures as small as possible. The smaller the figures, the easier the job. Moreover, small negative figures are preferable to large positive ones. How much shall we subtract? The golden rule is: A number as near the grand average as we can guess. A fair guess in this case would be 60 (keep it an easy number!). Making the subtractions and setting up a second compartment to our table which contains the squares of the reduced values, we arrive at the following table which contains all we need for our analysis:

	Items less 60				Squares of (Items less 60)			
	Package 1	Package 2	Package 3	Package 4	Package 1	Package 2	Package 3	Package 4
	6	−18	−6	18	36	324	36	324
	22	6	30	−6	484	36	900	36
	0	−30	0	0	0	900	0	0
	−10	0	21	−18	100	0	441	324
	0	−24	0	11	0	576	0	121
	30	−12	−9	−11	900	144	81	121
Totals	48	−78	36	−6	1,520	1,980	1,458	926

$T = 48 - 78 + 36 - 6 = 0$

$N = 6 \times 4 = 24$ items

Correction Factor $= \dfrac{T^2}{N} = \dfrac{0 \times 0}{24} = 0$

Between Sample Sum of Squares

(6 items in each total)

$\frac{1}{6}[48^2 + (-78)^2 + 36^2 + (-6)^2] - 0$

$= \dfrac{2,304 + 6,084 + 1,296 + 36}{6} - 0$

$= \dfrac{9720}{6} = 1,620$

There are 4 samples and therefore 3 degrees of freedom.

Total Sum of Squares

$[1,520 + 1,980 + 1,458 + 926] - 0$
$= 5,884$

There are 24 items and therefore 23 degrees of freedom.

Within Sample Sum of Squares

Is difference between Total Sum of Squares and Between Sample Sum of Squares, viz.

$5,884 - 1,620 = 4,264$

The degrees of freedom are the difference between the Total d.f. and the Between Sample d.f., viz.

$23 - 3 = 20$

We now collect our results together and calculate the Variance Estimates by dividing each sum of squares by its number of degrees of freedom.

TABLE OF ANALYSIS OF VARIANCE

Source of variation	Sum of squares	d.f.	Variance estimate
Between packages	1,620	3	540·0
Within packages	4,264	20	213·2
Total	5,884	23	

The variation between packages might be fortuitous, arising simply from the customer's uncertainty as to price without there being any real effect on price arising from the different packages. No use to fool ourselves that a more expensive package was helping price if this were not the case. Let us make a Null Hypothesis that differences in packaging have no effect on the customer's estimate of price and use the Variance Ratio test to see whether such a hypothesis is tenable in the face of the observed data. We get

$$F = \frac{540 \cdot 0}{213 \cdot 2} = 2 \cdot 5$$

The greater variance estimate has 3 degrees of freedom and the lesser estimate 20 degrees of freedom. The Table of the Variance Ratio shows that the 5% level of F is $3 \cdot 1$ and the 1% level $4 \cdot 9$. Hence, our observed value for F is well below the 5% level and therefore not significant of any departure from our Null Hypothesis. Our investigation has not succeeded in demonstrating convincingly that there is any difference between the packages in regard to price appeal. There may be such a difference, but further data would have to be collected to remove our scepticism in the matter.

We shall now bring in the control chart technique dealt with in Chapter 11 to throw further light on the Analysis of Variance technique. Our Table of Analysis of Variance gave us a Variance Estimate based on 20 degrees of freedom within samples equal to $213 \cdot 2$. The Variance Estimate based on 3 d.f. between samples was $540 \cdot 0$. According to our Null Hypothesis (which the data failed to refute) these are independent estimates of the variance in a common parent population. With the Null Hypothesis still standing, we may pool our estimates together based on $20 + 3 = 23$ d.f. We do this by dividing the total sum of squares by the total degrees of freedom and get

$$\hat{V} = \tfrac{5884}{23} = 256$$

The standard deviation of our hypothetical parent population is given by the square root of the variance, i.e.

$$\sigma = \sqrt{256} = 16$$

Now the standard deviation for the averages of samples of n items drawn from a population whose standard deviation for the individual items is σ is given by $\sigma \cdot \sqrt{n}$. In our case then, the standard deviation for the averages of our samples of six customers will be $16 \cdot \sqrt{6} = 6 \cdot 5$. Now we have already learnt that there is only about one chance in twenty of a deviation of more than two standard deviations from the average and only about three chances in a thousand of a deviation of more than three standard deviations from the average. Hence we only need to know the grand average and the sample averages in order to be able to plot a control chart for the sample (package) averages.

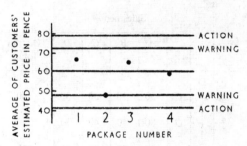

Fig. 99. Control Chart for analysis of variance in a market research problem on package appeal

The reader can quickly verify for himself that the grand average is 60d. and that the sample averages were

Package 1	68d.	Package 2	47d.
Package 3	66d.	Package 4	59d.

The Warning Limits for our control chart will be at

$$60 \pm 2(6 \cdot 5) = 60 \pm 13$$

The Action Limits will be placed at

$$60 \pm 3(6 \cdot 5) = 60 \pm 19 \cdot 5$$

The data are shown plotted in the control chart in Fig. 99. It will be seen that the points are quite well in control, it not being surprising that one point out of four should lie on the one chance in twenty limits.

The previous examples have been concerned with data classified according to a single criterion, e.g. type of package. Our next example will deal with data which are classified according to two criteria. Suppose a certain company had four salesmen, *A*, *B*, *C*, and *D*, each of whom was sent for a week into three types of area: country area, *C*, outskirts of a city, *O*, and shopping centre of a city, *S*. Their takings in pounds per week were as shown in the table.

| | | Salesmen | | | | |
		A	B	C	D	District totals
D i s t r i c t	C	30	70	30	30	160
	O	80	50	40	70	240
	S	100	60	80	80	320
Salesmen totals		210	180	150	180	

We can make a considerable saving in computational effort in this example by putting the data into 'coded form'. We have already had a simple case of coding when we reduced each item by a constant amount. There is another trick we can use, namely: to divide all items by a constant amount. What effect will this have on the variances? Evidently, if we divide each item by some number, c, then since the variance is calculated from the squares of the items the computed value of the variance in the coded data will be equal to the true variance divided by the square of the constant divisor, c. However, since our significance tests are carried out in terms of the *ratio* of variances, it is evident that the significance tests will be unaffected when all the items are divided by a constant amount. We thus get the following rule:

In carrying out an analysis of variance, we may code the data by addition, subtraction, multiplication or addition by constant amounts without in any way disturbing the significance tests.

This rule will be of tremendous assistance in our example. Let us code the data by (a) subtracting £50 from each of the takings and (b) dividing the result by 10. Thus, if we denote any actual takings by x, then the corresponding code value will be

$$x' = \frac{x - 50}{10}$$

Reducing the table of data to coded form, we get:

		Salesmen				
		A	B	C	D	District totals
Type of district	C	-2	2	-2	-2	-4
	O	3	0	-1	2	4
	S	5	1	3	3	12
Salesmen totals		6	3	0	3	Grand Total $= 12 = T$ Number of items $= 12 = N$

The Correction Factor will be $\dfrac{T^2}{N} = \dfrac{12 \times 12}{12} = 12$

Between Salesmen Sum of Squares. We find the sum of the squares of the salesmen totals, divide by the number of items that went to make up each salesmen total, and finally subtract the correction factor. We get

$$\tfrac{1}{3}[6^2 + 3^2 + 0^2 + 3^2] - 12 = \tfrac{54}{3} - 12 = 6$$

Between four salesmen there are 3 degrees of freedom.

Between District Sum of Squares. We find the sum of the squares of the district totals, divide by the number of items that went to make up each district total, and finally subtract the correction factor. We get

$$\tfrac{1}{4}[(-4)^2 + 4^2 + 12^2] - 12 = \tfrac{176}{4} - 12 = 32$$

Between three districts there are 2 degrees of freedom.

Total Sum of Squares. We find the sum of the squares of all the items in the table and subtract the correction factor. We get

$$[(-2)^2 + 2^2 + (-2)^2 + (-2)^2 + 3^2 + 0^2 + (-1)^2 +$$
$$2^2 + 5^2 + 1^2 + 3^2 + 3^2] - 12 = 74 - 12 = 62$$

Between 12 items there are 11 degrees of freedom.

Let us now collect our results together in a Table of the Analysis of Variance.

TABLE OF ANALYSIS OF VARIANCE

Source	Sum of squares	d.f.	Variance estimate
Salesmen	6	3	2
Districts	32	2	16
Residual	24	6	4
Total	62	11	

The reader will notice that besides the components of variation which we calculated, the table contains an extra entry under the title 'Residual'. Out of a total sum of squares equal to 62 the salesmen and district sources only accounted for $32 + 6 = 38$. This left still to be accounted for a sum of squares of magnitude $62 - 38 = 24$. This sum of squares which is a measure of the variation not explained by salesmen and district effects is entered as 'Residual'. Its degrees of freedom are the degrees of freedom not accounted for by salesmen and district effects.

Suppose now we make the Null Hypothesis that all the salesmen are equally good (condition that only obtains in a seller's market, but then applies with a vengeance), and that, moreover, it matters not at all whether we send our salesmen into country districts, shopping centres, or outskirts (the sort of condition that might obtain for all practical purposes either in a slump or in the off-season in a highly seasonal trade). Under such circumstances our three independent estimates of variance are all estimates of the variance of a common parent population where variability exists for reasons other than salesmen and district effects. They should therefore appear as compatible estimates under Snedecor's Variance Ratio Test. It is at once evident that the Variance Estimate based on the Salesmen degrees of freedom is not significantly greater than the Residual Variance Estimate. The reader can easily see for himself that if we compare the Districts Estimate with the Residual Estimate we get a Variance Ratio of $F = 4$, there being 2 degrees of freedom with the greater estimate and 6 degrees of freedom with the lesser estimate. Tables of the Variance Ratio give the value of the 5% level of F as approximately 5, and the 1% level as approximately 11. Our calculated value is not sufficient, therefore, to upset the Null Hypothesis. It would not be unreasonable – if we had no more to go on than these data – to believe that the salesmen were equally capable and that all districts were equally profitable to work. In order to establish the contrary of either of these propositions on a factual basis, we should need further data.

It is convenient at this point to look further into the precise nature of the 'residual' term in the previous example. Returning to our table of coded data we can quickly extract the following information:

| | Salesmen | | | |
	A	B	C	D
Salesman's average	2	1	0	1

| | District | | |
	C	O	S
District average	– 1	1	3

Grand average $= 1$

By subtracting the grand average from each of the salesmen's averages we get the amount by which each salesman's average departs from the grand average. A positive sign indicates that his average was above the grand average, a negative sign that his average was below the grand average.

DISCREPANCIES BETWEEN SALESMEN'S AVERAGES AND GRAND AVERAGE

	Salesmen			
	A	B	C	D
Discrepancy	1	0	-1	0

In like manner we can arrive at the following:

DISCREPANCIES BETWEEN DISTRICT AVERAGES AND GRAND AVERAGE

	District		
	C	O	S
Discrepancy	-2	0	2

If, now, we return to our table of coded takings, and subtract from each entry (being very careful about signs + and −) the discrepancy between its own salesman's average and the grand average, we shall have removed the specific salesmen's effect. The result will be:

	A	B	C	D
C	-3	2	-1	-2
O	2	0	0	2
S	4	1	+	3

Next we go through this table subtracting from each item (again being careful about signs) the discrepancy between its own district average and the grand average, in order, finally, to remove the specific district effect. The result this time is:

	A	B	C	D
C	-1	4	1	0
C	2	0	0	2
S	2	-1	2	1

The sum of squares calculated from this table will be the sum of squares introduced by variation other than that due to salesmen and district effect and should therefore equal what we have called the 'Residual' sum of squares. We compute the sum of squares by finding the sum of the squares of the items and subtracting the correction factor. We get

$$[(-1)^2 + 4^2 + 1^2 + 0^2 + 2^2 + 0^2 + 0^2 + 2^2 + 2^2 +$$
$$(-1)^2 + 2^2 + 1^2] - 12 = 36 - 12 = 24$$

This agrees with what we found before. A residual of the type we have just computed is called, for reasons which will later be apparent, the *Interaction* between the effects A and B, and is denoted by the symbol $A \times B$. It is one of the great merits of Analysis of Variance procedures that such interaction effects can be at once estimated and tested for. They come out naturally in the wash.

Before leaving this example, let us look at the data in control chart form. The residual variance estimate corresponds to a population standard deviation $\sigma = \sqrt{4} = 2$. The salesmen averages

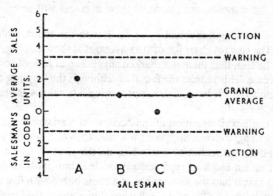

Fig. 100. Control Chart for analysis of variance in a sales department problem (salesmen effect)

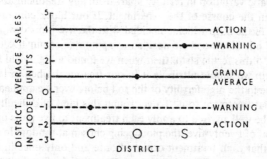

Fig. 101. Control Chart for analysis of variance in a sales department problem (districts effect)

are averages of three items, so the standard deviation for these averages will be $\frac{2}{\sqrt{3}} = 1.15$. Keeping in the coded form of the data, we should plot warning limits and the grand average plus or minus two standard deviations, i.e. at 1 ± 2.3. Action limits would go at the grand average plus or minus three standard deviations, i.e. at 1 ± 3.5. The control chart for salesmen's averages is shown in Fig. 100. It will be seen that they are in perfect control. In a similar way, since the district averages are the averages of four items, the standard deviation for these averages will be $\frac{2}{\sqrt{4}} = 1$, and the warning limits will go at 1 ± 2, with the action limits at 1 ± 3. The control chart for district averages is shown in Fig. 101. It will be seen that there is a marked suggestion of lack of control in this case. This reflects the fact that, although the variance ratio was below the 5 % level, it was approaching it (a value 4 as against the 5 % level of 5).

For our next illustration of the Analysis of Variance technique we turn to agriculture. Suppose we wished to investigate the effect of five different manurial treatments on the yield of wheat. We should take a block of land and subdivide it into plots of equal area so that it had the appearance of a chess board with five rows and five columns. One of the awkward things about field trials of this kind is that the soil in our experimental plot might show a systematic variation in fertility apart from any treatment applied by us in the course of the experiment. If our block contained a highly fertile strip which coincided with the five plots down one side of our block and we decided to apply one of our five treatments to this fertile strip, then when we found a high yield from this strip we should attribute it to our treatment when in fact it was due to the high fertility of the soil before ever we applied any manurial treatment to it. To get round this kind of difficulty we would be well advised to apply each treatment to five plots out of the total of twenty-five, the plots being chosen at random in such a way that each treatment occurred once and only once in each row and column of our chess board. Denoting the five treatments by the letters A, B, C, D, and E, one possible arrangement would be that shown in the following diagram, where the numbers are to be taken as the yields of wheat measured in bushels per acre.

A 13	B 9	C 21	D 7	E 6
D 9	E 8	A 15	B 7	C 16
B 11	C 17	D 8	E 10	A 17
E 8	A 15	B 7	C 10	D 7
C 11	D 9	E 8	A 15	B 11

For convenience in computing we shall code the yields by subtracting 10 bushels per acre in every case. The coded data are then as shown:

A	B	C	D	E	Row Totals
3	−1	11	−3	−4	6
D	E	A	B	C	
−1	−2	5	−3	6	5
B	C	D	E	A	
1	7	−2	0	7	13
E	A	B	C	D	
−2	5	−3	0	−3	−3
C	D	E	A	B	
1	−1	−2	5	1	4

Column Totals   2   8   9   −1   7   Grand Total $= T = 25$

Treatment Totals $\begin{cases} A & B & C & D & E \\ 25 & -5 & 25 & -10 & -10 \end{cases}$ Number of items $= N = 25$

Correction Factor $\dfrac{T^2}{N} = 25$

The Analysis of Variance then proceeds as follows:

Between Column Sum of Squares. Each column total is the sum of five items. Divide the sum of the squares of the column totals by the number of items going to make each total and subtract the correction factor. We get

$$\tfrac{1}{5}[2^2 + 8^2 + 9^2 + (-1)^2 + 7^2] - 25 = 14\cdot8 \text{ with 4 d.f.}$$

Between Row Sum of Squares. Each row total is the sum of five items. Divide the sum of the squares of the row totals by the number of items going to make up each row total and subtract the correction factor. We get

$$\tfrac{1}{5}[6^2 + 5^2 + 13^2 + (-3)^2 + 4^2] - 25 = 26 \text{ with 4 d.f.}$$

Between Treatment Sum of Squares. Each treatment total is the sum of five items. Divide the sum of the squares of the treatment totals by the number of items going to make up each treatment total and subtract the correction factor. We get

$$\tfrac{1}{5}[25^2 + (-5)^2 + 25^2 + (-10)^2 + (-10)^2] - 25 = 270 \text{ with 4 d.f.}$$

Total Sum of Squares. We find the sum of the squares of all the items in the table and subtract the correction factor. We get

TABLE OF SQUARED VALUES

9	1	121	9	16
1	4	25	9	36
1	49	4	0	49
4	25	9	0	9
1	1	4	25	1

Totals $\overline{16}$ + $\overline{80}$ + $\overline{163}$ + $\overline{43}$ + $\overline{111}$ = 413

Hence, subtracting the Correction Factor, we find

Total Sum of Squares = 413 − 25 = 388

Since there are altogether 25 items, there is a total of 24 d.f.

TABLE OF ANALYSIS OF VARIANCE

Source	Sum of squares	d.f.	Variance estimate
Columns	14·8	4	3·7
Columns	26	4	6·5
Treatments	270	4	67·5
Residual	77·2	12	6·4
Total	388	24	

The residual sum of squares is that portion of the total sum of squares not accounted for by row, column, or treatment effects. Inspection of the table of the Analysis of Variance shows at once

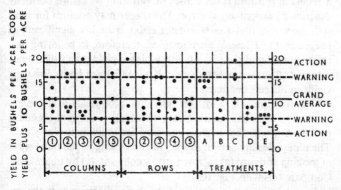

Fig. 102. Control Chart for latin square analysis on manurial treatment for wheat

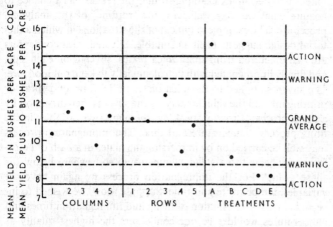

Fig. 103. Control Chart for row, column, and treatment averages in latin square analysis on manurial treatments

that there can be no question of the Estimates of Variance based on row or column degrees of freedom being significantly greater than the residual variance estimate. There is therefore no reason to suppose that there is any significant change in fertility of the soil across the rows or columns. Any apparent variation is simply a reflexion of those other causes of variation which we normally describe as experimental error. The reader may confirm for himself, however, that the treatment effect is highly significant as judged by the F test. We are justified, therefore, in believing that treatments A and C really do give a higher yield than other treatments, and may proceed to calculate confidence limits for their yields in bushels per acre.

This time we shall plot the individual plot yields in a control chart. The residual variance is 6·43 which gives us a standard deviation $\sqrt{6·4} = 2·5$ bushels per acre for individual plot yields. The plot yields are shown in Fig. 102 according to the three ways of looking at them: (a) by rows, (b) by columns, (c) by treatments. Compare this with Fig. 103.

An extremely useful design in Analysis of Variance is the so-called 'Factorial'. In order to illustrate this design type we shall take a fairly complex example so that the reader has a chance to acquire what we may well term the 'routine' of the analytical procedure. The example is typical of the situations in which a factorial design suggests itself as suitable. Silvered mica condensers are manufactured from small mica plates, silvered on each side, and finally impregnated with petroleum jelly to keep out moisture. The silver is applied to the mica plates in the form of a spray or printing ink and the vehicle carrying the silver is then driven off by a firing process. Broadly speaking, there are two variables in the firing process: temperature and time. The impregnation process may well be carried on by immersing the plates in a bath of petroleum jelly heated to a steady temperature somewhere below the 'flash point'. For the impregnation process we again have the variables, temperature and time. Suppose, now, we wished to investigate what combination of firing and impregnation times and temperatures would give our condensers the highest quality as measured by the 'loss angle' of the plates (the lower the loss angle, the better the condensers). To investigate this problem, we might choose three likely firing temperatures, three likely firing times, three likely impregnation temperatures, and three likely impregnation times. Altogether, our chosen conditions may be arranged into $3 \times 3 \times 3 \times 3 = 81$ different combinations, each of which constitutes a different manufacturing process. Suppose we decided to make up experimentally three condensers according to each of these 81 different processes, then there would be altogether 243 condensers to be made. There is no special reason why we should have chosen three levels for each of our conditions; we might, for instance, have had two firing times, three firing temperatures, four impregnation temperatures, and six impregnation times. Neither need we have made each process give us three condensers. We could have made only one condenser with each set of conditions or we could have made a dozen. We have a perfectly free hand to arrange our experiment in accordance with what seems good to us on technological grounds and economic in terms of the magnitude of the work involved in the experiment. The principles of analysis are always exactly the same as we shall indicate in our example.

We shall use the following notation:

Firing temperatures: H_1, H_2, and H_3

Firing times: T_1, T_2, and T_3

Impregnation temperatures: H_1, h_2, and h_3

Impregnation times: t_1, t_2, and t_3

The higher the subscript the longer the time or the higher the temperature

TABLE A1

Original data. Loss Angle in minutes of Condensers made under different combinations of Firing Time (T), Firing Temperature (H), Impregnation Time (t), and Impregnation Temperature (h). [Three values for each processing combination]

	T3									T2									T1								
	H3			H2			H1			H3			H2			H1			H3			H2			H1		
	t3	t2	t1	t3	t2	t1	t3	t2	t1	t3	t2	t1	t3	t2	t1	t3	t2	t1	t3	t2	t1	t3	t2	t1	t3	t2	t1
h1	6 4 8	5 9 4	7 6 8	10 9 10	10 10 8	7 6 8	10 9 6	10 10 8	9 11 12	6 8 6	7 9 5	7 8 6	6 8 7	5 9 7	7 6 8	11 7 5	10 8 7	9 8 7	9 7 11	12 8 6	10 9 11	12 9 8	9 11 8	10 11 10	14 10 11	10 11 9	12 10 13
h2	4 3 2	3 2 4	3 4 3	4 6 4	6 6 7	5 6 5	4 5 4	6 6 7	5 6 5	4 4 3	3 2 4	3 2 4	4 4 3	2 5 2	3 4 4	5 4 5	4 6 4	3 4 4	6 5 6	7 3 6	8 6 4	6 5 4	4 3 7	5 6 7	4 7 9	8 6 8	10 8 7
h3	6 4 3	6 2 2	3 2 4	3 4 4	3 5 4	3 4 3	3 4 4	3 5 4	4 4 2	3 2 1	2 4 2	2 1 3	2 2 1	1 1 3	2 1 2	4 3 2	1 2 4	3 2 3	3 4 5	6 3 4	4 5 3	4 9 7	5 4 7	6 5 5	7 5 5	5 4 6	6 5 7

Casual inspection of the results suggests that the grand average loss angle is about 5 minutes.

Each entry in the above Table is the Loss Angle of 1 condenser.

TABLE A2

Original data of Table A1 put into coded form by subtracting 5 minutes from each value

			h_1	h_2	h_3
T_1	H_1	t_1	7, 5, 8	5, 3, 2	-1, 0, 2
		t_2	5, 6, 4	3, -1, 3	0, -1, -1
		t_3	9, 5, 6	-1, 2, 4	2, 0, 0
	H_2	t_1	5, 6, 5	0, -1, 2	-1, 0, 0
		t_2	4, 6, 3	-1, -2, 2	0, -1, -2
		t_3	7, 4, 3	-1, 0, -1	-1, 4, 2
	H_3	t_1	5, 4, 6	3, -1, -1	-1, 0, -2
		t_2	7, 3, 1	2, -2, 1	-1, -2, -1
		t_3	4, 2, 6	-1, 0, -1	-2, -1, 0
T_2	H_1	t_1	4, 3, 2	-1, 0, 0	-2, -1, -2
		t_2	5, 3, 2	-1, -1, -1	-4, -3, -1
		t_3	6, 2, 0	0, -1, 0	-1, -2, -3
	H_2	t_1	2, -1, 3	-2, -1, -1	-3, -4, -3
		t_2	0, 4, 2	-3, 0, -3	-4, -4, -2
		t_3	-1, 3, 2	-1, -1, 1	-4, -3, -4
	H_3	t_1	2, 3, 1	-2, -3, -1	3, -4, -2
		t_2	2, 4, 0	-2, -3, -1	-1, -1, -3
		t_3	-1, 3, -1	-1, -1, 2	-2, -3, -4
T_3	H_1	t_1	4, 6, 7	0, -1, 0	-1, -1, -3
		t_2	5, 5, 3	-1, -1, 2	-2, 0, -1
		t_3	5, 4, 1	-1, 0, -1	2, -1, -1
	H_2	t_1	2, -1, 3	0, -1, 0	-1, -1, 2
		t_2	5, 5, 3	-1, -1, 2	2, 0, -1
		t_3	5, 4, 5	-1, -1, -1	2, -1, 1
	H_3	t_1	2, -1, 3	-2, -1, -2	2, 3, -1
		t_2	0, 4, -1	-2, -1, -1	-1, -3, -3
		t_3	-1, -1, 3	-1, -2, -3	-1, -1, 2

Each entry in the above table is the Loss Angle (coded) of 1 condenser.

TAKE NOTICE

The reader is asked to study the left-hand pages only, in order to see the formation of the different tables, until he reaches the bottom of page 410. He should then work his way back from the bottom of page 411, keeping to the right-hand pages and following the numbering of the calculations. Each calculation refers to the table which lies opposite to it on the left-hand page. The author apologizes for introducing Chinese methods, but the reader will soon see the advantage of the layout in making the computational procedure clear.

TABLE B

Obtained by totalling the repeat values ('replications') within each treatment combination

	T_1									T_2									T_3								
	H_1			H_2			H_3			H_1			H_2			H_3			H_1			H_2			H_3		
	t_1	t_2	t_3	t_1	t_2	t_3	t_1	t_2	t_3	t_1	t_2	t_3	t_1	t_2	t_3	t_1	t_2	t_3	t_1	t_2	t_3	t_1	t_2	t_3	t_1	t_2	t_3
h_1	20	15	20	16	13	14	15	11	12	9	10	8	6	6	6	6	6	5	17	13	10	6	13	14	6	3	3
h_2	10	7	5	3	-1	0	3	1	2	-1	-1	-1	-4	-6	-6	-6	-6	-4	1	4	-2	1	4	-1	1	3	-6
h_3	3	0	3	1	1	5	-3	-2	-3	-7	-8	6	-10	-10	-10	-9	-7	-9	-5	-3	-4	-4	-3	-4	-6	-5	-2

Explanation. In the top left-hand corner of Table A2 we find for the Loss Angles of the three condensers made with the treatment combination $T_1H_1t_1h_1$ the values

$$\begin{array}{c} 7 \\ 5 \\ 8 \end{array}$$

The sum of these is the entry 20 in Table B under $T_1H_1t_1h_1$.

Each entry in the above table is the sum of 3 loss angles.

CALCULATION 16

Total Sum of Squares and d.f. and Residuals

Sum the Squares of all the 243 items in Table A2 (page 397) and subtract the Correction Factor. The total Sum of Squares is

$$[7^2 + 5^2 + 9^2 + 5^2 + \ldots + (-1)^2 + (-3)^2 + (-2)^2] - 108 = 1,856$$

Between the 243 entries in Table A2 there will be a total of 242 d.f.

Residuals (Sum of Squares and d.f. associated with replication)

Subtract from the Total Sum of Squares the total of all the Sums of Squares found in Calculations 1–15.

Residual Sum of Squares $= 1,856 - (92 + 295 + 1,027 + 2)$
$$- (5 + 15 + 55 + 11 + 22 + 2) - (7 + 28 + 10 + 10) - 17 = 307$$

Subtract from the Total d.f. the total of all the d.f. in calculations 1–15.

Residual d.f. $= 242 - (4 \times 2 + 6 \times 4 + 4 \times 8 + 16) = 162$ d.f.

CALCULATION 15

$T \times H \times t \times h$ *Interaction Sum of Squares and d.f.*

Divide the sum of the squares of the 81 entries in Table B by the number of items going to make each entry. Subtract the Sums of Squares calculated for the T, H, t, and h effects, the $T \times H$, $T \times t$, $T \times h$, $H \times t$, $H \times h$, and $t \times h$ 'first order' interactions, and the $H \times t \times h$, $T \times t \times h$, $T \times H \times h$, and $T \times H \times t$ 'second order' interactions. Subtract the Correction Factor.

$$\tfrac{1}{3}[20^2 + 15^2 + 20^2 + \ldots + (-5)^2 + (-2)^2] - (295 + 92 + 2 + 1,027)$$
$$- (22 + 11 + 5 + 3 + 15 + 5) - (10 + 7 + 28 + 10) - 108 = 17$$

The T, H, t, and h effects each had 2 d.f. so the Interaction has $2 \times 2 \times 2 \times 2 = 16$ d.f.

TABLE C1
Obtained from Table B by summing over h

	T_1			T_2			T_3		
	H_1	H_2	H_3	H_1	H_2	H_3	H_1	H_2	H_3
t_1	33	20	15	1	-8	-9	13	3	-5
t_2	22	13	10	1	-10	-7	14	14	-8
t_3	27	19	11	1	-8	-8	4	9	-5

Explanation. The entry 33 under $T_1H_1t_1$ is obtained from the left-hand column
$\begin{array}{|c|}\hline 20 \\ \hline 10 \\ \hline 3 \\ \hline \end{array}$
under $T_1H_1t_1$ in Table B by adding the three values (each of which is the sum of 3 items already).

Each entry in the above table is the sum of 9 loss angles.

TABLE C2
Obtained from Table B by summing over T

	H_1			H_2			H_3		
	t_1	t_2	t_3	t_1	t_2	t_3	t_1	t_2	t_3
h_1	46	38	38	28	32	34	27	20	20
h_2	10	10	2	0	-3	-5	-8	-11	-8
h_3	-9	-11	-8	-13	-12	-9	-18	-14	-14

Explanation. Each entry is obtained from Table B by adding together the values found there for each treatment combination shown in Table C2, e.g. $46 = 20 + 9 + 17$.

Each entry in the above table is the sum of 9 loss angles.

CALCULATION 14

$T \times H \times t$ Interaction Sum of Squares and d.f.

Divide the sum of the squares of the 27 items in Table C1 by the number of items going to make up each entry. Subtract the Sums of Squares calculated for the T, H, and t effects. Subtract the Sums of Squares calculated for the $T \times H$, $T \times t$, and $H \times t$ Interactions. Subtract the Correction Factor.

$$\tfrac{1}{9}[33^2 + 20^2 + 15^2 + \ldots + 9^2 + (-5)^2]$$
$$- 295 - 92 - 2 - 22 - 11 - 11 - 108 = 10$$

The T, H, and t effects each had 2 d.f., so the Interaction had $2 \times 2 \times 2 = 8$ d.f.

CALCULATION 13

$H \times t \times h$ Interaction Sum of Squares and d.f.

Divide the sum of the squares of the 27 entries in Table C2 by the number of items going to make up each entry. Subtract the Sums of Squares calculated for the H, t, and h effects. Subtract the Sums of Squares calculated for the $H \times t$, $H \times h$, and $t \times h$ Interactions. Subtract the Correction Factor.

$$\tfrac{1}{9}[46^2 + 38^2 + 38^2 + \ldots + (-14)^2 + (-14)^2] -$$
$$92 - 2 - 1{,}027 - 3 - 15 - 5 - 108 = 10$$

The H, t, and h effects each had 2 d.f., so the Interaction had $2 \times 2 \times 2 = 8$ d.f.

TABLE C3
Obtained from Table B by summing over *t*

	T_1			T_2			T_3		
	H_1	H_2	H_3	H_1	H_2	H_3	H_1	H_2	H_3
h_1	55	43	38	27	18	17	40	33	12
h_2	22	2	6	− 3	− 14	− 16	3	4	− 17
h_3	5	7	− 8	− 21	− 30	− 25	− 12	− 11	− 13

Each entry is the sum of 9 loss angles.

TABLE C4
Obtained from Table B by summing over *H*

	T_1			T_2			T_3		
	t_1	t_2	t_3	t_1	t_2	t_3	t_1	t_2	t_3
h_1	51	39	46	21	22	19	29	29	27
h_2	16	7	7	− 11	− 13	− 9	− 3	2	− 9
h_3	1	− 1	4	− 26	− 25	− 25	− 15	− 11	− 10

Each entry is the sum of 9 loss angles.

CALCULATION 12

$T \times H \times h$ Interaction Sum of Squares and d.f.

Divide the sum of the squares of the 27 entries in Table C3 by the number of items going to make each entry. Subtract the Sums of Squares calculated for the T effect, H effect, and h effect. Subtract the Sums of Squares calculated for the $T \times H$, $T \times h$, and $H \times h$ Interactions. Subtract the Correction Factor.

$$\tfrac{1}{9}[55^2 + 43^2 + 38^2 + \ldots + (-11)^2 + (-13)^2]$$
$$- 295 - 92 - 1,027 - 22 - 5 - 15 - 108 = 28$$

The T effect, H effect, and h effect each had 2 d.f., so the Interaction d.f. $= 2 \times 2 \times 2 = 8$ d.f.

CALCULATION 11

$T \times t \times h$ Interaction Sum of Squares and d.f.

Divide the sum of the squares of the 27 entries in Table C4 by the number of items going to make each total. Subtract the Sums of Squares calculated for the T effect, t effect, and h effect. Subtract the Sums of Squares calculated for the $T \times t$, $T \times h$, and $t \times h$ Interactions. Subtract the Correction Factor.

$$\tfrac{1}{9}[51^2 + 39^2 + 46^2 + \ldots + (-11)^2 + (-10)^2]$$
$$- 295 - 2 - 1,027 - 11 - 5 - 5 - 108 = 7$$

The T effect, t effect, and h effect each had 2 d.f., so the Interaction d.f. $= 2 \times 2 \times 2 = 8$ d.f.

TABLE D1
Obtained by summing Table C2 over h

	H_1			H_2			H_3	
t_1	t_2	t_3	t_1	t_2	t_3	t_1	t_2	t_3
47	37	32	15	17	20	1	-5	-2

Note. The table could also be formed from Table C1 by summing over T.

Each entry is the sum of 27 loss angles.

TABLE D2
Obtained by summing Table C1 over t

	T_1			T_2			T_3	
H_1	H_2	H_3	H_1	H_2	H_3	H_1	H_2	H_3
82	52	36	3	-26	-24	31	26	-18

Note. The table could also be formed from Table C3 by summing over h.

Eech entry is the sum of 27 loss angles.

TABLE D3
Obtained by summing Table C1 over H

	T_1			T_2			T_3	
t_1	t_2	t_3	t_1	t_2	t_3	t_1	t_2	t_3
68	45	57	-16	-16	-15	11	20	8

Note. The table could also be formed from Table C4 by summing over h.

Each entry is the sum of 27 loss angles.

CALCULATION 10

$H \times t$ Interaction Sum of Squares and d.f.

Divide the sum of the squares of the items in Table D1 by the number of items going to make each entry. Subtract the Sums of Squares calculated for the H and t effects. Subtract the Correction Factor.

$$\tfrac{1}{27}[47^2 + 37^2 + 32^2 + \ldots + (-5)^2 + (-2)^2] - 92 - 2 - 108 = 3$$

There were 2 d.f. each for the H and t effects, so the d.f. for the Interaction are $2 \times 2 = 4$ d.f.

CALCULATION 9

$T \times H$ Interaction Sum of Squares and d.f.

Divide the sum of the squares of the items in Table D2 by the number of items going to make each entry. Subtract the Sums of Squares calculated for the T and H effects. Subtract the Correction Factor.

$$\tfrac{1}{27}[82^2 + 52^2 + 36^2 + \ldots + 26^2 + (-18)^2] - 295 - 92 - 108 = 22$$

There were 2 d.f. each for the T and H effects, so the d.f. for the Interaction are $2 \times 2 = 4$ d.f.

CALCULATION 8

$T \times t$ Interaction Sum of Squares and d.f.

Divide the sum of the squares of the items in Table D3 by the number of items going to make each entry. Subtract the Sums of Squares calculated for the T and t effects. Subtract the Correction Factor.

$$\tfrac{1}{27}[68^2 + 45^2 + 57^2 + \ldots + 20^2 + 8^2] - 295 - 2 - 108 = 11$$

There were 2 d.f. each for the T and t effects, so the d.f. for the Interaction are $2 \times 2 = 4$ d.f.

TABLE D4
Obtained from Table C4 by summing over *t*

T_1			T_2			T_3		
h_1	h_2	h_3	h_1	h_2	h_3	h_1	h_2	h_3
136	30	4	62	– 33	– 76	85	– 10	– 36

Note. The table could also be formed from Table C3 by summing over *H*.

Each entry is the sum of 27 loss angles.

TABLE D5
Obtained from Table C2 by summing over *t*

H_1			H_2			H_3		
h_1	h_2	h_3	h_1	h_2	h_3	h_1	h_2	h_3
122	22	– 28	94	– 8	– 34	67	– 27	– 46

Note. The table could also be formed from Table C3 by summing over *T*.

Each entry is the sum of 27 loss angles.

TABLE D6
Obtained from Table C2 by summing over *H*

t_1			t_2			t_3		
h_1	h_2	h_3	h_1	h_2	h_3	h_1	h_2	h_3
101	2	– 40	90	– 4	– 37	92	– 11	– 31

Note. The table could also be formed from Table C4 by summing over *T*.

Each entry is the sum of 27 loss angles.

CALCULATION 7

$T \times h$ Interaction Sum of Squares and d.f.

Divide the sum of the squares of the items in Table D4 by the number of items going to make each entry. Subtract the Sums of Squares calculated for the T and h effects. Subtract the Correction Factor.

$$\tfrac{1}{27}[136^2 + 30^2 + 4^2 + 63 + \ldots + (-10)^2 + (-36)^2]$$
$$- 295 - 1{,}027 - 108 = 5$$

The T effect had 2 d.f. and the h effect also 2 d.f. The d.f. for the Interaction is obtained as the product of the main effect d.f. $= 2 \times 2 = 4$ d.f.

CALCULATION 6

$H \times h$ Interaction Sum of Squares and d.f.

Divide the sum of the squares of the items in Table D5 by the number of items going to make each entry. Subtract the Sums of Squares calculated for the H and h effects. Subtract the Correction Factor.

$$\tfrac{1}{27}[122^2 + 22^2 + (-28)^2 + \ldots + (-27)^2 + (-46)^2]$$
$$- 92 - 1{,}027 - 108 = 15$$

The H effect had 2 d.f. and the h effect also 2 d.f. The d.f. for the Interaction is obtained as the product of the main effect d.f. $= 2 \times 2 = 4$ d.f.

CALCULATION 5

$t \times h$ Interaction Sum of Squares and d.f.

Divide the sum of the squares of the items in Table D6 by the number of items going to make each entry. Subtract the Sums of Squares calculated for the t effect and h effect. Subtract the Correction Factor.

$$\tfrac{1}{27}[101^2 + 2^2 + (-40)^2 + \ldots + (-11)^2 + (-31)^2]$$
$$- 2 - 1{,}027 - 108 = 5$$

The t effect had 2 d.f. and the h effect also 2 d.f. The d.f. for the Interaction is obtained as the product of the main effect d.f. $= 2 \times 2 = 4$ d.f.

14

TABLE E1
Obtained by summation from Tables D1, D3, or D6

t_1	t_2	t_3
63	49	50

Grand total $= T = 162$
for $N = 243$ items

Each entry is the sum of 81 loss angles.

TABLE E2
Obtained by summation from Tables D4, D5, or D6

h_1	h_2	h_3
283	-13	-108

Grand Total $= T = 162$
for $N = 243$ items

Each entry is the sum of 81 loss angles.

TABLE E3
Obtained by summation from Tables D2, D3, or D4

T_1	T_2	T_3
170	-47	39

Grand Total $= T = 162$
for $N = 243$ items

Each entry is the sum of 81 loss angles.

TABLE E4
Obtained by summation from Tables D1, D2, or D5

H_1	H_2	H_3
116	52	-6

Grand Total $= T = 162$
for $N = 243$ items

Correction Factor $= \dfrac{T^2}{N} = \dfrac{162 \times 162}{243} = \underline{108}$

Each entry is the sum of 81 loss angles.

N.B. Now start at the bottom of page 411 and follow the calculations
working backwards through the book to page 401 on right-hand pages.

CALCULATION 4

t Effect Sum of Squares and Degrees of Freedom

Divide the sum of the squares of the entries in Table E1 by the number of items going to make each entry ($=81$). Subtract Correction Factor ($=108$).

$$\tfrac{1}{81}[63^2 + 49^2 + 50^2]^{\cdot} - 108 = 2$$

Between three levels of t there are 2 degrees of freedom.

CALCULATION 3

h Effect Sum of Squares and Degrees of Freedom

Divide the sum of the squares of the entries in Table E2 by the number of items going to make each entry ($=81$). Subtract Correction Factor ($=108$).

$$\tfrac{1}{81}[283^2 + (-13)^2 + (-108)^2] - 108 = 1{,}027$$

Between three levels of h there are 2 degrees of freedom.

CALCULATION 2

T Effect Sum of Squares and Degrees of Freedom

Divide the sum of the squares of the entries in Table E3 by the number of items going to make each entry ($=81$). Subtract Correction Factor ($=108$).

$$\tfrac{1}{81}[170^2 + (-47)^2 - 39^2] - 108 = 295$$

Between three levels of T there are 2 degrees of freedom.

CALCULATION 1

H Effect Sum of Squares and Degrees of Freedom

Divide the sum of the squares of the entries in Table E4 by the number of items going to make each entry ($=81$). Subtract Correction Factor ($=108$).

$$\tfrac{1}{81}[116^2 + 52^2 + (-6)^2] - 108 = 92$$

Between three levels of H there are 2 degrees of freedom.

Collecting our results together, we form our Table of the Analysis of Variance, dividing each sum of squares by its appropriate number of degrees of freedom in order to form the column headed 'Variance Estimate'.

TABLE OF ANALYSIS OF VARIANCE

Nature of effect	Source	Sum of squares	d.f.	Variance estimate
Main factors	T ***	295	2	147·5
	H ***	92	2	46
	t	2	2	1
	h ***	1,027	2	513·5
Interactions between pairs of factors	TH *	22	4	5·5
	Tt	11	4	2·75
	Th	5	4	1·25
	Ht	3	4	0·75
	Hh	15	4	3·75
	th	5	4	1·25
Interactions between triplets of factors	Hth	10	8	1·25
	Tth	7	8	0·87
	THh	28	8	3·5
	THt	10	8	1·25
Interaction of all factors	$THth$	17	16	1·06
Replication	Residual	307	162	1·90
	Total	1,856	242	

We make a Null Hypothesis that all the effects named in our Table of the Analysis of Variance have a zero magnitude, so that in effect all the variance estimates listed in the last column are independent estimates of the same quantity estimated by the residual variance, viz. essentially an estimate of the magnitude of the 'experimental error.' The F test tells us whether the variance estimate based on any of our named sources of variation (i.e. *possible variation*) is so much greater than the variance estimate based on the residual (experimental) error that the observed variance ratio is very unlikely to have arisen by chance. If the F test gives a significant result, then our Null Hypothesis breaks down. It will be plain that in such case the variance estimate is *not* simply an estimate of the experimental error variance, but of that variance *plus* an extra variation introduced by the fact that in our experimental design we made the experimental conditions in question vary (e.g. if the Firing Temperature Variance Estimate proves significant, then that estimate includes not only experimental error but also the variation induced by the variation in Firing Temperature which was part of the experimental design).

Now it may be shown that if a second order interaction is significant it is not valid to test any first order interaction related to the significant second order interaction against the residual. For example, if the interaction $H \times T \times t$ proved to be significant, then it would not be permissible to test either the $H \times T$, the $H \times t$, or the $T \times t$ interaction against the residual. Likewise, if a first order interaction were to prove significant, then we should not be justified in testing any of the main factor effects related to that interaction against the residual. For example, if the $H \times T$ interaction were significant, then it would not be permissible to test either the H main effect or the T main effect against the residual. We shall say later what action it is proper to take when interactions arise that are significant.

It follows from what we have been saying that when we come to carry out the F test for the various effects in our Table of the Analysis of Variance we must first of all do the test for the highest order interactions – in this case the third order interaction, $H \times T \times h \times t$. Since the variance estimate associated with this is less than the residual variance estimate, there is no point in testing whether it is significantly greater. We pass, therefore, to the second order interaction group. The only one here with a chance of being significantly greater than the residual is the $T \times H \times h$ interaction, which gives a variance ratio $F = \dfrac{3 \cdot 50}{1 \cdot 90} = 1 \cdot 84$ for 8 and

162 d.f. When we consult the Tables of the Variance Ratio, however, this proves to be non-significant.

It may have occurred to the reader that, since the third and second order interactions have proved non-significant, then according to our Null Hypothesis they are estimates of Residual Error just as much as the effect specifically named as such in our table. We are therefore justified in pooling the second and third order interaction sums of squares with the residual sum of squares and dividing by the sum of the relevant degrees of freedom in order to get an improved estimate of the residual variance based on a greater number of degrees of freedom. Since we already have a large number of degrees of freedom for error in our present case, there is little to be gained apart from the reader learning that it can be done and how to do it. Since this is a very laudable objective, however, we shall do it for the reader's benefit before going any further.

	Sum of squares	d.f.
	10	8
	7	8
	28	8
	10	8
	17	16
	307	162
Totals	379	210

Revised Residual Variance Estimate $= \frac{379}{210} = 1\cdot8$

Let us now consider the first order interactions. The Table of Analysis of Variance tells us at once that only three interactions could possibly prove significant, viz. the $H \times h$, $T \times t$ and $T \times H$. It is easy to confirm that F is not significant at the 5% level for either $H \times h$ or $T \times t$ with 4 and 210 d.f. For the $T \times H$ interaction we find $F = \frac{5\cdot5}{1\cdot8} = 3\cdot1$ with 4 and 210 d.f. which the tables show to be significant at the 5% level though not at the 1% level. We can proceed no further until we have examined this.

Suppose, as suggested by the F test, that there is such an interaction. What does it mean? Quite simply that the T and H effects

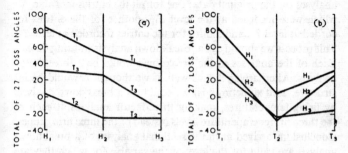

Fig. 104. Graphical representation of interaction between firing temperature and firing time in condenser problem (ref. table D2)

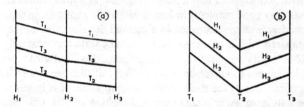

Fig. 105. What Fig. 104 might have looked like in the absence of interaction

are not independent in their effect on loss angle of the condensers. Some combinations of time and temperature are unexpectedly better or worse than we should expect. In Fig. 104 (a) and Fig. 104 (b) we see the interaction in graphical form by plotting the entries of Table D2. In the absence of interaction in (a) we should expect all three levels of T to follow the same kind of trend as we pass from H_1 to H_3. The trends need not all be straight lines, but they should all resemble each other. They might, for instance, have looked something as shown in Fig. 105 (a). Similar remarks apply to the (b) section of the diagram.

If we felt that such an interaction might occur in reality, we should then have to do repeat analyses of variance taking the interaction into account. We could do this by doing three separate analyses on the original data: one for all the entries in Table A2 which were recorded at the level T_1, another for the entries recorded at level T_2, and a third for the entries recorded at level T_3. This process we should call a 'breakdown analysis by firing times'. Each of the analyses in the breakdown would be a three-factor analysis. Alternatively (or as well, if we thought it would be instructive, as it sometimes is) we could do a breakdown analysis by firing temperatures, making three-factor analyses at each of the three firing temperature levels instead of the three firing times. Conclusions arrived at in the sectional analyses of a breakdown analysis are valid for the level of the variable for which they are carried out.

In our particular problem the interaction in question does not seem a very likely one. This is best seen in Fig. 104 (b) where the interaction suggests that a long firing time at a high temperature gives very good results (low loss angle) while a long firing time at a moderate temperature shows a marked deterioration in quality compared with a moderate time at a moderate temperature. As technologists we reject such a suggestion. This illustrates a point which cannot too often be stressed: that statistics need more than significance tests for their proper interpretation. It is inherent in the nature of experiments that odd-looking results will appear from time to time. Just as a new-born baby without experience of the world might regard the wickedness of a Borgia as something reasonably to be expected among popes, so the pure statistician would be unable to spot the oddity of our interaction. We must never lose sight of the fact that statistical techniques are instruments in our hand and – like all instruments of measurement – constantly to be suspected by the investigator of playing him false.

Having got rid of the necessity for doing a breakdown analysis in this case, we are now ready to look at the main effects. Testing these against the residual variance estimate, we find that all of them with the exception of t, the impregnation time, are significant. In fact, they all exceed the 0.1% level of F. It will be seen that they have been marked in the table of the analysis of variance with three asterisks (***) to indicate this level of significance. Two asterisks (**) would have indicated significance at the 1%

level, while a single asterisk (*) denotes significance at the 5% level. This is a very handy way for indicating which effects are important and how important they are.

To interpret the results, we turn to Tables E2, E3, and E4, where the main effects are displayed. Table E2 tells us that in order to get a low loss angle we should use the highest impregnation temperature in the range investigated. If there is a reasonable margin between this temperature and the flash point of the petroleum jelly it might be worth investigating whether the impregnation temperature could with advantage be raised even higher. Table E3 tells us that the moderate firing time is the best to use to get a low loss angle. The technician would also look out for possible reasons for the poorer results at the other times. At the lower firing time the reason might be that the vehicle in which the silver was carried in the spray paint or printing ink was not completely removed in the firing. The appearance of the plates might give some clue about the reasonableness of this assumption. The poorer result with the longer firing time is certainly obscure. Our investigation of the $T \times H$ interaction suggested that long firing time with high temperature gave very good results. It does not seem likely, therefore, that prolonged baking is causing any deterioration in the mica itself. Table E4 tells us that the best results will be obtained at the higher firing temperature. Again, we might bear in mind the possibility that an even higher firing temperature than any tried in the experiment might be a paying proposition. This would apply particularly if our firing cycles were rather long, since a higher temperature might well give a good result with an even shorter firing cycle than the present moderate one. A controlling factor here would ultimately be the temperature at which the mica would disintegrate, unless the duration of the firing cycle fell sufficiently rapidly as the temperature was raised. The fact that the impregnation time effect, t, proved non-significant tells us that it matters little what the duration of impregnation is, provided it is not less than our minimum. Table E1 certainly shows a tendency for the loss angle to fall as the impregnation time is prolonged, but this was not sufficiently marked to prove significant.

Our interim recommendation, then, would be that firing should be at the highest temperature H_3 for the medium duration T_2. This should be followed by impregnation at the highest temperature h_3 and the shortest impregnation cycle t_1 might be used as a time saver, though no harm would be done if the impregnation cycle were allowed to overrun. We should recommend that consideration be given to further investigation into the possibility of raising both firing and impregnation temperatures.

We have worked through this analysis in some detail, thinking aloud to ourselves, more or less as the statistician would as he did the analysis, in the hope that it may give the reader some insight into the spirit in which statistical analyses are carried out in practice. To conclude we shall show the data in control chart form for the four main effects. The residual variance we have estimated as 1·8 which corresponds to a standard deviation of $\sigma = \sqrt{1\cdot 8} = 1\cdot 4$ approximately. The entries in the four E tables are each the totals of 81 loss angles and correspond, therefore, to average values as shown in the following table (averages to one decimal place):

t_1	t_2	t_3	h_1	h_2	h_3	T_1	T_2	T_3	H_1	H_2	H_3
0·8	0·6	0·6	3·5	−0·2	−1·3	2·1	−0·6	0·5	1·4	0·6	−0·1

The standard deviation of the averages of samples of 81 items drawn from a population with standard deviation 1·4 will be $\frac{1\cdot 4}{\sqrt{81}} = 0\cdot 16$. Working in the coded data all the time, we find the grand average for 243 items with a grand total of 162 to be $\frac{162}{243} = 0\cdot 67$. The Warning Limits for our control chart for sample averages will therefore be set at $0\cdot 67 \pm 0\cdot 32$ and the Action Limits at $0\cdot 67 \pm 0\cdot 48$. Fig 106 shows the control chart with the averages plotted. It will be noted that the control chart bears out the analysis of variance (it is, of course, an analysis of variance in another form).

In order to exhibit our interaction $T \times H$ in control chart form, we argue as follows: Each entry in Table D2 is the sum of 27 loss angles; dividing each entry by 27 we get the following table of average values (1st decimal place).

T_1			T_2			T_3		
H_1	H_2	H_3	H_1	H_2	H_3	H_1	H_2	H_3
3·0	1·9	1·3	0·1	−1·0	−0·9	1·1	1·0	−0·7

If, now, from each entry we subtract:

(a) The discrepancy $(\bar{x}_T - \bar{x})$ between the average value of the T level in question and the grand average and

(b) the discrepancy $(\bar{x}_H - \bar{x})$ between the average value of the H level in question and the grand average;

then we should expect the modified entries to be distributed about the grand average with a standard deviation $= \dfrac{1\cdot4}{\sqrt{27}} = 0\cdot27$. The control chart limits would thus be

Warning $0\cdot67 \pm 0\cdot54$ Action $0\cdot67 \pm 0\cdot81$

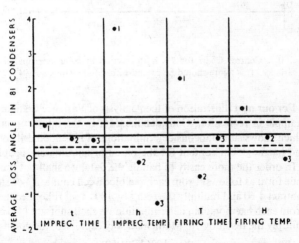

Fig. 106. Control Chart for analysis of variance of main effects in condenser loss angle problem

The subtraction of $(\bar{x}_T - \bar{\bar{x}})$ and $(\bar{x}_H - \bar{\bar{x}})$ in algebraic form is

$$- (\bar{x}_T - \bar{\bar{x}}) - (\bar{x}_H - \bar{\bar{x}}) = - \bar{x}_T - \bar{x}_H + 2\bar{\bar{x}}$$

Hence, what we have to do is to subtract from each entry the average value for its T level and the average value for its H level and, finally, add twice the grand average. The T level and H level averages are easily found from Tables E3 and E4. The reader may like to confirm for himself that the points plotted in the control chart in Fig. 107 are correct. It will be seen that the control chart agrees with the Analysis of Variance in showing the interaction a suspicious (5 %) level) rather than well established.

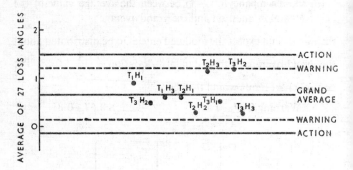

Fig. 107. Control Chart for $T \times H$ interaction in condenser analysis of variance. This figure should be compared carefully with Fig. 104

For our next illustration of the Analysis of Variance we take an example in regression. Consider the data in the following table which shows simultaneous determinations of red blood cell count and haemoglobin content for the blood of ten different people.

In order the more easily to handle the data, we shall put it into code form as follows. From each red blood cell count, X, we shall subtract 4·60 and multiply the result by 100 to get rid of decimals. From each haemoglobin determination we shall subtract 14·6 and multiply the result by 10. Mathematically expressed, the coding is

$$X_C = 100(X - 4 \cdot 60)$$
$$Y_C = 10(Y - 14 \cdot 6)$$

where X_c and Y_c denote the coded values of X and Y respectively.

X Red blood cells (millions per cubic millimetre)	Y Haemoglobin (grams per 100 cubic centimetres)
4·40	13·9
4·39	14·2
4·63	14·2
4·52	14·5
4·70	14·6
4·65	14·8
4·81	14·8
4·60	15·0
4·91	15·0
4·86	15·2

The table which follows shows the coded values together with the computation of sums of squares and products necessary for the computation of the regression coefficient and the correlation coefficient.

	X	Y	X^2	Y^2	XY
	−20	−7	400	49	140
	−21	−4	441	16	84
	3	−4	9	16	−12
	−8	−1	64	1	8
	10	0	100	0	0
	5	2	25	4	10
	21	2	441	4	42
	0	4	0	16	0
	31	4	961	16	124
	26	6	676	36	156
Totals	47	2	3,117	158	552
					$N = 10$ items

The correlation coefficient is given by

$$r^2 = \frac{(\Sigma xy)^2}{\Sigma x^2 . \Sigma y^2} \qquad \text{where} \begin{cases} \Sigma xy = \Sigma YX - \dfrac{\Sigma X . \Sigma Y}{N} \\[2mm] \Sigma x^2 = \Sigma X^2 - \dfrac{(\Sigma X)^2}{N} \\[2mm] \Sigma y^2 = \Sigma Y^2 - \dfrac{(\Sigma Y)^2}{N} \end{cases}$$

We have

$$\Sigma xy = \Sigma XY - \frac{\Sigma X . \Sigma Y}{N} = 552 - \frac{47 \times 2}{10} = 543$$

$$\Sigma x^2 = \Sigma X^2 - \frac{(\Sigma X)^2}{N} = 3,177 - \frac{47 \times 47}{10} = 2,896$$

$$\Sigma y^2 = \Sigma Y^2 - \frac{(\Sigma Y)^2}{N} = 158 - \frac{2 \times 2}{10} = 158$$

Hence $$r^2 = \frac{(\Sigma xy)^2}{\Sigma x^2 . \Sigma y^2} = \frac{543 \times 543}{2,896 \times 158} = 0.64$$

Hence $$\underline{r = \sqrt{0.64} = 0.80}$$

The Total Sum of Squares

$$\Sigma y^2 = \Sigma Y^2 - \frac{(\Sigma Y)^2}{N} = 158, \text{ as previously}$$

Regression Sum of Squares

The portion of the Total Sum of Squares accounted for by regression is

$$r^2 \Sigma y^2 = 0.64 \times 158 = 101$$

Residual Sum of Squares

The portion of the Total Sum of Squares not accounted for by regression is

$$(1 - r^2)\Sigma y^2 = (1 - 0.64)158 = 57$$

Alternatively

Residual Sum of Squares $= 158 - 101 = 57$

Degrees of Freedom

With $N = 10$, the Total d.f. $= 9$

A regression takes 1 d.f.

Hence, d.f. for the Residual $= 8$.

TABLE OF ANALYSIS OF VARIANCE

Source	Sum of squares	d.f.	Variance estimate
Regression	$r^2 \Sigma y^2 = 101$	1	101
Residual	$(1 - r^2) \Sigma y^2 = 64$	8	8
Total	$\Sigma y^2 = 158$	9	

If we make a Null Hypothesis that $r = 0$, then both our Variance Estimates are estimates of Residual (i.e. non-regression) variation. We have $F = \dfrac{101}{8} = 12 \cdot 6$ with 1 and 8 d.f. Tables of F show this value of F to be just in excess of the 1 % probability level. We conclude that the regression coefficient is significant.

In Chapter 16 we said the significance of r could be tested by calculating

$$\text{Student's } t = \frac{r\sqrt{N-2}}{\sqrt{1-r^2}} = \frac{0 \cdot 8\sqrt{8}}{\sqrt{1 - 0 \cdot 64}} = 3 \cdot 8$$

with $N - 2 = 10 - 2 = 8$ d.f.

Again we find that r reaches the 1 % level.

The next idea we shall illustrate is that of the Analysis of Co-variation, and for this purpose we shall revert to the Latin Square example dealt with on page 390. In that example we were investigating the yield of wheat under five different treatments and the Latin Square arrangement with the analysis of variance enabled us to remove any specific row and column effects due to differing fertility in the soil. The effect of this procedure, in general, will be to reduce the residual variation and so increase our precision of estimation and sharpen our significance test. Now suppose that in the year prior to our experiment the same twenty-five plots had been sown with wheat without the application of the five treatments which entered into our experiment. We shall imagine that the yields of the plots are known for this preliminary year to have been as shown in the following table.

INITIAL YIELDS OF WHEAT IN BUSHELS PER ACRE (X)

A 10	*B* 9	*C* 18	*D* 7	*E* 5
D 8	*E* 7	*A* 13	*B* 6	*C* 14
B 11	*C* 15	*D* 7	*E* 9	*A* 15
E 9	*A* 13	*B* 8	*C* 11	*D* 7
C 9	*D* 7	*E* 7	*A* 15	*B* 9

Subtracting 10 bushels per acre from each yield, we find the coded
yields as follows:

CODED INITIAL YIELDS IN BUSHELS PER ACRE MINUS 10

A 0	*B* −1	*C* 8	*D* −3	*E* −5
D −2	*E* −3	*A* 3	*B* −4	*C* 4
B 1	*C* 5	*D* −3	*E* −1	*A* 5
E −1	*A* 3	*B* −2	*C* 1	*D* −3
C −1	*D* −3	*E* −3	*A* 5	*B* −1

This is exactly similar in form to the table of coded yields
which we analysed for the treatments on page 391. The only difference is that in this case the letters are to be taken as denoting
the plots which in the actual experiment the following year are
to receive treatments *A*, *B*, *C*, *D*, and *E*. These preliminary yields
can be analysed in exactly the same way as the treatment yields
were analysed. We shall content ourselves with giving the results
of the analysis and leave it to the reader as an exercise to work out
for himself.

ANALYSIS OF VARIANCE FOR THE PRELIMINARY YIELDS

Source	Sums of squares	d.f.
Columns	4·6	4
Rows	13·4	4
Treatment positions	191·8	4
Residual	73·2	12
Total	283·0	24

For reference purposes we repeat here the coded yield table for the year for which the treatments were actually applied (picked up from page 391). If the reader will compare this table with the table of the coded yields for the preliminary year, a marked similarity of pattern will be observed. This is in no way surprising. A plot that crops well in the preliminary year has a start over a poor cropping plot when the manurial treatments are applied, and we should forecast that the good plots in the preliminary trial should, on the whole, do better than the poor plots when the treatments are applied, irrespective of the value of the treatments. If, then, we call the preliminary yields X and the second year (experimental) yields Y, we should expect that the X and Y values would exhibit a correlation – despite the disturbing effect of the different manurial treatments in the second year yields, Y.

CODED YIELDS WITH TREATMENTS APPLIED (Y)

A 3	B −1	C 11	D −3	E −4
D −1	E −2	A 5	B −3	C 6
B 1	C 7	D −2	E 0	A 7
E −2	A 5	B −3	C 0	D −3
C 1	D −1	E −2	A 5	B 1

If, therefore, we were to have a regression equation showing how the Y values are increased as the X values increase, we should have a means of calculating a correction to the yields when the treatment is applied, thereby eliminating initial bias due to unequal fertility in the individual plots. This regression equation is arrived at very simply by the Analysis of Co-variance (or, if you like, correlation). Just as the Analysis of Variance for the X values and the Y values was carried out by calculating the sums of squares of the X and Y values respectively, so the Analysis of Co-variance is arrived at by calculating the sums of products of corresponding X and Y values. Where the sums of squares were necessarily positive, the sums of products can sometimes be negative. This will be the case where we have a negative correlation (Y decreasing when X increases). In the analysis of variance we calculated sums of squares corresponding to rows, columns, treatments, residual, and total. We do exactly the same for sums of products in the analysis of co-variance. The degrees of freedom for the products are in every case equal to the degrees of freedom for the corresponding sum of squares. Taking the sources of variation in turn, we find the following:

Column Sum of Products

We set down corresponding column totals for the X and Y values taken from the coded yield tables and find the value of ΣXY, ΣX, and ΣY. The number of items corresponding to each grand total and product sum is $N = 25$, since there were twenty-five plots in our experiment. Each column total in the table which follows is the sum of five plot totals. The column totals are:

For X	-3	1	3	-2	0	$\Sigma X = -1$
For Y	2	8	9	-1	7	$\Sigma Y = 25$

Sum of products $-6 + 8 + 27 + 2 + 0 = 31$

We divide this quantity by the number of plots entering into each column total ($= 5$) and, finally, subtract a correction factor whose value is given by

$$\frac{1}{N} \Sigma X . \Sigma Y = \tfrac{1}{25}[(-1) \times 25] = -1$$

This same value for the correction factor will be used when we come to the sums of products for rows, residual, and total. In this case we find the sum of products corresponding to columns as

$$\tfrac{31}{5} - (-1) = 7 \cdot 2, \text{ with 4 degrees of freedom}$$

Row Sum of Products

Setting down row totals for X and Y, we get:

For X	-1	-2	7	-2	-3
For Y	6	5	13	-3	4

Sum of products $-6 - 10 + 91 + 6 - 12 = 69$

Dividing by 5, the number of plots in each row total, and subtracting our correction factor (-1 in this case), we find for the row sum of products:

$$\tfrac{69}{5} - (-1) = 14 \cdot 8, \text{ with 4 degrees of freedom}$$

Treatment Sum of Products

Setting down treatment totals for X and Y, we get:

For X	16	-7	17	-14	-13
For Y	25	-5	25	-10	-10

Sum of products $400 + 35 + 425 + 140 + 130 = 1{,}130$

Dividing by 5, the number of plots entering into each treatment total, and subtracting our correction factor, we find the treatment sum of products as:

$$\tfrac{1130}{5} - (-1) = 227, \text{ with 4 degrees of freedom}$$

Total Sum of Products

In order to get the total sum of products, we set up the following table which shows the products of the X and Y values for each of the twenty-five plots. These products are then totalled over the whole table and, finally, we subtract the correction factor.

0	1	88	9	20
2	6	15	12	24
1	35	6	0	35
2	15	6	0	9
-1	3	6	25	-1

[Derived from the coded yield tables for X and Y]

Summing the cell entries over the whole table, and subtracting our correction factor, we find for the total sum of products

$$318 - (-1) = 319, \text{ with 24 degrees of freedom}$$

We now set up our table of sums of squares and products by collecting together the sums of products just calculated and the sums of squares for the X values and the Y values which we computed when we did the analyses of variance for these values (reference: the analysis of variance tables on pages 392 and 425).

TABLE OF SUMS OF SQUARES AND PRODUCTS

Source	Sums of squares for X	Sums of products	Sums of squares for Y	d.f.
Columns	4·6	7·2	14·8	4
Rows	13·4	14·8	26·0	4
Treatments	191·8	227·0	270·0	4
Residual	73·2	70·0	77·2	12
Total	283·0	319·0	388·0	24

The Residual Sum of Products is obtained from those already calculated thus: Residual $= 319\cdot0 - 7\cdot2 - 14\cdot8 - 227\cdot0 = 70\cdot0$, as shown in the table.

We may now use the Residual Sum of Squares and Products to estimate the regression coefficient of Y on X, which will tell us how much advantage accrued to any plot in our testing of the various manurial treatments by virtue of higher initial fertility in the soil of that plot before any treatments were applied at all. The sums of squares and products in our table are sums of squares and products about the mean, since we have already applied the correction factor in computing them. To get the regression coefficient we divide the sum of products for the residual by the sum of squares in the X residual, thus:

$$b = \frac{\Sigma xy}{\Sigma x^2} = \frac{70 \cdot 0}{73 \cdot 2} = 0 \cdot 956$$

Armed with this knowledge, we could now go back to our table of coded yields, Y, for the treatment tests. We could work out from the preliminary yield figures for each plot how much the preliminary yield was in excess of the grand average preliminary yield per plot. We could then correct the yields, Y, by subtracting from each of them (to remove the initial advantage we subtract for an excess; for an initial deficiency we should add) the initial excess multiplied by the regression coefficient, $b = 0 \cdot 956$. Having adjusted all our yields in this way, we could then do a new analysis of variance on the adjusted yields. Fortunately, we can avoid all this work by thinking a little before we rush madly at the job.

For a plot whose preliminary yield is X against an average yield per plot of $\bar{X}$, the correction will be of magnitude $b(X - \bar{X})$, where b is the regression coefficient. For the deviation from the mean we may write $x = X - \bar{X}$ and the correction will then be bx. Hence if the yield of any plot under treatment is Y, then the adjusted yield will be $Y - bx$ which we may denote by Z. Our analysis on adjusted yields would be an analysis of variance for these quantities Z and would involve sums of squares of the form

$$\Sigma z^2 = \Sigma (Z - \bar{Z})^2$$

and since $\bar{Z} = \bar{Y}$, by virtue of the fact that the excess for the mean is by definition zero, we have

$$\Sigma z^2 = \Sigma (Y - bx - Y)^2 = \Sigma (y - bx)^2$$

i.e. $$\underline{\Sigma z^2 = \Sigma y^2 - 2b\Sigma xy + b^2 \Sigma x^2}$$

Hence, it follows that the analysis of variance for the corrected yields may be obtained at once from our table of sums of squares and products by following the instructions implicit in the formula for Σz^2 which we have just derived. As an illustration, we show the computation for the column sum of squares in the adjusted yields. Looking in the table for the sums of squares and products, we find:

$$\Sigma x^2 = 4 \cdot 6 \qquad \Sigma xy = 7 \cdot 2 \qquad \Sigma y^2 = 14 \cdot 8$$

and we know that $b = 0 \cdot 956$. For ease in computation, since the error is very small, we shall regard b as equal to unity in this example. We have

$$\Sigma z^2 = \Sigma y^2 - 2b\Sigma xy + b^2\Sigma x^2$$
$$= 14 \cdot 8 - 2(7 \cdot 2) + 4 \cdot 6 = 5 \cdot 0$$

The Computations for Row, Treatment, Residual, and Total Sums of Squares are made in turn in exactly the same way, and we arrive, finally, at the following table.

ANALYSIS OF VARIANCE ON ADJUSTED YIELDS

Source	Sum of squares	d.f.	Variance estimate
Columns	5·0	4	1·25
Rows	9·8	4	2·45
Treatments	7·8	4	1·95
Residual	10·4	11	0·95
Total	33·0	23	

It will be seen that the degrees of freedom are exactly as they were in the analysis on the unadjusted yields, except that one degree of freedom has now disappeared from the Residual. Why is this? The reason is not far to seek: we estimated our regression coefficient, b, from the residual section of our data, and in so doing we have to give up one degree of freedom. The first thing that strikes us is that in the analysis on adjusted yields the treatment effect turns out to be non-significant, where with the unadjusted yields it was significant. When we first analysed the data we were in the position of not having any information about the initial fertility of the plots. We did our best to control heterogeneity by rows and columns as a whole, by eliminating the sums of squares corresponding to these sources of variation. However, the analysis on adjusted yields shows that in this case the block of land on which the plots were laid out was very badly chosen from the point of view of homogeneity of fertility – so much so that treatments were apparently significantly different until we did our analysis of co-variance to eliminate this effect. We have here an extreme example, specially invented to illustrate our point. It is not likely that so extreme a case would often be met with in practice. Nevertheless, analysis of co-variance is a very powerful technique for adjusting yields in cases of this sort. A further point which should be carefully noted is the way in which the residual error variance estimate (experimental error) is reduced, thus increasing the precision of the whole experiment. The statistician gets tired of hearing people in certain industries say that while statistics is an excellent technique when materials like steel are being dealt with which are very uniform in their properties, it is of little use when materials of great variability are being examined. The whole essence of statistics is that it is the only way of tackling inherently variable data. Unless such data are dealt with statistically, they are not dealt with properly.

The Analysis of Co-variance is not confined to the adjustment of data to allow for variation in the fertility of the field plots in agricultural experiments. We might use it also in experiments designed to assess the gain in weight of human beings or animals fed on special diets so as to make special allowance for sex, initial weight, and other possible disturbing effects. The fact that we can eliminate this type of bias is a very important consideration in medical and biological experimentation in some cases. It is a common practice to restrict experiments to one litter of animals so as to keep down the heterogeneity of the 'plots' (experimental animals). Not only is this awkward when litters are small, but it is generally an undesirable thing for the reason that experiments restricted to one litter, one strain, or one anything else are strictly only assessing effects within their restricted area of experimentation. It follows that experimental results based on heterogeneous material – provided we make proper allowance for heterogeneity by a technique such as the analysis of co-variance – are much more likely to be of general applicability than results obtained on homogeneous material obtained by narrowing the field of investigation to particular groups or strains.

Yet again, the analysis of co-variance is extremely valuable when we wish to assess treatments for more than one factor simultaneously. For example, a certain treatment might be very successful in raising the weight of pigs; but, if the gain in weight were all fat, the result would not be best Danish bacon, but the sort of thing inexperienced amateurs produce when they feed a pig in their own backyard, ignoring scientific principles. Another example suitable for the analysis of co-variance would be the effect of certain manurial treatments on straw weight and grain weight in grain crops. In general, whenever any policy or treatment produces double effects both of which are of economic interest to us, the analysis of co-variance in a well-designed investigation would prove an illuminating way of looking at the data.

To conclude our brief introduction to the analysis of variation, we shall now give the reader the basic ideas behind the technique known as 'confounding', which, whatever its name may suggest at first sight, is a perfectly sensible and straightforward business with a very useful purpose. It will be appreciated that in factorial type experiments, even when each factor is tried at only two levels, the number of combinations of treatments involved in the experiment increases very rapidly as the number of factors is extended. In general, an experiment involving f factors, each at L levels, will involve us in Lf treatment combinations. To picture this in concrete terms, imagine we wish to try out 6 manurial treatments, each at 2 levels. Then we should need $2^6 = 2 \times 2 \times 2 \times 2 \times 2 \times 2 = 64$ plots of land in order to accommodate a single replication of the experiment. The block to contain so many plots must be of considerable area, and as the area of the block grows so also does the heterogeneity of the land within the block. It is true that we may often forgo replication of our blocks on the ground that higher order interactions in many cases are either non-existent or of little practical importance, so that the sums of squares and degrees of freedom associated with these higher order interactions may be taken as assessing residual error (=experimental error). If, however, the block size itself is too great for practical purposes, this is of no help to us. Confounding is a technique by which we forgo (wholly or in part) information about one or more interactions (believing on technical grounds that they are of little or no importance) and arrange that in exchange for this loss we shall be able to work with blocks of reduced size.

In order to see how this is done, we must familiarize ourselves with certain new methods of representing treatments. Consider an experiment in which we are going to have three factors A, B, C (e.g. manurial treatments) each at two levels. The symbols a, b, c will be used to denote the treatments where A, B, and C are at their higher levels respectively. When no small letter is mentioned it is to be taken that the factor mentioned is at its lower level (it may be that the lower level of a manurial treatment is complete absence of that treatment, of course). Thus, ab, bc, abc, and c denote plots receiving both A and B at their higher levels with C at its lower level; B and C at their higher levels with A at its lower level; A, B, and C all at their higher level; and C at its higher level with A and B at their lower levels, respectively. In a complete factorial layout there will be one plot which has all the treatments at their lower levels. For a reason which will be apparent in what follows, it is very convenient to denote this particular treatment combination by the symbol (1). In this notation, the eight treatment combinations to be used in our experiment may be denoted by the symbols:

$$abc, \ ab, \ ac, \ bc, \ a, \ b, \ c, \ (1)$$

Each treatment combination would occupy a plot of land, and the block containing the eight plots, as shown below, would constitute one complete replication.

abc	ab	ac	bc
a	b	c	(1)

In an experiment with fourfold replication there would be four such blocks, and so on. We shall ignore the question of replication.

Now look at our block on p. 433 which contains the eight treatment combinations. In what follows we shall be using the small letters which denote treatment combinations for the further purpose of signifying the yield (e.g. of corn). Clearly the difference between the yield a and the yield (1), viz. $a - (1)$ is a measure of the effectiveness of the treatment a as we pass from its lower to its higher level. Looking closer, we find other pairs of plots which also measure the same effect, viz. ab and b; ac and c; and, finally, abc and bc. In every pair mentioned we have two plots which have received identical treatment except in regard to the presence or absence of the high level of A. The reader should check carefully for himself that the eight plots in our block can also be broken up to give four pairs showing the effect of B and four pairs showing the effect of C. Consider now, again, the four pairs showing the effect of A. Clearly, if we add together the four yields of the plots which have received treatment a, and subtract from the total the total of the four remaining plots which have not had the benefit of this treatment, we still have a measure of the effectiveness of a, which may be represented as

$$[a + ab + ac + abc] - [b + c + bc + (1)]$$

Treat this as a little bit of algebra. We see that from the first bracket we can extract a factor a, thus getting

$$a[b + c + bc + 1] - [b + c + bc + 1]$$

The first part of the expression is identical with the second, except that it is modified by the presence of the factor a, which corresponds, of course, to the way in which we have measured the effect of the factor A by taking pairs of plots which differ only in the presence or absence of the letter a. Our algebraic expression may also be written as

$$a(b + 1)(c + 1) - (b + 1)(c + 1)$$

which in turn reduces to the form

$$(a - 1)(b + 1)(c + 1)$$

We have thus arrived at an easily remembered algebraic expression in factor form which, when expanded according to the ordinary rules of elementary algebra, tells us what plot yields are to be added and subtracted together in order to get a measure of the A effect as we pass from the lower level to the higher level of that factor. Notice that the minus sign occurs with the factor which we are estimating. In like manner, the B effect would be represented and measured by $(a+1)(b-1)(c+1)$ and the C effect by $(a+1)(b+1)(c-1)$.

The reader already knows enough, by this time, to realize that in an experiment of this type we should not only ask about the effect of the three main factors, but should also want to know about interaction effects. Is there a particular boost effect when we get particular combinations of factors? If so, how is it to be assessed in our new notation? We shall deal with this matter by considering the $A \times B$ interaction. There is an $A \times B$ interaction if the A effect is notably different according as the factor B is at its higher or lower level. The eight plots in our block again furnish us with the necessary information.

The plots with B at the higher level are:

$$abc, ab, bc, \text{ and } b$$

These may be subdivided as follows:

> *With A at the higher level*: abc and ab
> *With A at the lower level*: bc and b

Hence, the effect of A with B at the higher level may be measured as given by the expression $\underline{(abc+ab)-(bc+b)}$

The plots with B at the lower level are:

$$ac, a, c, \text{ and } (1)$$

These may be subdivided as follows:

> *With A at the higher level*: ac and a
> *With A at the lower level*: c and (1)

Hence, the effect of A with B at the lower level may be measured as given by the expression $\underline{(ac+a)-(c+1)}$.

If, now, we subtract the effect of A with B at the lower level from the effect of A with B at the higher level, we shall have a measure of the interaction of the factors A and B. Thus:

$$[(abc+ab)-(bc+b)]-[(ac+a)-(c+1)]$$

Treating this algebraically, we get

$$(abc + ab) - (bc + b) - (ac + a) + (c + 1)$$
$$= ab(c + 1) - b(c + 1) - a(c + 1) + (c + 1)$$
$$= (c + 1)(ab - b - a + 1)$$
$$= \underline{(a - 1)(b - 1)(c + 1)}$$

Here, then, we have an algebraic expression very similar in form to that which we found for the main effects. The only difference is that now we have two minus signs, one in each of the brackets containing the letters referring to the interaction we are to estimate. In like manner the $B \times C$ interaction would be represented by $(a + 1)(b - 1)(c - 1)$ and the $A \times C$ interaction by $(a - 1)(b + 1)$ $(c - 1)$. The reader will guess, rightly, that an interaction between all three factors will be represented by the expression $(a - 1)(b - 1)$ $(c - 1)$.

Before going any further, we must get a little practice in using this notation for the computation of sums of squares. Let us suppose that a double replication, three-factor experiment were carried out with each factor at two levels, and that the yields of the plots in the two blocks were as indicated below:

BLOCK I

abc	ab	ac	bc
2	3	1	4
a	b	c	(1)
2	1	4	3

BLOCK II

abc	ab	ac	bc
2	2	1	2
a	b	c	(1)
0	2	1	2

For Block I

Total $= 20$

Correction Factor $= \dfrac{20 \times 20}{8} = 50$

For Block II

Total $= 12$

Correction Factor $= \dfrac{12 \times 12}{8} = 18$

Grand Total, both blocks combined $= 32$

Grand Correction Factor, both blocks combined $= \dfrac{32 \times 32}{16} = 64$

Using, first, the technique already familiar, we shall divide the Total Sums of Squares into components corresponding to (a) Between Blocks and (b) Within Blocks Variation.

Total Sum of Squares

Square all yields for both blocks and subtract Grand Correction Factor.

Squares of Items

Block I: 4, 9, 1, 16, 4, 1, 16, 9   Total 60
Block II: 4, 4, 1, 4, 0, 4, 1, 4   Total 22

Total of Squares 82

Total Sum of Squares = 82 – 64 = 18

Between Blocks Sum of Squares

(Each block total is the sum of 8 items.)
$$\tfrac{1}{8}[20^2 + 12^2] - 64 = 68 - 64 = 4$$

Within Blocks Sum of Squares

Total of Squares of items in Block I = 60 and in Block II = 22
Using Block Correction Factors:

Within Block I Sum of Squares = 60 – 50 = 10
Within Block II Sum of Squares = 22 – 18 = 4

Total Within Blocks   = 14

These results may then be put in a table.

ANALYSIS OF VARIANCE BETWEEN AND WITHIN BLOCKS

Source	Sum of squares	d.f.
Between blocks	4	1
Within blocks	14	$2 \times 7 = 14$
Total	18	15

Now the within blocks variation, based on 14 degrees of freedom, includes the between treatment variation, based on 7 degrees of freedom. The remaining 7 degrees of freedom of the within block variation are assignable to error. Adding plot yields for corresponding plots in the two blocks, we find the treatment totals (each the sum of two items) to be:

abc	ab	ac	bc
4	5	2	6
a	b	c	(1)
2	3	5	5

And the treatment sum of squares then comes out as

$$\tfrac{1}{2}[4^2 + 5^2 + 2^2 + 6^2 + 2^2 + 3^2 + 5^2 + 5^2] - 64 = 72 - 64 = 8$$

The Analysis of Variance Table then becomes:

Source	Sum of squares	d.f.
Between blocks	4	1
Treatments	8	7
Residual (Error)	6	7
Total	18	15

Our next step is to use our new notation to help us to calculate the sums of squares corresponding to individual treatments, and, of course, the sum of these sums of treatment squares should be found equal to the Treatment Sum of Squares as given in the table above. The table of treatment totals will be the source of our information as to the numerical quantities required in our evaluation. It should be remembered that the value of the quantity arrived at using our algebraic formulae for treatments is based on the whole of the sixteen plots of our original experiment, and so to get the sum of squares corresponding to any one treatment we have to square the value given by the formula—and then divide the result by 16.

We shall show the working in full for the factor A and leave it to the reader to check for himself by expansion that the remaining factors are correct.

A effect: $(a-1)(b+1)(c+1)$

$$= abc + ab + ac - bc + a - b - c - (1)$$
$$= 4 + 5 + 2 - 6 + 2 - 3 - 5 - 5 = -6$$

To get the A effect sum of squares we square this and divide by 16, since it is based on the yields of 16 plots.

$$A \text{ effect sum of squares} = \tfrac{36}{16} = 2.25$$

The remaining effects are as shown in the table following:

Effect	abc ab ac bc a b c (1)	Total	Square	Sums of squares
B	$4+5-2+6-2+3-5-5$	4	16	1·00
C	$4-5+2+6-2-3+5-5$	2	4	0·25
$A \times B$	$4+5-2-6-2-3+5+5$	6	26	2·25
$A \times C$	$4-5+2-6-2+3-5+5$	-4	16	1·00
$B \times C$	$4-5-2+6+2-3-5+5$	2	4	0·25
$A \times B \times C$	$4-5-2-6+2+3+5-5$	-4	16	1·00
	Add A effect sum of squares as already found			2·25
	Total Sums of Squares for treatments			8·00

This agrees with the treatment sum of squares found previously. Whereas the previous calculation gave the sum of squares for all treatments, this has now given us the sums of squares for the individual treatments. Moreover, since each treatment was at two levels in the experiment, there is one degree of freedom for each of the treatment combinations in our table above. *It should be carefully noted that when this method of computing the sums of squares is used there is no question of having to apply any correction factor of the type* $\dfrac{T^2}{N}$ *as we have previously been in the habit of doing.*

We may now write out the full table of the analysis of variance for the data of our experiment, as follows:

TABLE OF ANALYSIS OF VARIANCE

Source	Sums of squares	d.f.	Variance estimate
Between blocks	4·00	1	4·00
Treatments			
A	2·25	1	2·25
B	1·00	1	1·00
C	0·25	1	0·25
$A \times B$	2·25	1	2·25
$A \times C$	1·00	1	1·00
$B \times C$	0·25	1	0·25
$A \times B \times C$	1·00	1	1·00
	— 8·00	— 7	— 1·14
Residual (Experimental Error)	6·00	7	0·86
Total	18·00	15	

In the investigation just dealt with, each block of land contained eight plots to accommodate the eight treatment combinations. It is reasonable to believe that blocks of half the area would exhibit greater internal uniformity. We may arrange our treatments in such half-size blocks without reducing the treatment plot size, provided that we are willing to forgo some of our information about interaction effects. We do this by confounding a chosen interaction with between plot differences, i.e. we put the chosen interaction on the same foundation (confound) as the between block effect, so that there is no way of disentangling the interaction from the block effect.

Let us consider first of all an experiment with a single replication in which, as before, we have three factors, A, B, and C, each at two levels. Using the notation just established, the treatment combinations will be

$$abc, ab, ac, bc, a, b, c, \quad (1)$$

In the previous experiment these all went into a single eight-plot block. This time, we are going to make two four-plot blocks and we shall allocate four treatment combinations to each block in such a way that one treatment effect will be indistinguishable from the between block effect. The usual thing is to sacrifice inter-actions of as high order as possible. Let us therefore agree in this case to sacrifice knowledge about the $A \times B \times C$ interaction. In our new notation, this interaction would be assessed as

$$(a-1)(b-1)(c-1) = [abc + a + b + c] - [ab + ac + bc + 1]$$

It follows that if we place in our first block the treatments shown in the first bracket and in our second block the treatments shown in the second bracket, we shall have an arrangement in which the chosen interaction is confounded with the between block effect. The experimental layout would be:

BLOCK I

abc	a
b	c

BLOCK II

ab	ac
bc	(1)

In practice, the treatments would be assigned to the plots within each block at random, e.g. by picking the treatments out of a hat as in a raffle. The reason for this randomization is to make sure that each treatment has an equal chance of being tested out on any particular plot of ground, thus eliminating bias which might be introduced through the conscious selection of the plots.

It will be plain enough that in the above arrangement the chosen interaction has indeed been lost. It still remains to show that the remaining treatment effects are unaffected by this arrangement. We shall illustrate this for the case of the A main effect and leave it to the reader to satisfy himself in similar fashion about the other treatments. Suppose that the soil in Block II is very fertile, so that each plot in that block would give an extra yield due to fertility bias of a magnitude which we shall represent by the symbol q. This is a between block difference, of course, The yields might then be denoted symbolically as follows:

15

BLOCK I   BLOCK II

abc	a
b	c

$(ab+q)$	$(ac+q)$
$(bc+q)$	$(1+q)$

Now the main effect A is represented by

$$(a-1)(b+1)(c+1) = [abc+ab+ac+a] - [bc+b+c+1]$$

Owing to the between block bias, however, we should actually evaluate:

$$[abc+(ab+q)+(ac+q)+a] - [(bc+q)+b+c+(1+q)]$$

It is clear that when the two brackets are subtracted the bias q will vanish. It follows, therefore, that with such an arrangement the main treatment A is unaffected by between block bias, whereas, in the case of the confounded interaction, the bias would have been associated with every treatment in one block and with none of the treatments in the other block. The reader will find that every treatment apart from the confounded interaction is unaffected by block bias in the experimental arrangement which we have designed.

Let us carry this confounding idea a little further. Suppose we allocate our treatments to four blocks of two plots each. In such a case, the blocks would be smaller than ever and therefore likely to be even more homogeneous in fertility. Of course, to reap this advantage there will be a price to pay. We shall have to sacrifice more of our treatment comparisons. The number to be sacrificed is equal to the number of degrees of freedom between our blocks. Between four blocks there are three degrees of freedom. Hence, we shall have to sacrifice knowledge about three effects. Now we are not completely free to choose which treatment effects we shall sacrifice. Suppose we choose to sacrifice the interaction $A \times B \times C$, as the highest order interaction, and decide that the $A \times B$ interaction might also be let go. Then it turns out that in choosing these two to be sacrificed we have automatically committed ourselves to losing the C main effect.

This is not at all obvious, at first sight, but the reader will soon be able to satisfy himself on that score when he knows a little more about confounding. He will be able to work out the fact from first principles. Meantime, there is a very simple rule, knowledge of which will make the reader as clever as the author in spotting these inevitable losses. This is it.

Regard the treatment symbols as algebraic expressions. Multiply together the expressions chosen for confounding. Replace every squared term in the answer by unity. The result is an interaction inevitably confounded by our initial choice.

Example. If we choose interaction ABC and interaction AB to be confounded, then we inevitably lose also

$$ABC \times AB = A^2B^2C = C$$

If the reader will try the matter out for himself, he will soon find that if he sacrifices the ABC interaction with any of the first order interaction, he is bound to lose one or other of his main effects. This is obviously unsatisfactory. The main effects would not have been introduced into the investigation at all unless we were interested in assessing them. There is a way out of the difficulty, however, provided we are willing to sacrifice all three of our first order interaction. If we choose to sacrifice the AB and the AC interactions, we shall inevitably lose also the interaction $AB \times AC = A^2BC = BC$. We shall still have the second order interaction available and the three main effects. We shall adopt this as a satisfactory arrangement for the purposes of illustration (very likely it would be unacceptable in practice and a complete revision of the experimental design would then be called for). The problem then arises: How do we allocate the treatments to our two-plot blocks so as to sacrifice the chosen interactions without losing the main effects and the second order interaction? This calls for a little explanation, but the idea is perfectly general and so worth learning. The procedure for finding one of our plots to start with – the leading block, we might sensibly call it – is as follows.

We take our eight treatment combinations

$$abc, ab, ac \ bc \ a, b, c, (1)$$

We then make a list of all the treatment combinations which have

an even number of letters in common with each of the interactions we propose to confound, thus:

Even number of letters in common with AB   abc   ab   c   (1)
Even number of letters in common with AC   abc   ac   b   (1)
Even number of letters in common with BC   abc   bc   a   (1)

The reader will not be puzzled by the appearance of the treatments *a*, *b*, *c*, (1) in our table when he recalls that zero is an even
number.

Comparing the results for the three interactions, we see that
there are only two treatment combinations which have an even
number of letters in common with all the interactions to be confounded, viz. *abc* and (1). These treatments will therefore be
taken as our leading block, which will appear as follows:

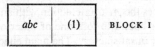

With our leading block found, the other blocks are easily arrived
at. We take any treatment that has not already been allocated to a
plot, e.g. *ab*. The treatments in the leading block are multiplied
by this treatment algebraically, any squared term being replaced
by unity, thus:

$$abc \times ab = a^2b^2c = c \text{ and } (1) \times ab = ab$$

In this way we arrive at our second block, which will be

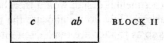

Again we look for a treatment which has not yet been allocated to
a plot, e.g. treatment *b*, and multiply the treatments in our leading
block by this treatment. This gives our third block as:

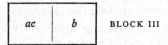

There are still two treatments left. These, of course, go to the fourth block:

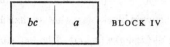

The layout for our confounded experiment is therefore:

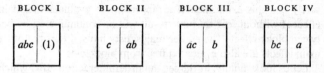

In practice the treatments should be allocated at random to the plots within their own block, so as to give every treatment an equal chance of being tested on each plot. In the full randomization, of course, we should decide which particular block of land was to be called Block Number I, which Block II, and so on by picking them out of a hat. In this way the introduction of conscious bias is avoided.

It remains to be seen now whether our procedure has, in fact, confounded the three first order interactions with between block effects, while at the same time leaving the three main effects and the second order interaction free from block bias. Let us suppose that relative to Block I, the other blocks have excess fertility p for Block II, q for Block III, and r for Block IV. The AB interaction is evaluated from

$$(a-1)(b-1)(c+1) = [abc+ab+c+1] - [ac+bc+a+b]$$

Allowing for block bias, we shall actually evaluate

$$[abc+(ab+p)+(c+p)+(1)]-[(ac+q)+(bc+r)+(a+r)+(b+q)]$$

It is at once evident that when we subtract the terms p, q, and r, which represent block bias, are not going to vanish. Hence, the interaction AB is confounded with between block differences, as we agreed it should be. In like manner, the reader may quickly satisfy himself that the other two interactions, AC and BC, are also confounded in this arrangement with between block differences.

Consider, now, the main effect A, which is assessed on the basis of

$$(a - 1)(b + 1)(c + 1) = [abc + ab + ac + a] - [bc + b + c + 1]$$

Allowing for between block bias, what we shall actually evaluate is

$$[abc + (ab + p) + (ac + q) + (a + r)] - [(bc + r) + (b + q) + (c + p) + 1]$$

When the brackets are subtracted, it is clear that the terms p, q, and r, which represent block bias, will vanish. Hence, we may safely use this experimental arrangement to evaluate the main effect A without fear that our result will be contaminated by between block effect. The reader may satisfy himself that the other main effects are also evaluated free from block bias.

Let us look, finally, at the second order interaction ABC which is evaluated from

$$(a - 1)(b - 1)(c - 1) = [abc + a + b + c] - [ab + ac + bc + 1]$$

Allowing for between block bias, what we shall actually calculate is

$$[abc + (a + r) + (b + q) + (c + p)] - [(ab + p) + (ac + q) + (bc + r) + 1]$$

Since, on subtraction, the block bias terms p, q, and r will vanish, we see that the experimental arrangement allows us to assess the second order interaction free from between block effects.

There is a logical end to this road. What happens if we try to work in blocks containing only one plot each, so as to get the maximum homogeneity? The price to be paid will be the sacrifice of a number of treatment comparisons equal to the number of degrees of freedom between blocks – in this case, with eight blocks, seven treatments would have to be sacrificed. What is left of our experiment? It is obvious, of course, that such greediness must be foolish. Every treatment would be associated with a block, and between block treatments would enter into every treatment assessment. Confounding is a purely commercial transaction. We pay the fair market price for what we buy. The advantage lies in the fact that the market is conducted on a barter basis. We pay a fair price in terms of things we do not specially want in return for something we do want. Which is all very jolly and above board.

In order to show the generality of the procedures, we shall now consider a four-factor experiment, with each factor tried at two levels. (It is possible to design confounded experiments when factors are at three levels, but for this more advanced technique the reader must refer to some of the texts mentioned in the bibliography.) If we denote the factors by the letters A, B, C, and D, then, with each factor at two levels, there will be sixteen possible treatment combinations. In our present notation, they may be represented by:

abcd	All treatments at high level
abc abd acd bcd	Three high and one low in each case
ab ac ad bc bd cd	Two high and two low in each case
a b c d	One high, three low in each case
(1)	All treatments at low level

For one complete replication the sixteen treatments would call for sixteen plots. If we decided that in the interests of greater block homogeneity we were well advised to work in two blocks of eight plots each, then this could be done by sacrificing any treatments contrast. Choosing the highest order interaction $ABCD$ to be sacrificed, we arrive at the plots to go into our leading block by collecting together those treatments which have an even number of letters in common with the interaction $ABCD$. In this way we find the leading block to be:

abcd	*ab*	*ac*	*ad*	*bc*	*bd*	*cd*	(1)	BLOCK I

It follows that the second block must be:

abc	*abd*	*acd*	*bcd*	*a*	*b*	*c*	*d*	BLOCK II

In practice the treatments would be assigned at random to the plots within their own block. The reader may confirm for himself that this arrangement allows us to evaluate every treatment comparison free from between block effect except the *ABCD* interaction which has been confounded. The demonstration is exactly the same in form as in the case of the three-factor experiment which we worked out in full.

Our single replication of sixteen plots can be arranged in other ways, however, if this suits our purpose. We might, for example, lay the experiment out in four blocks of four plots each, so as to increase the within-block homogeneity. Since there are three degrees of freedom between four blocks, this would involve us in the sacrifice of three treatment effects. The choice before us is wide in this case, and would ultimately rest on what treatments we felt on technical grounds to be of least interest to us in practice. Let us look at the possibilities, as they are shown in the table on page 449. If we decide to confound any interaction in the left-hand column of the table, and also at the same time any interaction along the top row of the table, then we commit ourselves, inevitably, to confounding the interaction shown in the body of the table. On our principle of trying to retain main effects and first order interactions, the choice becomes very much more restricted, this ideal being, in fact, impossible of attainment. Study of the table will convince the reader that the loss of at least one first-order interaction is inevitable. The arrangements in which this can be done are as follows:

	ABD	*ACD*	*BCD*	*AB*	*AC*	*AD*	*BC*	*BD*	*CD*
ABC	*CD*	*BD*	*AD*			*BCD*		*ACD*	*ABD*
ABD		*BC*	*AC*		*BCD*		*ACD*		*ABC*
ACD			*AB*	*BCD*			*ABD*	*ABC*	
BCD				*ACD*	*ABD*	*ABC*			

The above table is an excerpt from our full table. Actually it can be arrived at in very simple fashion if we remember that possible solutions must inevitably include two second order interactions. Putting these together in all possible pairs and finding the third interaction by the multiplication rule, we get:

	D	C	B	A	CD	BD	BC	AD	AC	AB	BCD	ACD	ABD	ABC
ABCD	ABC	ABD	ACD	BCD	AB	AC	AD	BC	BD	CD	A	B	C	D
ABC	ABCD	AB	AC	BC	ABD	ACD	A	BCD	B	C	AD	BD	CD	
ABD	AB	ABCD	AD	BD	ABC	A	ACD	B	BCD	D	AC	BC		
ACD	AC	AD	ABCD	CD	A	ABC	ABD	C	D	BCD	AB			
BCD	BC	BD	CD	ABCD	B	C	D	ABC	ABD	ACD				
AB	ABD	ABC	A	B	ABCD	AD	AC	BD	BC					
AC	ACD	A	ABC	C	AD	ABCD	AB	CD						
AD	A	ACD	ABD	D	AC	AB	ABCD							
BC	BCD	B	C	ABC	BD	CD								
BD	B	BCD	D	ABD	BC									
CD	C	D	BCD	ACD										
A	AD	AC	AB											
B	BD	BC												
C	CD													

ABC	*ABD*	*CD*	*ABD*	*ACD*	*BC*
ABC	*ACD*	*BD*	*ABD*	*BCD*	*AC*
ABC	*BCD*	*AD*	*ACD*	*BCD*	*AB*

Let us now choose for the purposes of illustration the set *ABC*, *BCD*, and *AD*

In order to find our leading block, we have to pick out those treatments which have an even number of letters in common with each of the interactions to be confounded. Doing this we arrive at the following table:

Even number in common with		Treatment combination							
ABC	*abd*	*acd*	*bcd*	*d*	(1)	*ab*	*ac*	*bc*
BCD	*abd*	*acd*	*abc*	*a*	(1)	*bc*	*bd*	*cd*
AD	*abd*	*acd*	*bc*	*b*	*c*	*ad*	(1)	*abcd*

Inspection of the table shows that the treatments which have an even number of letters in common with the interactions to be confounded are *abd*, *acd*, *bc*, and (1). Our leading block thus becomes

abd	*acd*	*bc*	(1)	BLOCK I

This does not include the treatment combination *a*, so we multiply through the leading plot treatments, substituting unity for any squared terms, and find

bd	*cd*	*abc*	*a*	BLOCK II

The treatment combination *b* has not yet been allocated. Multiplying through the leading block treatments by *b*, we get

ad	*abcd*	*c*	*b*	BLOCK III

The treatment d has not yet occurred. Multiplying through the leading block by d, we find

ab	ac	bcd	d

BLOCK IV

The experimental layout would then be as shown:

BLOCK I

abd	bc
(1)	acd

BLOCK II

bd	abc
a	cd

BLOCK III

c	b
ad	abcd

BLOCK IV

bcd	ac
ab	d

So far we have only considered confounding in single replication experiments. It is evident that, if we have more than one replication, the range of possibilities will be at once increased. There will exist the opportunity of confounding one treatment effect in one of the replications and quite different treatment effects in other replications. In this way, there is no need to sacrifice all knowledge about a confounded effect. The ideas follow quite naturally from what we have already learnt, so we shall illustrate the technique by working a numerical example, in which there are three factors A, B, and C, each at two levels, and in which the treatment combinations ABC and BC are confounded, each in one only of the two replications of the experiment. Before dealing with the numerical analysis, let us design the experimental layout as the investigator would have to do before starting the experiment.

Consider the first replication in which we are to confound the ABC interaction. One block will contain those treatment combinations having an even number of letters in common with the interaction ABC, and will therefore appear as

| (1) | ab | ac | bc | BLOCK I |

For the second block we shall have, therefore:

| abc | a | b | c | BLOCK II |

Considering next the second replication, one block will have those treatments containing an even number of letters in common with the interaction BC, and will therefore appear as

| (1) | a | bc | abc | BLOCK III |

The second block in this replication must therefore be

| ab | ac | b | c | BLOCK IV |

Imagine, now, that the experiment has been performed and that the yields were as shown in the following schematic:

FIRST REPLICATION

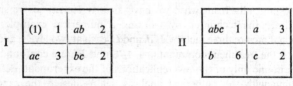

I

| (1) | 1 | ab | 2 |
| ac | 3 | bc | 2 |

II

| abc | 1 | a | 3 |
| b | 6 | c | 2 |

Block Total $T = 8$
Block Correction Factor
$$\frac{T^2}{N} = \frac{64}{4} = 16$$

Block Total $T = 12$
Block Correction Factor
$$\frac{T^2}{N} = \frac{144}{4} = 36$$

SECOND REPLICATION

III
(1) 2	a 3
bc 3	abc 8

IV
ab 6	ac 10
b 7	c 5

Block Total $T = 16$
Block Correction Factor

$$\frac{T^2}{N} = \frac{256}{4} = 64$$

Block Total $T = 28$
Block Correction Factor

$$\frac{T^2}{N} = \frac{784}{4} = 196$$

Grand Total for all blocks $T = 64$

Grand Correction Factor $\dfrac{T^2}{N} = \dfrac{4096}{16} = 256$

The reader should by now be able to follow the following computation without difficulty:

Total Sum of Squares

Square all items and subtract the grand correction factor.

Block	I items squared		$1 + 4 + 9 + 4 =$	18
Block	II	,,	,,	$1 + 9 + 36 + 4 =$	50
Block	III	,,	,,	$4 + 9 + 9 + 64 =$	86
Block	IV	,,	,,	$36 + 100 + 49 + 25 =$	210

Total of squares of items $= 364$
Total Sum of Squares $= 364 - 256 = 108$ with 15 d.f.

Between Blocks Sum of Squares

Derived from squares of block totals and grand correction factor, remembering that each block total is the sum of 4 items.

$$\tfrac{1}{4}[64 + 144 + 256 + 784] - 256 = 312 - 256 = 56$$

Between blocks sum of squares $= 56$ with 3 d.f.

Within Blocks Sum of Squares

Derived by subtracting between blocks sum of squares from the total sum of squares, thus: $108 - 56 = 52$ with $15 - 3 = 12$ d.f.

Alternatively. We may derive it directly by subtracting from the sum of the squares of the items in any block (see total sum of squares computation) the block correction factor. Then sum the results for all blocks thus:

Block I 18 – 16 = 2 with 3 d.f. within the block
Block II 50 – 36 = 14 with 3 d.f. within the block
Block III 86 – 64 = 22 with 3 d.f. within the block
Block IV 210 – 196 = 14 with 3 d.f. within the block

Total within blocks = 52 with 12 d.f. within the blocks

Now this within blocks sum of squares includes the treatment sum of squares and the residual error sum of squares. Our next step is to get the sum of squares for all the treatments individually and combined.

Treatment Sum of Squares

Firstly, those treatments which are not confounded with between block differences. To evaluate these we can utilize all the blocks.

$$A = (a - 1)(b + 1)(c + 1)$$
$$= [abc + ab + ac + a] - [bc + b + c + (1)]$$

Summing the treatment yields over every block, we find:

$$A = [9 + 8 + 13 + 6] - [5 + 13 + 7 + 3] = 8$$

We get the A sum of squares by squaring this result and dividing by 16, the number of plots on which the contrast is based. Hence the A sum of squares is $\frac{64}{16} = 4$. Since the factor A was at two levels in the experiment, there is 1 d.f.

The following table shows the computation for all the unconfounded contrasts. The layout is self-explanatory.

	abc ab ab bc a b c (1)	Total = T	T^2	$\dfrac{T^2}{16}$
A	9 + 8 + 13 – 5 + 6 – 13 – 7 – 3	8	64	4·00
B	9 + 8 – 13 + 5 – 6 + 13 – 7 – 3	6	36	2·25
C	9 – 8 + 13 + 5 – 6 – 13 + 7 – 3	4	16	1·00
AB	9 + 8 – 13 – 5 – 6 – 13 + 7 + 3	–10	100	6·25
AC	9 – 8 + 13 – 5 – 6 + 13 – 7 + 3	12	144	9·00

(Unconfounded) Total treatment sum of squares, with 5 d.f. = 22.50

We can estimate the *BC* sum of squares from Blocks I and II, since the interaction was left unconfounded in these blocks. Summing over the blocks in the first replication only, therefore, we find:

	abc *ab* *ac* *bc* *a* *b* *c* (1)	T	T^2	$\dfrac{T^2}{8}$
BC	$1 - 2 - 3 + 2 + 3 - 6 - 2 + 1$	-6	36	4·50

This is with 1 d.f., since each of the main factors *B* and *C* have only one degree of freedom, so that the interaction has $1 \times 1 = 1$ d.f.

The *ABC* interaction may be assessed from the second replication, since it was left unconfounded there. Summing as before over the eight plots, we find:

	abc *ab* *ac* *bc* *a* *b* *c* (1)	T	T^2	$\dfrac{T^2}{8}$
ABC	$8 - 6 - 10 - 3 + 3 + 7 + 5 - 2$	2	4	0·50

This again is based on 1 d.f.

Collecting together the treatment sums of squares, we have:

	Sum of Squares
A	4·00
B	2·25
C	1·00
AB	6·25
AC	9·00
BC	4·50
ABC	0·50

Treatment Total   27·50 with 7 d.f.

Residual Sum of Squares

This is found as the difference between the within blocks sum of squares and the treatment sum of squares, viz.

$$52 - 27{\cdot}50 = 24{\cdot}50 \text{ with } 12 - 7 = 5 \text{ d.f.}$$

We may now draw up the table of the analysis of variance.

TABLE OF ANALYSIS OF VARIANCE

Source	Sum of squares	d.f.	Variance estimate
Blocks	56·00	3	18·67
Treatments			
A	4·00	1	4·00
B	2·25	1	2·25
C	1·00	1	1·00
AB	6·25	1	6·25
AC	9·00	1	9·00
BC	4·50	1	4·50
ABC	0·50	1	0·50
Error	24·50	5	4·90
Total	108·00	15	

NOW TRY YOUR SKILL AT ANALYSIS OF VARIANCE

1. The following table shows the annual death rate by quarters of the year and by decades according to the Registrar General. Carry out a between-row and column analysis to establish season and long-term trend.

	March	June	September	December
		Quarter ended		
1901/10	17·1	14·6	13·8	15·4
1911/20	17·2	13·6	11·8	14·9
1921/30	15·5	11·7	9·5	11·8
1931/40	15·8	11·6	9·8	12·0

2. In the chapter on Time Series Analysis, we got the following results for quarterly takings as a percentage of the current trend. Carry out an analysis of variance between quarters to establish formally that there is a real seasonal effect:

	1st Quarter	2nd Quarter	3rd Quarter	4th Quarter
Year 1	-44	$+ 2$	$+134$	-13
Year 2	-60	$+13$	$+112$	-33
Year 3	-67	-10	$+ 70$	$+ 8$
Year 4	-48	-51	$- 90$	$- 9$

3. If, in an experiment, we decide to confound the interactions AB and AC, what other effect must inevitably be sacrificed? Lay out an experimental arrangement for four factors A, B, C, and D, with each factor at two levels, in which this particular set of effects may be confounded with between block differences.

4. Design an experimental layout in which three treatments are considered each at two levels, there being two replications of treatment combinations with the AB interaction confounded in one replication and the AC in the other replication.

20

Statistics Desirable

'This is the end of tears: No more lament.' SOPHOCLES

It would be ungracious of us to leave the reader who has valiantly suffered our attempt to explain statistical methods without some word of farewell. Statistics is not the easiest of subjects to teach, and there are those to whom anything savouring of mathematics is regarded as for ever anathema. We have tried to keep these lost souls in mind by keeping the more formidable aspects of mathematical statistics as far in the background as possible. For this reason, we hope that some of those who have laboured with us will not be happy that the time has come to part. After all, the whole point of a book such as this is that it sets out to create an interest in its subject-matter. We shall be well content if some, at least, of our readers, while glad enough to be rid of the present author and his efforts, will at any rate have seen sufficient of the light to wish to go to those better teachers whose names we have placed in the bibliography as if in a roll of honour.

There are certain matters which we would place before the reader's attention before leaving him to his own thoughts. In the first place, the fact that men are very fond of collecting figures, quoting from them and drawing conclusions (legitimate and otherwise) on them as a foundation. We feel that the man who says 'Give me the figures' is worthy of respect; that propaganda well armed with numerical data is sincere – even if it may still be misleading. This attitude we find in every aspect of our lives, whether it be in the field of sport or the world of business. There is something very sad in the disparity between our passion for figures and our ability to make use of them once they are in our hands. How often we find ourselves in the same position as the child who has a lovely chemistry set for Christmas but who lacks the knowledge to do anything but mix anything and everything together, making a fine old mess in the process. There is an art in handling figures, just as in handling chemicals. We do not set ourselves up as chemists without studying the laws of chemistry.

Neither are we likely to make much of a job of anything but the simplest data without proper study of the means of handling them.

The trouble arises from the fact that, while we are not all taught chemistry at school, we are all taught arithmetic. Now there are in arithmetic four things to learn: addition, subtraction, multiplication, and division. That is all. Most of our time at arithmetic in school is devoted to applying these four operations to a variety of circumstances: thus arise the problems in weights and measures, fractions, decimals, proportion, and all the rest. It is constantly impressed upon us that arithmetic is an exact science; that all the problems in our textbooks have an answer, which is an exact one and may (if our teachers are modern enough so to pamper us) be found in the back of the book. The nearest we get to anything like statistics is when we learn to work approximations (a dying art, alas!). But even in such cases we are sternly reminded that we are only getting a rough idea of an exact answer which we could (were it not that we are now on Chapter 14) work out exactly.

Far be it from me to decry the ardour with which our masters and mistresses drive this into our thick skulls. It is all necessary. What I grumble about is the fact that they seem positively afraid of doing anything that is not capable of an exact solution. This is indeed a sorry preparation for the life of the real world. Apart from the bank clerk counting someone else's coppers with grimy fingers, it is doubtful whether there is any single case where the full precision of which arithmetic is capable is of the slightest use. What training do we receive even in the basic ideas of handling statistical data, which is the very lifeblood of everyday life? There is much that could be done with children of even average intelligence before the age of fifteen. But the schoolmasters must learn first. And a jolly interesting class subject they can make of it if they will. They will be doing a job of inestimable value if they will train their students to have some critical faculty in the face of arithmetic. Teach them the art of crossing out 114·72 and replacing it with 100. My experience is that people have a sort of religious awe about figures. They feel there is something impious in interfering in any way with an answer that has once been worked out.

How many hearts have been saddened when the physics master puts his pencil through the accurate answer! It is strange how lads of sixteen and seventeen think it quite daring fun to make gross approximations. Stranger still to see them at so advanced an age surprised that crude approximations in the parts of a problem can lead to a quite decent answer, provided the sacrilege is carried out with all the cunning of the devil himself.

Half of the corruption of political life may be due to malice aforethought on the part of the politicians. The other half is certainly due to their having an unhealthy respect for figures – a positive fear of attacking them when they lend colour to their own party's dogmas. Men have been martyred for the difference between two wrong answers. In business, too, men have lost face for the same reason and had to wait until the following year before the disgrace had sufficiently worn down for them to be given a well merited rise.

Really, the slipshod way we deal with data is a disgrace to civilization. Never have so many data been collected in files and left unanalysed. Never have so many data been taken out of files and misread. Yet it is easy enough to learn the arts of interpretation; to learn when it is safe to say definitely one thing or another; to learn when judgement must be suspended.

A very little consideration shows that there is scarcely a hole or corner of modern life which could not find some application, however simple, for statistical theory and show a profit as a result. It has something to offer the man who specializes in any of the branches of management in industry. It offers assistance to the man responsible for purchasing and goods inward inspection. In the hands of the cost accountant or the time and motion study man it acts as a hone to sharpen traditional tools. For the inspector in a production plant it offers the only possible realization of the true philosophy of inspection and, not surprisingly, does the job with greater efficiency and in a more revealing manner. It is a positive encouragement to the customer in that it holds out the promise of goods produced under controlled conditions, so that they are at once better and more consistent in quality. In the research laboratory it is a powerful adjunct, offering optimum criteria for the assessment of data, eliminating wishful thinking, and yielding principles of experimental design which face the fact of experimental error and make possible the highly desirable objective of experimenting with a great diversity of combinations of the factors under test. Perhaps most important of all, it enables research to leave the controlled conditions of the laboratory and proceed in the rough and tumble of the factory, where, after all, the results of experimental work have finally to be turned into production processes reasonably immune from trouble.

Consider, for a moment, some of the fields where the techniques may be applied. There is scope and often real necessity for them in leather tanning, in the paper-making mill, and in the preparation of pharmaceutical products. It is applied in glass technology, in rubber technology, and in the manifold branches of applied chemistry and metallurgy on which we so much depend for the comforts of modern civilization. We find it in steel works, in agricultural research, and in the textiles industry – the latter still offering enormous scope to those who have the courage to apply statistical techniques to hosiery production problems and the like. It is made use of by the telephone engineer both in the design of equipment and in the manufacture of components to close limits. It has been applied even to traditional handicrafts like glass blowing. In the field of mechanical engineering it has a great part to play both for quality control of quantity produced articles and for the sampling inspection of components and raw materials. Insurance, public health, road safety research, operational research into building techniques, selection of students for higher education aptitudes, personnel selection, and market research all depend on the application of sound statistical principles. It is a promising tool for the meteorologist, for the biologist, and for the student of sociology. Constantly, new techniques are being developed as the science is used in more and more fields of endeavour. Each field raises new problems and calls for new techniques and modification of old ones to suit its own peculiarities. There is unceasing cross fertilization between applied statistics and mathematical statistics. Mathematical principles spread out in ever widening circles of practical application; diverse techniques developed in varying fields by practical men are unified and strengthened by the mathematicians.

At bottom it boils down to this: wherever anything is measured numerically, wherever there is an attempt, however rough, to assess anything in the form of numbers, even by the simple process of counting, then there begins to arise the necessity for making judgements as to the significance of the data and the necessity for traffic rules by which the flow of information may proceed smoothly and purposefully. In a word, there is the need for statistics. The application of scientific method to every phase of industry (which is a phenomenon of rapidly growing proportions) inevitably has brought about an increase in measurement of every kind. It is widely accepted now that, even if in the present state of knowledge and in the hurlyburly of production we are able to measure what we are dealing with only roughly, it is far better to make some rough measurement than no measurement at all. The fantastic success of physics – which is by definition the science of measurement – has stirred workers in every field to try to emulate this success in their own field by similar methods. No doubt it is true that the methods of physics are not applicable in all other fields. The fact remains that in many cases it is only now being tried out, and is certain to bring great rewards in many cases. The very fact that this great adventure in measurement is of necessity rough, that very often we are unaware of the underlying structure of the universe our measurements are sampling, is the true explanation of why statistical techniques are becoming so widely adopted in every industrial country.

Britain has a proud record in the development of statistics. Yet already a rather familiar story is being retold. Other countries, notably the United States, are more alive to the practical value of these techniques. To the American industrialist 'there's gold in them thar formulae'. This book is meant as a small contribution to bringing statistical methods before the attention of those who were raised earlier in history, as well as those who are responsible for the future of our industries. It is not that I recommend statistics as a panacea – such things do not exist, but it is a development worthy of the attention of all who have the application of scientific method to our industries at heart. It is one more tool which many, though not all, will find valuable. What about you?

Every man who has attained success in his walk of life tends to grow contented. His success is taken as proof of the essential rightness of his ideas. And rightly so, maybe, so long as we remember that William the Conqueror was also right at the Battle of Senlac Hill. Those who have not yet attained success are (among my readers) those whom it awaits as they grow older – and as the older men retire. These young men tend to believe that anything new is better, simply because it is new. I have advice for young and old which I hope they will ponder.

If you are young, then I say: Learn something about statistics as soon as you can. Don't dismiss it through ignorance or because it calls for thought. Don't pass into eternity without having examined these techniques and thought about the possibility of application in your field of work, because very likely you will find it an excellent substitute for your lack of experience in some directions. It will curb your over-enthusiasm. If you are older and already crowned with the laurels of success, see to it that those under your wing who look to you for advice are encouraged to look into this subject. In this way you will show that your arteries are not yet hardened, and you will be able to reap the benefits without doing overmuch work yourself. Whoever you are, if your work calls for the interpretation of data, you may be able to do without statistics, but you won't do so well. If my efforts in this book have helped you to some measure of understanding about the subject, I am sure you will thank me and forgive the bluntness of my advice. If not, then I am sorry for everything.

Bibliography

Economic Control of Quality of Manufactured Products by W. A. Shewhart (Macmillan). One of the classics on quality control. Excellent study of the philosophical aspects of quality.

Engineer's Manual of Statistical Method by L. E. Simon (John Wiley & Sons). Full of the common-sense observations one expects from an engineer. An excellent book in its general reading matter for anyone. Essentially a book for practical men.

Statistics by L. H. C. Tippett (Home University Library). A very simple introduction to basic ideas written in readable form.

Methods of Statistics by L. H. C. Tippett (Williams & Norgate). Suitable for the research worker rather than the commerce or production man.

Statistical Quality Control by E. L. Grant (McGraw Hill). A detailed manual of quality control techniques.

Statistical Methods in Research and Production (Oliver & Boyd for Imperial Chemical Industries, Ltd.) A readable account of the more common methods including analysis of variance.

Industrial Experimentation by K. A. Brownlee (H.M.S.O.). Essentially a book of method with lots of worked examples. Ideal for those who learn better from practice than precept.

Advanced Theory of Statistics by M. G. Kendall (Charles Griffin). Essentially a book for the mathematician. The standard reference book for theory.

Design of Experiments by R. A. Fisher (Oliver & Boyd). A book you can read, when experienced, over and over again and still profit from, but assumes far too much for the novice.

Statistical Methods for Research Workers by R. A. Fisher (Oliver & Boyd). Recommended as a classic rather than a book to learn the subject from.

Introduction to Modern Statistical Methods by P. R. Rider (John Wiley & Sons, Inc.). A neat and compact account of the more usual techniques applicable in research.

B.S. 600R. Quality Control Charts by B. P. Dudding and W. J. Jennett (British Standards Institution),

Sampling Inspection Tables by H. F. Dodge and H. G. Romig (Chapman & Hall). Tables for single and double sampling schemes both for lot quality and average quality protection.

Statistical Techniques in Market Research by R. Ferber. (McGraw-Hill). A comprehensive account in readable form.

Mathematics of Statistics by J. F. Kenney (Chapman & Hall, Ltd.). This is in two volumes. The first calls for very little maths and covers more or less the ground common in commercial courses. The second takes a sudden leap forward in mathematical standard.

Mathematical Statistics by C. E. Weatherburn (Oxford University Press). The presentation of the subject is elegant and will appeal to those with degree standard mathematics.

Applied Statistics by Croxton and Cowden (Pitman). This is the book I should recommend above all others to the commerce or economics student. It goes to a good standard, keeps its feet on the ground, and provides plenty of examples.

Sequential Analysis of Statistical Data: Applications by the Statistical Research Group of Columbia University (Columbia University Press). A practical account of the methods of sequential analysis by those who developed them. Well presented and readable.

Tables for Statisticians and Biometricians by Karl Pearson (Cambridge University Press).

Statistical Tables for Agricultural, Biological, and other Research Workers by Fisher and Yates.

Probability and its Engineering Uses by T. C. Fry (Van Nostrand). A very attractive book for the engineer who likes his mathematics and a practical problem to which to apply it.

Sampling Inspection by the Statistical Research Group of Columbia University (Columbia University Press). Principles, procedures, tables, and operating characteristics for single, double, and sequential sampling. A first-rate manual.

Methods of Correlation Analysis by M. Ezekiel (John Wiley & Sons). An extensive treatise on methods, excellently presented and using no more than elementary algebra.

Experimental Designs by W. G. Cochran and G. M. Cox (John Wiley & Sons). Gives an extensive collection of designs of proved value with notes on the advantages and limitations of each. Each design is accompanied by a plan, by instructions for its use in practice, and by an account of the appropriate statistical analysis.

Methods of Statistical Analysis by C. H. Goulden (John Wiley & Sons). An excellent book dealing with the principal techniques for those who have already done some statistics, but are not mathematicians.

Statistics by N. L. Johnson and H. Tetley (Cambridge Univ. Press), 3 vols. Written specially for actuaries, but strongly recommended to any with stronger than usual mathematics who want a good account of the theory.

Statistical Method from the viewpoint of Quality Control by W. A. Shewhart and W. E. Deming (Graduate School, Department of Agriculture, Washington). An elementary philosophical discussion of the fundamental principles worth careful study.

Statistical Methods by G. W. Snedecor (Iowa State College Press). An expert exposition of the most common techniques up to Covariance Analysis and Curvilinear Regression, based on elementary algebra and the practical approach.

Statistical Techniques in Agricultural Research by D. D. Paterson (McGraw-Hill). Equally valuable to those who are not agriculturalists.

Introduction to Statistical Method by B. C. Brookes and W. F. L. Dick (Heinemann). Essentially a school or college text. Gives an excellent account of the subject from the beginning up to the elementary principles of Experimental Design. Includes a handsome collection of mathematical and practical exercises with solutions.

Introduction to the Theory of Statistics by G. U. Yule and M. G. Kendall (Griffin). A standard work, recently revised, which can confidently be recommended to those whose interest lies in the theoretical aspects.

Quality Control: Principles, Practice and Administration by A. V. Feigenbaum (McGraw Hill). The best book for Management to read.

Applied Statistics. (Oliver and Boyd for R. Statist. Soc.) A journal of application in all fields. Recommended for circulation in firms.

Industrial Quality Control. (Am. Soc. for Quality Control). Recommended as a circulating journal.

Quality Control Handbook by J. Juran (McGraw Hill). Deals exhaustively with the whole subject and a wide range of applications.

Statistical Method in Biological Assay by D. J. Finney (Griffin). The best book for those specializing in bioassay.

Statistical Methods in Electrical Engineering by D. A. Bell (Chapman & Hall). Not nearly so narrow as its title might imply.

Control Chart Technique when Manufacturing to a Specification by B. P. Dudding and W. J. Jennett (British Standards Institution). Should be read in conjunction with *B.S.*600*R.*

Introduction to Mathematical Statistics by P. G. Hoel (Chapman & Hall). Mathematics not too advanced and style unusually lucid.

Cambridge Elementary Statistical Tables by D. V. Lindley and J. C. P. Miller (C.U.P.). Quite comprehensive for the price.

Design and Analysis of Industrial Experiments by O. L. Davies (Oliver & Boyd). A major work, full of practical examples and practical comment.

Design and Analysis of Experiments by M. H. Quenouille (Griffin). Emphasis on methods of experimentation rather than on methods of analysis.

Technological Applications of Statistics by L. H. C. Tippett (Williams & Norgate). A very well written book that will repay careful study.

Sampling Inspection by Variables by Bowker and Goode (McGraw-Hill). Strongly recommended to those who have need for ready-made sampling plans for variables inspection.

Answers

(1) $\frac{1}{6}$.   (2) (4.3.2.1) $(\frac{1}{52} \cdot \frac{1}{51} \cdot \frac{1}{50} \cdot \frac{1}{49})$.   (3) 17$s$. 6d.

(4) Two factors, 10. Three factors, 10.   (5) 64.

(6) *No Orchids* forbidden, 5. Compulsory, 10. Free choice, 15. Note that $15 = 5 + 10$. General Rule: $NCR = (N-1)CR + (N-1)C(R-1)$.

(7) 56, 7, 20, 720.   (8) 630.

(9) Statesmen $\frac{9!}{2!2!2!}$ Procrastinator $\frac{14!}{3!2!2!2!}$ Both $\frac{23!}{4!3!3!3!2!2!2!}$

(10) 32.31.30 . . . 24.23.

(1) $\frac{1}{2}(n+1)$.   (2) 50·1.   (3) H.M. = 24 m.p.g., A.M. = 25 m.p.g.

(4) 52·6.   (5) 16$\frac{3}{4}$ lb., but arithmetic avg. preferable.

(1) $\bar{x} = 50·1$, $s = 0·305$.   (2) M.D. = 0·25.   (3) I.Q.R. = 0·5.   (4) 61%.

(1) $\bar{x} = 9·5$, $s = 1·25$.   (2) 9·25.   (3) 9·47.

(1) (*a*) 0·904, (*b*) 0·091, (*c*) 0·995, (*d*) 0·005, (*e*) 0·096.

(3) Not rash. Probability is only 0·001.   (4) 1:1:2.   (5) 20%.

(1) Odds 30 to 1 against so many deaths if treatment harmless and patients typical.

(2) Results so bad have only 1% chance without definite cause.

(3) About one chance in ten.

(4) Taking '5 and over' as equal to 7, the expectation is $z = 2·08$ approx. and the approx. expected frequencies for 0, 1, 2 etc. particles are, 37, 78, 82, 57, 30, 12, 4.

(1) (*a*) 15–33, (*b*) 18–30, (*c*) 21–27.

(3) $\frac{1}{8}$ inch.   (4) 0·002 inch.